Music, Politics and Society in Ancient Rome

Music was everywhere in ancient Rome. Wherever one went in the sprawling city, the sound of singing and piping, drumming and strumming was never far out of earshot. This book examines the role of music in Roman politics and society, focusing on the period from the Roman conquest of Greece in the second century BCE to the end of the reign of Nero in 68 CE. Drawing on a wide range of literary texts, inscriptions and material artefacts, Harry Morgan uncovers the tensions between elite and popular attitudes towards music, and shows how music was exploited as a tool by political leaders and emperors. Far from being a marginal aspect of daily life, music was fundamental to Roman political culture and social relations, shaping debates about class, gender and ethnicity. The book will be of interest to students and scholars of ancient music and Roman history.

HARRY MORGAN is a lecturer in Ancient History at Harvard University.

Music, Politics and Society in Ancient Rome

HARRY MORGAN

Harvard University

CAMBRIDGE
UNIVERSITY PRESS

Shaftesbury Road, Cambridge CB2 8EA, United Kingdom

One Liberty Plaza, 20th Floor, New York, NY 10006, USA

477 Williamstown Road, Port Melbourne, VIC 3207, Australia

314–321, 3rd Floor, Plot 3, Splendor Forum, Jasola District Centre, New Delhi – 110025, India

103 Penang Road, #05–06/07, Visioncrest Commercial, Singapore 238467

Cambridge University Press is part of Cambridge University Press & Assessment, a department of the University of Cambridge.

We share the University's mission to contribute to society through the pursuit of education, learning and research at the highest international levels of excellence.

www.cambridge.org
Information on this title: www.cambridge.org/9781009232319

DOI: 10.1017/9781009232326

© Harry Morgan 2023

This publication is in copyright. Subject to statutory exception and to the provisions of relevant collective licensing agreements, no reproduction of any part may take place without the written permission of Cambridge University Press & Assessment.

First published 2023

A catalogue record for this publication is available from the British Library

Library of Congress Cataloging-in-Publication data
Names: Morgan, Harry (Historian) author.
Title: Music, politics and society in ancient Rome / Harry Morgan.
Description: [1.] | New York, NY : Cambridge University Press, 2022. | Includes bibliographical references and index.
Identifiers: LCCN 2022036811 (print) | LCCN 2022036812 (ebook) | ISBN 9781009232333 (hardback) | ISBN 9781009232319 (paperback) | ISBN 9781009232326 (epub)
Subjects: LCSH: Music, Greek and Roman–History and criticism. | Music–Political aspects–Rome–History–To 476. | Music–Social aspects–Rome–History–To 476.
Classification: LCC ML169 .M87 2022 (print) | LCC ML169 (ebook) | DDC 780.937–dc23/eng/20220802
LC record available at https://lccn.loc.gov/2022036811
LC ebook record available at https://lccn.loc.gov/2022036812

ISBN 978-1-009-23233-3 Hardback
ISBN 978-1-009-23231-9 Paperback

Cambridge University Press & Assessment has no responsibility for the persistence or accuracy of URLs for external or third-party internet websites referred to in this publication and does not guarantee that any content on such websites is, or will remain, accurate or appropriate.

Contents

List of Figures [*page* vii]
Acknowledgements [x]
List of Abbreviations [xii]

Introduction [1]
Approaching Roman Music [3]
Sources of Evidence [6]
Terminology [11]
Greek and Etruscan Influences on Roman Music [18]
Sound, Space and Social Control [26]
Sensing Music, Embodying Music [30]
The Status of Musicians [34]
Chapter Outline [39]

1 The Games of L. Anicius Gallus and the Cultural Politics of Music in the Second Century BCE [42]
Triumphal Politics and Spectacle Culture in Mid-Republican Rome [49]
Battle of the Bands: Anicius' Martial Soundtrack [55]
Music and Morality in Polybius' *Histories* [62]
Scipio, Cato and the Roman Opposition to Greek Music [72]
Banning the *Ludus Talarius*: A Case of Roman Musical Censorship? [77]
Conclusion [81]

2 Popular Music and Popular Politics in the Late Republic [83]
Cicero on the Music of the Roman Theatre [86]
The Musical Experience of Pompey's Theatre [98]
The Role of Music in Late-Republican Oratory and Rhetorical Invective [104]
Gaius Gracchus and the *Fistula* [110]
Publius Clodius: Harpist, Chorus-Leader, Entertainer Extraordinaire [115]
Nec Tam Musicus: Piso, Philodemus and the Epicureans [122]
The *Onos Lyras*: Varro's Satire on Music [129]
Conclusion [139]

3 Augustus, Apollo's Lyre and the Harmony of the Principate [142]
Apollo Citharoedus on the Palatine [144]
Apollo Citharoedus and the Commemoration of Actium [153]

Antony, Cleopatra and the Triumph over Dionysian Music [160]
Tuning the World [173]
Sound, Ritual and the Citharodic Experience [178]
A 'Golden Age' of Music? [184]
Conclusion [189]

4 Nero and the Age of Musomania [191]
'O Apollo, O Augustus': Making Sense of a Musical Emperor [198]
The Master's Songbook: *Neroniana Cantica* and Popular Music at Rome [206]
Water-Organs, Bagpipes and the Lure of the Arena [215]
Musomania in a Young Man's World [224]
Conclusion [238]

Epilogue [239]

Bibliography [249]
Index [279]

Figures

0.1 Mosaic panel by Dioscurides of Samos showing masked actors playing musical instruments (*tibiae*, *cymbala* and *tympanum*). Based on an episode from Menander's *Theophoroumene*. From the Villa of Cicero, Pompeii; ca. 100 BCE.   [*page 7*]

0.2 Facsimile of a Roman *cornu* found at Pompeii, produced by the Belgian instrument-maker Victor-Charles Mahillon (1841–1924).   [10]

0.3 Pair of bronze cymbals linked by a chain; Pompeii, first century CE.   [10]

0.4 Roman *sistrum*, made of bronze or copper alloy; first or second century CE.   [11]

0.5 Performance by the group 'Ludi Scaenici' at the Festival Tarraco Viva; Tarragona, Spain.   [12]

0.6 A *tibia* from Roman Syria, made of bone with bronze and silver facing and decorative chalcedony bulb, L. 23⅛ in. (58.6 cm); ca. 1–500 CE.   [16]

0.7 Detail of mosaic panel showing a dancer and *tibia* player. One of five panels with circus and arena scenes, from Sta. Sabina on the Aventine, Rome; third century CE.   [16]

0.8 Wall painting from Herculaneum depicting a ceremony of the cult of Isis. A figure in a mask performs a sacred dance, accompanied by a female *tympanum*-player dressed in white, who stands behind him, and a throng of attendants with *sistra*; ca. 1–79 CE.   [19]

0.9 Wall painting with seated woman holding a *cithara*, from Room H of the Villa of P. Fannius Synistor at Boscoreale; ca. 50–40 BCE.   [25]

0.10 Marble funerary relief depicting a priest of Cybele with *cymbala*, *tympanum* and Phrygian *tibia*; from Lavinium, Rome; ca. mid-second century CE.   [34]

1.1 Bas-relief from Osuna (Urso), Spain, representing a *cornicen*; early first century BCE.   [57]

1.2 Marble bas-relief showing musicians and armed dancers leading captives in a triumph or ovation; mid-first century BCE.   [59]

List of Figures

2.1 3-D model of the Theatre of Pompey, general view, looking southeast. [99]
2.2 3-D model of the Theatre of Pompey, view of stage and *cavea*. [100]
2.3 Wall painting depicting a musical concert; Herculaneum, Italy, ca. 1–79 CE. [108]
2.4 Wall painting depicting Pygmies at an outdoor banquet. A seated *tibicen* playing a Phrygian pipe accompanies scenes of sex and drinking. From the House of the Doctor, Pompeii, ca. 59–79 CE. [109]
3.1 Terracotta plaque from the sanctuary of Apollo on the Palatine, showing Apollo and Diana adorning a sacred pillar; ca. 30 BCE. [148]
3.2 Apollo, Diana and Latona received by Victoria on the Palatine; Augustan marble relief. [149]
3.3 Apollo, Diana and Latona on the Sorrento Base; Augustan/early imperial period. Sorrento. [150]
3.4 Apollo with cithara and quiver depicted on a fragment of a wall painting from the House of Augustus. [151]
3.5 Marble statue of Augustus from Prima Porta; after a bronze original, ca. 20 BCE. [152]
3.6 Apollo Citharoedus overlooking the Battle of Actium; Medinaceli Reliefs, detail of panel; second quarter of first century CE. [156]
3.7 Denarius struck by C. Antistius Vetus, 16 BCE, Rome mint. Obverse: head of Augustus. Reverse: Apollo with lyre in left hand and *patera* in right hand, pouring a libation over an altar. [157]
3.8 Aureus of Augustus, 15–13 BCE, Lugdunum mint. Observe: head of Augustus. Reverse: Apollo with plectrum in right hand and lyre in left hand. [158]
3.9 Aureus of Augustus, 11–10 BCE, Lugdunum mint. Observe: head of Augustus, laureate. Reverse: Apollo with *patera* in right hand and lyre in left hand. [159]
3.10 Wall painting illustrating the musical contest between Apollo and Marsyas; from Herculaneum, 60–79 CE. [162]
3.11 Bronze as of Domitian, 88 CE. Rome mint. Observe: head of Domitian, laureate. Reverse: Domitian sacrifices over an altar in front of a temple, accompanied by a *tibicen* and *fidicen*. [183]
4.1 Poster for the silent motion picture *Quo Vadis* (1913) showing Nero fiddling while Rome burns. [193]

4.2 Bronze as of Nero, 62–68 CE. Rome mint. Observe: head of Nero, radiate. Reverse: (Nero as?) Apollo Citharoedus, singing and playing *cithara*. [204]

4.3 Medallion depicting an organist and *cornicen* on amphitheatre mosaic from Roman villa at Nennig, near Trier, Germany; second or third century CE. [220]

4.4 Copper alloy contorniate, minted in Rome, late fourth or fifth century CE. Observe: head of Nero, laureate, with palm-branch countermark. Reverse: *hydraulis* with a figure standing facing on the left, with legend LAVRENTI NICA (the victory of Laurentius). [221]

4.5 Terracotta figurine from Alexandria, Egypt, ca. 200 CE, showing a pair of musicians. [223]

4.6 Terracotta figurine from Alexandria, Egypt, first century CE, showing a female organ-player wearing a diadem and a macrophallic dwarf playing the *tuba*. [224]

4.7 Wall painting of a banquet scene, from Room 15 of the House of the Triclinium, Pompeii (V.2.4). [231]

4.8 Wall painting of a banquet scene, from Room 15 of the House of the Triclinium, Pompeii (V.2.4). [232]

Acknowledgements

This book has its origins in a conversation with Jerry Toner, my then Director of Studies at Churchill College, Cambridge, back in 2014. I was taking a final-year undergraduate course on 'Popular Culture in the Ancient Roman World', co-taught by Jerry and Mary Beard, and approached Jerry about writing a research paper on the topic of music and the non-elite. We both initially had doubts about the feasibility of such a project: after all, how much do we really *know* about Roman music? As I started to gather evidence for the paper, however, it became clear that what we know about Roman music cannot be summarised adequately in just a few pages. What began as a tentative foray into unknown territory blossomed into an eight-year voyage of discovery; from the undergraduate essay was spawned a doctoral thesis, and from the doctoral thesis a monograph. I am grateful to Jerry for setting me on this path of exploration – and for opening my eyes to the wonderful world of the Roman *plebs*. I am also indebted to Nicholas Purcell, my doctoral supervisor at Oxford, who inspired me to ask more probing questions of Roman culture than I had ever thought possible. This book would not have come to fruition without their guidance.

Many colleagues and friends lent their support to the project along the way. Anna Clark, Matthew Leigh, Leah Lazar and Andrew Stiles helped to shape my research in its formative stages, while Katherine Clarke and Catharine Edwards offered generous and insightful feedback on the finished thesis. Kathleen Coleman, Tim Moore, Lauren Curtis and Sinclair Bell read drafts of the book and provided valuable critique. My work has benefited immensely from their expertise.

The two anonymous readers for Cambridge University Press offered many helpful suggestions. Michael Sharp was a pleasure to work with throughout the production of the book. Andrew Gu provided exemplary assistance with the editing and proof-reading of the manuscript.

I would like to thank my parents for nurturing my two great passions in life – ancient history and jazz music – both of which have left their mark on this book.

My wife, Melissa, has been by my side since the inception of the project. Mastering the arcane ways of the ancient historian is no mean feat for an immunologist, and yet she has more than risen to the challenge! Her thirst for knowledge remains a constant source of inspiration.

This book is dedicated to my grandparents, who instilled in me a fascination with the past and its music.

Abbreviations

Abbreviations of ancient authors follow the conventions of the *Oxford Classical Dictionary* (4th ed., 2012). All texts are taken from the Loeb Classical Library volumes, published by Harvard University Press. Translations are my own, unless otherwise noted. I use the following abbreviations:

AE	*L'Année Epigraphique* (1888–).
BMCRE	H. Mattingly, *Coins of the Roman Empire in the British Museum* (1923–).
BMCRR	H. A. Grueber, *Coins of the Roman Republic in the British Museum* (1910).
BNP	H. Cancik, C. Salazar *et al.* (eds.), *Brill's New Pauly* (Leiden, 2002–2010).
CIL	*Corpus Inscriptionum Latinarum* (ed. T. Mommsen *et al.*, 1863–).
EJ^2	V. Ehrehberg and A. H. M. Jones (eds.), *Documents Illustrating the Reigns of Augustus and Tiberius* (Oxford, 2nd ed., 1976).
FD	*Fouilles de Delphes* (Paris, 1902–).
FGrH	F. Jacoby, *Fragmente der griechischen Historiker* (1923–).
FRHist	T. J. Cornell (ed.), *Fragments of the Roman Historians* (Oxford, 2013).
IG	*Inscriptiones Graecae* (1873–).
ILLRP	*Inscriptiones Latinae Liberae Rei Publicae* (ed. A. Degrassi, 1957–63).
ILS	*Inscriptiones Latinae Selectae* (ed. H. Dessau, 1892–1916).
Inscr.It.	*Inscriptiones Italiae* (Rome, 1931–).
LIMC	*Lexicon Iconographicum Mythologiae Classicae* (ed. H.-C. Ackermann and J.-R. Gisler, 1981–99).
LSJ	H. G. Liddell, R. Scott and H. S. Jones, *A Greek-English Lexicon* (9th ed., Oxford, 1940).
LTUR	*Lexicon Topographicum Urbis Romae* (ed. E. M. Steinby, 1993–2000).
OCD	S. Hornblower, A. Spawforth and E. Eidinow (eds.), *The Oxford Classical Dictionary* (4th ed., Oxford, 2012).

OGIS	W. Dittenberger, *Orientis Graeci Inscriptiones Selectae* (Leipzig, 1903–05).
OLD	P. G. W. Glare (ed.), *Oxford Latin Dictionary* (2nd ed., Oxford, 2012).
ORF	H. Malcovati, *Oratorum Romanorum Fragmenta Liberae Rei Publicae* (4th ed., 1976).
PIR^2	E. Groag, A. Stein *et al.*, *Prosopographia Imperii Romani saec. I. II. III.* (Leipzig, 1930–).
RGE	R. K. Sherk, *Rome and the Greek East to the Death of Augustus* (Cambridge, 1984).
RIC	H. Mattingly, E. A. Sydenham *et al.*, *The Roman Imperial Coinage* (London, 1923–67).
RPC	M. H. Crawford, *Roman Republican Coinage*, 2 vols. (Cambridge, 1974).
SEG	*Supplementum Epigraphicum Graecum* (1923–).
Syll.^{3}	W. Dittenberger, *Sylloge Inscriptionum Graecarum*, 3rd ed. (1915–24).
TLL	*Thesaurus Linguae Latinae* (Leipzig, 1900–).

Introduction

Music was everywhere in ancient Rome. Wherever one went in the sprawling city – in houses, on the street, in theatres and amphitheatres, shops and bars, temples and marketplaces – one encountered signs of musical life. Busking musicians, dispersed along busy thoroughfares, competed for the attention of passers-by.[1] Travellers entertained themselves by humming cheerful jingles.[2] Labourers and shopkeepers sang while they worked.[3] At night, taverns came alive with singing and piping, strumming and drumming.[4] Wealthier patrons meanwhile, were serenaded by bands of musicians as they dined in their homes.[5] For every occasion, for every season and for every time of day, there was music. And every member of Roman society – whether old or young, male or female, rich or poor – played their part in keeping this vibrant musical culture alive.

But music, to the Romans, was never purely incidental. It had the power to captivate hearts and minds, to educate and enlighten, to forge communities and mould citizens. 'Music is connected with knowledge of things divine', writes Quintilian in his *Institutes of Oratory* (composed ca. 95 CE), 'and no one can doubt that some men famous for wisdom have been devotees of music'.[6] For centuries, music-making brought the Roman people together in the pursuit of religious and artistic expression. It was through song that the Romans paid tribute to the gods; it was from song that poetry was born. According to Quintilian, music even held the key to Rome's ascendancy as a military power: 'What else is the function of

---

[1] Cf. Sen. *Ep.* 56.4, discussed below in the section 'Sound, Space and Social Control'. The orator Dio Chrysostom describes a piper busking and holding lessons in a crowded street in Alexandria (*Orat.* 20.9–10).
[2] Hor. *Sat.* 1.5.15–17; Juv. 10.22; Aus. *Mosella* 165–8. Augustine (*En. In Ps.* 66.5–6) speaks of travellers singing to ward off the terrors of the night, even at the risk of alerting robbers.
[3] Varro ap. Non. 56M; Verg. *Georg.* 1.293–4; Tib. 2.1.65–6; Ov. *Trist.* 4.1.5–14; Quint. *Inst.* 1.10.16; Aug. *En. 2 in Ps.* 18.2; Wille 1967: 107–9; Horsfall 2003: 45.
[4] Ps.-Verg. *Copa* 3–4; Hor. *Ep.* 1.14.25–6; Philostr. *VA* 4.39, 4.42; Sidon. 8.11.3, ll. 49–54. On tavern music, see Morgan 2017.
[5] See Bonaria 1983; Jones 1991; Morgan 2019.
[6] Quint. *Inst.* 1.10.11–12: *musicen cum divinarum etiam rerum cognitione esse coniunctam ... atqui claros nomine sapientiae viros nemo dubitaverit studiosos musices fuisse.*

trumpets and horns in our legions? The more forceful their sound, the more does Roman military glory prevail over the rest.'[7]

And yet, to many Romans – Quintilian included – music also posed a real and present danger to society. In the eyes of Cicero, writing in the middle of the first century BCE, singing in the forum constituted 'a great perversion' (*magna perversitas*) of societal norms, an action strongly discordant with civilized behaviour.[8] It was imperative, therefore, that the right kinds of music were heard in the right places and at the right times. Members of the upper classes, Cicero maintained, should sing only when it was appropriate.[9] As early as the 180s BCE, a Roman magistrate was publicly reprimanded by a prominent senator for 'singing whenever he feels like it' (*cantat ubi collibuit*).[10] Moral strictures of this sort are commonplace in Roman literature. Men and women are accused of enjoying music *too* enthusiastically or playing instruments *too* skilfully. What inspired this rhetoric of contempt? Why did singing and playing instruments generate such intense feelings of anxiety, indignation and shame among generations of Roman citizens? What were the criteria for distinguishing 'good' music from 'bad'? And who was responsible for determining these criteria?

This book examines the role that music played in the political and social landscape of ancient Rome. It does not purport to be a comprehensive history of Roman music as such. Rather, it is intended primarily as a study of how Roman attitudes to music evolved throughout the mid-to-late Republic and early Principate, and how music was used as a political tool by Roman elites during this period. Since the vast majority of the extant written sources from the Roman world were produced by members of the educated upper classes, it is much easier to reconstruct the musical experiences and attitudes of those at the very top of society than those lower down. However, the elite's interactions with music had far-reaching consequences for the urban populace at large. This book asks not only what Roman leaders thought about music and how they used music, but also how their use of music in turn affected wider social attitudes and practices.

---

[7] Quint. *Inst.* 1.10.14–15: *quid autem aliud in nostris legionibus cornua ac tubae faciunt? quorum concentus quanto est vehementior, tantum Romana in bellis gloria ceteris praestat*. On the role of music in the Roman army, see Vincent 2016: 15–117.

[8] Cic. *Off.* 1.145: *ea, quae multum ab humanitate discrepant, ut si qui in foro cantet, aut si qua est alia magna perversitas, facile apparet*.

[9] Cf. Cic. *De Orat.* 3.87, discussed below in the section 'The Status of Musicians'.

[10] Cato fr. 114–15 Malcovati = Macr. *Sat.* 3.14.9.

Approaching Roman Music

Although the centrality of music in the cultural life of the ancient Romans has long been recognised, the intersections between music, politics and society at Rome have not received sufficient attention.[11] The study of Roman music, in general, has languished by comparison with the study of Greek music, which has in recent decades blossomed into a vibrant field of scholarship.[12] Indeed, Roman music has traditionally been dismissed as little more than a crude derivative of Greek music – a topic worthy of antiquarian interest, perhaps, but devoid of any real historical or musicological importance. This theory, which has its roots in the intellectual currents of the eighteenth and nineteenth centuries, is predicated on a long-outdated notion of the moral and aesthetic superiority of Greek culture over Roman.[13] The Romans, being a pragmatic and bellicose people, are said to have developed a taste for music only through exposure to, and appropriation of, the civilizations of conquered peoples (especially the Greeks and Etruscans). So, in the entry on 'music' in the *Oxford Classical Dictionary*, published in 1949, it is stated that 'in the whole range of Latin literature we find only the most commonplace and conventional references to music, and ... nowhere is there any indication that the Romans regarded music as anything more than a tolerable adjunct of civilized life'.[14] John Landels reaches a similar conclusion in his book

---

[11] Notable early treatments of the subject include: Eximeno 1774; Hawkins 1776; Burney 1789; Zell 1829; Rowbotham 1888; Machabey 1936; Antcliffe 1949.

[12] See especially Barker 1984, 1989; West 1992; Mathiesen 1999; Wilson 1999, 2002, 2004; Murray and Wilson 2004; Csapo 2004; Murray and Wilson 2004; Csapo and Wilson 2009; Hagel 2009; Power 2010; D'Angour and Philipps 2018; Weiss 2018; Rocconi and Lynch 2020. Much research has been conducted under the auspices of the MOISA Society for the Study of Ancient Greek and Roman Music, founded by Andrew Barker in 2007. The bibliography listed on the organisation's website (www.moisasociety.org) displays a striking imbalance in favour of Greek music, as do the articles published in the MOISA-affiliated journal *Greek and Roman Musical Studies*, established in 2013. In Comotti's book *Music in Greek and Roman Culture*, the chapter on Roman music occupies a mere eight pages (Comotti 1989: 48–55). Creese 2006 and Rocconi 2015 provide helpful overviews of ancient Greek and Roman music, but focus largely on the former.

[13] See Hawkins 1776: xxvi: 'Neither [the Romans'] religious solemnities, nor their triumphs, their shows or theatrical representations, splendid as they were, contributed in the least to the improvement of music either in theory or practice: to say the truth, they seemed scarcely to have considered it as a subject of speculation.'; Burney 1789: 474: 'It was long the fate of our own country, like that of the ancient Romans, to admire the polite arts more than cultivate them.' The influential Belgian musicologist François-Auguste Gevaert argued in his *Histoire et théorie de la musique de l'antiquité* (1875) that the rise of the Roman Empire marked the nadir of music history, separating the apogee of Greece and the revival of Christianity.

[14] Mountford 1949: 585; echoed in Mountford 1964: 198: 'There is no evidence to suggest that Rome contributed much that was vital to the history of musical development.' Similar views are

Music in Ancient Greece and Rome (1999): 'In dealing with the role of music in Roman life, we shall not be looking at the emergence of a new and totally different musical culture. It would be fair to say that the Romans did not attempt to develop a musical identity of their own.' The reader is even assured that 'the Romans themselves do not seem to have been troubled or embarrassed by their lack of interest and proficiency in music'![15]

Not all scholars have been so dismissive. In 1967, the German philologist Günther Wille published a weighty monograph entitled *Musica Romana: die Bedeutung der Musik im Leben der Römer*. In the book, Wille sought to challenge the prevailing view of the Romans as an innately unmusical people. His approach was simple yet ambitious: to document every identifiable reference to music in the entire corpus of Latin literature, supplemented by inscriptions and material artefacts. The product of this endeavour is an impressive anthology of more than four thousand texts, laid out over some seven hundred pages. Coincidentally, just two years before the publication of *Musica Romana*, the art historian Günther Fleischhauer published an extensive catalogue of musical images from Rome and Etruria, comprising some eighty illustrations with accompanying descriptions.[16] The two works did much to raise the profile of the subject in the face of continued scholarly efforts to undermine its value. However, while Wille succeeded in demonstrating the pervasiveness of music in Roman culture, his treatment of the evidence was inadequate in several respects. *Musica Romana* provides an object lesson in the privileging of quantity over quality: each page is crammed with copious references to primary source material, and yet the author's broad thematic deployment of this material allows virtually no scope for analytical discussion. Sensitive issues of philological and historical importance are passed over in silence. Moreover, many of Wille's arguments in favour of the 'originality' of Roman music (such as the theory that Horace's lyric poems were set to melodies) do not hold up to scrutiny.[17] Above all, then, *Musica Romana* sounded a clarion call for further research in this area.

Only in the last few decades have scholars begun to comb through the vast body of evidence which Wille and Fleischhauer so painstakingly assembled nearly sixty years ago. Classical philologists such as Nevio Zorzetti, Thomas Habinek and Denis Feeney have attempted to trace the

---

expressed by Celentano 1913: 245; Birt 1928: 380; Friedländer 1936: 347; Sachs 1944: 272; Bonaria 1983: 119–20; Pöhlmann 2010: 31.

[15] Landels 1999: 172.   [16] Fleischhauer 1965.
[17] See the criticisms raised by McKinnon 1968 and Borthwick 1969.

origins of Latin literature back to an archaic Roman song culture, whose existence is first posited by Cato the Elder.[18] Thanks to the pioneering work of Timothy Moore, we now have a much deeper appreciation of the vital contribution of song and dance to the Roman theatre.[19] Studies have also demonstrated how music enhanced Roman audiences' experience of gladiatorial games and chariot races by punctuating moments of tension or climax.[20] Jörg Rüpke, Christophe Vendries and others have done much to illustrate the role of the sensorium, and sound especially, in shaping participants' experience of religious rituals in Rome, stressing, for instance, the association of different kinds of music with different sanctuaries and cults.[21] Nicholas Horsfall has drawn attention to the importance of music in the culture of the Roman *plebs*, emphasising in particular the strong connection between song and memory.[22] Finally, the lives of musicians in the Roman world have been the subject of no fewer than four monographs, including, most recently, Alexandre Vincent's *Jouer pour la cité: une histoire sociale et politique des musiciens professionnels de l'Occident romain*.[23]

The growing body of scholarship devoted to Roman music attests to the great potential of this subject to enrich our understanding of the ancient world. Nonetheless, it would not be an overstatement to say that we have barely scratched the surface of the evidence. Above all, there remains an urgent need for a systematic analysis of what we might call the 'cultural politics' of Roman music – that is, the attitudes, discourses and ideologies generated by, and in response to, musical practices. Following the model of Wille's *Musica Romana*, scholarly discussions have tended to filter the sources through a synoptic lens. As a consequence, they have promoted a largely homogeneous view of Roman musical culture, with little variation across time and space. However, as I argue in this book, the Roman musical experience was marked by conflict, contradiction and change. It is true that many aspects of Roman music-making, such as the use of certain instruments and the organisation of musical performances, remained constant over several centuries. However, we should not assume that the Romans' attitudes towards and interactions with music were unaffected by broader social, cultural and political developments. On the contrary, as we shall see,

---

[18] Zorzetti 1991; Habinek 2005; Feeney 2016.
[19] Moore 2012, 2016, 2021. See also Guidobaldi 1992; Péché and Vendries 2001.
[20] See Simpson 2000; Fagan 2011: 225–7; Coleman 2018.
[21] Rüpke 2018: 17–18; Brulé and Vendries 2001; Vendries 2004; Fless and Moede 2007.
[22] Horsfall 2003.   [23] Baudot 1973; Bélis 1999; Scoditti 2009; Vincent 2016.

Roman engagements with music are inextricably bound up in complex and evolving discourses on morality, class, ethnicity, gender and sexuality. By paying closer attention to these discourses, we can gain a more nuanced and more fully contextualised view of music's place in Roman society.

Sources of Evidence

Understanding the musical experience of historical peoples is a task fraught with difficulty. In the case of ancient Rome, the difficulty is compounded by the fact that we know relatively little about the actual melodies that were heard by listeners some two millennia ago. There are, nevertheless, various sources of evidence which help us to understand the role of music in Roman life. Of particular importance for the purposes of this book are literary texts which contain descriptions of musical performances, accounts of the history of music, or reflections on the theoretical, ethical and political significance of music. Passages of this nature crop up in a wide variety of genres, but are chiefly found in speeches, histories, poems and philosophical treatises. Of course, there is much that does not survive. The loss of the treatise on music written by M. Terentius Varro, the great scholar and polymath of the first century BCE, is particularly regrettable. Contained in the seventh book of his *Disciplinae* (Disciplines), the *De Musica* was widely consulted by later musicologists, including Augustine, Martianus Capella and Boethius.[24] Varro's contemporary, Cicero, is a more eloquent witness; his views on music have been particularly neglected and will be considered at length in Chapter 2.

There are two additional sources of evidence that contribute to our understanding of Roman musical culture – namely, epigraphy and art. The lives of musicians are documented in hundreds of funerary inscriptions from across the Roman world. These range from simple records of the deceased's name and profession to elaborate verse epitaphs commemorating the individual's attainments. Many musicians belonged to professional associations, known as *collegia*, which set up inscriptions publicly memorialising their participation in civic festivals and religious cults.[25] As Vincent shows, this rich body of evidence attests to the integration of many freed or freeborn musicians into Roman society, affording an impression that is in many ways diametrically opposed to that conveyed by the literary

---

[24] See Jacobsson 2017 on Augustine; Heilmann 2007 and Caldwell 1981 on Boethius.
[25] See Péché 2001; Vincent 2008; Giovagnoli 2014.

Figure 0.1 Mosaic panel by Dioscurides of Samos showing masked actors playing musical instruments (*tibiae*, *cymbala* and *tympanum*). Based on an episode from Menander's *Theophoroumene*. From the Villa of Cicero, Pompeii; ca. 100 BCE. Photo by DEA Picture Library / De Agostini via Getty Images.

sources.[26] Scenes of music-making are also ubiquitous in Roman art.[27] For example, portrayals of singers and musicians in Pompeian wall-paintings and mosaics can help us to visualise what a musical performance looked like from the perspective of Roman audiences, supplementing the eyewitness accounts of contemporary authors (see Fig. 0.1). Additionally, the appearance of musical imagery on statues and coins often carries distinct political resonances. The representations of Apollo in Augustan and Neronian iconography are particularly revealing in this respect, as will be discussed in Chapters 3 and 4 respectively.

Although this book is not primarily concerned with uncovering the actual sounds of Roman music, it will be necessary at various points to engage with the practical and technical aspects of Roman song and instrumental performance. It seems worthwhile, therefore, to examine briefly

---

[26] Vincent 2016. [27] See Fleischhauer 1965; Emerit *et al.* 2017; Gétreau 2021.

how one might approach such a topic. There are three main types of evidence which aid in the reconstruction of Roman music: extant examples of ancient Greek musical notation; Roman dramatic texts from the late third and second centuries BCE that were originally set to music; and archaeological remnants of musical instruments. The best insights can be gleaned from examining all three types of evidence together.

Around sixty examples of notated Greek music survive from antiquity. Interestingly, the majority of these examples are preserved on stone or papyrus fragments from the Roman Empire, including several hymns attributed to Mesomedes, the court musician of the emperor Hadrian.[28] The interpretation of Greek musical notation is made possible by the survival of a treatise written by the late-antique Egyptian scholar Alypius. Entitled *Introduction to Music* (*Eisagoge Mousike*), the treatise lists the correspondence of each symbol to its respective note on the Greek musical scale. This has allowed modern experts to produce accurate renderings of ancient melodies, which, when performed on replica instruments, afford a remarkably realistic impression of ancient Greek music as it would have sounded some two millennia ago. However, if we wish to understand the indigenous musical traditions of Roman Italy, Greek notation can only take us so far. First, the Greek system of musical notation was, as far as we know, never repurposed by composers of Latin songs.[29] Second, musical notation does not seem to have been in widespread use in Greco-Roman antiquity, but rather was developed by and for a small number of professional practitioners.[30] Third, the fact that Latin and Greek had different systems of accentuation is likely to have resulted in a significant degree of melodic variation: songs set to Latin words are unlikely to have used the same melodies as songs set to Greek words.[31]

For further insights, we can turn to the comedies of Plautus and Terence. The musical complexity of Roman drama has been brilliantly illuminated by Moore in a series of pathbreaking publications, including

---

[28] The extant documents are published in Pöhlmann and West 2001. Yuan 2005 and West 2007 discuss musical fragments discovered subsequently. Johnson 2000a and 2000b deal specifically with two Roman-era fragments. On the hymns of Mesomedes, see Whitmarsh 2004.

[29] Päll 2004 discusses a curious graffito from Pompeii, consisting of a string of fifteen letters (RIITOTATOTOTATO), some of which have symbols written above them. The symbols resemble Greek musical notation. However, as Moore (2012: 13 n. 29) points out, 'the letters are not Latin ... but either onomatopoetic syllables or additional musical symbols'. The graffito evokes parallels with Ennius' onomatopoetic description of the trumpet (*Ann.* fr. 451 Skutsch: *at tuba terribili sonitu taratantara dixit*), suggesting that the author of the text may have been attempting to capture the sound (and pitch?) of a brass instrument.

[30] Pöhlmann and West 2001: 1.   [31] See Moore 2012: 94–5.

most notably his monograph *Music in Roman Comedy*, published in 2012. We know from various sources that performances of Roman comedy were accompanied by a pipe-player (*tibicen*). The actors, meanwhile, did not simply recite their lines, but also sang and danced. More specific information about the plays' musical accompaniment comes from *didascaliae*, production notes preserved in the manuscripts of Plautus and Terence. For example, the *didascaliae* preceding Terence's *Phormio* state that 'Flaccus, the slave of Claudius, produced the music on unequal pipes (*tibiis inparibus*) through the whole play'.[32] The plays themselves also contain valuable clues as to the nature of the musical accompaniment. Analysing the metrical arrangements of the texts allows us to distinguish between verses that were sung (*cantica*) and verses that were recited (*deverbia*).[33] We can therefore determine when the music started and stopped, and on this basis draw inferences about how Plautus and Terence used music to enhance the dramatic effect of their plays (for example, by accentuating certain plotlines or character traits). Additionally, as Moore's recent research has shown, the metres of Roman comedy can provide insights into an audience's musical memories within a play and between different plays, based on their recollections of different musical patterns.[34]

Dozens of musical instruments from the Roman period have been brought to light in archaeological excavations. Finds have been made throughout Italy and Sicily, and in sites as far removed as Gaul and the Levant.[35] At Pompeii alone, archaeologists have discovered fifteen pipes (*tibiae*), five trumpets (*cornua*), and a large number of cymbals (*cymbala*), drums (*tympana*) and rattles (*sistra*) (see Figs. 0.2, 0.3 and 0.4).[36] We also have the remains of three water-organs (*hydraulae*), uncovered at Aquincum (modern Budapest), Dion (in northern Greece) and Aventicum (modern Avenches, Switzerland) during the twentieth century.[37] Though often extremely fragmentary, these artefacts provide valuable information about what ancient instruments looked like and

---

[32] On the *didascaliae*, see Moore 2012: 8–9.
[33] By Moore's calculation (2012: 16), *cantica* make up over 66 per cent of Plautus' verses and about 52 per cent of Terence's.
[34] Moore 2021.
[35] For music archaeology in Italy and Sicily, see Castaldo 2012; Bellia 2012. For music archaeology in Gaul, see Homo-Lechner, Pinette and Vendries 1993. Braun 2002 and Waner 2014 examine finds from the Levant.
[36] For general discussions of Pompeian instruments, see De Simone 1999; Melini 2012, 2014. On the *tibiae*, see Hagel 2008; on the *cornua*, Vendries 2020.
[37] On the Aquincum organ, see Hyde 1938; Kaba 1976. On the Dion organ, see Markovits 2003: 97–8; Beschi 2009: 256–7; Stroux 2009: 267–9. On the Aventicum organ, see Jakob *et al.* 2000.

10   *Introduction*

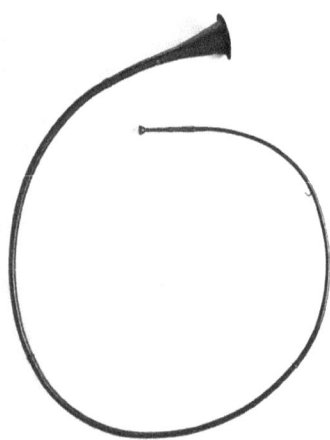

Figure 0.2 Facsimile of a Roman *cornu* found at Pompeii, produced by the Belgian instrument-maker Victor-Charles Mahillon (1841–1924). © New York Metropolitan Museum of Art.

Figure 0.3 Pair of bronze cymbals linked by a chain; Pompeii, first century CE. Museo Archeologico Nazionale, Naples. Photo by DeAgostini / Getty Images.

how they were made. It has also been possible to manufacture playable replicas based on surviving ancient models, allowing us to 'hear' Roman music as it might have originally sounded (see Fig. 0.5).[38]

---

[38] The Italian group 'Ludi Scaenici', founded by Cristina Majnero and Roberto Stanco, stages performances of 'reconstructed' ancient Roman music. The group consists of five musicians, who play a variety of replica instruments, and two dancers. Further information about the

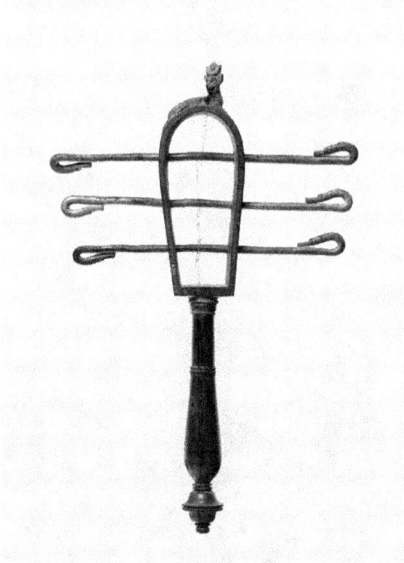

Figure 0.4 Roman *sistrum*, made of bronze or copper alloy; first or second century CE; now in the New York Metropolitan Museum of Art. The top of the instrument is decorated with a cat and two suckling kittens – an ornamental feature typical of Roman *sistra* – perhaps evoking the goddess Bastet. © New York Metropolitan Museum of Art.

Terminology

The Romans had no single word for what we could call 'music'. The Greek concept of *mousike* encompassed not only 'music' in the modern sense of the term, but also drama, poetry and dance. In Latin, *musica* and its derivatives have a different set of meanings. Roman writers typically refer to the *ars musica* or *scientia musica* as a way of denoting the discipline of music theory, which was divided according to the Greek model into the three sub-fields of harmonics, rhythmics and metrics.[39] To the Romans, then, a *musicus* (from the Greek *mousikos*) was one skilled in music theory,

---

group can be found on their website: http://www.ludi-scaenici.it/ludeng.html (accessed 11 May 2021).

[39] The term *musica* is most frequently used as an adjective, modifying either *ars* or *scientia*, although it is also attested as a substantive noun: cf. Nep. *Epam.* 1.2, *praef.* 1; Cic. *Fin.* 3.5, *De Orat.* 1.217; Varro, *Ling.* 9.111; Vitr. 1.1.3, 1.1.8; Sen. *Ep.* 88.4; Plin. *HN* 7.204; Quint. *Inst.* 1.4.4, 1.10.12, 1.10.15, 1.10.20, 1.10.27; Suet. *Nero* 20.1, *Titus* 3.2.

Figure 0.5 Performance by the group 'Ludi Scaenici' at the Festival Tarraco Viva; Tarragona, Spain. Photo: Rafael López Monné. Credit: Ludi Scaenici, courtesy of Cristina Majnero.

not necessarily a practising musician.[40] However, the term *musicus* also came to mean someone who was generally 'cultured'.[41] Its antonym, *amousos*, could be used equally of someone 'unmusical' (that is, lacking in musical cultivation) or of someone 'uncultured'.[42] It is important, therefore, to pay close attention to the specific contexts in which these words are used in order to determine their precise meaning.

Roman terminology pertaining to music can be divided into three main categories: Greek technical terms in transliteration (e.g. *musica*, *harmonia*, *symphonia*, *melodia*), Latin translations of Greek technical terms (e.g. *intervalla*, *accentus*) and indigenous Latin words (e.g. *carmen*, *cantus*, *modus*, *numerus*).[43] An author's use of a given term was influenced by

---

[40] Cf., e.g. Quint. *Inst.* 2.14.4; Cic. *De Orat.* 1.44, 3.58; *Rep.* 2.18; *Tusc.* 1.4, 1.19; Sen. *Ep.* 87.12; Colum. 1 *praef.* 5. The term *musicarius* is attested in a small number of inscriptions, where it seems to mean 'one who plays music': *CIL* 2.2241, 6.4454, 6.9650/51, 9648, 9649, 12.3344.

[41] Cf. Cic. *Pis.* 22 (*nec tam musicus*); Plaut. *Mostell.* 287 (*musice hercle agitis aetatem, ita ut vos decet*); *TLL* s.v. 'musicus', vol. VIII, 1702, 1–1705, 32 (Oomes).

[42] Varro, *Men.* 350 (*amusiam*); Vitr. 1.1.13 (*amusos*); Gel. *NA* 1.5.2–3 (*amousos*). On the various meanings of *amousia*, see Harmon 2003; LeVen 2012.

[43] For a comprehensive glossary of Roman musical terms, see Scoditti 2010.

various factors, including adherence to a particular Greek source, generic conventions and the date of writing. Cicero comments on the fact that the Romans preferred to borrow the Greek words for 'music', 'philosophy', 'rhetoric' and so on, 'although they might have been translated into Latin' (*quamquam Latine ea dici poterant*), on the grounds that these words 'have been familiarised through use' (*usu percepta sunt*).[44] Vitruvius, writing in the 20s BCE, observes that in his time there were still no Latin equivalents for many Greek musical terms.[45] However, as will become clear throughout this book, the fact that Roman thinkers continued to employ Greek loanwords to express musical ideas does not necessarily mean that their conception of music was wholly indebted to the Greeks. In dealing with Roman arguments about music, it is important to establish which elements derive from Greek models and which elements reflect independent thinking on the part of the Roman author(s) in question.

Deciphering Latin musical terminology presents various challenges. Commonly used words like *modus* and *numerus* have a wide semantic range, and it is not always easy to ascertain their precise meaning in a given context. *Modus* (literally 'measure'), when applied to music, can describe either rhythm or melody, or both.[46] Likewise, *numerus* (number) is conventionally linked to rhythm, but in some cases it appears to be more closely associated with melody or harmony.[47] At the same time, we must be wary of conflating the ancient term *harmonia* with our modern concept of 'harmony'. In both Greek and Latin, *harmonia* referred to an agreeable progression from one note to another; it dealt with 'the intervals between sounds'.[48] Harmony as we know it pertains not to the intervals between musical notes, but to a combination of notes sounded simultaneously to produce chords and chord progressions. While both the ancient and modern definitions have an aesthetic dimension, in that they emphasise

---

[44] Cic. *Fin.* 3.5.
[45] Vitr. 5.4.1. According to Boethius (*Inst.* 1.26), many Greek musical terms were first translated into Latin by Ceionius Rufius Albinus, consul and then urban prefect in 335 CE, who wrote a treatise on music (now lost).
[46] Cf. *TLL* s.v. 'modus', Vol. VIII, 0, 1252, 43–1321, 73 (Brandt).
[47] Cf. *OLD* s.v. 'numerus' 13 (a rhythm or cadence) and 15 (musical strains, melody). The latter usage is restricted to plural forms: e.g. Cic. *Leg.* 1.11 (*numeros in cantu cecinerat*); Prop. 2.22.16 (*cur aliquis ... Phrygis insanos caeditur ad numeros?*); Verg. *Ecl.* 9.45 (*numeros memini, si verba tenerem*).
[48] Cic. *Tusc. Disp.* 1.41 (*ex intervallis sonorum*). The Latin transliteration *harmonia* retains the same technical sense as the Greek ἁρμονία; cf. also Cic. *Rep.* 1.16.9, *Tusc. Disp.* 1.24; Vitr. 5.4.3; Quint. *Inst.* 1.10.12.

the pleasing effect of 'harmonious' music, the system of chord-based harmony is generally regarded as an invention of the late Middle Ages.

Descriptive terms for music, like *flexus* (bending) and *fractus* (broken), pose an additional set of interpretative issues, since it is often unclear whether they are being used in a technical or rhetorical sense. The idea of 'bending' music seems to have developed in Greek discourse as a reaction to the so-called New Music of the late fifth century BCE.[49] The term *kampe* (bend) is associated in the first instance with melodic modulation (the Greek lyric poet Pindar speaks of a 'bending melody', *kampylon melos*), but it was also used metaphorically as an indictment of the moral laxity of the New Music (contrasted with the simplicity of traditional music).[50] In Latin descriptions of music, words like *flexus* or *modulatio* often have a similarly negative connotation.[51] For example, while singers and orators alike are encouraged to employ vocal 'bending' for the sake of pleasing the ears of their listeners, they are also warned against excessive use of this technique, on the grounds that too much 'bending' was unmanly and undignified. Similarly, the term *fractus* (or *infractus*), when used in connection with music, entails what Maud Gleason describes as a kind of 'semantic double-determination': 'words or voices that are "broken" are weak, and therefore feminine; rhythms that are "broken" (in Greek, *keklasmenoi*) soil the dignity of prose with the unmanly ethos of certain lyric metres'.[52] Instead of looking in vain for the precise technical application of certain musical terms, therefore, we must root out their polyvalent meanings within broader Greek and Roman discourses on morality, sexuality and aesthetics.

The Romans employed various words for song, including *carmen, cantus, cantio* and *canticum*.[53] These words pose notorious problems for the modern interpreter. Since the Latin language does not draw a sharp distinction between singing and speaking, it is often extremely difficult, if not impossible, to determine whether the usage of *carmen* or *cantus* in a given text denotes an action that we would consider 'musical'. According to Thomas Habinek, who tackles this issue at length in his book, *The World of Roman Song: From Ritualized Speech to Social Order* (2005), the verb

---

[49] See Hagel 2009: 270–1; Franklin 2013.
[50] Pind. fr. 107a1–3 Snell-Maehler, quoted in Plut. *Mor.* 748b.   [51] See Moore 2012: 94.
[52] Gleason 1995: 112. For the use of *fractus/infractus* in reference to literary composition and rhetorical delivery, cf. Sen. *Contr.* 7.4.8 (*non tantum emollitae compositionis sunt, sed infractae*); Sen. *Ep.* 114.1 (*explicatio ... infracta et in morem cantici ducta*); Juv. 2.111–12 (*fracta voce loquendi libertas*); Gell. *NA* 3.5 (*vocem ... infractam*).
[53] For terminology associated with professional singers in Rome, see Caruso 2008.

canere (to sing) and its cognates 'describe speech made special through the use of specialized diction, regular meter, musical accompaniment, figures of sound, mythical or religious subject matter, and socially authoritative performance context: in effect, speech that has been ritualized'.[54] Thus, the verbs *canere* and *cantare* indicate, in Habinek's opinion, a kind of 'marked' language, in contradistinction with verbs like *loqui* (to speak), which indicate 'unmarked' language. To add to the complexity, Habinek imposes a further division between *canere* and *cantare*: whereas *canere* refers to marked language in a general sense, *cantare* is used specifically for 'the repetition or reperformance of someone else's authorizing performance'.[55] Habinek's framework is useful in highlighting the integral role of song in the formation of Roman social ritual. However, it is of limited value in shedding light on the historical realities of Roman musical performance. When we encounter an instance of 'marked' or 'authorizing' discourse, how are we to know that singing is involved, especially if we lack external context? A remark in Cicero's treatise *De Legibus* illustrates the problem. In passing, Cicero describes the Twelve Tables, an early Roman law code, as a *carmen necessarium*, which he was required to learn as a boy.[56] Nicholas Horsfall, in his study of Roman plebeian culture, takes this remark as straightforward evidence for the use of music as a mnemonic aid in the Roman classroom – just as Augustine, much later, recalled chanting his times tables and Jerome the letters of the alphabet.[57] However, it is possible that Cicero never actually *sang* the Twelve Tables. As Habinek points out, verbal formulae which required 'specialized diction' could be classified as *carmina* on the basis that they were differentiated from everyday (unmarked) speech. In such cases, the sources unfortunately raise more questions than answers.

Finally, there are terms relating to musical instruments.[58] Here we find ourselves on firmer ground. By far the most important instrument in the Roman world was the *tibia* (*aulos* in Greek), a reed pipe usually played in pairs (see Figs. 0.6 and 0.7). The *tibia* was used in many types of civic and religious rituals, including sacrifices, theatrical performances and funerals.[59] A male player of the *tibia* was called a *tibicen*, a female player

---

[54] Habinek 2005: 61–2.   [55] Habinek 2005: 66.
[56] Cic. *Leg.* 2.59 (*discebamus enim pueri duodecim ut carmen necessarium*).
[57] Horsfall 2003: 11; cf. August. *Conf.* 1.13.22 (*unum et unum duo, duo et duo quattuor, odiosa cantio mihi erat*); Jer. *Ep.* 107.4.2 (*et non solum ordinem teneat litterarum, et memoria nominum in canticum transeat*).
[58] For a general overview of this subject, see Bélis 1988a.
[59] Cf. Ov. *Fast.* 6.13: *cantabat fanis, cantabat tibia ludis, cantabat maestis tibia funeribus*. For the role of the *tibia* in the Roman theatre specifically, see Péché 1998.

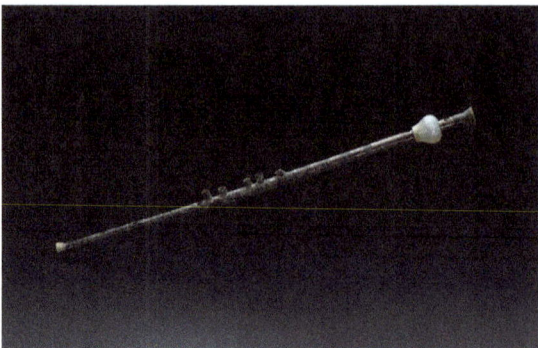

Figure 0.6 A *tibia* from Roman Syria, made of bone with bronze and silver facing and decorative chalcedony bulb, L. 23⅛ in. (58.6 cm); ca. 1–500 CE. © New York Metropolitan Museum of Art.

Figure 0.7 Detail of mosaic panel showing a dancer and *tibia* player. One of five panels with circus and arena scenes, from Sta. Sabina on the Aventine, Rome; third century CE. Museo Pio Clementino, Vatican Museums. Credits: Photo Scala, Florence / Art Resource NY.

a *tibicina*.⁶⁰ Other wind instruments employed by the Romans include the panpipe (*fistula* in Latin, *syrinx* in Greek);⁶¹ the transverse flute (*tibia obliqua* in Latin, *plagiaulos* in Greek);⁶² the water-organ (*hydraulis*);⁶³ and the bagpipe.⁶⁴

Next to the *tibia* in importance was the *cithara* (*kithara* in Greek). The *cithara* typically had seven strings and was played with a plectrum in the right hand, while the left hand was used for dampening the strings. *Citharae* were showpiece instruments, designed for concert performance.⁶⁵ A player of the *cithara* was called a *citharista* or *citharoedus*; the latter term refers specifically to a musician who sang while playing the *cithara*.⁶⁶ Although it is conventional to translate *cithara* as 'lyre' (as I shall do in this book), there were other types of lyres in Rome besides the *cithara*. Amateurs and students usually opted for the smaller, bowl-shaped tortoise-shell lyre known in Greek as a *chelys* (*lyra* or *fides* in Latin) or its baritone version, the *barbitos*.⁶⁷ The Romans were also familiar with a variety of harps of eastern origin. These included the *sambuca*, a type of arched harp, the *trigonon*, a triangular harp, and the *pandura*, a kind of lute.⁶⁸

---

⁶⁰ Greek αὐλητής (masculine), αὐλητρίς (feminine). *Tibiae* came in various shapes and sizes; the most common variant was the *tibia Phrygia* (Phrygian pipe), which had a horn fitted to the end of one pipe: see Moore 2012: 56–63; Bélis 1986.

⁶¹ Though associated primarily with pastoral settings, *fistulae* were also used to accompany theatrical performances. Ciotti (1950) discusses an Italian relief representing a *fistulator* (player of the panpipes) as part of an orchestral ensemble for a pantomime performance.

⁶² Like the *fistula*, the transverse flute had strong pastoral connotations, though it is much less frequently attested: see West 1992: 112–3; Landels 1999: 71–2.

⁶³ The *hydraulis* was invented in Alexandria in the Hellenistic period and became popular in Rome during the early imperial period: see Perrot 1971; Markovits 2003; Morgan 2022.

⁶⁴ There are two known words for bagpiper: *utricularius* (Suet. *Nero* 54) and *ascaules* (Mart. 10.3.8). Strangely, there is no recorded Greek or Latin term for the instrument itself. On the history of the bagpipes, see Baines 1960; Calvo-Sotelo 2015.

⁶⁵ Literary and artistic depictions show that they were often very large in size and could be inlaid with precious metals and gems. The Roman historian Ammianus Marcellinus complains of the construction of 'giant lyres as large as carriages' in the fourth century (*lyrae ad speciem carpentorum ingentes*; 14.6.18).

⁶⁶ On the Greek art of *kitharoidia*, see Power 2010.

⁶⁷ Confusingly, the terms *lyra* and *fides* are sometimes used synonymously with *cithara*, especially in poetic texts. 'Lyre-player' = *fidicen* (Cic. *Nat. D.* 3.32, *Fam.* 9.22.3; Hor. *Sat.* 4.3.23, 4.6.25, *Ep.* 1.9.33); *fidicina* (Plaut. *Stich.* 380, *Epid.* 47 and *passim*; Gell. *NA* pr.1.11.4; *SHA Verus* 8.11); *lyristes* (Plin. *Ep.* 1.15.2, 9.17.3, 9.36.3, 9.40.2).

⁶⁸ 'Harp-player' = *psaltes* (Quint. *Inst.* 1.10.18); *psaltria* (e.g. Ter. *Ad.* 388 and *passim*; Cic. *Tusc.* 3.46, *Sest.* 116; Livy 39.6.8; Juv. 6.337); *sambucistria* (a transliteration of the Greek σαμβυκίστρια) appears once in Livy 39.6.8; at Plaut. *Stich.* 381, *sambucae* are 'female players of the *sambuca*'. The term *spadix* is also used to refer to a kind of stringed instrument: Poll. *Onom.* 4.59; Quint. *Inst.* 1.10.31 makes reference to *spadicae* (female players of the *spadix*); see further Barker 1989: 294 n. 31.

The generic term for 'harp' in Latin is *psalterium*.[69] Harp-players are most often found in convivial settings, reflecting their traditional presence in Greek symposia, although they also took part in certain religious rituals.[70]

Horns and trumpets constitute another important category of instruments. There were three main types: the *tuba*, a long, straight trumpet with a flared bell, made typically of bronze or brass; the *cornu* (or *bucina*), a curved horn (Fig. 0.2); and the *lituus*, a straight trumpet with a curved end. The players of these instruments were called *tubicines, cornicines* and *liticines* respectively; *aenatores* was also used as a generic term for brass-players.[71] In the textual sources they feature most prominently in military settings, accompanying the daily routines of the army camp or giving signals on the battlefield.[72] *Cornicines* and *tubicines* also participated in triumphs, processions (*pompae*), funerals, chariot-races and gladiatorial contests.[73]

The most widely used percussion instruments in Rome were hand drums (*tympana*), cymbals (*cymbala*) and castanets (*crotala*). We also encounter the so-called *scabellum* (or *scabillum*), a type of clapper made of wood or metal that was worn on the foot (see Fig. 0.7), and the *sistrum*, a hand-held rattle associated with the cult of Isis (Figs. 0.4 and 0.8). With the exception of the *scabellum*, which was usually played in theatrical settings by male *tibicines*, percussionists tended to be women. This is reflected both by the preponderance of feminine nouns in Latin (*tympanista, cymbalista, crotalistria*, etc.) and by the common depiction of female percussionists in Roman art.[74]

Greek and Etruscan Influences on Roman Music

It has become axiomatic in modern scholarship to speak of Roman music as simply an amalgamation of Greek and Etruscan music. In support of this

---

[69] Cf. *ORF* 21.30 = Macr. *Sat.* 3.14.6; Cic. *Har. resp.* 44; Varro, *Ling.* 8.61; Quint. *Inst.* 1.10.31.

[70] *Psaltriae* took part in the mystery rites of the Bona Dea cult: Plut. *Caes.* 10.1 and Juv. 6.337, referring to Clodius' intrusion on the rites in 62 BCE. For an in-depth study of Roman stringed instruments, see Vendries 1999.

[71] *Tubicen* corresponds with the Greek σαλπιγκτής (also spelled σαλπικτής or σαλπιστής); *cornicen/bucinator* with βυκανητή (Polyb. 2.29.6; Dion. Hal. *Ant. Rom.* 4.18.3) or βυκανιστής (Polyb. 30.22.11).

[72] See Alexandrescu 2010.   [73] Vincent 2016. Ziolkowski 1999 examines the origins of the *tuba*.

[74] *Tympanista*: Apul. *De Deo Socratis* 14.8. *Cymbalista*: Pet. *Sat.* 22.6, 23.1; Apul. *De Deo Socratis* 14.8; *CIL* 6.4627. *Crotalistria*: Prop. 4.8.39; Pet. *Sat.* 55.6.6. On the *scabellum*, see Bélis 1988b. There was a *collegium scabillariorum* at Rome: *CIL* 6.33193, 6660. Another *collegium scabillariorum* was active in Puteoli in the second century CE: *CIL* 10.1642, 1643, 1649. See also *AE* 2005, 439, for an inscription referring to a notable in Spoletum who provided a troupe of *scamelarii* (= *scabillarii*?) for the local theatre.

Figure 0.8 Wall painting from Herculaneum depicting a ceremony of the cult of Isis. A figure in a mask performs a sacred dance, accompanied by a female *tympanum*-player dressed in white, who stands behind him, and a throng of attendants with *sistra*; ca. 1–79 CE. Museo Archeologico Nazionale, Naples. Credit: Prisma Archivo / Alamy Stock Photo.

idea, scholars have pointed to three factors in particular: the Greek and Etruscan origins of Roman instruments; the dependence of Roman musicological thought on earlier Greek models; and the prevalence of Greek-derived names in the prosopography of Roman musicians. However, these considerations are of limited value in assessing the social and political dynamics of Roman musical culture over the *longue durée*. In recent decades, scholarly advances in the fields of philology, philosophy, history and archaeology have opened up a range of nuanced perspectives on the cultural interface between imperial Rome and the Greek East. The phenomenon of Hellenisation, it is now understood, was not simply the hegemonic appropriation of a subject culture, as satirised in the immortal verse of Horace, *Graecia capta ferum victorem cepit* (conquered Greece took its savage victor captive).⁷⁵ Rather, it invoked a bilateral process of borrowing and exchange. Crucially, the transmission of culture through time and space changed how that culture was received and reproduced in its new setting. Thus, to insist on the derivative character of Roman music is to cling onto an outdated notion of what 'Roman culture' represents. What is more, it ignores the basic fact that music reflects the specific historical contexts of its creation.⁷⁶ The study of Roman music cannot be reduced to a discussion of musical instruments, performance styles and techniques. We must cast our net more broadly, to look not only at the different ways in which music was consumed, but also at the societal, cultural, political and psychological factors which conditioned how music was experienced and imagined by people of different ages, genders and social classes.

There can be little doubt that the Romans were exposed to foreign musical influences at an early stage in their history through contact with the Hellenised communities of Etruria and northern Italy. Evidence from pottery and tomb paintings attests to the use of music in Etruscan rituals as early as the seventh century BCE.⁷⁷ A wide range of instruments is represented in Etruscan art and archaeology, including double-pipes, panpipes, transverse flutes, trumpets, lyres and castanets. When this music made its way south to Latium cannot be clearly determined. Of course, it is likely that the Romans' earliest encounters with Etruscan music have left no trace in the archaeological record.⁷⁸ Strabo, the Greek geographer of the first century CE, goes so far as to describe Etruria as the source of 'all music publicly used by the Romans' (μουσικὴ ὅση δημοσίᾳ χρῶνται Ῥωμαῖοι), but he unfortunately does not elaborate on this statement.⁷⁹ The earliest tangible evidence for musical interaction between Rome and Etruria dates from the fourth century BCE. A number of engraved bronze boxes (*cistae*) from Latium, produced mostly during the fourth century, represent pipe-playing satyrs accompanying female dancers in the performance of scenes from Euripidean tragedy. Similar Dionysiac imagery can be

---

[75] Hor. *Ep.* 2.1.156.   [76] See Trietler 1999: 366.
[77] On Etruscan music, see Tobin 2013; Carrese, Li Castro and Martinelli 2010.
[78] Powley 1996 offers some useful reflections on the relationship between Etruscan and Roman music, although his discussion is necessarily impressionistic given the paucity of direct evidence.
[79] Strabo 5.2.2.

found on contemporary red-figure vase paintings from Etruria and Campania.[80] In addition, the historian Livy, describing the first theatrical performances in Rome in 364 BCE, records that 'dancers, summoned from Etruria, dancing to tunes provided by a *tibicen*, performed proper dances in the Etruscan manner, without any singing and without imitating the action of singers' (*sine carmine ullo, sine imitandorum carminum actu ludiones ex Etruria acciti, ad tibicinis modos saltantes, haud indecoros motus more Tusco dabant*).[81] Regardless of the overall historical accuracy of Livy's account, the suggestion that Etruscan music influenced the development of Roman drama seems creditable on a priori grounds, and is broadly consistent with the impression afforded by the material culture from Latium and the surrounding regions.[82]

Despite the strong ties between Roman and Etruscan music, the Romans saw themselves first and foremost as the inheritors of a Greek musical tradition, which predated the foundation of Rome itself.[83] The Greeks' devotion to music was legendary. As Cicero writes, 'musicians flourished in Greece; everyone would learn music, and whoever was unacquainted with it was not regarded as fully educated' (*in Graecia musici floruerunt, discebantque id omnes, nec qui nesciebat satis excultus doctrina putabatur*).[84] As with Etruscan music, documenting the Hellenic influence on early Roman music is exceedingly difficult. We must rely for the most part on literary texts written during the height of the Roman Empire. A particularly interesting source is Dionysius of Halicarnassus, a Greek historian and teacher of rhetoric who migrated to Rome in around 30 BCE. Dionysius' magnum opus, entitled *Roman Antiquities*, traces the history of Rome from its beginnings down to the time of the First Punic War. In one section of the work, Dionysius describes the customs of the Arcadians, a Greek people who came from their homeland to settle on the site where Romulus would later establish the city of Rome. The Arcadians, Dionysius explains, brought with them to Italy 'music played on instruments which are called lyres (λύραι), *trigona* (τρίγωνα) and pipes (αὐλοί), the previous people having used no musical devices apart from pastoral panpipes (σύριγξι

---

[80] See Wiseman 2008: 85–139.   [81] Livy 7.2.4.
[82] Livy's narrative on the origins of the Roman *ludi* has been interpreted by some scholars as an aetiology of the pantomime, which was introduced to Rome during Livy's lifetime and gained popularity thanks to its promotion by the emperor Augustus: see, e.g. Jory 1981. Some of the details may derive from an earlier work by the first-century BCE writer Varro (Moore 2012: 2).
[83] Cf. Cic. *Rep.* 2.18: *in id saeculum Romuli cecidit aetas, cum iam plena Graecia poetarum et musicorum esset.*
[84] Cic. *Tusc. Disp.* 1.4; cf. *De Orat.* 3.197.

ποιμενικαῖς)'.⁸⁵ Dionysius goes on to relate how the twins Romulus and Remus, after finding shelter near the Palatine Hill, were given a Greek education by the native settlers, who taught them 'letters, music (μουσικήν) and the use of Greek arms'.⁸⁶ As Andrew Barker rightly points out, this narrative is far from a reliable record. Not only is it reminiscent of other Greek accounts of the development of 'primitive' societies, but it also aligns with the broader aim of Dionysius' historiographical project – namely, to establish the Greek lineage of the Romans and their customs.⁸⁷ Nevertheless, Dionysius' account highlights the complex role of music in the cultural memory of Rome's inhabitants. On the one hand, his attempt to write *mousike* into the story of Rome's foundation shows how the Greek and Roman musical traditions were viewed as historically intertwined: Roman *mousike* is presented by Dionysius as both originating from and developing in tandem with Greek *mousike*. On the other hand, we can see Dionysius responding here to sceptical readers, both Greek and Roman, who saw music as a late, and therefore relatively minor, addition to the Roman cultural scene. Cicero, for all his admiration of Greek *musici*, freely admitted that the Romans had been slow to adopt the Greek arts of poetry, music and geometry, choosing to focus instead on oratory.⁸⁸ In reality, Hellenic influence on Roman music was both continuous and pervasive, and most likely began long before the advent of recorded history.

The expansion of the Roman Empire during the second century BCE had a particularly profound impact on Rome's relationship with Greek music. Through a series of stunning victories – over the Carthaginian general Hannibal in 201, the Seleucid King Antiochus III in 188, the Macedonian king Perseus in 168 and the Achaean League in 146 – Rome cemented its place as the political and cultural epicentre of the Mediterranean world. Musicians, like many other professionals, flocked to Rome in droves from all over the Greek East in search of patronage and employment. Livy comments revealingly on the mass migration of female harp-players (*psaltriae sambucistriaeque*) to Rome following the triumph of Cn. Manlius Vulso in Asia Minor in 186. For Livy, the arrival of these performers in the capital symbolised the Romans' newfound taste for

---

⁸⁵ Dion. Hal. *Ant. Rom.* 1.33.4–5.   ⁸⁶ Dion. Hal. *Ant. Rom.* 1.84.5.   ⁸⁷ Barker 2017: 70.
⁸⁸ Cic. *Tusc. Disp.* 1.3–5. Cicero elsewhere (*De Orat.* 3.197) provides evidence of an indigenous Roman musical tradition going back to the time of Numa, the second king of Rome, but he seems to present it as separate from Greek music rather than as a direct offshoot of it. On the musical institutions of Numa, cf. also Plut. *Num.* 17. 3, *Quaest. Rom.* 55.

imported luxuries and contributed ultimately to the moral decay of the Roman aristocracy.[89]

No doubt inspired by the influx of highly skilled musicians from abroad, an increasing number of Roman citizens, many from the upper echelons of society, decided to take up musical pursuits themselves. Although we lack quantitative data for the number of Romans who received musical training in any given period, the profusion of individual examples speaks to a widespread and long-lasting tradition of amateur music-making. Children born into noble or wealthy families were frequently taught to sing, dance and play instruments as part of their education; as adults, they continued to perform privately in the company of friends and relatives.[90] Women were probably afforded greater access to musical instruction than men. Indeed, musicality seems to have been regarded by many as a distinctly feminine virtue. For example, Cornelia, wife of Pompey the Great, was admired for her skill at playing the lyre.[91] And at the turn of the second century CE, the Younger Pliny boasted of having his verses sung to the accompaniment of the *cithara* by his wife Calpurnia, 'with no musician to teach her but the best of masters, love'.[92] Nevertheless, we should not underestimate the number of men who possessed some degree of musical proficiency. The Roman general Sulla was said to be an excellent singer.[93] Lucius Norbanus, the consul of 19 CE, was an avid trumpeter.[94] We also know of several Roman emperors who were talented musicians.[95]

---

[89] Livy 39.6.7–8. Cf. Polyb. 31.25.4, on the popularisation of 'musical entertainments' (ἀκροάματα) after the Third Macedonian War, and Hor. *Ars P.* 208–19, on the 'greater licence' (*licentia maior*) and 'luxury' (*luxuriem*) enjoyed by musicians in the wake of Rome's imperial conquests.

[90] Greek music-teachers remained in high demand during the late Republic and early Principate, and evidently catered for both a male and female clientele: cf. Colum. *De Re Rust.* 1. pr. 5; Sen. *Ep.* 90.19; Musonius Rufus, *Discourse* 5. On the role of music in Roman education, see Bonner 2012: 44, 77; Hagel and Lynch 2015: 408–9.

[91] Plut. *Pomp.* 55.1.

[92] Plin. *Ep.* 4.19.4: *non artifice aliquo docente, sed amore qui magister est optimus*. Female musicians belonged to all ranks of society. An epitaph from Rome commemorates Auxesis, a citharode (*citharoeda*) and 'excellent wife' (*optima coniux*) of Gaius Cornelius Neritus (*CIL* 6.10125). A verse epitaph from the Spanish town of Segobriga (second century CE) is dedicated to the enslaved *citharoeda* Iucunda by her mother Nigella; the deceased is represented as a lyre-player on her tombstone (*AE* 2007, 805). Musicality was also a trait of the elegiac *puella docta* (Hemelrijk 1999: 81–4): note especially Horace's praise of the 'sweet singing' of Licymnia (*dulcis ... cantus*; 2.12.13–14), identified by the scholiast as Maecenas' wife Terentia (Ps.-Acro ad Hor. *Od.* 2.12.13–20).

[93] Macr. *Sat.* 3.14.10: *L. Sylla, vir tanti nominis, optime cantasse dicatur.*   [94] Dio Cass. 57.18.3.

[95] Caligula: Philo *Leg.* 44, 79, 96; Suet. *Calig.* 11, 54.1; Dio Cass. 59.29; Aur. Vict. *Caes.* 3.12; cf. Philo *Leg.* 42, describing his 'boyish' (μειρακιωδέστερον) enthusiasm for dancers and mimes. Titus: Suet. *Tit.* 3. Hadrian: *SHA Hadr.* 14.8. Marcus Aurelius: *SHA Marc. Aur.* 2.2. Commodus: *SHA Comm.* 1.8. Elagabalus: *SHA Heliogab.* 32.8. Alexander Severus: *SHA Alex. Sev.* 27.5, 27.9.

Most notorious of all, of course, was the much-maligned Nero; he was remembered by later generations simply as *citharoedus princeps*, 'the emperor who sang to the lyre'.[96]

One did not need to know how to sing or play an instrument to be considered a connoisseur of music. Roman elites could also display their wealth and cultural sophistication by patronising Greek musicians.[97] The staging of private musical concerts, known as *symphoniae*, became fashionable during the late Republic and early Principate, inspiring a craze for musically trained slaves (*symphoniaci*).[98] The Romans' penchant for such entertainment is reflected in the decoration of their houses. Pompeian wall paintings often depict musicians engaged in performance, dressed in fine clothing and playing expensive instruments. A particularly well-preserved example comes from the villa of Publius Fannius Synistor at Boscoreale (Fig. 0.9). Dated to around 40–30 BCE, it shows a seated woman holding a large, gilded lyre, while a younger girl stands behind her. The identity of the pair has been disputed, but the most persuasive interpretation is that they represent a Macedonian queen and her daughter or younger sister.[99] By commissioning artistic depictions of music-making like the one found at Boscoreale, Roman patrons were able to create an air of luxury in their house while advertising their cultural sophistication to visitors.

The rise of philhellenism affected not only how Roman elites made and listened to music, but also how they engaged with it intellectually. Music came to be valued as an edifying pursuit – 'a most beautiful art' (*ars pulcherrima*), in the words of Quintilian – because of its venerable association with Greek learning (*paideia*).[100] By the time of Cicero, if not earlier, the study of music theory (as distinct from musical performance) had become a valuable, even necessary, component of an aristocratic education.[101] An aspiring orator could be expected to know the technical terms for the different strings of the lyre and the different

---

[96] Juv. 8.198.

[97] Pliny the Younger (*Ep.* 7.4.9) boasts that his verses were sung and accompanied on the *cithara* and *lyra* by Greek musicians.

[98] For the term *symphoniacus* (one who performs in a *symphonia*), see Bélis 1999: 61–72; Vincent 2016: 169–71; Morgan 2019: 260–6. Linderski 2003 examines an unusually sophisticated epitaph of a *symphoniacus* which seems to contain an eschatological injunction. See also Panayotakis 1995: 60, discussing the prominence of slave musicians in Petronius' *Cena Trimalchionis*.

[99] See Power 2010: 68–70.   [100] Quint. *Inst.* 1.10.17.

[101] Music was one of the nine 'liberal arts' (*artes liberales* or *disciplinae*) which comprised the Roman aristocratic curriculum, along with grammar, dialectic, rhetoric, geometry, arithmetic, astronomy, medicine and architecture.

Figure 0.9 Wall painting with seated woman holding a *cithara*, from Room H of the Villa of P. Fannius Synistor at Boscoreale; ca. 50–40 BCE; New York Metropolitan Museum of Art, Rogers Fund, 1903 (03.14.5). © New York Metropolitan Museum of Art.

intervals.[102] Architectural experts like Vitruvius applied the Pythagorean principle of harmonic ratios to optimise the design of theatres and other buildings.[103] Music theory also became a bedrock of the Roman philosophical tradition. From studying the precepts of Plato and Pythagoras, Aristotle and Aristoxenus, Roman thinkers such as Cicero, Varro and Seneca the Younger gained an appreciation of how music affected the soul in both positive and negative ways and altered the character of political states.

---

[102] Cf. Quint. *Inst.* 1.10.1–33, with Hagel 2009: 134.
[103] Cf. especially Vitr. *Arch.* 5.5, on the use of tuned resonating jars in theatres; discussed by Hagel 2009: 251–5. Walden 2014 discusses the place of musical theory in Vitruvius' work more generally.

And yet, the spread of Greek musical culture also generated long-lasting and deep-rooted tensions in Roman society. In Roman discourse, music-making became associated with a set of undesirable traits, such as sexual depravity, effeminacy, luxury and vulgarity, all of which were regarded as quintessentially 'Greek' flaws. However, the Romans conceded that some forms of Greek music were more harmful than others. One could object to music on moral or aesthetic grounds while still championing the benefits of a musical education (and, even then, there was considerable disagreement about what kind of musical education was best).

In assessing Roman attitudes to music, therefore, it is vital that the content of the sources is weighed against broader considerations of genre, audience, authorial bias and historical context. The attitudes of Cicero and his friend T. Pomponius Atticus provide a case in point. In the *Life of Atticus* by Cornelius Nepos, we read that Atticus never exhibited a single musical entertainer at his banquets, such was his concern for avoiding needless extravagance.[104] In a similar vein, Cicero in his speeches frequently accuses his opponents of singing and dancing in order to cast aspersions on their moral character.[105] And yet, we know for a fact – thanks to Cicero's letters – that the philhellene Atticus not only owned his own musician (named Phemius after the Homeric citharode), but also went to great lengths to equip him with a rare musical instrument from Asia Minor, enlisting the help of Cicero, who was serving as governor of Cilicia at the time, to help him find it.[106] Furthermore, when Cicero wrote to Atticus in July 54 BCE with news of Caesar's exploits in Britain, he complained of a lack of captives 'trained in literature or music' (*litteris aut musicis eruditos*); if Atticus wished to acquire musical slaves, he would have to look elsewhere.[107] Taken as a whole, these passages remind us that the Romans' relationship with Greek music was much more ambivalent and idiosyncratic than historians have tended to assume.

Sound, Space and Social Control

The recent proliferation of scholarship on the senses in antiquity has transformed our understanding of how sound structured the Romans'

---

[104] Nep. *Att.* 14.1 (*nemo in convivio eius aliud acroama audivit*); cf. *Ep.* 1.2.
[105] See, e.g. Corbeill 1996: 135–9; Horsfall 2003: 32, 35; Laurence 2009: 115–7.
[106] Cic. *Att.* 5.50.9, 5.21.9, 6.1.13. The instrument in question was almost certainly a Phrygian pipe (*tibia Phrygia*): see further discussion in Morgan 2019.
[107] Cic. *Att.* 4.16.7.

interactions with the urban environment.[108] However, the role of music within the Roman sensorium has not yet been fully explored. In one sense, of course, music is (and was) a 'universal language'.[109] In an age before recording technology, music broke down the barriers, both conceptual and concrete, which separated those at the top of the social hierarchy from those lower down. Amorphous and ephemeral, its presence could not easily be confined within spatial or temporal bounds. Moreover, unlike many of the sensual pleasures enjoyed by Rome's affluent elite (foodstuffs, perfumes, fine clothing, etc.), the delights of music could be freely enjoyed by all. To experience the best music Rome had to offer, one simply had to go to the theatre and listen.[110]

For the Roman governing class, who spent much of their time conducting business in public, the inescapable presence of music in the urban environment was a source of both temptation and irritation. Roman elites placed a premium on silence (a luxury afforded to them by virtue of the fact that they owned large houses which insulated them from the external noises of the city) and viewed the music of the *plebs* – the music of the street-corner, the theatre, the circus and the tavern – as a threat to that silence.[111] Privileging the intellectual order of the *ars musica*, by contrast, served to confine music to the silent realm of the library, closing it off to the disorderly, uneducated masses. Accordingly, Roman writers typically portray the people's music as a kind of noise pollution. In a famous passage from his *Moral Letters*, Seneca the Younger describes the various sounds

---

[108] See Devereux 2006; Toner 2009: 123–61; Betts 2011; Toner 2014; Hartnett 2016; Vincent 2017a and 2017b; Laurence 2017; Veitch 2017; Butler and Nooter 2018; Platts 2020.

[109] The idea of music as a 'universal language' has long been of interest to musicologists: see, e.g. Nettl 2005: 42–9.

[110] Cf. Plut. *Mor.* 706a–c, describing the popular obsession with music and *aulos*-playing in his own time: προῖκα καὶ ἀμισθὶ τῶν ἡδονῶν πάρεστι πολλαχόθεν ἀρύτεσθαι καὶ ἀπολαύειν, ἐν ἀγῶσιν, ἐν θεάτροις, ἐν συμποσίοις, ἑτέρων χορηγούντων· ὅθεν ἕτοιμον τὸ διαφθαρῆναι τοῖς μὴ βοηθοῦντα καὶ παιδαγωγοῦντα τὸν λογισμὸν ἔχουσι (it is frequently possible to procure and enjoy such delights free, without any expenditure at all – at the festivals, in the theatres, or at dinners, where others foot the bills. In this way it is easy for the hearers to be corrupted, since they do not have the calculation of the costs to rescue and discipline them; trans. Minar, Sandbach and Helmbold). The mixed composition of Roman theatre audiences is taken for granted by most scholars, especially following the completion of Rome's first stone theatre in 55 BCE (on which, see Chapter 2). Fontaine (2010: 184–5) argues that the audiences who attended plays in the time of Plautus (ca. 200 BCE) were 'predominantly elite'; see, however, the counterarguments of Richlin 2017: 17–19. Comic prologues address an audience of different social backgrounds, including both free citizens and slaves: cf., e.g. Plaut. *Poen.* 5–35; Ter. *Hec.* 28–48.

[111] As Laurence (2017: 75) puts it, there was a consensus that 'sounds had their place and some places in the city should be kept free of some sounds'.

which could be heard from his apartment above a bath complex. Standing out amidst the din of passing traffic, the groans of weightlifters in the *palaestra* and the cries of street vendors was a busking musician warming up on little flutes and pipes at a nearby fountain (*hunc qui ad Metam Sudantem tubulas experitur et tibias*). Far from being a pleasant diversion, the musician merely added to the cacophony: he was supposed to be making music, but all he did was make a racket (*nec cantat sed exclamat*).[112]

Loud music produced within the household had the potential to spill out onto the street, penetrating into public spaces where it was unwelcome.[113] Cicero ridicules a flamboyant resident of the Palatine who employed so many musicians at his dinner-parties 'that the whole neighbourhood echoes with the sound of voices and strings and pipes and nocturnal revels'.[114] It was a source of great annoyance to Seneca that those who attended musical concerts at the houses of friends would go about in public afterwards humming the melodies they had heard – 'a proceeding which interferes with their thinking and does not allow them to concentrate upon serious matters'.[115] From the perspective of Cicero and Seneca, music of this kind not only contributed to the noise pollution plaguing the city of Rome, but also blurred the boundary between work and play, *negotium* and *otium*. Those who sang in the Forum committed a 'great perversion' (*magna perversitas*), according to Cicero, precisely because they were claiming for their own personal leisure a space which represented both the literal and symbolic centre of Roman civic life.[116]

The use of music in public religious ceremonies was subject to particularly stringent controls. The resonant tones of the *tibiae* were deemed essential for ensuring the efficacy of sacrifice, drowning out any extraneous

---

[112] Sen. *Ep.* 56.4. Cf. Hor. *Ep.* 1.14, contrasting the peace and quiet of the countryside with the 'noise' (*strepitum*) of a pipe-playing courtesan (*meretrix tibicina*) in a city tavern.

[113] On noise as a feature of Roman street life, see Hartnett 2016.

[114] Cic. *Rosc. Am.* 134: *animi et aurium causa tot homines habet ut cotidiano cantu vocum et nervorum et tibiarum nocturnisque conviviis tota vicinitas personet*.

[115] Sen. *Ep.* 123.9: *qui audierunt symphoniam ferunt secum in auribus modulationem illam ac dulcedinem cantuum, quae cogitationes inpedit nec ad seria patitur intendi*; cf. *Brev.* 12.4.

[116] Cic. *Off.* 1.145; cf. also Artem. 1.76.7: τὸ δὲ ἐν ἀγορᾷ ἢ πλατείαις ᾀσματολογεῖν πλουσίῳ μὲν ἀσχημοσύνας καὶ καταγέλωτας σημαίνει, πένητι δὲ μανίαν (giving renditions of songs in the marketplace or the streets signifies disgrace and ridicule for a rich man, and for a poor man insanity; trans. Thonemann 2020: 66). Cf. also Lucian's criticism of the debauched philosopher Polemo for parading through the middle of the *agora* night and day to the music of pipes (*Bis accusatus* 17).

noise which might detract from the sanctity of the ritual.[117] Indeed, without the constant accompaniment of the *tibicen*, the entire ceremony could be deemed null and void.[118] For the worshippers of Bacchus, Isis and Cybele, music took on a very different, yet equally significant, ritual meaning. Whereas traditional Roman sacrifices featured just a single *tibicen*, who occupied a stationary position next to the officiants, the ceremonies devoted to these 'foreign' deities involved a varied assortment of drums, cymbals, rattles and pipes.[119] The frenetic noise of these instruments, accompanied by the loud chanting and wailing of worshippers, was supposed to have induced a state of ecstasy in those who heard them. On certain days of the year, the priests of Cybele would dance through the streets, begging alms and playing drums while their followers accompanied them on pipes. Their ability to transgress public norms in this way reflected their status as social outsiders. According to Dionysius of Halicarnassus, a senatorial decree passed during the republican period prohibited 'any native Roman citizen from processing in a spangled robe begging alms to the music of the pipes (καταυλούμενος) or celebrating the goddess' orgies in the Phrygian manner'.[120]

Disturbances to the sonic order were not always problematic, however. There were certain official occasions, such as the triumph or the Saturnalia, which facilitated a temporary suspension of social order, allowing for the controlled expression of sounds that would under normal circumstances be considered disruptive. Triumphs provided an opportunity for the populace to come together in communal celebration. Brass musicians played a prominent role in the procession, escorting the soldiers, captives and spoils on their journey through the city. The soldiers themselves would sing humorous songs which poked fun at their general.[121] The festivities which

---

[117] Plin. *HN* 28.11: *tibicinem canere, ne quid aliud exaudiatur.* Suet. *Tib.* 70.3 presents the absence of a *tibicen* at a sacrifice as highly unusual. For artistic representations of *tibicines* in sacrifices, see Fless 1995; Huet 2007.

[118] Cic. *Har. resp.* 23: *an si ludius constitit aut tibicen repente conticuit . . . ludi sunt non rite facti.*

[119] Cf. the description of a procession of Isis in Apul. *Met.* 11.9. The cult of Cybele seems to have had its own companies of musicians and dancers: *CIL* 6.2264 (*tympanistria*), 9.1538 (*cymbalistria*), 14.408 (*tibicen*), 6.2265 (*sodales ballatore[s]*).

[120] Dion. Hal. *Ant. Rom.* 2.19.3–5; for discussion of this passage, see Latham 2012: 101–2.

[121] On music in the triumph, see the section 'Battle of the Bands: Anicius' Martial Soundtrack' in Chapter 1.

accompanied the Saturnalia in December included 'drinking, noise and games and dice, electing kings and feasting slaves, singing naked and clapping frenzied hands'.[122] The Saturnalian king could command the guests to 'shout out something disgraceful about himself, to dance naked, to pick up the woman playing pipes and carry her three times around the house'.[123] Music clearly added much to the carnivalesque atmosphere of these occasions.

Professional musicians even had their own festival. Held annually on 13 June, the so-called Lesser Quinquatrus (*Quinquatrus Minusculae*) featured a riotous parade of pipe-players through the streets of Rome. During the parade, the pipe-players wore masks and long robes and sang light-hearted verses before gathering at the temple of Minerva, the patron goddess of pipe-playing, on the Aventine Hill.[124] The origins of the festival were attributed to a famous, and possibly fictitious, incident in 311 BCE, when the pipers' guild (*collegium tibicinum*) staged a walk-out in response to some unfair restrictions which had been imposed on them by the Roman political authorities.[125] Knowing that the Romans would be unable to perform the correct religious rites without their assistance, the pipe-players absconded in protest to the nearby town of Tibur. Eventually, the Senate managed to trick the *tibicines* into returning by getting the Tiburtines to ply them with wine until they passed out in a drunken stupor. They then proceeded to load the musicians onto wagons and drove them back to Rome under cover of darkness. The festivities of the Lesser Quinquartus – the noise, the gaudy costumes and general merriment – served as a reminder of this episode and of the *tibicines*' indispensable role within the civic community.

Sensing Music, Embodying Music

Like their Greek forebears, the Romans believed that music elicited complex mental and physical responses in human beings. They conceptualised

---

[122] Luc. *Sat.* 2.
[123] Luc. *Sat.* 4; cf. Epict. *Diss.* 1.25.8. Pliny the Younger retreated to his private chambers during the Saturnalia to escape the 'merry shouts' (*festisque clamoribus*) that echoed through the rest of the house (*Ep.* 2.17.24).
[124] Varro, *Ling.* 6.17; Festus 149L; Censorinus, *DN* 12.2.
[125] Livy 9.30.5–10; Ov. *Fast.* 6.649–710; Val. Max. 2.5.4; Plut. *Quaest. Rom.* 55. The sources differ on what caused the controversy: Livy and Plutarch state that the *tibicines* were prohibited from holding their traditional annual feast in the temple of Jupiter, while Ovid suggests that the dispute arose as a result of a restriction on the allowable number of *tibicines* at funerals. For modern discussions of this episode, see Pailler 2001; Dupont 2004; Buchet 2010; Barja de Quiroga 2018.

the act of listening to music not only as a sensory experience, but also as a psychological and embodied experience. Sounds 'invaded the body, and they were capable of corrupting – or alternatively, of cultivating – minds'.[126] This phenomenon was not limited to auditory stimuli: tastes, sights and smells also worked upon the body in powerful ways.[127] However, ancient sources give an indication of the particular potency of music in relation to other sensations. 'Nothing is so akin to our minds as rhythms and melodies (*numeri atque voces*)', writes Cicero; 'they arouse and inflame us, soften us and calm us down, and often lead us to laughter and to sadness'.[128] Hence the need for caution, according to Plutarch: 'Melody and rhythm take us captive and corrupt us by means of concoctions more pungent and varied than the products of any cook or perfumer, overwhelming our senses . . . Therefore, we must be especially wary of these pleasures; they are extremely powerful, because they do not, like those of taste and touch and smell, have their only effect in the irrational and "natural" part of our mind, but lay hold of our faculty of judgement and prudence.'[129]

So great was music's influence over the mind and body that it was even thought to possess miraculous healing properties.[130] The physician Asclepiades of Bithynia, who counted Cicero among his clients, is said to have often used music to treat cases of phrenitis.[131] Celsus, the Roman medical writer active during the reign of Tiberius, prescribes 'music, cymbals and loud noises' (*symphoniae et cymbala strepitusque*) for patients suffering from depression (*tristes cogitationes*).[132] Listening to music was also recommended by Rufus of Ephesus (ca. 100 CE) as a cure for lovesickness.[133] The remedial benefits of music were not limited to diseases of the mind. According to the second-century writer Aulus Gellius, the sound of the *tibiae* was useful for alleviating the symptoms of gout and for treating snakebites.[134] Not all kinds of music were therapeutic, however. 'The sound of music congests the head' (*cantilenae sonus caput impleat*), explains the late-antique physician Caelius Aurelianus, and 'in some cases music

---

[126] Hendy 2013: 80. Thus, Quintilian (*Inst.* 1.10.22) speaks of music working both 'through sounds' (*in vocibus*) and 'through the body' (*in corpore*).
[127] See Toner 2014: 3.   [128] Cic. *De Orat.* 3.197.   [129] Plut. *Mor.* 705f–706b.
[130] On therapeutic uses of music in antiquity, see West 2000; Provenza 2020.
[131] Censorinus, *DN* 12.4; Martianus Capella 9.926.   [132] Celsus, *De medicina* 3.18.10.
[133] Quoted in a tenth-century Arabic text: see Burnett 1993: 3–4. By contrast, the Christian bishop Ambrose of Milan inveighs against 'deadly songs' (*mortiferi cantus*) which induce feelings of amorousness (*mentem emolliant ad amores*; *Hexaemeron*, 3.1.5 = PL 14. Col. 157).
[134] Gell. *NA* 4.13.

arouses men to madness' (*accendat aliquos in furorem*).[135] One unfortunate patient, diagnosed by Galen with 'delirium' (*paraphrosyne*), imagined that a troupe of pipers had taken up residence in a corner of his house. The man cried out for them to leave, but the musicians kept on playing regardless, 'so that they neither let up during the night, nor were in the least bit silent throughout the whole day'.[136]

Music, then, had the power not only to invigorate and inspire, but also to debilitate and derange, to loosen minds and weaken bodies. An anecdote in Cicero's treatise *De Consiliis Suis* serves as a cautionary tale of the dangers of musical intoxication. The philosopher Pythagoras, walking along the street one day, stumbled upon a gang of drunken youths. 'Aroused by the playing of the pipes, as often happens', the men were trying to break down the door of a respectable lady's house. Sensing the danger, Pythagoras instructed the *tibicina* to play a different melody, and when she did so, 'the slow pace of the rhythms and solemn character of the music calmed their uncontrolled aggression'.[137] Though the story is obviously apocryphal, it is informative for several reasons. Firstly, it reflects a widely held belief in antiquity that the younger generation was particularly susceptible to the corrupting effects of music. Secondly, the story highlights the strong association in Greek and Roman culture between the pleasures of music, wine and sex. Thirdly, and perhaps most importantly, the story demonstrates the connection between the consumption of music and the performance of Roman masculinity. In Cicero's time, men were expected to display self-control at all times. Since one's capacity for self-control was thought to be conditioned by one's environment, it mattered what kinds of music one was accustomed to hearing. Initially, the sound of the pipes encourages the rowdy behaviour of the youths. It is only when they are exposed to music of a more sedate and solemn character that they are able to regain the composure that is expected of them as adolescent men.

---

[135] Caelius Aurelianus, *On Chronic Diseases* 1.176, trans. Drabkin 1950: 557. Conversely, the second-century Greek medical writer Aretaeus used the ability to be 'roused by the pipe' (ἐγείρονται δὲ αὐλῷ) as a basis for discerning whether someone was mentally sane: Aretaeus, *On the Symptoms of Chronic Diseases* 1.6.

[136] Galen, *On the Differentiae of Symptoms*, VII.60–1K, trans. Johnston 2006: 191. King 2013 discusses an intriguing passage in Galen's *Epidemics* about a man who had a phobia of the *aulos*.

[137] Cic. *De Consiliis suis* fr. 3, p. 339 Müller = FRHist 39 F6: *cum vinolenti adolescentes tibiarum etiam cantu, ut fit, instincti, mulieris pudicae fores frangerent, admonuisse tibicinam ut spondeum caneret Pythagoras dicitur; quod cum illa fecisset, tarditate modorum et gravitate cantus illorum furentem petulantiam resedisse.* For variants of this story, cf. Quint. *Inst.* 1.10.32; Gal. *De Hipp. et Plat.* 9.5; Sext. Emp. *Math.* 6.8; Iambl. *De Vita Pythagorica* 112. In Galen's version, the subject is Damon, Socrates' teacher.

As noted earlier, it is common in both Greek and Latin literature for some kinds of music to be associated with a softening effect on both mind and body and other kinds with a hardening effect. This language of 'softening' and 'hardening' is heavily implicated in ancient discourses on gender: hardness (*robur*) is equated with virility, and softness (*mollitia*) with femininity. We have already seen, for example, how the blare of horns and trumpets was thought to strengthen the manly resolve of soldiers in battle. Conversely, the theatre is often criticised for promoting emasculating tunes and rhythms. Thus, Quintilian draws a distinction between proper 'macho' types of music (traditional banquet songs, military fanfares, songs to accompany manual labour, and so on) and the 'effeminate' (*effeminata*) music of the contemporary stage, 'corrupted by shameful melodies' (*inpudicis modis fracta*); the latter, he claims, has 'destroyed any vestige of manly strength left in us' (*quid in nobis virilis roboris manebat excidit*).[138] Three centuries later, the historian Ammianus Marcellinus bemoaned the fact that Roman soldiers had abandoned the traditional war chant in favour of 'effeminate ditties' (*cantilenas ... molliores*), doubtless picked up from the theatre.[139]

Beyond the realm of public entertainment, the gendering of music was also reinforced in the religious sphere. The cults of Cybele, Isis and Bacchus were notorious for driving worshippers into a music-induced frenzy. Instruments like the *sistrum*, the rattle beloved by the followers of Isis, and the *tibia Phrygia*, the distinctive curved pipe associated with the rites of Cybele, created a powerfully charged sonic atmosphere, ideal for stimulating minds and loosening bodies; the 'Phyrigan pipe' was said to 'breathe life into bones with its liquid spirit'.[140] Music, in these contexts, facilitated not only the relaxation of social inhibitions, but also the subversion of conventional gender roles. For example, Juvenal imagines the wailing of the effeminate *galli* (the castrated priests of Cybele) drowning out the voices and drums of their lower-ranking followers, while Seneca the Younger refers to them as 'half-men' (*semiviri*) driven out of their minds 'upon

---

[138] Quint. *Inst.* 1.10.31. For similar terms applied to the music of the stage, cf. Sen. *Contr.* 1.22 (*carminibus enervata*); Sen. *Ep.* 101.13 (*carmen effeminatum*); Tac. *Ann.* 14.15 (*gestus modosque haud virilis*), 14.20 (*fractos sonos*); Tert. *De Spect.* 25.3 (*effeminati tibicinis*).

[139] Amm. Marc. 22.4.6. Note also the antithesis drawn by Seneca the Elder and Younger between the *symphonia* and the *classicum*, a traditional melody played in the army camp: Sen. *Con.* 9.2.14; Sen. *Ep.* 51.12.

[140] Lucr. 2.620: *Phrygio stimulat numero cava tibia mentis*; Var. fr. 131 Bücheler: *Phrygius per ossa cornus liquida canit anima*; cf. Var. *Sat. Men.* fr. 149 Astbury. The earliest extant reference to a player of the Phrygian pipe in Latin literature occurs in the second-century historian Cassius Hemina (*FRHist* 6 F28: *mulier cantabat tibiis Phrygiis et altera cymbalissabat*).

Figure 0.10 Marble funerary relief depicting a priest of
Cybele with *cymbala*, *tympanum* and Phrygian *tibia*; from Lavinium, Rome; ca.
mid-second century CE. Musei Capitolini, Centrale Montemartini, Inv. S. 1207. Photo
by DEA / A. Dagli Orti / De Agostini via Getty Images.

command' (*ex imperio*) by the sound of the *tibiae*.[141] In effect, the loud singing and instrumental music which accompanied the public rites of the *galli* served as an audible marker of their liminal status in-between the masculine and feminine spheres (see Fig. 0.10).

The Status of Musicians

Although musical expertise was widely frowned upon by the Roman upper classes, men and women of lower status who chose to practice music professionally enjoyed relatively good social and economic prospects. As Alexandre Vincent has highlighted, many musicians in Rome belonged to the respectable middling ranks of society, performing important functions in the army, law courts, political assemblies and other civic settings. These musicians were social insiders, with access to the same opportunities for long-term employment, financial success and community-building that were available to other urban professionals in the Roman

---

[141] Juv. 6.515–6; Sen. *Ep.* 108.7.

world.¹⁴² However, the musicians whose lives are foregrounded in Vincent's study represent in many ways a privileged group. At the opposite end of the spectrum were enslaved musicians, sometimes called *symphoniaci*, who were employed by their owners (or rented out) to provide entertainment at parties and other social gatherings. Cicero refers quite frequently in his speeches to the buying, selling and exchanging of *symphoniaci* among wealthy senators, especially those stationed in the East.¹⁴³ Horace portrays a slave-dealer at a market in Rome advertising a young boy who 'will sing for you over your cups in an unpolished yet charming manner' (*canet indoctum sed dulce bibenti*).¹⁴⁴ Similarly, in a scene from the *Life of Aesop*, an anonymous biography dating from the second century CE, a merchant arrives on the Greek island of Samos with several slaves in tow, including one trained as a musician. In preparation for the auction, 'he dressed the musician, who was good-looking, in a white robe, put light shoes on him, combed his hair, gave him a scarf for his shoulders and put him on the selling block'.¹⁴⁵ Remarkably, we have evidence from the first and second centuries CE of musical slaves from the Roman Empire being traded as far east as India and China, where they were offered to local potentates as exotic gifts.¹⁴⁶

The stain of slavery was one of several factors which brought the musical profession into disrepute. Even for those musicians who were not enslaved, the very fact that they were implicated in the world of commercial entertainment marked them out as socially inferior in the eyes of many citizens. The stereotype of the money-grubbing, upstart musician looms large in Roman literature. For instance, Juvenal belittles a popular lyre-player of the

---

[142] Vincent 2016. See especially the inscriptions from the Meta Sudans, uncovered during the early 1990s, which attest to the involvement of the *collegium aenatorum* in the erection of a monument for the imperial cult: Panella 1996: 30–62.

[143] Cf., e.g., Cic. *Pis.* 22, 83; *Caec.* 55; *Mil.* 55. In 385 CE, the emperor Theodosius I went so far as to issue a decree expressly prohibiting the buying, training or selling of female lyre-players (*fidicinae*): C.Th. 15.7.10; *Epit. de Caes.* 48.10. Whether this law was enacted on moral grounds, or out of a practical concern for ensuring the availability of entertainers for public performances, has been disputed (Webb 2013: 387).

[144] Hor. *Ep.* 2.2.9.   [145] *Life of Aesop* 21 (trans. Daly 1961).

[146] The anonymous *Periplus Maris Erythraei*, dating probably from the mid-first century CE, records slave musicians (μουσικά) being imported from Roman Egypt to the Indian market town of Barigaza for King Nahapana, along with precious silverware, female concubines, fine wine, expensive clothing and perfumes (49:16.26; Casson 1989: 16); cf. Strabo 2.99, recording an attempted shipment of slave musicians from Gades (modern Cádiz in Spain) to India in the late second century BCE. Ancient Chinese records state that in 120 CE musicians and jugglers were sent from the eastern Roman empire to China along the sea-route: Hirth 1975: 36–7, 179–80.

time by referring to him as 'one who sells his voice to the praetors' (*vocem vendentis praetoribus*). In a similar vein, Martial describes the vocations of the *citharoedus* and *choraules* as 'money-making arts' (*pecuniosae artes*).[147] Those who made a living at other people's expense were said, according to one Roman proverb, to 'live the life of a pipe-player' (αὐλητοῦ βίον ζῆς).[148] Many musicians doubtless struggled to make ends meet (another proverb speaks of the poor as having a 'piped out life' (βίος ἐξηυλημένος) as though worn out by piping for a living).[149] The music industry was, and always has been, a high-stakes business. But the risk of failure was offset by the promise of immense riches. Juvenal sneers at the upward mobility of professional horn-players (*cornicines*) – 'the permanent followers of country shows, their rounded cheeks a familiar sight through all the towns' – who, despite their humble origins, had attained a status rivalling members of the municipal aristocracy. Having started out accompanying gladiatorial shows, they had now accumulated the resources to produce gladiatorial shows in their own name ('after all, they're the type that Fortune raises up from the gutter to a mighty height whenever she fancies a laugh').[150] Exaggerated though this description may be, there is no question that some musicians were extremely well paid: in the time of Martial, the citharode Pollio earned enough money to purchase a luxurious estate on the outskirts of Rome.[151]

Like prostitutes, actors and gladiators, musicians aroused feelings of both intense desire and intense suspicion.[152] They were judged not only by the quality of the music they produced, but also by their physical beauty. This extended beyond the clothes they wore (although the musician's

---

[147] Juv. 6.380; Mart. 5.59.9–10.
[148] Pseudo-Diogenianus, *Popular Proverbs* 3.14 (ed. Leutsch and Schneidewin 1839: 216).
[149] *Epitome of Zenobius' Proverbs* 2.64 (ed. Leutsch and Schneidewin 1839: 49). For the association of this proverb with poverty, see Morgan 2007: 47. Alternatively, the expression could refer to the wearing out of *aulos* reeds through frequent use.
[150] Juv. 3.34–40.
[151] Mart. 3.20.18. Pollio no doubt made a handsome profit from his stage performances, but he also apparently hired out his services as a music teacher to the sons of wealthy Romans for exorbitant fees (Juv. 7.176–7).
[152] The strong affinity between musicians and prostitutes in Roman culture is underscored by a sarcophagus in the British Museum belonging to a certain Marcus Sempronius Nikokrates, a poet and lyre-player who also sold prostitutes for a living (his epitaph describes him as 'a merchant of beautiful women' (ἔμπορος εὐμόρφων)). He was clearly successful in this enterprise, judging from the expensive funerary monument which he was able to commission for himself. See *IG* XIV 2000 = *IGUR* 1326 (Rome, second or third century CE); examined at length in Vendries 2001.

costume was certainly integral to his or her aesthetic appeal).[153] As performers, musicians put their bodies on show for the titillation and gratification of Roman audiences.[154] With this public exposure came both celebrity and notoriety.[155] In his sixth satire, Juvenal imagines flocks of female admirers swooning over their favourite lyre-players, collecting their plectrums as souvenirs and even praying to the gods on their behalf.[156] Though Juvenal's depiction is surely fanciful, it speaks to a general fixation in Roman discourse on the sexual potency of musical performers.[157] Enslaved musicians and dancers were especially prone to being objectified in this way, since their bodies were sexually violable by law. One of Martial's *Epigrams* is devoted to a female slave named Telethusa, who was 'skilled at performing lascivious gestures to Baetican castanets and dancing to tunes from Gades'.[158] Similarly, in Statius' representation of a theatrical spectacle during the reign of Domitian, 'the cymbals and jingling Gades' (*cymbala tinnulaeque Gades*) provide the soundtrack to the dancing of 'Syrian troupes' (*agmina Syrorum*) and 'buxom showgirls from Lydia' (*Lydiae tumentes*). Lest we be left in any doubt about the sexual availability of these foreign starlets, we are assured by the poet that their services are 'easily bought' (*faciles emi*).[159]

It is little surprise, then, that Roman elites came to associate musical expertise with extreme social degradation. Upper-class Romans who spent too much time in the company of musicians, or whose skill at singing or playing instruments resembled that of a consummate professional,

---

[153] In addition to *Life of Aesop* 21 (quoted earlier in this section), note the description of a citharode at *Rhet. Her.* 4.47: *optime vestitus, palla inaurata indutus, cum chlamyde purpurea variis coloribus intexta, et cum corona aurea magnis fulgentibus gemmis inluminata, citharam tenens exornatissimam auro et ebore distinctam* (beautifully dressed, wearing a gold-embroidered robe, with a purple mantle interlaced with various colours, and with a golden crown illumined with large gleaming jewels, and holding a lyre decorated with golden ornaments and set off with ivory). On the costume of musicians, see further Power 2010: 11–12; Ercoles 2014.

[154] For this idea applied to actors, see Edwards 1997: 68.

[155] Cf. *Digest* 48.5.25[24] pr. Macer, on Augustus' law against singers and dancers caught in adultery (discussed in Chapter 3). Power (2010: 79) comments on the absence of evidence for citharodes being officially subject to *infamia*, but in general *infamia* could be applied to anyone who sang or danced on the public stage: cf. Cic. *Rep.* 4.10 (= August. *de Civ. Dei* 2.14.ext.); Edwards 1997. Tacitus' description of Nero's lyre-playing as a *foedum studium* (a disgraceful pursuit is also suggestive in this regard (*Ann.* 14.14.1).

[156] Juv. 6.380–95.   [157] See Power 2010: 50–7.   [158] Mart. 6.71.1–2.

[159] Stat. *Silv.* 1.6.67–71. Syria and Gades were renowned for their exotic entertainers: Fear 1991; Morgan 2017.

attracted a great deal of censure. Cicero's comparison of the two individuals Valerius and Numerius Furius is indicative in this regard:

> *Valerius cotidie cantabat; erat enim scaenicus: quid faceret aliud? at Numerius Furius, noster familiaris, cum est commodum, cantat; est enim paterfamilias, est eques Romanus; puer didicit quod discendum fuit.* (Cic. Orat. 3.87)

> Valerius used to sing every day, and naturally so, being a professional; but our friend Numerius Furius sings when it suits him, for he is the head of a household and a Roman equestrian; he learnt what was appropriate when he was a boy.

Cicero does not actually state what occasions were 'appropriate' (*commodum*) for a Roman equestrian to sing: he simply took it for granted (and assumed that his readers would too) that a well-born citizen should know what kinds of musical pursuits were or were not acceptable for someone of Numerius' rank. Suitable occasions for singing might have included banquets, religious festivals and weddings.[160] In his speech *On Behalf of Murena*, Cicero suggests that dancing was a natural accompaniment to a debauched feast and was allowable to the extent that it represented an occasional indulgence.[161] The key point here is that music was considered a luxury, not a pleasure to be taken at liberty; the serious duties of business and politics always came before the casual enjoyment of song and dance.

Although, in general, music-making seems to have been policed more strictly for men than for women, there are a few notable exceptions. Particularly revealing is Sallust's criticism of the noblewoman Sempronia in his monograph on the Catilinarian conspiracy of 63 BCE. A notorious associate of Catiline, Sempronia is accused of 'playing the lyre and dancing more elegantly than is appropriate for a respectable woman' (*psallere [et] saltare elegantius quam necesse est probae*).[162] The commentary on this passage by the fifth-century Roman writer Macrobius is instructive: what Sallust objected to, Macrobius explains, was not the fact that Sempronia

---

[160] On banquet songs (*carmina convivalia*), see Zorzetti 1990; Feeney 2016: 213–18. The singing of hymns was a traditional feature of Roman religion (Hahn 2011: 244). For example, the duties of the Salii and Arval Brethren involved processing through the city while singing and dancing: cf. Livy 1.20.4; Dion. Hal. *Ant. Rom.* 2.70.1–5. For music at weddings, see Hersch 2010: 239–42.
[161] Cic. *Mur.* 13.
[162] Sall. *Cat.* 25.2. On the identity of Sempronia, see Syme 2016: 173–81. It is interesting that Sallust opts for the word *psallere*, rather than *citharizare* (preferred by Nepos); according to Power (2010: 130 n. 315), 'Sallust probably wants the word to evoke the louche world of the professional *psaltria* ... and so underline the impropriety of Sempronia's (Greek) cultural enthusiasms.'

danced, but the fact that she did so 'with aplomb' (*optime*).[163] Again, what is at stake here is the idea that, while occasional singing or dancing was admissible in certain situations, a freeborn Roman should not aspire to professional levels of musicianship, especially if he or she was of aristocratic birth.

Roman responses to music were therefore conditioned by a variety of factors, including the cultural politics of Hellenism, conceptions of sound and its place within the urban environment, the perceived influence of music on the human mind and body, and the categorisation of music-making as an 'infamous' profession. Music pointed up a fundamental set of distinctions – between Roman and non-Roman, free and slave, elite and plebeian, young and old, male and female – which structured social relations and political discourses. For this reason, the study of music has much to offer the historian of ancient Rome.

Chapter Outline

The following chapters are framed around four substantive case studies, each focusing on a different period of Rome's history: the middle Republic (Chapter 1); the late Republic (Chapter 2); the Augustan Principate (Chapter 3); and the Neronian Principate (Chapter 4). My decision to concentrate on these four periods was partly contingent on the availability of source material. We lack direct testimonies for Roman musical culture prior to the second century BCE; the evidence for the late Republic and early Principate, on the other hand, is relatively plentiful. However, there are also methodological reasons for adopting a narrower chronological focus. The narrative of this book opens in 167 BCE with a performance given by Greek musicians in Rome during the height of the empire's expansion and ends circa 67 CE with a performance (or rather a series of performances) given by a Roman musician – an emperor, no less – in the heart of Greece. The reign of Nero seemed to provide a natural endpoint, in that it marked not only the end of the Julio-Claudian dynasty but also the culmination of over two centuries of musical interaction between Greece and Rome, anticipating the cultural florescence of the Second Sophistic. Although I will draw on later sources where appropriate in order to support my arguments, a full discussion of Roman musical culture in the

---

[163] Macr. *Sat.* 3.14.5: *Semproniam reprehendit non quod saltare sed quod optime scierit.* Cf. Serv. *ad Aen.* 8.646, commenting disdainfully on Tullia Minor's predilection for singing and dancing.

High Empire and Late Antiquity, taking into consideration the extensive corpus of early Christian writings on music, would require a very different set of sources and approaches from those employed in this book, and therefore is afforded only minimal treatment here.[164]

Chapter 1 takes as its central focus the triumphal games given by the Roman praetor L. Anicius Gallus in 167 BCE. The chapter deconstructs Polybius' hostile account of this event by exploring how he represents the role of music in the spectacle. The first part of the chapter examines how Anicius manipulated the musical dynamics of the spectacle in order to amplify the importance of his triumph. The second part uses the episode as a springboard for investigating broader developments in Greek and Roman musical culture during the second century. As well as discussing the general treatment of music in Polybius' *Histories*, I consider how the dissemination of Greek musical culture during this period sparked a reaction from senior members of the Roman political elite, as evidenced by the fragmentary speeches of Cato the Elder and Scipio Aemilianus.

Chapter 2 looks at the role of music in the political contests of the late Republic. Taking Cicero's discussion of music in the *De Legibus* as a point of departure, I argue that Cicero's comments need to be seen against the background of major changes in the culture of Roman spectacle in the 50s BCE – most notably, the construction of Pompey's stone theatre. Furthermore, the chapter identifies points of overlap in the critical discourse focused on musical entertainment and the hostile characterisations of the so-called *populares*. This collapsing of the boundaries between popular music and popular politics provides an important new angle on the political struggles of the late Republic.

Chapter 3 is devoted to the relationship between Octavian/Augustus and Apollo's incarnation as *citharoedus* (lyre-player). The main contention of the chapter is that the Augustan period fostered a revival of music which resonated with and to some degree embodied a restorative political message. Not only did Augustus integrate images of Apollo Citharoedus into his own imagery (both in Rome and in the commemorative monuments around the gulf of Actium), but he also exploited *harmonia* as a metaphor for his newly established regime, imbuing musical rituals like the *Ludi*

---

[164] Whitmarsh (2004) examines the relationship between Hadrian and the musician Mesomedes. For a comprehensive survey of musical culture in Late Antiquity (including Christian material), see Eberhardt 2018. Other notable studies include Quaesten 1983; Cosgrove 2006; Page 2010; Shaw 2011: 441–89; Grig 2013. Webb (2013) deals specifically with the status of professional musicians in Late Antiquity. McKinnon (1987) compiles and translates various early Christian writings on music.

Saeculares of 17 BCE with powerful symbolic resonances. The chapter also makes a case for seeing Mark Antony's use of music as a key part of a project to present himself through the symbolic language of Hellenistic kingship, against which Octavian in turn defined his own musical 'programme'.

Chapter 4 examines the reign of the notorious musician-emperor Nero. The chapter offers a comprehensive survey of the ancient material relating to Nero's performances, stressing also his important role behind the scenes as producer, composer and choreographer. Building on the recent 'performative turn' in Neronian studies, I argue that Nero used music not to satisfy some narcissistic or tyrannical bent, as has traditionally been maintained, but rather as part of a self-conscious strategy for the negotiation and representation of imperial power. Nero's music-making responded to, and drew energy from, the cultural interests of both the ordinary Roman people and the young metropolitan elite. In this way, I suggest, Nero succeeded in creating and disseminating an original musical language, which repackaged elements of Greek culture into a distinctly Roman product optimised for popular consumption.

Finally, in the epilogue, I bring together the arguments of the four chapters in order to assess broader changes and continuities in Roman musical culture during the period under consideration. While the ideological frameworks underpinning musical discourses remained largely constant over time, and competing political actors continued to use music for their own ends, I show that the gradual evolution of Roman society and politics prompted new types of engagement with music. This has important ramifications for our understanding of Rome's relationship with Greek culture, as well as the interactions between elites and non-elites.

1 | The Games of L. Anicius Gallus and the Cultural Politics of Music in the Second Century BCE

In the autumn of 167 BCE, the praetor Lucius Anicius Gallus returned to Rome in the wake of a glorious victory in the province of Illyria. Messengers and hostages had already reached the capital, and the general's arrival alongside his lieutenant Octavius was a cause for national celebration.[1] A triumph was promptly voted by the Senate and referred to the popular assembly for formal ratification.[2] Anicius, however, was not content with this singular honour. He planned to crown the festivities with a theatrical extravaganza. A star-studded line-up of musicians, dancers and prize-fighters was specially brought over from Greece for the occasion and a massive wooden stage erected in a circus near the Tiber.

The Greek historian Polybius witnessed the spectacle in person and recorded what he saw. His detailed account survives only thanks to its preservation in Athenaeus' *Deipnosophistae*, a miscellaneous compendium of dinner-party trivia composed during the early third century CE. The passage reads as follows:

> Λεύκιος δὲ Ἀνίκιος, καὶ αὐτὸς Ῥωμαίων στρατηγήσας, Ἰλλυριοὺς καταπολεμήσας καὶ αἰχμάλωτον ἀγαγὼν Γένθιον τὸν τῶν Ἰλλυριῶν βασιλέα σὺν τοῖς τέκνοις, ἀγῶνας ἐπιτελῶν τοὺς ἐπινικίους ἐν τῇ Ῥώμῃ παντὸς γέλωτος ἄξια πράγματα ἐποίησεν, ὡς Πολύβιος ἱστορεῖ ἐν τῇ τριακοστῇ. μεταπεμψάμενος γὰρ τοὺς ἐκ τῆς Ἑλλάδος ἐπιφανεστάτους τεχνίτας καὶ σκηνὴν κατασκευάσας μεγίστην ἐν τῷ κίρκῳ πρώτους εἰσῆγεν αὐλητὰς ἅμα πάντας. οὗτοι δ' ἦσαν Θεόδωρος ὁ Βοιώτιος, Θεόπομπος, Ἕρμιππος, [ὁ] Λυσίμαχος, οἵτινες ἐπιφανέστατοι ἦσαν. τούτους οὖν στήσας ἐπὶ τὸ προσκήνιον μετὰ τοῦ χοροῦ αὐλεῖν ἐκέλευσεν ἅμα πάντας. τῶν δὲ διαπορευομένων τὰς κρούσεις μετὰ τῆς ἁρμοζούσης κινήσεως προσπέμψας οὐκ ἔφη καλῶς αὐτοὺς αὐλεῖν, ἀλλ' ἀγωνίζεσθαι

---

[1] Upon receiving news of the victory, the Senate decreed a three-day period of public thanksgiving (Livy 45.3.1–2). For the dispatch of messengers and hostages, cf. Livy 44.32.4–5. Anicius and Octavius arrived at Rome a few days after L. Aemilius Paullus (Livy 45.35.4); Paullus was still touring Greece in the early part of the autumn (Livy 45.27.5; Briscoe 2012: 28–9), so the arrival of Anicius and Octavius must have taken place not long before Paullus' triumph on 27–29 November 167 BCE (3–5 September 167 BCE in the Julian calendar).

[2] Livy 45.35.4.

μᾶλλον ἐκέλευσεν. τῶν δὲ διαπορούντων ὑπέδειξέν τις τῶν ῥαβδούχων ἐπιστρέψαντας ἐπαγαγεῖν ἐφ᾽ αὑτοὺς καὶ ποιεῖν ὡσανεὶ μάχην. ταχὺ δὲ συννοήσαντες οἱ αὐληταὶ καὶ λαβόντες [...] οἰκείαν ταῖς ἑαυτῶν ἀσελγείαις μεγάλην ἐποίησαν σύγχυσιν. συνεπιστρέψαντες δὲ τοὺς μέσους χοροὺς πρὸς τοὺς ἄκρους οἱ μὲν αὐληταὶ φυσῶντες ἀδιανόητα καὶ διαφέροντες τοὺς αὐλοὺς ἐπῆγον ἀνὰ μέρος ἐπ᾽ ἀλλήλους. ἅμα δὲ τούτοις ἐπικτυποῦντες οἱ χοροὶ καὶ συνεπεισιόντες τὴν σκηνὴν ἐπεφέροντο τοῖς ἐναντίοις καὶ πάλιν ἀνεχώρουν ἐκ μεταβολῆς. ὡς δὲ καὶ περιζωσάμενός τις τῶν χορευτῶν ἐκ τοῦ καιροῦ στραφεὶς ἦρε τὰς χεῖρας ἀπὸ πυγμῆς πρὸς τὸν ἐπιφερόμενον αὐλητήν, τότ᾽ ἤδη κρότος ἐξαίσιος ἐγένετο καὶ κραυγὴ τῶν θεωμένων. ἔτι δὲ τούτων ἐκ παρατάξεως ἀγωνιζομένων ὀρχησταὶ δύο εἰσήγοντο μετὰ συμφωνίας εἰς τὴν ὀρχήστραν, καὶ πύκται τέτταρες ἀνέβησαν ἐπὶ τὴν σκηνὴν μετὰ σαλπιγκτῶν καὶ βυκανιστῶν. ὁμοῦ δὲ τούτων πάντων ἀγωνιζομένων ἄλεκτον ἦν τὸ συμβαῖνον. περὶ δὲ τῶν τραγῳδῶν, φησὶν ὁ Πολύβιος, ὅ, τι ἂν ἐπιβάλωμαι λέγειν, δόξω τισὶ διαχλευάζειν. (Polyb. 30.22 = Athen. 14.615)

After conquering the Illyrians and taking captive their king, Genthius, along with his children, the Roman general Lucius Anicius presented games (*ludi*) in Rome in celebration of his victory. He conducted proceedings in a completely ridiculous fashion, as Polybius reports in the Thirtieth Book [of his *Histories*]. For, having summoned the most celebrated performers from Greece and built an enormous stage in the circus, he first brought on all the pipe-players at once. These were Theodorus of Boeotia, Theopompus, Hermippus, and Lysimachus – the superstars of the day. He positioned them centre-stage and ordered them to accompany the chorus all together as an ensemble. While they were performing their routine in harmony with the choral dance, he interrupted to inform them that they were playing badly and instructed them to show a more competitive edge. They were confused as to his meaning, until one of the lictors explained that they should turn around and have a go at each other and make it look like they were fighting. The pipe-players quickly grasped what he meant and, after receiving [an order?] which suited their own proclivity for licentiousness, created utter pandemonium. They got the group of dancers in the middle to turn en masse and face those on the outside. Then, proceeding to blow meaningless and discordant notes on their instruments, they advanced towards each other in turn. The dancers responded to them and, mounting the stage all together, charged at the opposing group and then turned around and retreated in ranks. And when, right on cue, one of the dancers gathered up his robes, spun around and raised his fists in boxing-style against the piper who was advancing towards him, the spectators erupted in rapturous applause and shouting. While the performers were still competing in battle lines, two dancers were introduced into the *orchestra* accompanied by a band, and four boxers mounted the stage along with trumpeters and horn-players. The scene with all these people struggling together was unbearable. 'As for the tragic actors', says Polybius, 'if I tried to describe them some people will think that I am joking.'

What are we to make of this bizarre charade? Polybius' review is hardly flattering: the impresario Anicius is written off as a bumbling buffoon, arrogantly interrupting his headline artists in the middle of their set for no apparent reason; the hapless lictor attempts to restore order, but merely adds to the confusion; and the whole performance descends into an unruly fracas, with dancers, musicians and boxers all vying for the spectators' attention. Modern verdicts have been similarly scathing. 'A confused burlesque and near riot'; 'an undignified masquerade'; a 'clumsy' and 'tactless' production which 'backfired': these are just some of the terms which scholars have used to describe Anicius' games in recent decades.[3]

However, as Erich Gruen pointed out nearly three decades ago, there is much more to Polybius' narrative than meets the eye.[4] Why would a supposedly inept Roman general with little appreciation of the performing arts have gone to the trouble of procuring the services of the finest musicians that Greece had to offer – it is stated twice that they were 'very famous' (ἐπιφανέστατοι) – only then to let the performance be derailed by the whims of his audience? And why, at any rate, should we assume that this audience was on the verge of rioting, as has been suggested? The hooliganism of the Roman spectators may have appalled Polybius, but in the context of the dramatic head-to-head between the dancer and the piper, their clapping and cheering make much better sense as an expression of approval than of disdain. 'Far from letting matters slip out of his hands, Anicius dictated them from start to finish'.[5] The show was no flop. It was designed to make an impact, and by all accounts it succeeded in doing so.

If we recognise that Anicius' production had a logical design, this raises the question as to what that design was, and why the performance offended Polybius to the extent that it did. As Gruen underlines, we must be mindful of how Anicius exploited the national divide between his Greek hirelings on the one hand and his Roman compatriots on the other. 'Exploitation' is the operative word here. The spectacle functioned, in Gruen's words, as 'a stunning display of Roman power to exploit Hellenic culture'.[6] In particular, Gruen highlights how the degrading treatment suffered by

---

[3] Beacham 1991: 48; MacMullen 1991: 421 n. 6; Edmondson 1999: 88; Brennan 2000: 337 n. 222; Ferrary 2017: 458.
[4] Gruen 1993: 215–18.   [5] Gruen 1993: 217.   [6] Gruen 1993: 248.

the Greek musicians at the hands of the praetor engendered in the Roman audience a 'sense of cultural superiority' in the face of a common (Greek) enemy.[7] The whole thing was a 'conscious parody', intended to be read as such by all who saw it. It was thus bound to offend a patriotic Greek observer like Polybius, who was unfamiliar with the Roman theatre and was in any case naturally ill-disposed towards the Romans, having been taken hostage by them just a few months earlier following the defeat of the Macedonian king Perseus.

Gruen's theory of 'conscious parody' has been developed more recently by George Fredric Franko in an article entitled '*Anicius vortit barbare*: The Scenic Games of L. Anicius Gallus and the Aesthetics of Greek and Roman Performance'. Franko's central argument is that Anicius designed his show based on the tried-and-tested model of a Plautine comic drama. Like Plautus, he 'twisted' Greek culture to suit Roman tastes, transforming it into 'raw material for Roman fun' and thereby 'triumphing through subversion and reconfiguration for a Roman audience'.[8] To support this argument, Franko draws attention to the fact that Anicius' triumph took place during the Quirinalia festival.[9] The Quirinalia is associated by some ancient authors with the so-called Feast of Fools (*feriae stultorum*), which fell on the same date.[10] This festival served, in Franko's view, as an atmospheric backdrop to the festivities in 167, inspiring and authorising the mayhem. Franko also reaffirms Gruen's view that the show was scripted specifically to appeal to the 'chauvinistic' and 'xenophobic' tendencies of a Roman audience.[11] It is no surprise, then, that a proud Greek like Polybius failed to see the funny side.

Franko is surely right to emphasise the importance of mockery and subversion in Anicius' games. Scholars such as Linda-Marie Günther have attempted to downplay the comedic aspects of the show, claiming that it represented not a 'parody' but a 'parable' of the Greeks' political servility to Rome, acted out by the tame musicians.[12] However, this interpretation is unconvincing. It is telling that Athenaeus presents the episode in a section of the *Deipnosophistae* dealing specifically with the subject of joking and laughter. Anicius is introduced alongside several other political leaders who were unusually fond of jokes, including the Macedonian kings Demetrius Poliorcetes and Philip II, and the Roman dictator Sulla.[13] Perhaps most

---

[7] Gruen 1993: 217–18.   [8] Franko 2013: 348, 353.
[9] Livy 45.43.1: *L. Anicius Quirinalibus triumphavit de rege Gentio Illyriisque*.
[10] Cf. Fest. 304L, 418L; Plut. *Quaest. Rom.* 89.   [11] Franko 2013: 345.   [12] Günther 2002.
[13] Athen. 14.613d–615a. On the relationship between music and comedy in Book 14, see Ceccarelli 2000.

revealingly, the anecdote concludes with the banqueters all in hysterics ('everyone burst out laughing at these Anician spectacles', πάντων ἀνακαγχασάντων ἐπὶ ταῖς Ἀνικίοις ταύταις θέαις).[14] For Athenaeus and his readers, there was no question that this performance was supposed to make its audience laugh.

In my view, however, the Plautine model can only get us so far. Roman comedies were, of course, highly musical affairs, with sung *cantica* and the ever-present accompaniment of the pipe-player (*tibicen*). But the fact remains that the plays of Plautus and Terence originated as written texts; they derived their entertainment value from wordplay and dialogue as much as from music and dance. Anicius' production, on the other hand, was predominantly non-verbal, at least as far as we can gauge from the surviving account (we hear of the involvement of tragic actors, but this seems to have followed later in the proceedings). At any rate, it is doubtful that the Feast of Fools had the general currency which Franko ascribes it. Ovid, in the *Fasti*, connects the *feriae stultorum* not with the Quirinalia, but with the Fornicalia, an obscure festival held in honour of Fornax, the goddess of the oven.[15] This hardly seems a likely pretext for the antics of a theatrical performance. In short, while Plautine comedy may provide a suitable framework for understanding certain aspects of what Anicius was doing, it is only one of several possible points of comparison.

Above all, what has been missing from the scholarship is a recognition of the peculiar musicality of Anicius' spectacle. Polybius' account is extraordinary precisely because it represents one of the few eyewitness descriptions of a musical performance to have survived from Roman antiquity. It therefore affords historians a rare opportunity to examine how a Roman politician and impresario manipulated sound and choreography to convey a particular message to a particular audience. That the musical soundtrack of Anicius' games comes across so powerfully is no coincidence; it reflects a conscious emphasis on the part of both Anicius (as producer) and Polybius (as narrator). This raises two interrelated questions. First, what was Anicius trying to achieve through his innovative use of music and dance? And second, why did Polybius choose to foreground this musical episode in his *Histories*?

---

[14] Athen. 14.615e. Worth noting here is the pun on ταῖς Ἀνικίοις ταύταις θέαις: *anikios* in Greek means 'unbeatable', but it is also the adjectival form of Anicius' name (hence, 'these Anician spectacles').

[15] Ov. *Fast.* 2.513–32.

Before we can start to address these questions, however, there is a more fundamental issue that must be considered. As I noted at the start of this chapter, Polybius' account of Anicius' games survives only in the much later work of Athenaeus. It is unclear whether the account that has come down to us represents an accurate record of what Polybius actually wrote, as opposed to an adapted or abridged version. For example, is the phrase παντὸς γέλωτος ἄξια (literally 'worthy of much laughter/ridicule') Polybius' or Athenaeus'? To be sure, Athenaeus was not interested in presenting his readers with a joined-up historical narrative, but selected excerpts primarily on the basis of their thematic content.[16] Moreover, he did not have access to a definitive 'first edition' of Polybius, but made use of later copies which doubtless varied from one to another.[17] Further alterations to the text could have been made by Athenaeus himself, or by a later copyist of the *Deipnosophistae*. Dominique Lenfant's study of the Herodotean passages in the work has shown how Athenaeus is prone to changing, adding or removing certain words for reasons of dialect, syntax and context.[18] Christopher Pelling's examination of the use of Xenophon has highlighted similar trends.[19] In most cases, however, Athenaeus' alterations are cosmetic; very rarely do they deviate substantially from the 'authoritative' version of the text, insofar as it has been transmitted independently through the manuscript tradition. We have no such 'authoritative' text to rely on for the passage under consideration in this chapter. Nevertheless, it should be noted that Athenaeus credits his source on two occasions in the text: the first reference gives the exact book in Polybius' *Histories* from which the passage has been excerpted (ὡς Πολύβιος ἱστορεῖ ἐν τῇ τριακοστῇ), while the second purports to be a verbatim citation (φησὶν ὁ Πολύβιος). Of course, these statements alone do not prove that the text is 'authentically' Polybian. But on the basis of the evidence presented above, it seems safest to conclude that Athenaeus has reproduced the main elements of Polybius' narrative, albeit with the potential for slight linguistic or syntactic modifications here and there. It is also very likely that the criticism of Anicius, including in the phrase παντὸς γέλωτος ἄξια, comes from Polybius rather than from Athenaeus and/or his interlocutor.

---

[16] See Pelling 2000; Zecchini 2007; Wilkins 2007.
[17] Polybius is one of the historians most often consulted by Athenaeus; his work is cited around thirty times in the *Deipnosophistae*. Walbank (2000: 161) suggests that the Polybian excerpts may have been gathered second-hand from a lexicon of some kind.
[18] Lenfant 2007: 68–70.   [19] Pelling 2000: 188–90.

The following discussion is divided into five sections. The first two sections focus on the spectacle itself. I begin by addressing a set of issues relating to the date and location of the games. Establishing where and when the event took place is important because it allows us to draw more informed inferences about Anicius' intentions. It is also important to consider the political context of the games. By comparing Anicius' show with other *ludi* staged during this period by victorious Roman generals (*triumphatores*), we can see how the praetor sought to engage in a competitive dialogue with his senatorial rivals – most notably, M. Fulvius Nobilior and L. Aemilius Paullus. In the second section, I dissect the various components of the spectacle, paying particular attention to the use of music and choreography. I argue that Anicius, in devising his *ludi*, subtly incorporated sounds and sights that were reminiscent of other militaristic ceremonies – especially the triumph – in order to amplify the sense of occasion that accompanied his Illyrian victory. In effect, Anicius blended the elements of a military procession with those of a theatrical performance, producing a memorably subversive spectacle that immortalised his achievements as a general.

The third section deals with the representation of the games in Polybius' *Histories*. The question of why Polybius chose to foreground the musicality of Anicius' *ludi* cannot be answered simply by reverting to the 'culture shock' argument made by Gruen and other scholars. A more productive line of enquiry, I suggest, is to examine the role of music in the *Histories* more broadly. The account of Anicius' games is, in fact, one of several passages in which Polybius passes judgement on musical performances both past and present. Taken together, these passages highlight the importance of music in Polybius' moralising narrative. The self-degradation of the Greek performers was offensive to the historian not simply because it upset his sense of national pride, but because it illustrated the moral degeneracy of contemporary music. I argue, moreover, that Polybius' conservative stance on music was influenced by contemporary trends in Greek civic ideology and philosophical discourse.

The final two sections of the chapter situate Anicius' games within the broader musical milieu of second-century Rome. Despite the paucity of evidence for Roman attitudes to music in this period, there is still much that can be gleaned from the extant sources. Firstly, we can draw comparisons between Anicius' spectacle and the Greek-inspired musical performances put on by Aemilius Paullus and Fulvius Nobilior. Secondly, we can use Polybius' critique of the games to shed light on the attacks on music made by Scipio Aemilianus and Cato the Elder. We can only imagine how the likes of Scipio and Cato might have responded to Anicius' games. Yet there were at least some members of the Roman political establishment who objected vociferously to, and even legislated against, certain kinds of popular musical entertainment. The games of 167 may have been well-received by the general public, but that does not necessarily mean *all* Roman spectators approved.

Triumphal Politics and Spectacle Culture in Mid-Republican Rome

The date of Anicius' games cannot be established with certainty. Since we do not know where exactly in Book 30 the episode was situated, we must resort to circumstantial details in Livy's history in order to reconstruct a basic chronology. Livy informs us that Anicius' triumph took place on the Quirinalia of 166 BCE.[20] This festival was held each year on 17 February.[21] However, the year 166 was intercalary, and so the Quirinalia will have fallen in the Julian calendar on 19 November 167, or, if 167 was also intercalary, on 11/12 December.[22] The renowned Polybian scholar F. W. Walbank asserts in his commentary on the *Histories* that Anicius' games 'were probably the result of a *votum* [that is, a vow to a deity made prior to or during the Illyrian campaign], and quite distinct from his triumph'.[23] But it seems difficult to explain the phrase ἀγῶνας ... τοὺς ἐπινικίους as anything other than a direct allusion to the triumph on the Quirinalia: the opening reference to Anicius' praetorian command ('Ρωμαίων στρατηγήσας) and the capture of Genthius and his children (αἰχμάλωτον ἀγαγὼν Γένθιον ... σὺν τοῖς τέκνοις) makes the connection almost explicit.

The temporal relationship between the triumph and the games therefore requires elucidation. Walbank reached the conclusion that the games must have taken place several days or weeks after the triumph. Subsequent scholarship has generally concurred with this view. However, the assumption that the games served as a sequel to the triumph is problematic, for reasons which have not been sufficiently acknowledged. In presiding over the spectacle, Anicius was acting in the capacity of an *imperator* (a general invested with a formal command, or *imperium*). Not only did he appear as Genthius' conqueror, but he also possessed lictors (τῶν ῥαβδούχων) in his

---

[20] Livy 45.43.1: *L. Anicius Quirinalibus triumphavit de rege Gentio Illyriisque.*
[21] Ov. *Fast.* 2.475; Scullard 1981: 78–9.   [22] Cf. Livy 45.44.3; Walbank 1979: 445.
[23] Walbank 1979: 446.

retinue. The involvement of these officials would be extremely odd if the triumph had already taken place and Anicius had formally relinquished his command.[24] The most likely scenario, therefore, is that the games were either held on the same day as the triumph, while Anicius still retained *imperium*, or they were held beforehand, with the praetor's army still encamped on the Campus Martius.[25]

The fact that Anicius was acting as *imperator* would also have restricted the range of theatrical venues that were accessible to him. Polybius mentions the erection of a large stage 'in the circus' (ἐν τῷ κίρκῳ), without specifying *which* circus is meant.[26] Scholars have assumed that Polybius must be referring here to the Circus Maximus, the place where many of the city's annual festivals were celebrated.[27] On the face of it, this seems a reasonable assumption; the racetrack would have afforded ample space for a *scaena* (stage), while the spectators could have watched from the available seats, just as they watched *ludi scaenici* on other occasions from the steps of temples.[28] However, the identification with the Circus Maximus is flawed in one key respect: the Circus Maximus lay inside the *pomerium* (the sacred boundary of the city) and so was effectively out-of-bounds for an incumbent *imperator*. Moreover, there is no reason to assume that Anicius had any intention to 'accommodate the audience in tiered seats', as Sander Goldberg claims.[29] The Greek word *skene* refers simply to a wooden 'stage-building' and need not imply the existence of a larger *cavea* (auditorium).[30] It is certainly possible that some spectators sat on benches, but this cannot be taken for granted: indeed, ancient authors indicate that it was not unusual in the mid-second century for Roman theatre-goers to stand rather than sit.[31]

---

[24] Lictors were regularly in attendance at the Roman theatre during this period (cf. Plaut. *Poen.* 18), but it would have been highly irregular for a lictor to intervene in the performance without the authorization of the presiding magistrate to whom he was formally attached.

[25] Livy (45.35.4) informs us that a plebiscite had been passed enabling Anicius and his colleague Octavius to retain *imperium* within the city on the day of their triumph. For the suggestion that the games might have taken place immediately after the triumph, see Brennan 2000: 337 n. 22.

[26] The Greek loanword κίρκος (= Lat. *circus*) appears for the first time in this passage and is found nowhere else in Polybius: see *LSJ*, s.v. κίρκος, IV.

[27] See most recently Franko 2013: 344; Wiseman 2015: 58; Feeney 2016: 147; Champion 2018: 38.

[28] Literary and archaeological evidence confirms that by the 160s BCE the Circus Maximus already possessed permanent tiers of seating, as well as a central enclosure decorated with various monumental structures: see Humphrey 1986: 72; Manuwald 2011: 42.

[29] Goldberg 1995: 39.   [30] Cf. *LSJ*, s.v. σκηνή, II.

[31] Cf. Livy, *Per.* 48: *populusque aliquamdiu stans ludos spectavit*; Val. Max. 2.4.2 (*sedensve ludos spectare vellet*); Tac. *Ann.* 14.20 (*stantem populum spectavisse*). On occasions when seating was

On this basis, we might postulate that Anicius' games took place not in the Circus Maximus, but in Rome's other circus, the Circus Flaminius, created by the censor C. Flaminius Nepos in 221 BCE.[32] As 'a broad open space unencumbered by *spina* [a central barrier], *carceres* [starting barriers] or terraces of public seats', the Circus Flaminius was more than capable of housing a large *skene*.[33] It also met the necessary criterion of being located beyond the *pomerium*, lying on the Campus Martius near to the river Tiber where Anicius' troops would have disembarked. The Circus Flaminius would have been an appropriate choice of venue for several reasons. We know that it was used as the setting for the annual Plebeian Games, which included dramatic performances.[34] Furthermore, in 179, the consul M. Aemilius Lepidus commissioned an 'auditorium and stage' (*theatrum et proscaenium*) in front of the temple of Apollo in the Circus Flaminius. The appearance of this structure is unknown (in fact, it was probably never completed), but it seems to have been intended as a permanent venue for hosting the *Ludi Apollinares*.[35] The Circus Flaminius also served as a starting point for triumphal processions and as a place where triumphal spoils were deposited. Plutarch describes how, during the triumph of Aemilius Paullus in 167, 'the people erected scaffolding in the horse-racing stadia, which the Romans call "circuses"' (ὁ μὲν δῆμος ἔν τε τοῖς ἱππικοῖς θεάτροις, ἃ Κίρκους καλοῦσι ... ἰκρία πηξάμενοι) in order to watch the procession – these 'circuses' were presumably the Circus Maximus and Circus Flaminius.[36] A year later (or shortly thereafter), Cn. Octavius built 'a portico at the Circus Flaminius' (*porticus ad circum Flaminium*) from the spoils of his naval triumph against the Macedonian king Perseus.[37] The Circus Flaminius therefore possessed strong links to

---

provided, temporary benches would have been the norm: Moore 1994; Gruen 1993: 207–8; Goldberg 1998.

[32] Livy, *Per.* 20: *C. Flaminius censor ... circum Flaminium exstruxit*.
[33] Wiseman 1974: 4. On the topography of the Circus Flaminius, see Wiseman 1974, 1976; Richardson 1992: 83; Viscogliosi 1993b.
[34] Cf. Val. Max. 1.7.4, 4.4.8; Manuwald 2011: 43. The Circus Flaminius was also used for *ludi funebres* in 174 BCE (Livy 41.28.11).
[35] Five years later, in 174 BCE, the censors Q. Fulvius Flaccus and A. Postumius Albinus commissioned 'a stage to be provided for aediles and praetors' in the Circus Flaminius (*scaenam aedilibus practoribusque praebendam*; Livy 41.27); this project too was aborted for unknown reasons: see Manuwald 2011: 57–8; Popkin 2016: 189–90.
[36] Plut. *Aem.* 32; cf. Livy 35.39; Beard 2007: 101–2. In 187, the consul M. Fulvius Nobilior commemorated his victory in Aetolia by presenting his soldiers with military decorations in the Circus Flaminius: Livy 39.5.13–17. Note also Plut. *Luc.* 37 (Lucullus' triumph in 63) and Sen. *De ben.* 5.16.5 (Caesar pitching camp in the Circus Flaminius in 49).
[37] Plin. *HN* 34.13; Vell. 2.1.2; Festus 188L.

both the *ludi* and the triumph. Accordingly, it would have been an opportune space for hosting a quasi-military performance of the kind witnessed by Polybius.

The Illyrian triumph of 167 was the third such event to have taken place in Rome in the space of just three months. The naval triumph of Octavius was, by Livy's estimate, something of a dull affair, lacking in both prisoners and spoils.[38] But the magnificent triumph of L. Aemilius Paullus over king Perseus had gone down in history as one of the finest spectacles the city had ever witnessed.[39] Subsequent *triumphatores* struggled to compete. Paullus' conquest came at the cost of a long and hard-fought campaign. Anicius' subjugation of Illyria, by contrast, was completed after barely a month of skirmishing.[40] The disparity between the two generals is astutely observed by Livy:

> *similia omnia magis visa hominibus quam paria; minor ipse imperator, et nobilitate Anicius cum Aemilio et iure imperii praetor cum consule conlatus; non Gentius Perseo, non Illyrii Macedonibus, non spolia spoliis, non pecunia pecuniae, non dona donis comparari poterant.* (Livy 45.43.2–3)
>
> Men saw in each detail a resemblance, but no equality. The commander himself was the lesser, both in public esteem, as an Anicius compared with an Aemilius, and in rank of office, a praetor rather than a consul. Genthius could not be compared to Perseus, the Illyrians to the Macedonians, nor the spoils of the one to those of the other, nor the money, nor the gifts to the soldiers.

Not that there was anything inherently contemptible about Anicius' triumph. As Livy points out: 'The Illyrians were a nation formidable both by land and sea, who felt secure in their strong fortified positions, and Anicius had thoroughly subjugated them in a few days and captured their king and all his family'. Nor was the booty unimpressive. The problem, rather, was one of timing, for 'the memory of the Macedonian triumph was still fresh not only in people's minds but almost before their eyes'.[41]

---

[38] Livy 45.42.1 (*sine capitivis fuit, sine spoliis*).
[39] Diod. 31.9.1 (λαμπρὸς θρίαμβος). Paullus' triumph took place on 27–9 November (3–5 September in the Julian calendar): *CIL* I² p. 48. The naval triumph of Cn. Octavius took place shortly thereafter on the Kalends of December (6 September in the Julian calendar): Livy 45.42.2; Walbank 1979: 440.
[40] A helpful synopsis of the Illyrian campaign can be found in Wilkes 1992: 173–5. On the triumph itself, cf. Livy 45.39.2–4; Vell. Pat. 1.9.5; App. *Ill.* 2.9.
[41] Livy 45.43.1.

Livy's comments provide a revealing insight into the competitive dynamics of Roman public spectacle during the second century BCE. As Rome gradually extended her hegemony over the Hellenistic East, there emerged a small but powerful clique of pre-eminent statesmen who vied with one another to win over the hearts and minds of their fellow citizens. As well as having to contend with the recent memory of Paullus' triumph (and the less memorable, but not negligible, triumph of Octavius), Anicius could recall a string of triumphal honours conferred on victorious generals of the not-so-distant past: M. Fulvius Nobilior in 187, Cn. Manlius Vulso in 186, Ti. Sempronius Gracchus in 178, C. Claudius Pulcher in 177, M. Aemilius Lepidus in 175 and C. Cicerius in 172 – to name only a few.[42] Having a triumph to one's name was all well and good, but in the crowded arena of Roman politics it was no longer a guaranteed route to immortality. Now, more than ever, the *triumphator* needed to put on a show.[43]

Anicius was not the first Roman general to sponsor a theatrical performance involving Greek artists. In 186, following his conquest of Ambracia, the consul M. Fulvius Nobilior presented votive games in Rome, which, according to Livy, showcased 'a large number of artists from Greece' (*multi artifices ex Graecia*) and featured for the first time in Rome a contest of athletes and a wild-beast hunt.[44] In the same year, L. Scipio celebrated his victory in the Antiochene War by producing a spectacle which featured 'artists gathered from all over Asia' (*congregatosque per Asiam artifices*).[45] When Anicius sent for 'the most distinguished performers from Greece' (τοὺς ἐκ τῆς Ἑλλάδος ἐπιφανεστάτους τεχνίτας), he knew that he was following in the footsteps of political heavyweights.

The legacy of Fulvius Nobilior is worth considering more closely. Fulvius' commitment to promoting Greek culture extended beyond the

---

[42] Cf. Livy 39.7.1–4, 41.7.1–3, 41.13.6–7, 42.21.6–7.

[43] On the competitive dynamics of public spectacles in the republican period, see Edmondson 1999: 77; Bell 2004: 156; *contra* Gruen 1993: 188–97.

[44] Livy 39.22.2. Livy does not specify where the games were held, but the Circus Flaminius is a strong possibility.

[45] Livy 39.22.10. Gruen (1993: 195–6) argues that these *artifices* were 'artisans' (i.e. manual labourers) rather than 'stage-performers', on the grounds that there was already a plentiful supply of performers in Italy who could have been recruited for this purpose. However, it is hard to explain what role the *artifices* would have played in Scipio's games if they were not actually taking part in the performances as musicians or actors (why else would Livy have mentioned them?). Indeed, their prestige surely derived from the fact that they were foreign artists, specially imported for the pleasure of the Roman people. On the popularity of *ludi Graeci* in the late-republican period, see Crowther 1983.

showcasing of Greek artists on the Roman stage; for he also dedicated a temple next to the Circus Flaminius in honour of Hercules and the Muses. This temple, known commonly as the Aedes Herculis Musarum, has generated a great deal of scholarly debate, mainly focusing on the date of the temple's foundation (the *communis opinio* favours 187, the year of Fulvius' triumph, but 189 and 179 have also been canvassed) and its connection with the Roman 'guild of playwrights and actors' (*collegium scribarum et histrionum*), which is believed to have established its headquarters in the temple.[46] Nothing remains of the monument today, although its location is identifiable based on fragments of the Severan Marble Plan. We know from literary sources that the temple was adorned with cult statues depicting the nine Muses and Hercules playing the lyre, taken as spoils during the Ambracian campaign.[47] In the eyes of Cicero, these spoils were a testament to the fact that Roman generals, 'while still virtually armed', were concerned with 'cultivating the name of poets and temples of the Muses'.[48] By transforming the Circus Flaminius into a monumental arena for his own philhellenic self-fashioning, Fulvius articulated a vision for Roman culture in which *mousike* (defined in the broad sense of music, poetry and drama) was to play a central role.

The games of Aemilius Paullus provide another illustration of the political importance of Greek culture to Roman generals in this period. In the aftermath of his stunning victory over king Perseus at the Battle of Pydna in 168, Paullus made the decision to postpone his return to Italy, and instead visited the city of Amphipolis, the cultural epicentre of northern Greece, where he presided over a great theatrical bonanza. Paullus replicated, with remarkable precision, the traditional format of a Greek agonistic festival, bringing together 'a multitude of artists of every kind from all over the world' (*artificum omnis generis ... ex toto orbe terrarum multitudo*).[49] According to Livy, the fact that the consul had planned the

---

[46] See Richardson 1977; Viscogliosi 1996; Sciarrino 2004a; Rüpke 2006; La Rocca 2006; Hardie 2007; Heslin 2015: 202–7; Russell 2016: 139–45.

[47] For the cult statues, cf. Plin. *NH* 35.66; Ov. *Fast.* 6.812, *Ars Am.* 3.168; Eumenius, *Paneg.* 9.7.3. The statues appear to be depicted on coins minted by Pomponius Musa in 56 BCE: *RRC* 410/1, pl. 50; Marabini Moevs 1981. For Hercules' association with music and the Muses, see Dugas 1944; La Rocca 2006: 103–5; *LIMC* 4.1.810–17, nos. 1438–74.

[48] Cic. *Arch.* 27: *in qua urbe imperatores prope armati poetarum nomen et Musarum delubra coluerunt*. This is an allusion to Fulvius' patronage of Ennius, whose *Annales* are thought to have ended with Fulvius' dedication of the temple of Hercules Musarum: Skutsch 1968: 18–21.

[49] Livy 45.32.9. On the games at Amphipolis, cf. Polyb. 30.14; Plut. *Paul.* 28.3–5; Ferrary 1988: 560–5; Gruen 1993: 247; Edmondson 1999: 79–80. On Paullus' philhellenism more generally, see Gruen 1993: 245–8.

games 'a long time in advance' (*ex multo ante preparato*) stood as a testament to his unrivalled *prudentia*, at a time when the Romans were still 'inexperienced' (*rudes*) in the theatrical arts.[50] In effect, Paullus' achievement was to recognise and exploit the natural affinity between the roles of *imperator* and impresario; as he often professed, 'the person who knows how to conquer in war also knows how to organise a banquet and to prepare games'.[51]

Like his illustrious predecessors, Anicius understood the need to capitalise on his moment in the spotlight. He realised that there were political rewards to be reaped from sponsoring a Greek-inspired theatrical production on a lavish scale. However, he chose to target his games not at a Greek audience in a Greek city, as Paullus had done, but at a Roman audience in the city of Rome. He may have done so with the deliberate intention of overshadowing Paullus, as has been argued persuasively by Jonathan Edmondson.[52] After all, Rome was surely a much better place for an ambitious politician to make a splash than the far-flung city of Amphipolis. The games of Fulvius Nobilior provided a shining example in this regard. More importantly, Rome was also the place where the triumph took place and, if Livy's comments are to be believed, the praetor had good reason to suspect that this event might otherwise have slipped under the radar. Anicius could not afford simply to imitate Paullus: he had to be bolder, more original, more creative. Introducing Greek performers to an 'inexperienced' audience might have been a gamble, but there is certainly no reason to assume that this gamble backfired.[53]

Battle of the Bands: Anicius' Martial Soundtrack

How, then, did Anicius create a show that eclipsed what Roman audiences had witnessed before? As I argued at the beginning of this chapter, the tendency to draw comparisons with Plautine comedy has led scholars to underestimate the novelty of Anicius' production. A more helpful approach, I suggest, is to look at how Anicius incorporated musical influences from *outside* the theatre – most importantly, the triumph – in order to heighten the impact of his spectacle. In particular, I will contend that

---

[50] Livy 45.32.8–10; cf. Plut. *Aem.* 28.7–9; Diod. 31.8.9.
[51] Polyb. 30.14; Livy 45.32.11; Plut. *Aem.* 28.9; Diod. 31.8.13. [52] Edmondson 1999: 83.
[53] Anicius was elected to the consulship in 160 BCE (Cic. *Brut.* 287; Broughton 1952: 529), though it is unclear to what extent the games of 167 contributed to his later political success.

Anicius used musical effects to create an audible juncture between the games and the triumph. This strategy served as a way of amplifying the importance of his military victory and thus reinforcing his political prestige (*auctoritas*).

Those who attended the circus with Polybius would have been left in no doubt that they were witnessing a quasi-military display. The lictor initially orders the musicians and dancers 'to simulate a battle' (ποιεῖν ὡσανεὶ μάχην). As the choreography unfolds, the movements begin to resemble those of a battle line (παράταξις) advancing and retreating in neat array. The musical accompaniment, 'meaningless and discordant' (ἀδιανόητα καὶ διαφέροντες), provides a fitting soundtrack to the chorus' shenanigans. Then, at the last moment, four boxers (πύκται τέτταρες) enter the fray. They are accompanied by an unnumbered group of brass-players (σαλπιγκτῶν καὶ βυκανιστῶν, equivalent to *tubicines* and *cornicines* in Latin). The role of these musicians is not immediately apparent. In Rome, as in Greece, brass instruments were synonymous not with the theatre but with the army.[54] It is likely that the trumpeters would have completely drowned out the sound of the pipers, who seemingly kept on playing regardless.[55]

Not all of Anicius' audience will have experienced the din of battle (although there may have been large numbers of soldiers in attendance). But the vast majority will have witnessed a triumph, and it is likely that the sight and sound of the musicians would have prompted recollections of just such an occasion. The music of the *tuba* and *cornu* played an important role in reinforcing the martial atmosphere of the triumph (see Fig. 1.1).[56] Trumpeters were typically the first thing that spectators saw and heard during a triumphal procession. For example, they led the procession on the

---

[54] Cf. Polyb. 6.35.12 and 14.3.6, on the uses of the *bukane* (*cornu*) and *salpinx* (*tuba*) in the Roman army camp. The martial association of the trumpet is highlighted by an anecdote in Cassius Dio's history (57.18.3), concerning the consul Lucius Norbanus. At dawn on the first day of his consulship in 19 CE, Norbanus cheerfully greeted his morning callers by playing a loud note on his trumpet. This alarmed the unsuspecting visitors, who mistook the sound as a signal for battle. Cf. Livy 25.10.4, describing the consternation caused by a *tuba* 'being heard in the theatre' during the capture of Tarentum in 211 BCE: the trumpet was probably used to call for silence before a theatrical show, but the Roman soldiers mistook it for a military signal. On the use of brass instruments in the Roman army, see Vincent 2016: 15–117.

[55] Cf. Luc. *Rh.Pr.* 13, describing an orator who can drown out other speakers 'as effectively as the trumpet drowns out pipes' (τούς γε ἄλλους τοσοῦτον ὑπερφωνοῦντα εὑρήσεις ὁπόσον ἡ σάλπιγξ τοὺς αὐλούς).

[56] On the role of music in the triumph, see Vincent 2016: 172–82. In addition to the examples discussed below, notice the conspicuous presence of musicians in the sham 'triumph' staged by the Parthians in celebration of their victory at Carrhae in 53 BCE (Plut. *Crass*. 32).

Figure 1.1 Bas-relief from Osuna (Urso), Spain, representing a *cornicen*; early first century BCE. Museo Arqueológico Nacional, Madrid, inv. 38417. Photo by DEA / G. Nimatallah / De Agostini via Getty Images.

first day of Aemilius Paullus' triumph, 'as they did in war'.[57] They appeared again on the third and final day, when, according to Plutarch, they played not a marching or processional fanfare, but a call to arms, 'such as the Romans use to rouse themselves to battle'.[58] Musicians also feature in Appian's account of the triumph of Scipio Africanus in 201 BCE.[59] As usual, trumpeters led the vanguard. Next came the general himself, followed by lictors clad in purple robes and a chorus of lyre-players and pipers (χορὸς κιθαριστῶν τε καὶ τιτυριστῶν), who marched 'in regular order with song and dance' (βαίνουσιν ἐν τάξει μετὰ ᾠδῆς καὶ μετ' ὀρχήσεως).[60]

---

[57] Diod. Sic. 31.8.10: προηγοῦντο δὲ αὐτῶν ὡς ἐν πολέμῳ σαλπιγκταί.
[58] Plut. *Aem.* 33.1: μέλος οὐ προσόδιον καὶ πομπικόν, ἀλλ' οἵῳ μαχομένους ἐποτρύνουσιν αὐτοὺς Ῥωμαῖοι, προσεγκελευόμενοι.
[59] App. *Pun.* 66.
[60] The word τιτυριστῶν is a hapax, probably deriving from τιτύρινος αὐλός, 'shepherd's pipe': cf. *LSJ*, s.v. τιτύρινος. However, the term may be related to τίτυρος ('satyr-dances', *pace* Wiseman 1994: 76; see further Smith 1970.

Appian is the only ancient author who explicitly mentions the participation of lyre-players and pipe-players in a Roman triumph. This has prompted speculation about whether string instruments and *tibiae* featured routinely in triumphal processions or only on certain occasions. Censorinus indicates that *tibicines* took part in triumphs, but does not say how often or in what capacity.[61] On the other hand, Plutarch claims that the use of *salpinktai* instead of *auletai* was one of the features which distinguished the triumph from the ovation, its lesser counterpart, stating that 'the *aulos* is an instrument of peace (εἰρήνης μέρος)'.[62] For example, we are told that Marcellus' ovation in 211 BCE featured 'a very large number of pipe-players' (αὐλητῶν μάλα πολλῶν).[63] Moreover, a sculptural relief from Rome, dating from the first century BCE, shows a pair of *tibicines*, a *fidicen* (lyre-player) and a group of armed dancers involved in a procession (Fig. 1.2). An association with the ovation (or, less likely, the triumph) is suggested by the fact that the musicians wear crowns on their heads and are trailed by three captives with their arms tied behind their backs.[64] Thus, while the evidence precludes definitive conclusions, the logical inference is that *tibicines* and *fidicines* were involved *occasionally* in triumphs, but certainly not as a matter of course. The quintessential triumphal instruments were always the *tuba* and *cornu*.

In addition to its military soundtrack, the triumph was also noted for its choreography. Appian foregrounds the role of dance and mime in giving life to the spectacle and eliciting the laughter of spectators. During Scipio's triumph, one member of the chorus, positioned 'in the middle' (ἐν μέσῳ) and decked out in a long purple cloak and gold jewellery, 'caused laughter by making various gestures, as if he were dancing in triumph over the enemy' (σχηματίζεται ποικίλως ἐς γέλωτα ὡς ἐπορχούμενος τοῖς πολεμίοις). According to Mary Beard, 'the man's actions here cast the celebration of

---

[61] Censorinus, *De die nat.* 12 (*in sacris aedibus adhiberetur non cum tibicine Marti triumphus ageretur*). Also worth considering here is the case of the Roman general Gaius Duilius. In recognition of being the first Roman citizen to celebrate a naval triumph in 260 BCE, Duilius was granted the right to be escorted home from dinner each night by a pipe-player and a torch-bearer. According to Florus (1.18.10–11), this entourage provided Duilius with 'a kind of daily triumph'; in the words of Östenberg (2015: 16–17), 'the flutist(s) [sic] would have recalled and evoked the triumph itself, in which Duilius also had moved through the city accompanied by music'. However, while Duilius' post-dinner celebration may have been reminiscent of the triumph, it was something fundamentally different, and cannot be taken as evidence for the involvement of *tibicines* in the triumph itself. Cf. *ILS* 55 = *Inscr. It.* XIII.3, 13; Cic. *Sen.* 44; Livy, *Per.* 17; Sil. *Pun.* 6.667–70; Val. Max. 3.6.4 (noting uniquely that Duilius was also accompanied by a *fidicen*); Amm. Marc. 26.3.5; *De vir. ill.* 38.
[62] Plut. *Marc.* 22.4.   [63] Plut. *Marc.* 22.2.   [64] See further discussion in Latham 2016: 32–3.

Figure 1.2 Marble bas-relief showing musicians and armed dancers leading captives in a triumph or ovation; mid-first century BCE. Raccolta di antichità Baldassini-Castelli, courtesy of the Università degli studi di Urbino "Carlo Bo" (Anna Santucci).

victory as comic parody'.[65] Further comparisons can be drawn with the famous account of the *Ludi Romani* by Dionysius of Halicarnassus, derived from the third-century Roman historian Fabius Pictor. Dionysius begins by describing the war-dances which opened the games. The dancers who took part were equipped with weapons and armour, and were accompanied by an ensemble of pipe-players and lyre-players.[66] They were followed by a second chorus of dancers, who impersonated satyrs (in the manner of a Greek dance called the *sicinnis*) and 'ridiculed and mimicked the serious movements of the others, turning them into laughter-provoking performances' (κατέσκωπτόν τε καὶ κατεμιμοῦντο τὰς σπουδαίας κινήσεις ἐπὶ τὰ γελοιότερα μεταφέροντες).[67] After these choruses came 'a multitude of lyre-players and many pipe-players' (μετὰ δὲ τοὺς χοροὺς τούτους κιθαρισταί τ' ἀθρόοι καὶ αὐληταὶ πολλοί).[68] Though not pertaining directly to the triumph, Dionysius' account is helpful in highlighting the traditional role of music, dance and mimicry in Roman military celebrations.

---

[65] Beard 2003: 34.
[66] Dion. Hal. *Ant. Rom.* 7.72.5. On the role of these musicians, see Barker 2017: 77–80.
[67] Dion. Hal. *Ant. Rom.* 7.72.10.   [68] Dion. Hal. *Ant. Rom.* 7.72.13.

The spectacles of the triumph and the *Ludi Romani* are reminiscent of Anicius' games in several ways. Polybius' narrative plays out in sequential episodes, each act appearing in turn as though part of a moving procession. Particularly significant is the inclusion of *tubicines* and *cornicines*, which recalls the military-style music heard during the *pompa triumphalis*. The martial choreography, intended to evoke the movements of a battle-line, also mirrors the role of mimetic dancing during the triumph. Furthermore, the triumph was associated with a particular kind of licence (*licentia*), whereby the normal rules and restrictions of public life were temporarily suspended. Appian comments that 'in a triumph everybody is free and is allowed to say what he pleases'.[69] This freedom of speech was exemplified by the so-called *carmina triumphalia*, ribald songs sung by the parading soldiers in mockery of their general.[70] With its irreverent humour and subversive use of music, Anicius' production seems to owe much to the *licentia* of the triumph.

The use of brass musicians in a military-style spectacle is also evocative of gladiatorial contests (or *munera*). Literary and iconographic sources highlight the rousing effect of music (especially brass instruments) on both the combatants and spectators in the arena.[71] Admittedly, these sources were produced at a time when gladiatorial *munera* had become a major industry and were housed in large purpose-built amphitheatres (the earliest evidence for the participation of musicians in gladiatorial contests dates from the end of the Republic). In Polybius' day, gladiatorial displays were staged on a much more modest scale. However, there is no reason to doubt that music featured in earlier *munera*. Gladiators were first exhibited in the mid-third century BCE at the funerals of wealthy Roman aristocrats, and we have evidence for the involvement of musicians in Roman and Etruscan funerals from as early as the fifth century BCE.[72]

---

[69] App. *Pun.* 66.

[70] Livy (45.43.8) mentions the jovial songs that were sung about Anicius by the soldiers who took part in his triumph. *Carmina triumphalia* are also described in connection with the triumphs of Gnaeus Manlius (Livy 39.7.3), Aemilius Paullus (Plut. *Aem.* 34) and Julius Caesar (Suet. *Iul.* 49, 51; Dio Cass. 43.20.2). Dionysius of Halicarnassus states that the songs were 'improvised' (ποιήματα αὐτοσχέδια; *Ant. Rom.* 7.72.11).

[71] See Simpson 2000; Fagan 2011: 225–7; Coleman 2018.

[72] According to tradition, gladiatorial games were first displayed at the funeral of L. Iunius Brutus Pera in 264 BCE: Livy, *Periochae* 16; Val. Max. 2.4.7; Serv. *ad Aen.* 3.67. On the musical background of Roman *munera*, see Coleman 2018: 7. A law in the *Twelve Tables* prohibited more than ten *tibiae* at a funeral (Cic. *Leg.* 2.59). Note also the appearance of musicians in Etruscan funerary art from the fifth century BCE: Holliday 1990.

Clearly, then, Anicius' spectacle was no ordinary comedy. Breaking the rules at almost every turn, it challenged the very idea of what constituted public entertainment in a Roman setting. The praetor presented the semblance of normality only to confound his audience's expectations in hilarious fashion. He was also able to play with the parameters of time and space in ways that the dramatists of the time could not. The custom of Roman *ludi* dictated that musical and dramatic performances should be kept separate in the running order from athletic and gladiatorial events. When Terence staged the premiere of his play *The Mother-in-Law* at the *Ludi Megalenses* of 165, the performance was cut short after the crowd's attention was diverted to the boxers and tightrope-walkers who were due to perform later that day. Undeterred, Terence arranged for a second debut to coincide with the funeral of Aemilius Paullus in 160, but this too was disrupted when a rumour arose that a gladiatorial show was about to take place, at which point a crowd flocked in and started shouting and jostling for places.[73] Roman audiences could be tough to please. But where Terence had stumbled, Anicius sensed an opportunity. He employed the same medley of performers that had proven popular at previous festivals (musicians, dancers and fighters) and packaged them together in an all-singing, all-dancing spectacular. This was, in effect, a whole day's entertainment rolled into one. We might estimate that by the end of the performance there were some forty or fifty individuals on stage. But Anicius did not stop there. Having distorted the temporal and spatial divisions between the acts, he also conflated the roles of the individual performers: musicians played the part of actors; dancers played the part of boxers; and boxers played the part of dancers. Polybius' narrative breaks off before we have time to learn what happened next. But to judge from the closing sentence, the role of the tragic actors was anything but tragic (περὶ δὲ τῶν τραγῳδῶν, φησὶν ὁ Πολύβιος, ὅ τι ἂν ἐπιβάλωμαι λέγειν, δόξω τισὶ

---

[73] Cf. Ter. *Hecyr.* 4–5, 33–42. Exactly what happened on these two occasions remains disputed. The traditional view that the audience deserted the theatre en masse midway through the performance was convincingly refuted by Gilula (1978) and Sandbach (1982). An alternative theory is that the crowd seated in the theatre grew impatient and demanded that the events scheduled for later in the programme be brought forward (*pace* Parker 1996). Or perhaps the influx of newcomers into the theatre agitated an audience that was already on edge (*pace* Goldberg 1995: 40–3). See also Lada-Richards 2004, who analyses the prologue of the *Hecyra* through the lenses of 'authorial pride', 'identity construction' and 'theatrical self-definition'. Franko (2013: 358) goes so far as to read the prologue as a subtle swipe at what he calls 'Anician-style entertainment', but it seems unreasonable in my view to speak of a single spectacle – especially one so unusual – as constituting a recognisable 'style' of entertainment.

διαχλευάζειν).⁷⁴ And what better occasion to produce such an outlandish and uproarious spectacle than during a triumph, when, as Appian reminds us, 'everybody is free and is allowed to say what he pleases'?

Music and Morality in Polybius' *Histories*

In the thirty years since the publication of Gruen's seminal monograph *Culture and National Identity in Republican Rome*, scholars have tended to frame Polybius' reaction to Anicius' games in terms of a clash between Greek and Roman national identities. In the words of Sander Goldberg, 'Polybius, as a new and involuntary resident of Rome, was no dispassionate observer, and his own inexperience with Roman ways fed a natural but perhaps hasty indignation ... It was certainly not a Greek show, which is why it offended Polybius, who came to it with inappropriate expectations'.⁷⁵ Franko makes a similar point: 'Polybius was a hostile witness who likely came to the show with unsuitable expectations that significantly distorted his assessment.'⁷⁶ What Polybius *expected* to see, according to this argument, was a tasteful Roman rendition of a Greek musical contest, in keeping with the precedent set by Fulvius Nobilior and Aemilius Paullus; instead, what he actually saw was a tasteless parody, which made a mockery of the Greek cultural traditions he had fought to protect.

However, even if Polybius did come to the Roman circus with inappropriate expectations, this does not fully explain in my view why Anicius' games are treated so prominently, and so negatively, in the *Histories*. The notion that Polybius underwent a culture shock is both reductive and misleading. It is important to note that Polybius often paints Roman customs in a favourable light. In general, his outlook on Roman culture is not that of a hostile and reluctant captive, but that of a curious and knowledgeable insider.⁷⁷ Indeed, as Craige Champion underlines in his book *Cultural Politics in Polybius' Histories*, the representation of the Romans in Polybius' work is ambiguous and does not map straightforwardly onto national or ethnic paradigms: 'Polybius at times represents the

---

⁷⁴ The verb διαχλευάζειν (to make a mockery of, or to talk insultingly to) appears elsewhere in Polybius at 38.8.13, describing the tyrannical behaviour of the Carthaginian general Hasdrubal, and at 18.4.4, describing Philip's mockery of Phaeneas.
⁷⁵ Goldberg 1995: 38–9.   ⁷⁶ Franko 2013: 345.
⁷⁷ Cf., e.g. Polyb. 6.56, comparing the religious practices of Greeks and Romans.

Romans as a civilized people possessing Hellenic virtues ... while in other passages he obliquely suggests the barbarism of the Romans'.[78]

On a separate note, there is strong evidence to suggest that the theatrical cultures of Greece and Rome, far from being diametrically opposed, were in fact engaged in close dialogue with one another at the time Polybius was writing. Scholarship has highlighted how the institution of new civic festivals in parts of the Greek East provided a central mechanism of cultural and political exchange between local Greek communities and the Roman state. Much has been written about the introduction of 'Roman games' (*Romaia*) in places such as Chios, Delphi, Xanthos and Thebes.[79] The inscription pertaining to the games at Xanthos, set up by the Lycian League in 188 BCE, states that the crowns for each contest were 'dedicated at the altar of [the goddess] Rome'. We are also given the name of a Roman victor in the chariot-races, Gaius Octavius Pollio, who identifies himself as a citizen of the Lycian town of Telmessos.[80] Particularly noteworthy is an inscription from Delos, dating from only a couple of years before Anicius' games (169 BCE), which lists among the performers at a local festival 'an actor of Latin comedies or mimes' (ῥωμαϊστής). He performed alongside tragic and comic actors, aulodes, citharists and citharodes, dancers and even a magician (wonder-worker).[81] Thus, while it may be fair to say that Anicius' show contained certain elements that were distinctive to the Roman theatre of the second century, the idea that it would have been completely alien to a Greek observer is unfounded.[82]

The Greek versus Roman polarity breaks down even further if we examine what Polybius has to say about music elsewhere in his history. Most significantly, in Book 31, the historian identifies 'musical

---

[78] Champion 2004: 4.
[79] Chios: *SEG* 30, 1073; Salvo 2013. Delphi: *Syll.*³ 611.6. Xanthos: Robert 1978. Thebes: Knoepfler 2004. Further references in Salvo 2013: 136 n. 44; van Nijf 2001: 320. Polybius (2.12.8) tells us that Romans had been participating in the Isthmian Games at Corinth since 228 BCE.
[80] Robert 1978.
[81] *IG* XI.2 133. The term ῥωμαϊστής is attested only in this inscription. Ferri (2008) derives it from ῥώμη, 'strength' (a ῥωμαϊστής being 'one who performs feats of strength for entertainment'), but the evidence he adduces in support of this theory is tenuous. The association with Roman theatrical culture seems more plausible (see Robert 1983).
[82] Music, dance and comedy had long played a central role in Greek theatrical performances; Polybius no doubt witnessed many such performances in his native Megalopolis. A year or two before Anicius' games, in fact, the city of Delphi put on a festival of auletes, citharodes, comedians and dancers. None of them actually 'competed'; they performed for a fee, just as they did in Rome: *SEG* 50, 725; text, translation, and commentary in Prêtre 2000. See further discussion in Slater 2004: 150–1 and 2007: 43, noting the exorbitant salary of fifteen thousand drachmas received by the *choraulae*.

performances and drinking parties and the extravagance they involve' (ἀκροάματα καὶ πότους καὶ τὴν ἐν τούτοις πολυτέλειαν) as the key factors which precipitated the moral decline of the Roman aristocracy in the aftermath of the Third Macedonian War. *Acroamata* is a rather nebulous term (it can refer to anything 'heard'), but the context specifically calls to mind the musical entertainments of the symposium. The fact that Polybius goes on to describe these *acromata* as a vestige of '*Greek* immorality' (τὴν τῶν Ἑλλήνων ... εὐχέρειαν) strengthens this association.[83] In fact, Polybius refers to the private consumption of music several times throughout the *Histories* in order to cast certain characters in a negative light. In Book 14, for example, he attacks king Ptolemy Philadelphus (309/8–246 BCE) for bestowing excessive favours on female piper-players and mime-actresses.[84] Similarly, in Book 23, the Messenian leader Deinocrates is criticised for partaking in 'love affairs, drinking deep from an early hour and listening to musicians (τοῖς ἀκροάμασι τὰς ἀκοὰς ἀνατεθεικώς)', while carrying out a diplomatic mission to Rome in 184/3 BCE. In one episode, Deinocrates is reprimanded by the stern Roman general T. Quinctius Flamininus:

> ἰδὼν γὰρ αὐτὸν παρὰ πότον ἐν μακροῖς ἱματίοις ὀρχούμενον, παρ' αὐτὰ μὲν ἐσιώπησε, τῇ δ' αὔριον ἐντυγχάνοντος αὐτοῦ καί τι περὶ τῆς πατρίδος ἀξιοῦντος "ἐγὼ μέν, ὦ Δεινόκρατε, πᾶν" ἔφη "ποιήσω τὸ δυνατόν· ἐπὶ δὲ σοῦ θαυμάζω πῶς δύνῃ παρὰ πότον ὀρχεῖσθαι, τηλικούτων πραγμάτων ἀρχὴν κεκινηκὼς ἐν τοῖς Ἕλλησιν." (Polyb. 23.5.11–12)

> For once when Flamininus saw him at a party dancing in a long robe, he remained silent at the time, but when Deinocrates came to see him the next day and made some request about Messene, he said, 'I will do what I can, Deinocrates; but as for you I am amazed how you can dance at parties, after having set in motion matters of such importance for Greece.'

Deinocrates is portrayed in this vignette as the stereotypical debauchee, wallowing in music and donning effeminate costume. Flamininus, by contrast, is the ideal Roman philhellene – respectful of the Greeks' cultural heritage and political autonomy, but impervious to the seductions of the symposium and its attendant luxury.[85]

Polybius' aversion towards Greek sympotic music can also be seen in his portrayal of the Seleucid king Antiochus IV Epiphanes. In the summer of 166, Antiochus presided over a series of extravagant royal banquets in the

---

[83] Polyb. 31.25.4. [84] Polyb. 14.11 = Athen. 13.756c.
[85] In Plutarch's version of the story (*Flam.* 17.3), which is closely modelled on Polybius', Deinocrates is accused by Flamininus of singing as well as dancing. For Flamininus' philhellenism, cf. Polyb. 18.46.

suburb of Daphne in Syrian Antioch. These banquets provide the subject of a memorable set-piece narrative in Book 30:

> Ὁ δὲ χειρισμὸς ἐγίνετο τῶν πραγμάτων δι' αὐτοῦ τοῦ βασιλέως ... καὶ περιπορευόμενος οὗ μὲν προσεκάθιζεν, οὗ δὲ προσανέπιπτε· καὶ ποτὲ μὲν ἀποθέμενος μεταξὺ τὸν ψωμόν, ποτὲ δὲ τὸ ποτήριον ἀνεπήδα καὶ μετανίστατο καὶ περιῄει τὸν πότον, προπόσεις λαμβάνων ὀρθὸς ἄλλοτε παρ' ἄλλοις, ἅμα δὲ καὶ τοῖς ἀκροάμασι προσπαίζων. προϊούσης δ' ἐπὶ πολὺ τῆς συνουσίας καὶ πολλῶν ἤδη κεχωρισμένων, ὑπὸ τῶν μίμων ὁ βασιλεὺς εἰσεφέρετο ὅλος κεκαλυμμένος καὶ εἰς τὴν γῆν ἐτίθετο ὡς εἷς ὢν δῆτα τῶν μίμων. καὶ τῆς συμφωνίας προκαλουμένης, ἀναπηδήσας ὠρχεῖτο καὶ ὑπεκρίνετο μετὰ τῶν γελωτοποιῶν, ὥστε πάντας αἰσχυνομένους φεύγειν. (Polyb. 30.26.4–9 = Athen. 5.195d–f)

> The king handled all the details personally ... He walked around and sat next to someone here, or lay down beside someone else there; and sometimes he set down a bit of food when he was in the middle of eating it, or a glass of wine, and leapt up, went off somewhere else, and circulated through the party, receiving toasts standing next to various people, while simultaneously laughing at the entertainment. When the party had gone on for a long time and many people had already left, the king was carried in by the mime-actors with his face entirely concealed, and was set on the ground as if he were actually one of them. When the band summoned him, he leapt up and began to dance and to act along with the comedic performers; everyone was so embarrassed that they tried to flee. (Trans. Olson 2007, with slight alterations)

These banquets capped off a month of public games, gladiatorial shows and wild-beast fights in the Seleucid capital.[86] Antiochus went to great lengths to ensure that his festival matched the scale and grandeur of the games put on by Aemilius Paullus at Amphipolis a year earlier. What is more, he opened the celebrations with a spectacular military procession, which consciously emulated aspects of the Roman triumph (the procession was headed by a battalion of five thousand young men dressed in Roman armour).[87] Polybius was left in no doubt that Antiochus had fallen short of Paullus' example: not only were the celebrations excessive, and the king's involvement in them wholly inappropriate, but they had been funded through acts of theft and sacrilege.[88] Instead, Polybius seems to have lumped Antiochus with another Roman general, one who shared his taste

---

[86] Cf. Polyb. 30.25.1–26.1.
[87] Antiochus' fondness for emulating Roman customs is also highlighted at Polyb. 26.1.4–6.
[88] Polyb. 30.26.9.

for theatrics. If Walbank's reconstruction of Book 30 is correct, the account of the games at Daphne was situated only three chapters before the account of Anicius' games.[89] It is certainly tempting to read the two episodes together. Both spectacles feature a large cast of performers and deploy the same distinctive combination of music and mimicry. And in both spectacles the organisers play an unusually prominent role, cavorting with the performers while poking fun at members of the audience. Antiochus is the star of his own farce: he 'jokes with the musicians', 'acts alongside the comedic performers', and even plays the part of a mime-actor.[90] Like Anicius, he saves the big musical finale until the last minute (τῆς συμφωνίας προκαλουμένης), and it is at this point that the burlesque reaches its show-stopping climax: the horrified onlookers all head for the exit and the soiree comes to an abrupt end.[91]

In Polybius' *Histories*, therefore, music functions primarily as a way of pointing up the moral flaws of Greek, as well as Roman, leaders. The Romans, in developing their newfound taste for *acroamata*, are shown to have fallen victim to a pre-existing Greek vice – namely, *poluteleia*, 'extravagance' or 'luxury'. This is not to suggest that Anicius' games necessarily reminded Polybius of the entertainments of a Seleucid or Ptolemaic royal symposium, although I would not discount that possibility. Rather, the point that needs to be emphasised is that Polybius' presentation of Anicius' games cannot be understood simply through the lens of national identity. Indeed, if the point of the Anicius episode was to foreground the *Roman* abuse of Greek culture, it is hard to see why Polybius would have presented the Greek auletes who starred in the games in such an unsympathetic light. Although the musicians appear to be acting at the praetor's behest, it is *they* who are ultimately blamed for causing the pandemonium (μεγάλην ἐποίησαν σύγχυσιν). Far from expressing

---

[89] Walbank 1979: 33.

[90] The version in Diodorus Siculus (31.16.3) adds that Antiochus 'performed the kind of dances that usually provoke laughter and hoots of derision' (ὠρχεῖτο τῶν ὀρχήσεων τὰς γέλωτα καὶ χλευασμὸν εἰωθυίας ἐπισπᾶσθαι).

[91] For this kind of aposiopesis, caused by banqueters fleeing a feast, cf. Suet. *Aug.* 70; Hor. *Sat.* 2.8; Pet. *Sat.* 78.8; Lucian, *Merc. Cond.* 18. Gowers (1993: 197) compares noisy scenes at the end of mimes, citing Cic. *Cael.* 65 (*scabilla concrepant*). For a contrasting archetype, cf. Athen. 4.142f (= Phylarchus *FGrH* 81 F44), on the banquets of the Spartan king Cleomenes: ἀκρόαμα δὲ οὐδὲν οὐδέποτε παρεισεπορεύετο, διετέλει δ' αὐτὸς προσομιλῶν πρὸς ἕκαστον καὶ πάντας ἐκκαλούμενος εἰς τὸ τὰ μὲν ἀκούειν, τὰ δὲ λέγειν αὐτούς, ὥστε τεθηρευμένους ἀποτρέχειν ἅπαντας (no musical entertainment was ever brought in, and Cleomenes himself spent his time talking to each of his guests and urging them all to say or listen to this or that, with the result that they were all captivated by him when they left.).

reluctance or dismay, the performers readily acquiesce in the charade, taking a knowing role in the choreography and prompting the raucous behaviour of the spectators. Though the text is damaged, Polybius leaves us in no doubt about the dubious character of these men, stating that they were naturally 'predisposed to acts of licentiousness' (οἰκείαν ταῖς ἑαυτῶν ἀσελγείαις).[92]

To gain a better understanding of the relationship between music and morality in Polybius' *Histories*, it is helpful to examine a famous passage from Book 4 in which Polybius gives an account of the Cynaethean people of Arcadia. Polybius makes much of the fact that the Cynaetheans were the first and only people in Arcadia to abandon the ancestral custom of musical education. As a result, their community gradually degenerated to a state of 'savagery' (ἀγριότης), 'cruelty' (ὠμότης) and 'lawlessness' (παρανομία), while the rest of Arcadia flourished thanks to the continued musical devotion of its inhabitants:

> μουσικὴν γάρ, τήν γε ἀληθῶς μουσικήν, πᾶσι μὲν ἀνθρώποις ὄφελος ἀσκεῖν, Ἀρκάσι δὲ καὶ ἀναγκαῖον. οὐ γὰρ ἡγητέον μουσικήν, ὡς Ἔφορός φησιν ἐν τῷ προοιμίῳ τῆς ὅλης πραγματείας, οὐδαμῶς ἁρμόζοντα λόγον αὑτῷ ῥίψας, ἐπ' ἀπάτῃ καὶ γοητείᾳ παρεισῆχθαι τοῖς ἀνθρώποις· οὐδὲ τοὺς παλαιοὺς Κρητῶν καὶ Λακεδαιμονίων αὐλὸν καὶ ῥυθμὸν εἰς τὸν πόλεμον ἀντὶ σάλπιγγος εἰκῇ νομιστέον εἰσαγαγεῖν, οὐδὲ τοὺς πρώτους Ἀρκάδων εἰς τὴν ὅλην πολιτείαν τὴν μουσικὴν παραλαβεῖν ἐπὶ τοσοῦτον ὥστε μὴ μόνον παισὶν οὖσιν ἀλλὰ καὶ νεανίσκοις γενομένοις ἕως τριάκοντ' ἐτῶν κατ' ἀνάγκην σύντροφον ποιεῖν αὐτήν, τἆλλα τοῖς βίοις ὄντας αὐστηροτάτους. ταῦτα γὰρ πᾶσίν ἐστι γνώριμα καὶ συνήθη, διότι σχεδὸν παρὰ μόνοις Ἀρκάσιν οἱ παῖδες ἐκ νηπίων ᾄδειν ἐθίζονται κατὰ νόμον τοὺς ὕμνους καὶ παιᾶνας, οἷς ἕκαστοι κατὰ τὰ πάτρια τοὺς ἐπιχωρίους ἥρωας καὶ θεοὺς ὑμνοῦσι. μετὰ δὲ ταῦτα τοὺς Τιμοθέου καὶ Φιλοξένου νόμους μανθάνοντες χορεύουσι κατ' ἐνιαυτὸν τοῖς Διονυσιακοῖς αὐληταῖς ἐν τοῖς θεάτροις, οἱ μὲν οὖν παῖδες τοὺς παιδικοὺς ἀγῶνας, οἱ δὲ νεανίσκοι τοὺς τῶν ἀνδρῶν. καὶ παρ' ὅλον δὲ τὸν βίον ἐν ταῖς συνουσίαις ταῖς κοιναῖς οὐχ <οὕτω ποιοῦνται τὰς ἀγωγὰς> διὰ τῶν ἐπεισάκτων ἀκροαμάτων ὡς δι' αὑτῶν, ἀνὰ μέρος ᾄδειν ἀλλήλοις προστάττοντες. καὶ τῶν μὲν ἄλλων μαθημάτων ἀρνηθῆναί τι μὴ γινώσκειν οὐδὲν αἰσχρὸν ἡγοῦνται, τήν γε μὴν ᾠδὴν οὔτ' ἀρνηθῆναι δύνανται διὰ τὸ κατ' ἀνάγκην πάντας μανθάνειν, οὔθ' ὁμολογοῦντες ἀποτρίβεσθαι διὰ τὸ τῶν αἰσχρῶν παρ' αὐτοῖς νομίζεσθαι τοῦτο. καὶ μὴν

---

[92] Feeney's claim that the musicians 'have not the remotest idea what is going on' misses the point (Feeney 2016: 149); they could hardly have been caught unawares. The vanity and debauchery of pipe-players was proverbial. Livy writes that *tibicines* were 'generally greedy for wine' (*vino, cuius avidum ferme id genus est*; 9.30.9); note also the anecdotes about the disreputable Theban aulete Ismenias: Plin. *HN* 37.6–8; Plut. *Per.* 1.5.

ἐμβατήρια μετ' αὐλοῦ καὶ τάξεως ἀσκοῦντες, ἔτι δὲ ὀρχήσεις ἐκπονοῦντες μετὰ κοινῆς ἐπιστροφῆς καὶ δαπάνης κατ' ἐνιαυτὸν ἐν τοῖς θεάτροις ἐπιδείκνυνται. (Polyb. 4.20.4–12 = Athen. 14.626a–d)

> Making music – genuine music, I mean – is beneficial for everyone, but for Arcadians it is a necessity. We should not regard music, as Ephorus suggests in his preface, in an untypically hasty assertion, as a human invention designed merely to beguile and charm. Nor should we think that there was no thought involved when the ancient Cretans and Spartans replaced the trumpet, as their time-keeping instrument in war, with the pipes. Nor should we suppose that the earliest Arcadians had no good reason for incorporating music into Arcadian life so thoroughly that not only children, but also young men up to the age of thirty, are required to make it their constant companion, even though in all other respects their lives are very harsh. It is a familiar and well-known fact that, almost uniquely, Arcadian children are taught from their earliest childhood to sing in the prescribed manner the traditional songs and paeans with which each community hymns its local heroes and gods. Later, they learn the measures of Philoxenus and Timotheus, and every year they put on a keenly contested dance competition in their theatres, accompanied by pipe-players supplied by the Guild of Dionysus. The contest has a junior section for boys, and a senior section for young men. Moreover, throughout their lives their entertainment in private social settings consists not of hired players, but of themselves, with each of them obliged, when his turn comes around, to sing to the others. It is no disgrace, in Arcadia, to deny knowledge of any other subject, but they cannot deny their musical abilities, since all of them have had to learn it. Nor is it acceptable for someone to give music up, because that is what is considered disgraceful there. The young men also drill to the accompaniment of rhythmically played pipes, and practise their dancing, in the public eye and at public expense, on display to their fellow citizens. (Trans. Waterfield 2010)

In many ways, the contrast between the festival of the Arcadians and the Roman games of 167 could not be starker.[93] The Arcadian festival has no ties to any particular sponsor but is organised expressly 'as a matter of communal concern and public expense' (μετὰ κοινῆς ἐπιστροφῆς καὶ δαπάνης); it serves to honour the gods, not a mortal benefactor. Its performers are native citizens of Arcadia rather than foreign luminaries. The Arcadians take pains to banish all extraneous influences, instilling music in their own young 'from infancy' (ἐκ νηπίων) and thereby perpetuating a venerable indigenous tradition of musical pedagogy. They do not

---

[93] For a brief comparison of the two episodes, see Champion 2018.

pit the contestants against one another in an outlandish melee, but assign them a rightful place in the programme, with the children competing in 'the junior contests' (τοὺς παιδικοὺς ἀγῶνας) and the young men in 'the senior contests' (τοὺς τῶν ἀνδρῶν). There is no pretend fighting, no false impression of *taxis*; these war-dances are the real thing, conducted with the utmost solemnity as a corrective to 'luxury and excess' (τρυφῆς καὶ περιουσίας).[94] In short, the Arcadian festival epitomises what Polybius considers to be 'genuine music' – music designed not to 'beguile and charm', but to edify and benefit mankind.[95]

Polybius was by no means alone among his contemporaries in voicing concerns about the direction in which musical culture was headed. As Andrew Barker explains, from the fourth century BCE onwards, Greek writers 'seem to have recognised the real importance of music in earlier Greek culture, by contrast with the situation in their own time, when music outside strictly religious contexts was construed, for the most part, as nothing but a form of trivial entertainment'.[96] It is instructive to compare Polybius' writings with those of his younger contemporary, Posidonius of Apamea. In one fragment from his *Histories* preserved by Athenaeus, Posidonius characterises his Syrian compatriots as a nation of debauched music-lovers. Enjoying a life of carefree luxury, they spent most of the day being 'continually entertained by pipe-playing accompanied by the sound of the loud-twanging lyre, with the result that whole cities resounded with such noises'.[97] In another passage, Posidonius criticises the people of Apamea for taking with them on campaign 'donkeys loaded with wine and food of all kinds, beside which lay flutes (φωτίγγια) and single pipes

---

[94] A nuanced discussion of the whole passage can be found in Prauscello 2009: 188–94. In Greek culture, war-dances (ἐμβατήρια) were associated especially with conservative Spartan *mousike* (Csapo 2004: 242), but they also had a place in traditional Roman culture: cf. Dion. Hal. *Ant.* 2.70.5, 3.32.4, on the ancient martial dances of the Salii, accompanied by the *auloi*.

[95] Polybius' criticism of Ephorus of Cyme, the fourth-century BCE historian, at 4.20.4 is hard to interpret. The surviving fragments of Ephorus' work provide only vague clues about his views on music. Parmeggiani (2011: 87–91) speculates that, by rejecting the divine origins of music in his preface, Ephorus aimed to distance his historiographical method from the practice of poets, who typically began their works by invoking the Muses (and, by extension, the 'musical' tradition they inspired). On the other hand, we know that Ephorus wrote about the positive influence of music on the communities of Crete and Sparta, and, indeed, the fact that Polybius mentions Crete and Sparta as analogues to Arcadia suggests that he may have used Ephorus' account as a model: Ephorus F 149 = Strabo 10.4.16, with discussion in Barker 2014: 52–5.

[96] Barker 2014: 87.

[97] Posidonius, *FGrH* 87 F10 = F62 Edelstein-Kidd (Athen. 5.210e–f): καταυλούμενοι πρὸς χελωνίδος πολυκρότου ψόφους, ὥστε τὰς πόλεις ὅλας τοῖς τοιούτοις κελάδοις συνηχεῖσθαι.

(μοναύλια), instruments of revelry rather than of war'.[98] Further parallels can be drawn between Polybius and two other Hellenistic writers on music history – namely, Artemon of Cassandreia and Phillis of Delos. Artemon wrote a treatise entitled *On the Artists of Dionysus*, in which he commented on the recent disappearance of certain ancient musical practices.[99] Similarly, a quotation attributed to Phillis of Delos discusses how the early citharodes produced 'marching and dance steps' (ἐμβατηρίους καὶ χορευτικάς) when they performed, recalling Polybius' description of the military drills practised by the Arcadians (ἐμβατήρια μετ' αὐλοῦ καὶ τάξεως ἀσκοῦντες).[100] Although the nature of Phillis' work is obscure, it is very likely, as Timothy Power points out, that Phillis was 'nostalgic for old-time music, and thus was likely biased against the "new" citharodes'.[101]

The nostalgia for 'old-time' music among Polybius' contemporaries is also well-documented in the epigraphic records of civic festivals during the late Hellenistic period. An honorific decree from Delphi, dating from 118 BCE, praises two visiting musicians for presenting the 'measures of the old poets' (ἀριθμοὺς τῶν ἀρχαίων ποιητᾶν) and commends them for contributing to the teaching of children (διδασκαλίαν τῶν παίδων) during their stay.[102] The Delphians' interest in promoting traditional music is highlighted by two further decrees, both inscribed during the first half of the second century BCE: the first mentions a virtuoso citharodic rendition of Euripides' *Bacchae* given by Satyros of Samos, while the second honours the citharodes Thrason and Socrates, brothers from Aegira, who presented concerts featuring 'lyric compositions of ancient poets' (τῶν λυρικῶν συστημάτων ... [τ]ῶν ἀρχαίων πο[ητ]ᾶν).[103] A particularly popular composer was Timotheus of Miletus, the citharode and dithyrambic poet of the late Classical period.[104] The Nemean Games of 205 BCE featured an acclaimed performance of Timotheus' *Persians*.[105] In around 170 BCE, a

---

[98] Posidonius, *FGrH* 87 F2 = F54 Edelstein-Kidd (Athen. 4.176b–c): Ποσειδώνιος δ' ὁ ἀπὸ τῆς στοᾶς φιλόσοφος ἐν τῇ τρίτῃ τῶν Ἱστοριῶν διηγούμενος περὶ τοῦ Ἀπαμέων πρὸς Λαρισαίους πολέμου γράφει τάδε ... ὄνους ἐφελκόμενοι γέμοντας οἴνου καὶ βρωμάτων παντοδαπῶν, οἷς παρέκειτο φωτίγγια καὶ μοναύλια, κώμων οὐ πολέμων ὄργανα.

[99] Artemon *ap*. Athen. 14.636b–e.   [100] Phillis of Delos *ap*. Athen. 1.21–2.

[101] Power 2010: 141 n. 341.

[102] *Syll.*³ 703, ll. 8–10. The text states that the performers 'gave displays through the musical art' (ἐπιδείξεις ἐποιήσαντο ... διὰ τὸς μουσικὰς τέχνας), but does not specify what musical discipline they specialised in (the beginning of the inscription is lost).

[103] *FD* III 3.128 (200–175 BCE), III 1.49 (ca. 165 BCE).

[104] Branded as a revolutionary in his own lifetime, Timotheus became synonymous in later centuries with a lost heyday of *mousike*: see Csapo and Wilson 2009; Prauscello 2009.

[105] Paus. 8.50.3; Plut. *Philop.* 11.

citharode from Teos served as a foreign ambassador to Crete and was honoured by his hosts for having performed a selection of Timotheus' repertoire in the theatre, 'as befits an educated man' (ὡς προσῆκεν ἀνδρὶ πεπαιδευμένωι).[106] It is worth recalling here that Polybius names Timotheus along with Philoxenus as the composers most venerated by the Arcadians.

Polybius' account of Anicius' games can thus be better understood when situated in relation to other musical passages in the *Histories*, as well as in the context of contemporary Greek reflections on the proper uses of music. Music, for Polybius, was not some incidental fact of life, unaffected by the vicissitudes of history; on the contrary, it determined the very fate of humanity. In his work, the historian maps out an ideal vision for the state (*politeia*) in which *mousike* performs a prescribed social and political function. Not just any music will do, however. Only the right kind of music – 'real music' – can bring about the requisite conditions for a stable society. Centuries of Greek philosophising had built up a rich store of images and ideas from which Polybius was able to draw insights.[107] Plato, as is well known, placed great emphasis in his writings on the affective power of music. He argued that for a democratic society to function effectively, it needed to promote a simple, traditional kind of *mousike*, which instilled decent civilized values in those who performed and listened to it. Conversely, innovations in musical culture were to be avoided at all costs, since they risked disturbing the natural order and rupturing the fabric of civic life.[108] It is not hard to see why these ideas might have appealed to Polybius.[109] The abuses which Plato had diagnosed as the cause of Athens' moral decline were, at least in their outward manifestation, not dissimilar to those which had reduced the once civilized Cynaetheans to their barbarian state and had turned powerful rulers like Antiochus IV into corrupt tyrants. Now, perhaps more than ever, it was necessary to hark back to the austere traditions of the past and do away with the over-the-top

---

[106] *I.Cret.* I.viii.11, V.xxiv.1; commentary in Chaniotis 2009 and Barker 2011.

[107] The idea that musical modes (*nomoi*) had the power to alter the character (*ethos*) of the listener in both positive and negative ways was first expounded by the Athenian philosopher Damon in the fifth century BCE: see Wallace 2004.

[108] Cf. especially the discussion of *theatrokratia* at *Laws* 700c–701a; see here Wallace 1997; Pelosi 2010: 39–77; Gülgönen 2014. For the idea of *theatrokratia* exploited elsewhere, cf. Arist. *Pol.* 1341b; Aristox. *Elem. Harm.* 41.4–5; Plut. *Phoc.* 8.5; Luc. *Harmonid.* 1–3. Cf. also Pl. *Rep.* 397a–b, on mimesis as a trait of the 'vulgar' musician.

[109] The influence of Platonic models on Polybius' political philosophy is most apparent in his account of the Roman 'mixed constitution': cf. Polyb. 6.5.1–6.9.14; Walbank 2002: 201–3. See also Burghart 2018 on the references to Plato's *Republic* at Polyb. 7.13.7.

mimeticism and vulgar showmanship that had come to define musical theatre, both Greek and Roman, in the present day.

Scipio, Cato and the Roman Opposition to Greek Music

The question of how best to regulate the use of music within the civic community exercised the minds of Romans as well as Greeks. Our evidence for Roman attitudes to music in the second century BCE is exiguous, to say the least, but it is not devoid of insights. Most notably, the late-antique author Macrobius in his discussion of Roman dance preserves two crucial testimonies in the form of speeches given by Scipio Aemilius and Cato the Elder. While we should be wary of inferring a senatorial opposition to Anicius' games on the basis of these testimonies alone, the texts nonetheless expose deep tensions and fault lines within Roman musical culture during this period. Negative attitudes towards certain types of Greek music can be detected during the early part of the second century and seem to have become increasingly trenchant over the following decades. By the end of the century, as we will see, the popularity of Greek-inspired musical entertainment was considered sufficiently dangerous by the Roman censors that it warranted direct legal intervention.

The first of the two passages quoted by Macrobius comes from a speech given by Cato the Elder in 183 BCE. In the excerpt, Cato censures the plebeian tribune Marcus Caelius for engaging in unseemly theatrical antics, including singing and dancing:

> *descendit de cantherio, inde staticulos dare, ridicularia fundere ... praeterea cantat ubi collibuit, interdum Graecos versus agit, iocos dicit, voces demutat, staticulos dat.* (Macr. Sat. 3.14.9 = fr. 114–115 Malcovati)

> He dismounts from his nag, and right then and there strikes little poses and spouts jokes ... Moreover he sings whenever he feels like it, and sometimes performs Greek verses, tells jokes, changes his voice and strikes little poses.

This fragment has often been adduced as evidence of Cato's virulent opposition to Hellenism. The reference to 'Greek verses' (*Graecos versus*) is certainly consistent with this notion.[110] However, there is more at stake in

---

[110] On the context of the speech, cf. Gell. *NA* 1.15.9; Cugusi and Sblendorio Cugusi 2001: 304–9; Sciarrino 2004b: 339. On Cato's attitude to 'Hellenism', see Astin 1978: 157–81; Gruen 1993: 52–83.

Cato's rhetoric than an opposition to Greek culture. Caelius is accused of indulging in undignified pursuits which are deemed incompatible with his status as a Roman magistrate. Singing, performing lewd dances, cracking jokes and impersonating characters are the stock trades of the professional entertainer.[111] According to Thomas Habinek, the phrase *voces demutat* implies speaking in a high-pitched (and thus effeminate) voice, while *staticulos dat* is evocative of cinaedic dancing. In Plautus' *Persa*, for instance, the slave Sagaristio mocks the pimp Dordalus by calling on him to dance 'a little pose' (*staticulum*).[112]

Despite Macrobius' claim that Cato considered singing 'unbecoming for a serious person' (*cantare non serii hominis*), he was clearly not averse to music-making in principle. A fragment from Cato's lost history, the *Origines*, makes reference to a type of Roman 'banquet songs' (*carmina convivalia*), the origins of which allegedly dated back to the earliest days of the Republic.[113] Cato describes the *carmina* as follows: 'It was customary among our ancestors for banqueters to sing, one after another, of the merits and virtues of famous men to the accompaniment of the pipe.'[114] One must be careful not to assign too much credence to the historicity of these songs, especially given our limited knowledge of Cato's oeuvre; we are dealing here with ideological constructs, not historical truths.[115] Rather, what should be emphasised is the way in which Cato's idealistic vision of Rome's musical heritage brings into sharper focus the negative exemplarity of Caelius' behaviour. By harking back in the *Origines* to an age when Rome's musical culture was pure and austere, Cato was articulating a vision not only of how things *were* in the past but also of how things *ought to be* in the present and future – just as Polybius, in recalling the historical customs of Arcadian *mousike*, was passing negative judgment on the musical practices of his own time. The *carmina convivalia* were, in essence, a moral corrective for those who, like Caelius, 'sang whenever they felt like it'.

The second passage quoted by Macrobius comes from a speech delivered by Scipio Aemilianus in 129 BCE against the judiciary law (*lex iudiciaria*)

---

[111] See Milanezi 2000: 401–3 and 2004: 193–5 on the *gelotopoios* (laughter-maker).
[112] Plaut. *Pers.* 824; Habinek 2005: 199; see also Sciarrino 2004b: 339. On *cinaedi*, see below.
[113] On the *Origines*, see Astin 1978: 211–39; Gotter 2009.
[114] Cato FRHist F113 = Cic. *Tusc. Disp.* 4.3: *gravissimus auctor in Originibus dixit Cato morem apud maiores hunc epularum fuisse, ut deinceps, qui accubarent, canerent ad tibiam clarorum virorum laudes atque virtutes*; cf. Cic. *Tusc. Disp.* 1.3, *Brut.* 175.
[115] See Zorzetti 1990; Feeney 2016: 213–18.

of Tiberius Gracchus.[116] In the speech, Scipio chastises members of the Roman upper classes for educating their children in the musical arts:

> *docentur praestigias inhonestas: cum cinaedulis et sambuca psalterioque eunt in ludum histrionum, discunt cantare, quae maiores nostri ingenuis probro ducier voluerunt: eunt, inquam, in ludum saltatorium inter cinaedos virgines puerique ingenui. haec cum mihi quisquam narrabat, non poteram animum inducere ea liberos suos homines nobiles docere: sed cum ductus sum in ludum saltatorium, plus medius fidius in eo ludo vidi pueris virginibusque quinquaginta, in his unum (quod me reipublicae maxime miseritum est) puerum bullatum, petitoris filium non minorem annis duodecim, cum crotalis saltare quam saltationem inpudicus servulus honeste saltare non posset.* (Macr. Sat. 3.14.7 = fr. 30 Malcovati)

> They're taught disreputable tricks, they go to acting school together with effeminate dancers toting this and that kind of harp, they learn to sing – things our ancestors wished to be considered disgraceful for freeborn children. They go to dancing school, I say, freeborn maidens and boys, in a crowd of effeminate dancers! When someone told me this, I could not believe that noble men were teaching their own children these things; but when I was taken to a dancing school, for goodness sake, I saw more than fifty boys and girls there, and among these – this above all made me grieve for our republic – one of them a boy wearing the amulet of the well-born, the son of an office-seeker, not less than twelve years old, doing a dance with castanets that it would disgrace a shameless little slave to dance.

According to Macrobius, this passage testifies to the fact that during the republican period 'nobles' sons and – disgraceful to say – unmarried daughters also counted learning to dance a worthwhile pursuit'.[117] However, we should be cautious about taking Scipio's words at face value, reported as they are by an author writing some five centuries later. Even if Macrobius' source is accurate, the polemical nature of the speech makes it very difficult to extract reliable historical information. The image of

---

[116] Why Scipio chose to discuss music in a speech attacking the Gracchan judiciary bill is something of a mystery. Proposed in the aftermath of the highly contentious *lex Sempronia agraria* of 133, the *lex iudiciaria* sought to assign formal powers of adjudication to the land-commissioners charged with carrying out Tiberius' redistribution programme (cf. App. *B Civ.* 1.19). It is possible that Scipio's denunciation of music was originally part of a larger diatribe aimed at exposing the dangers of Greek luxury. Tiberius proposed to fund his land reform by appropriating revenues acquired from the recent Roman annexation of Pergamum. Accordingly, Scipio may have linked this influx of foreign wealth with an uptake of luxury among Roman elites, as reflected by the increased demand for Greek music and dance (see Dillon and Garland 2015: 372).

[117] Macr. *Sat.* 3.14.6: *nobilium vero filios et, quod dictu nefas est, filias quoque virgines inter studiosa numerasse saltandi meditationem testis est Scipio Africanus Aemilianus.*

dancing schools at every street corner, filled to capacity with the sons and daughters of music-loving senators, is without doubt a rhetorical exaggeration. Nevertheless, it would be naïve to assume that Scipio's invective is entirely divorced from reality, especially in light of his claim to be drawing on first-hand observations (*cum ductus sum in ludum saltatorium ... vidi*). The high demand for foreign musicians in second-century Rome is taken for granted by Polybius (as discussed above in the section 'Music and Morality in Polybius' Histories').[118] Livy, similarly, comments on the influx of female string-players (*psaltriae sambucistriaeque*) to Rome following the triumph of Cn. Manlius Vulso in 186 BCE – a detail which he may have derived from the second-century annalist L. Calpurnius Piso Frugi.[119] Furthermore, in Plautus' *Stichus*, which was first performed in 200 BCE, one of the characters makes reference to female lyre-players, pipers and harpists (*fidicinas, tibicinas, sambucas*) as items found among the cargo of a trading ship.[120] It would be reasonable to infer from these passages that the rise of Rome as a centre of cultural and economic exchange resulted in a considerable increase in the number of elite Roman children who received a musical education, even if this practice never became ubiquitous, as Scipio's comments suggest.

Scipio's polemic hinges upon the association between music-making, social degradation and sexual deviance. The implication is that the future leaders of the Republic were partaking in trivial and demeaning activities that were practised by the salaried professional or, worse still, by lowly slaves. Scipio focuses his criticism especially on the *cinaedi* who frequented the dancing schools along with the sons and daughters of well-to-do senators (the use of the diminutive *cinaeduli* underscores his contempt). The term *kinaidos* originated in the Hellenistic period as a label for an effeminate dancer who performed lewd gestures while playing various percussion instruments.[121] In the comedies of Plautus, *cinaedi* are

---

[118] Polyb. 31.25.4.
[119] Livy 39.6.7–8; cf. Calpurnius Piso Frugi *FRHist* F36 (= Plin. *HN* 34.14), claiming that Manlius Vulso popularised expensive dining furniture at Rome after his conquest of Asia.
[120] Plaut. *Stich*. 380–1. Plautus (*Rud*. 43) refers to a *ludus fidicinius*, 'a school for harpists', as a training ground for would-be prostitutes; however, this may be a figment of the playwright's imagination or a reflection of the *fabula palliata*'s Greek setting. Titinius, the second-century BCE writer of *fabulae togatae* (comic plays set in Italy), wrote plays called *The Female Harp-Player or Girl from Ferentinum* (*Psaltria sive Ferentinatis*) and *The Female Pipe-Player* (*Tibicina*): Ribbeck 1873: 146–7, 152.
[121] Williams 2010: 193. For the Hellenistic origins of *kinaidos*, cf. Athen. 14.620e. A papyrus letter from Hibeh, dated to 245 BCE, contains an interesting description of a *kinaidos* in the context of preparations for a local festival: 'Send us also Zenobius the effeminate dancer with his drum, cymbals and castanets (Ζηνόβιον τὸν μαλακὸν ἔχοντα τύμπανον καὶ κύμβαλα καὶ κρόταλα), for the women want him for the festival; and let him be dressed as well as possible.' (*P.Hib*. I.54)

associated with the louche dance scenes that often feature at or near the end of the play.[122] Later on, the term came to refer more broadly to someone who performed illicit sexual acts or who played the passive role in intercourse.[123] The thought of a high-born Roman child being escorted around the city by a harp-wielding *cinaedulus* would therefore have horrified conservative elites, who saw the presence of such lowlifes in aristocratic society as a threat to traditional Roman mores.

The stigma which Scipio and his peers attached to musical expertise is further highlighted by an anecdote in Plutarch's *Moralia* relating to the consular elections of 142 BCE.[124] Among the contenders for the consulship was a certain Quintus Pompeius. Pompeius was eminently well-qualified for the office in all respects but one: 'He was rumoured to be the son of a pipe-player' (ἐδόκει δὲ ὁ Πομπήιος υἱὸς αὐλητοῦ γεγονέναι). Initially, Pompeius had declared that he would not be campaigning, instead offering to lend his support to Scipio's protégé Laelius. However, it later emerged that he had been going around town soliciting votes. Laelius was caught completely off-guard, but not Scipio. On hearing of Pompeius' deception, he is said to have remarked: 'It is our own stupidity that is to blame; for, just as if we were intending to call not upon men but upon gods, we have been wasting all this time waiting for a pipe-player!' (ἀβελτερία γε ... ἡμῶν, καθάπερ οὐκ ἀνθρώπους μέλλοντες ἀλλὰ θεοὺς παρακαλεῖν, πάλαι διατρίβομεν αὐλητὴν ἀναμένοντες). Innocuous though this remark may seem, it says much about the notoriety of professional musicians in Roman society. To a member of the senatorial elite, the notion of a pipe-player's son ascending to the highest office of the Republic was completely unthinkable.[125]

At a time when Greek learning (*paideia*) was becoming an increasingly valued commodity at Rome, we should not be surprised to find educated senators espousing ethical ideas about music in their speeches and writings. For all his anti-hellenic posturing, Cato was steeped in the teachings of Plato and Pythagoras.[126] He was also personally acquainted with Polybius, and, according to some scholars, shared with him a close intellectual

---

[122] See Moore 2012: 106–14; cf. also Lucil. fr. 33 (Nonius 5.6): *stulte saltatum te inter venisse cinaedos.*

[123] See Richlin 1993; Gleason 1995: 64–6; Corbeill 2004: 120–2; Clarke 2005; Habinek 2005: 177–200; Williams 2010: 193–214.

[124] Plut. *Mor.* 200c.

[125] For the negative associations of being a 'son of a musician', cf. Plut. *Roman Sayings, Flam.* 21.6 (ὁ τοῦ κιθαρῳδοῦ), *Pomp.* 36.3 (ψάλτου τινὸς ... θυγάτηρ); *Acta Isidori* 4, col. 3, 7–12 (ed. Musurillo 1954: 19, 25: μουσικῆς [υἱ]ός).

[126] See Gruen 1993: 58–9.

affinity.[127] The same might be said of Scipio. When Polybius speaks of Roman noblemen being led astray by 'musical performances and drinking parties', he does so in order to throw light on the exemplary character of his protégé. The historian describes his relationship with Scipio as being like 'that of father and son or near relations' (πατρικὴν καὶ συγγενικὴν); indeed, we are told that 'the young man never left Polybius' side and preferred his company to anyone else'.[128] Of course, this claim should be taken with a pinch of salt: Polybius was understandably eager to stress his connection to the scion of a great republican dynasty, the son of the illustrious L. Aemilius Paullus and future nemesis of Carthage.[129] Nevertheless, Scipio's concerns about the moral and pedagogical function of music resonate strongly with the issues voiced by Polybius and other Greek writers. Roman attitudes to Greek music did not emerge in a vacuum, therefore, but were probably influenced by long-standing Greek discourses on music.

Banning the *Ludus Talarius*: A Case of Roman Musical Censorship?

For the most part, the senatorial opposition to music was confined to the spheres of literature and rhetoric. Rarely, it seems, did the Roman political authorities attempt to impose legal sanctions on musical culture. In 115 BCE, however, the Roman censors took the drastic measure of banning certain types of theatrical entertainment from the city, which they deemed inimical to the interests of the state. Our information comes from a short entry in a chronicle written by the sixth-century author Cassiodorus:

> his conss. L. Metellus et Cn. Domitius censores artem ludicram ex urbe removerunt praeter Latinum tibicinem cum cantore et ludum talarium. (Cass. Chron. 2, p. 31 f. Mommsen)[130]
>
> During the consulship of these men, the censors L. Metellus and Cn. Domitius excluded from the city the *ars ludicra*, with the exception of the Latin pipe-player and singer, and the *ludus talarius*.

This text raises major interpretative problems. There is uncertainty surrounding the significance of *ars ludicra* (a generic term for 'the performing arts'), the contested reading of *ludum talarium* (a kind of theatrical entertainment) and the identity of the 'Latin pipe-player'

---

[127] See, e.g., Nicolet 1974: 243–55.   [128] Polyb. 31.24.12–25.1.   [129] Sommer 2013: 308.
[130] According to Jory (1995: 150–1), Cassiodorus may have derived this information from Livy or Varro.

(*Latinus tibicen*). The interpretation of *ludus talarius* presents perhaps the greatest difficulty. The manuscript reading *ludum talanum* makes little sense and is almost certainly corrupt. Mommsen's emendation, *ludus talarius*, is to be preferred over the alternative *ludus Atellanus*. However, since the *ludus talarius* is mentioned by only a handful of ancient writers, there is very little that can be said about it with any confidence. The name *talarius* probably derives from *tunica talaris*, an ankle-length robe which was presumably worn by the actors who specialised in this kind of performance.

In an article published in 1995, John Jory makes a persuasive case for interpreting *ars ludicra* as a general term for 'professional entertainment' or 'show business', arguing that the censorial edict of 115 constituted 'a restriction on the activities of professional performers in Rome', the majority of whom hailed from the Greek East.[131] Jory proposes, moreover, that the *ludus talarius* originated as a form of Italian sub-dramatic performance and became an important forerunner to the imperial pantomime. The genre was exempted from the ban, according to Jory, because, like the *Latinus tibicen cum cantore*, it represented a home-grown Roman product: 'what the censors were doing was banning from the stage full-scale professional dramatic entertainment, above all comedy and tragedy, the origins of which were not Roman but Greek'.[132]

Attractive though this explanation may seem, it is based on very shaky evidence. The Roman character of the *Latinus tibicen cum cantore* is not difficult to discern, even if the precise significance of the adjective *Latinus* remains uncertain.[133] However, Jory's notion of the *ludus talarius* as a Roman or Italian genre is contingent on a tenuous connection with the so-called *planipedia*, a type of Latin mime which is even more obscure than the *ludus talarius*.[134] The matter is complicated further by the ambiguous nature of Cassiodorus' syntax. The words *ludum talarium* could be taken

---

[131] Jory 1995: 145; supported by Moore 2012: 28–9; cf. Cic. *Rep.* 4.10. For the *fabulae Atellanae* and its distinction from *ars ludicra*, cf. Livy 7.2.12.

[132] Jory 1995: 151.

[133] The *collegium tibicinum Romanum* traced its origins back to Numa: Plut. *Numa* 17.2–3. Cf. the 'strike of the *tibicines*' episode: Livy 9.30.5–10, Ov. *Fast.* 6.657–692, Val. Max. 2.5.4, Plut. *Quaest. Rom.* 55. The phrase *Latinus tibicen* might refer to a musician who accompanied traditional Roman theatrical genres like the *fabula palliata*, in contrast with the imported Greek *auletai* who featured, for example, at Anicius' *ludi*: see Garelli-François 2000: 96–102; Moore 2012: 29.

[134] The evidence for the *planipedia* derives mainly from late-antique grammarians: see Jory 1995: 149–50, with references.

either in apposition with *Latinum tibicinem cum cantore* (as favoured by Jory) or as the direct object of *removerunt* (excluded). If we take *ludum talarium* with *removerunt*, as I believe we should, this would mean that the *ludus talarius* was in fact *included* in the censors' ban along with the *ars ludicra*.[135] The case for the *ludus talarius* as a protected Italian theatrical genre thus becomes untenable.

References to the *ludus talarius* in other sources support the idea that the *ludus talarius* was included in the ban on *ars ludicra*. Most significantly, the second-century CE author Fronto refers to a censorial ban relating specifically to the *ludus talarius*:

> *laudo censoris factum, qui ludos talarios prohibuit, quod semet ipsum diceret, cum ea praeteriret, difficile dignitati servire, quin ad modum crotali aut cymbali pedem poneret.* (Fronto, Orat. 10, p. 157 van den Hout)
>
> I praise the action of the censor, who banned *ludi talarii*, in view of the fact that he said that he found it difficult to maintain his dignity when he passed by a performance and not to keep step to the beat of the castanets or cymbals.

Fronto unfortunately does not specify when and by whom this ruling was enacted. If, as seems likely, he was thinking of the ban of 115, then we have clear evidence that the *ludus talarius* was prohibited in conjunction with the *ars ludicra*.[136] The notoriety of the *ludus talarius* is also emphasised strongly by Cicero and Quintilian. Cicero includes 'dancers and the whole *ludus talarius*' (*saltatores totumque ludum talarium*) in his list of 'sordid trades' (*sordides artes*) in the *De Officiis*.[137] This suggests that dancing was an integral part of the *ludus talarius*, and that the performers who took part in it were stigmatised on account of the fact that they received remuneration for their *ars*. Quintilian provides additional evidence for the musical accompaniments of the *ludus talarius*. He connects the genre with the deplorable 'sing-song' style of Asiatic oratory current in his day, stating that 'if this [style] is held to be at all acceptable, there is no reason why we should not accompany the voice with the lyre, the pipes, or

---

[135] For this argument, see Leppin 1992: 186–8; Slater 1994: 127; Garelli-François 2000: 88.

[136] The fact that Fronto refers only to a single censor has led some to suppose that Cato was the instigator of the ban, and thus that Fronto and Cassiodorus were describing separate incidents (in some editions, *Censor* is capitalised). However, Garelli-François (2000: 101) suggests that the ban of 115 was associated specifically with L. Metellus; hence Fronto could refer to one censor as the primary instigator of the ban.

[137] Cic. *Off.* 1.150; cf. *Att.* 1.16.3: *non enim umquam turpior in ludo talario consessus fuit.*

indeed – and this would be more suitable for such atrocities – the cymbals?'[138] The impression conveyed by Cicero and Quintilian is of a noisy and boisterous performance, not dissimilar to the kind of Greek-style musical entertainments singled out by Polybius and others as a new and unwelcome addition to Rome's cultural scene.[139] The fact that *ludi talarii* were still being performed in Cicero's and Quintilian's day need not preclude the idea that the genre had been subject to an earlier ban which had since fallen into abeyance. It is certainly hard to see why the censors would have gone to the trouble of protecting a genre that would be so vehemently condemned by Roman moralists of later generations.

What, then, was the motivation behind the ban of 115? Jory speculates that the censors were motivated by 'a desire to save money'.[140] Another possibility is that the censors viewed some types of theatrical performance as a threat to social order, fearing that the actors involved might voice statements that were politically controversial or inflammatory.[141] However, the most likely explanation in my view is the one given by Fronto. Fronto explicitly cites moral scruples about music as the reason for the ban: the percussive sounds of the castanets and cymbals (*crotali aut cymbali*) distracted the censor as he went about his official business and prevented him from walking at a stately pace (in Roman elite culture, the gait was considered a marker of *dignitas*, and dancing represented the antithesis of proper masculine comportment).[142] It could be argued that Fronto's explanation does not accurately represent the intentions of the censor himself. But the important point is that, from Fronto's perspective, the *ludus talarius* challenged Roman assumptions about what constituted appropriate

---

[138] Quint. *Inst.* 58–59: *quod si omnino recipiendum est, nihil causae est cur non illam vocis modulationem fidibus ac tibiis, immo mehercule, quod est huic deformitati propius, cymbalis adiuvemus.*

[139] Garelli-François (2000: 99–100) draws a connection between the *ludus talarius* and the so-called *magoidoi*, a Greek category of lyric mimes who specialised in verse songs accompanied by loud percussive music and comic gestures (cf. Athen. 14.620e, 621c; Strabo 14.1.41). It would be unwise to push this comparison too far, given the scarcity of evidence pertaining to the *magoidoi*, but the idea of the *ludus talarius* as a Greek-inspired type of performance is compelling in my view. Cf. Suet. *Cal.* 54.2: *magno tibiarum et scabellorum crepitu cum pallio purpureo talarique tunica versaretur in conviviis muliebribus.*

[140] Jory 1995: 152.   [141] See Manuwald 2011: 53–4.

[142] Compare the controversy surrounding the proposal to erect a stone theatre in Rome in 154 BCE; according to the ancient sources, the controversy revolved around concerns about the effect of 'Greek pleasures' on Roman masculinity and morality: Val. Max. 2.4.2. Moral concerns also lie behind the legal restrictions imposed on the *convivium* in this period (e.g. the *lex Orchia* of 182 BCE): cf. Cato *ORF*, fr. 139–146; Macr. *Sat.* 3.17; Lintott 1972: 631–2. In the 350s CE, the emperor Theodosius I outlawed the exhibition of female lyre-players at private banquets: *C.Th.* 15.7.10; *Epit. de Caes.* 48.10.

music-making. Echoing the speeches of Scipio and Cato, his testimony highlights how Roman anxieties about music's effect on mind and body influenced ideas about masculinity, social status and the uses of public space.

Conclusion

This chapter has examined the games of L. Anicius Gallus as a window onto the cultural politics of music in the second century BCE. Polybius' account of this extraordinary spectacle repays close attention, since it affords a unique insight into how a musical performance in republican Rome looked and sounded to a foreign observer. However, while there has been no shortage of interest in this episode in recent decades, scholars have overlooked the particular importance of music in explaining both the intentionality behind Anicius' spectacle and its presentation in Polybius' *Histories*.

The games of 167 highlight how music could operate as an effective currency through which to articulate one's claim to a place in the crowded and highly competitive staging of military glory. Faced with the embarrassing prospect of being upstaged by rival *triumphatores*, Anicius masterminded a performance which skilfully combined elements of a Plautine comedy, a triumph and a gladiatorial contest. The praetor assembled a veritable 'who's who' of Greek artists; he paraded them in a venue with strong ties to the recent triumphal games of Fulvius Nobilior and Aemilius Paullus; and, on the eve (if not the day) of the Illyrian triumph, he made them take part in an uproarious mock battle replete with its own military-style musical accompaniment. The fact that the performance took place in conjunction with Anicius' triumph on the Quirinalia would have created a strong temporal link between the two events. The triumphal connection was also underscored topographically by the use of the Circus Flaminius, a performance space with strong links to the triumph. The message of *Graecia capta*, of Greek culture being taken captive, was thus embedded in the very soundtrack of Anicius' show.

Anicius' games represented everything that Polybius detested about contemporary music. Whereas his Arcadian compatriots used music to inculcate moral decency and a respect for tradition, Anicius' production was a mere charade – pleasing to the uneducated ear, perhaps, but devoid of the qualities that in Polybius' view defined 'real music'. The historian's aversion to the spectacle, however, cannot be explained simply along national or ethnic lines. Rather, as I have sought to demonstrate, the Anicius episode has an exemplary function in reinforcing the association between music and morality in the *Histories*. The importance which Polybius assigns to music generally in his work reflects wider trends in the intellectual and civic culture of the Hellenistic world.

At the same time, the Anicius episode invites broader reflection on what we might call the 'Hellenisation' of Roman musical culture during the second century BCE. Egert Pöhlmann, a leading authority on ancient music, has spoken of 'a process of mutual assimilation of Greek and Roman music, which began early in republican times' and resulted in 'a Greco-Roman musical idiom, a common musical language'.[143] On the face of it, the appearance of Greek pipe-players on the Roman stage in 167 would seem to represent a significant milestone in this process of musical acculturation. And yet, as I argue throughout this book, the tendency to portray the Romans as passive consumers of Greek music is deeply flawed. While it is certainly true that Greek musicians and music teachers were highly valued by the philhellenic Roman elite throughout the second century, their assimilation into Roman society was neither seamless nor inevitable. Anicius' show can be seen as one stage in a series of Roman experimentations with Greek musical culture in this period, many of them instigated by successful generals who sought to convert the cultural capital of Hellenism into social and political capital at Rome. These experimentations undoubtedly succeeded in elevating the status of *mousike* at Rome. And yet, they also exposed a deep ideological rift within the upper classes. Scipio Aemilianus and Cato the Elder were outspoken in their dislike of certain types of Greek music and regarded the transfer of such cultural 'booty' as a threat to the integrity of Roman morals. Thus, rather than speaking of a single 'Greco-Roman musical idiom' in the second century, we might more accurately speak of a plurality of Greek and Roman musical idioms, which reflected the conflicting attitudes and priorities of different individuals, both in Rome itself and throughout the Mediterranean world.

---

[143] Pöhlmann 2010: 34.

2 | Popular Music and Popular Politics in the Late Republic

ὃ δὲ δὴ μέγιστον ἁπάντων, ὅτι καὶ κατά τινας καιροὺς ἀμουσοτέρων τῶν προστατῶν τῆς πολιτείας πεπειραμένη τῶν ὑπὸ Πλάτωνος ἐν Πολιτείᾳ λόγῳ χρησμῳδουμένων ἔργῳ πεπείραται, ἐν μέσαις ἀγυιαῖς καὶ ἱερῶν κάλλεσιν ὠμοτάτην τῶν πολιτῶν κατ' ἀλλήλων ἐσιδοῦσα μιαιφονίαν.

Most remarkable of all, when at various times Rome had, as leaders of the state, men deficient in musical cultivation, it experienced in practice what Plato in his *Republic* had prophesied, and saw its citizens murdering one another most brutally in the middle of its streets and among the beauties of its temples.
                               Aristides Quintilianus, *On Music* 2.62 (trans. Barker)

In the second book of his treatise *On Music*, the Greek writer Aristides Quintilianus conjures up a harrowing vision of Rome locked in a Platonic dystopia, ravaged by violence and internecine strife. Citizens murder one another in broad daylight. Temples are besmirched with blood. And all because the leaders of the state (τῶν προστατῶν τῆς πολιτείας) in their ignorance failed to heed the warnings of Plato about the dangers of music. What brought the Roman *politeia* to its knees, according to Aristides, was not civil discord as such, but rather a lack of musical cultivation (*amousia*) among the governing class. Without a proper respect for music's affective power, Aristides asserts, the politicians led their people into vice and lawlessness, bringing the Roman state to the verge of collapse.[1]

The idea that music played a significant role in the political upheavals of the late Republic is one which very few modern scholars have taken seriously. In the copious scholarship on late-republican Rome, musical

---

[1] Although Aristides does not situate his description within a specific chronological framework (the uncertainty surrounding the author's date complicates the issue), we cannot read the passage without thinking of the dark days of the late Republic (Mathiesen 1983: 126 n. 101; Barker 1989: 465). The origins of civil war in Rome were strongly associated with the reforms of the Gracchi: see Wiseman 2010, citing Vell. Pat. 2.3.3 among other sources. Aristides' reference to Cicero's *De Re Publica* at the start of the digression on Roman music (2.61) strengthens the republican association.

themes have received only superficial treatment. Elizabeth Rawson's seminal monograph *Intellectual Life in the Late Republic* is a case in point. 'Musical theory', Rawson argues, 'was a highly abstract subject, with limited connection with musical practice (to the impoverishment of both)'; it was, accordingly, a subject 'to which only lip-service was paid'.[2] That, as far as Rawson is concerned, is the end of the matter: historians of the late Republic have little reason to concern themselves with music, because music was of little concern to the Romans themselves.[3]

And yet, contrary to modern assumptions, the last century of the Republic has provided us with an abundance of evidence for the role of music in Roman life. Much of this evidence derives, as we might expect, from the hand of Marcus Tullius Cicero, the renowned orator, philosopher and statesman whose presence looms so large over this entire period.[4] In 1948, the American classicist P. R. Coleman-Norton catalogued over one hundred references to music in the Ciceronian corpus alone, publishing his findings in an article suggestively titled 'Cicero Musicus'. These references – culled from Cicero's speeches, letters and treatises on philosophy and rhetoric – afford an unrivalled insight into the musical experiences and attitudes of a well-educated upper-class Roman of the first century BCE. From the *Tusculan Disputations*, we learn that Cicero spent several years studying under the blind Stoic philosopher Diodotus, who, while residing in Rome as Cicero's house guest, gave demonstrations of Pythagorean theory on the lyre.[5] Those years of study evidently paid dividends. Already at the turn of the second century CE, Cicero was considered an influential authority on the *ars musica*.[6] Musical theorists of later centuries, from Aristides Quintilianus to Augustine, drew inspiration from his works.[7]

It is astonishing, then, that Cicero's comments on music have elicited almost no scholarly attention since Coleman-Norton's study. In the recently published volume *Music and Philosophy in the Roman Empire*,

---

[2] Rawson 1985: 156, 167.
[3] See also Mountford 1964: 202: 'Nowhere else, even in his philosophical works, does Cicero offer anything except conventional and second-hand references to music'; Delattre 1998: 231 n. 102: 'the subject of music is never taken up by Cicero – far less treated by him – for itself.'
[4] As noted by Levene (2005: 31), Cicero's writings make up more than seventy-five per cent of extant Latin literature from the period 90–40 BCE.
[5] Cic. *Tusc. Disp.* 5.113: *Diodotus Stoicus caecus ... fidibus Pythagoreorum more uteretur*. Cicero probably acquired his knowledge of the *ars musica* from various philosophical mentors, both in Rome and in Greece, including Phaedrus, Philo of Larissa and Posidonius of Rhodes.
[6] Cf. Tac. *Dial.* 30.4: *itaque hercule in libris Ciceronis deprehendere licet ... non musicae ... scientiam ei defuisse*.
[7] Aristides Quintilianus, *De Musica* 2.61–62 (discussed below in the section 'Cicero on the Music of the Roman Theatre'); Augustine, *Contra Iul. Pelag* 5.23 = FRHist 39 F6a (a fragment from Cicero's *De Consiliis Suis*).

edited by Francesco Pelosi and Frederico Petrucci, Cicero's name appears only a handful of times, with the majority of the chapters focusing on much later authors such as Sextus Empiricus, Plotinus and Porphyry, most of whom were writing in Greek.[8] Historians have occasionally mined Cicero's oeuvre for musical testimonia, but, with only a few exceptions, have failed to address the full implications of this material, generally quoting passages out of context with little regard to the author's literary aims and historical context.[9]

The same can be said of the other musical writings produced in Italy during Cicero's lifetime. The biographies of Cornelius Nepos, the poetry of Lucretius and the philosophical treatises of Philodemus all exhibit a strong preoccupation with music, both in theory and in practice. Especially noteworthy is the contribution of that most elusive of Roman writers, Marcus Terentius Varro. Among his voluminous bibliography, Varro published a full-blown treatise on music (sometimes referred to as the *De Musica*), which he included in a series of nine books on the liberal arts known collectively as the *Disciplinae*. This work no longer survives, but it is cited quite frequently by later writers on music and probably served as the primary model for Augustine's still extant *De Musica*.[10] Fortunately, the range of Varro's musicological interests can be gauged from his surviving works and fragments.[11] Another major witness is Philodemus of Gadara, an Epicurean philosopher and poet who migrated to Italy in around 80 BCE. He, too, produced a study 'On Music' (*Peri Mousikes* in Greek). Long consigned to oblivion, this fascinating text was partially rediscovered during excavations of the library of the Villa of the Papyri near Herculaneum, the probable home of Philodemus' patron, L. Calpurnius Piso Caesoninus. Though the papyrus scrolls containing the text were excavated in the mid-eighteenth century, it is only relatively recently that

---

[8] Pelosi and Petrucci 2021.
[9] Typical examples of this synoptic approach are Wille 1967: 192–5; Guidobaldi 1992: 15, 30; Comotti 1989: 50–2; Horsfall 2003: 39. Porter (2018) explores the relationship between music and the tradition of sublime criticism in Cicero's rhetorical treatises, but eschews a wider discussion of Cicero's attitudes toward music.
[10] Augustine's famous definition of music as 'the science of modulating well' (*scientia bene modulandi*; *De Musica* 1.2.2) is often, though insecurely, attributed to Varro's *De Musica*: see Holzer 1890; Rawson 1985: 167–8; Brennan 1988: 272; Shanzer 2005: 102. Testimonia for the *De Musica* are collected by Ritschl (1877).
[11] In addition to passages discussed below, cf. Varro, *Ling.* 5.91, 5.117, 6.75, on the etymology of certain musical terms. Unplaced Varronian fragments dealing with musical themes include: Cassiodorus, *De Musica* 8.15, on the notes of the tetrachord; Martianus Capella, *De Nuptiis Philologiae et Mercurii* 9.928, on the 'Islands of the Nymphs' in Lydia moved by the sound of *tibiae*; and Augustine, *De Doctrina Christiana* 2.16.26, on the tripartite division of sound into vocal, blown and struck.

scholars have been able to decipher their contents.[12] Taken as a whole, this rich body of evidence casts serious doubt on the notion that music was an insignificant aspect of Roman culture during the late Republic.

The time is ripe, then, for a thorough re-examination of music's place in the world of Cicero. This chapter represents a first step towards that goal. I propose to use Cicero's testimony as a basis for shedding light on contemporary attitudes to music, especially in the context of theatre and entertainment. More specifically, I will attempt to show that the late-republican discourse on music operated along two major ideological axes – a political axis, on the one hand, and a philosophical axis, on the other. Taking the discussion of music in the *De Legibus* as a starting point, I argue that Cicero's conception of music was not simply a derivative of Plato's, as has generally been assumed. Rather, his comments must be seen against the background of two major developments: first, the construction of Pompey's theatre in 55; and second, the intensifying political conflict between the *optimates* – the self-styled 'best men', who favoured the interests of the Senate – and the *populares*, who favoured the people. The careers of Gaius Gracchus and Publius Clodius provide revealing examples of *populares* who used music to enhance the impact of their political messaging.

The second part of the chapter challenges Rawson's theory that music was a minor and uncontroversial aspect of Roman intellectual culture during the first century BCE. Cicero's views on music were formulated not in an ideological vacuum, but in dialogue with those of prominent Epicureans such as Philodemus and Piso. There is also compelling evidence in the form of Varro's satire *Onos Lyras* (*Donkey [Hears] the Lyre*) that debates about music engaged a wider segment of the Roman population than traditionally thought. In summary, while we need not go so far as to endorse Aristides's claim that the Republic collapsed due to a lack of musical cultivation among its leading citizens, I hope to demonstrate that music did in fact play a significant role in cementing and reflecting the political and social divisions of the late Republic.

Cicero on the Music of the Roman Theatre

In the second book of his treatise *De Legibus* (*On the Laws*), composed probably in the late fifties BCE, Cicero discusses what he considers to be

---

[12] The most comprehensive and up-to-date edition of the text is Delattre 2007.

the best way of celebrating the Roman games.[13] Dividing the *ludi publici* into two categories – *ludi circenses* (circus shows) and *ludi scaenici* (theatrical shows) – he proceeds to outline an ideal set of legal statutes which, in his view, ought to govern their existence:

> *iam ludi publici quoniam sunt cavea circoque divisi, sint corporum certationes cursu et pugillatu et luctatione, curriculisque equorum usque ad certam victoriam circo constitutis, cavea cantu vacet et fidibus et tibiis, dummodo ea moderata sint ut lege praescribitur.* (Cic. Leg. 2.38, ed. Powell 2006)

> Since the public games are divided between the theatre and the circus, in the circus let there be athletic contests in running, boxing and wrestling, and horse-races established with a clearly defined goal, and let the theatre resound with singing, lyres and pipes, provided that these are regulated in accordance with the law.

Cicero – or, properly speaking, the interlocutor 'Marcus' – goes on to explain why the music of the theatre should be subject to legal regulation. He launches into a lengthy philosophical excursus on the nature and causality of musical revolution, modelled on the teachings of Plato but incorporating first-hand observations of theatrical performances in Rome:

> *adsentior enim Platoni, nihil tam facile in animos teneros atque molles influere quam varios canendi sonos, quorum dici vix potest quanta sit vis in utramque partem; namque et incitat languentes et languefacit excitatos, et tum remittit animos tum contrahit. civitatumque hoc multarum in Graecia interfuit, antiquum vocum conservari modum; quarum mores lapsi ad mollitias pariter sunt immutati cum cantibus, aut hac dulcedine corruptelaque depravati, ut quidam putant, aut cum severitas eorum ob alia vitia cecidisset, tum fuit in auribus animisque mutatis etiam huic mutationi locus. quamobrem ille quidem sapientissimus Graeciae vir longeque doctissimus valde hanc labem veretur; negat enim mutari posse musicas leges sine mutatione legum publicarum; ego autem nec tam valde id timendum nec plane contemnendum puto. illud quidem <video>: quae solebant quondam compleri severitate iucunda Livianis et Naevianis modis, nunc ut eadem exsultent, <et> cervices oculosque pariter cum*

---

[13] On the date of the *De Legibus*, see MacKendrick 1989: 77–9; Zetzel 1999; Dyck 2004: 5–7; Caspar 2011. The *communis opinio* is that Cicero left the text incomplete in 51 when he departed for his governorship of Cilicia and never returned to it under the changed political circumstances of the 40s. Cornelius Nepos alludes to the work in a fragment of his book *On Latin Historians*, written in the late 30s, suggesting that it may have been published posthumously.

modorum flexionibus torqueant. graviter olim ista vindicabat vetus illa Graecia, longe providens quam sensim pernicies illapsa civium <in> animos malis studiis malisque doctrinis repente totas civitates everteret, si quidem illa severa Lacedaemo nervos iussit, quos plures quam septem haberet, in Timothei fidibus incidi. (Cic. Leg. 2.38–39, ed. Powell)

For I agree with Plato that nothing so easily flows into young and impressionable minds as the various notes of the musical scale; it is hard to express the extent of their power in one way or the other. For music animates the indolent and calms the excited; it causes spirits to relax at one moment and then restrains them the next. Many states in Greece considered it important to preserve the ancient style of music; yet their morals changed along with their songs and slid into decadence as a result. Either they were corrupted by the sweet seductiveness of music, as some people think, or, once the stringency of their morals was undermined by their other vices, then their ears and minds became changed, leaving room for this musical change too. For this reason, the wisest and by far the most learned man in Greece was greatly afraid of this decline. For he denies that the laws of music can be changed without bringing about a change in the laws of the state. However, I for one do not think that this should be feared so greatly, although it should not be overlooked completely either. Indeed, <we see> how the theatre, which once used to be filled with the tunes of Livius and Naevius, pleasing in their simplicity, is now filled with people who leap up and toss their heads and roll their eyes in time with the twists and turns of the music. In the old days, Greece used to punish such behaviour harshly, anticipating far in advance how the deadly plague might sink gradually into the minds of citizens and suddenly overturn entire states with evil pursuits and evil ideas – if, indeed, it is true that stern Sparta ordered the strings above the number of seven to be cut off the lyre of Timotheus.

This is, at first glance, a passage which evades straightforward interpretation. The synthesis of legal theory, moral philosophy and anecdotal historiography is highly idiosyncratic and has been met with a great deal of scepticism by modern critics. The classicist James Mountford, writing in 1964, went so far as to reject the entire passage as 'a piece of vacillating urbanity', which demonstrates 'no flicker of personal musical experience or conviction'.[14] Timothy Moore sensibly adopts a more cautious approach: 'we must always be wary of references to the "good old days" in Roman literature, and Cicero's words are suspiciously reminiscent of the criticisms of the "New Music" made by Plato, Cicero's principal inspiration in the

---

[14] Mountford 1964: 202; see also Williams 1968: 338: 'Cicero is simply adapting Plato's ideas to Rome'.

Laws, and by other Greek conservatives'.[15] To be sure, the shadow of Plato ('the wisest and by far the most learned man in Greece') looms large throughout Cicero's discussion.[16] As noted in Chapter 1, Plato argued resolutely in his *Laws* against the democratisation of musical culture, which, he believed, provided a platform for the Athenian masses to rise up and overthrow their superiors. Another important model was Aristoxenus of Tarentum. Like Plato, Aristoxenus voiced concerns about the corrupting effects of 'popular music' (ἡ πάνδημος αὕτη μουσική), arguing that it was necessary to preserve the memory of 'what music used to be like' (οἵα ἦν ἡ μουσική) at a time when 'the theatres have become completely barbarised' (τὰ θέατρα ἐκβεβαρβάρωται).[17] The influence of these ideas on Cicero's analysis of the Roman *ludi* is readily discernible.

The Greek background of the *De Legibus* is not the only factor which casts doubt on Cicero's account. Moore has rightly questioned the extent to which Cicero was reliably informed about the music of early Roman drama. There is plenty of evidence attesting to the revival of old tragedies in the first century BCE, but, as Moore points out, changes in Latin diction and performance conventions would have resulted in a very different musical experience.[18] Cicero was certainly familiar with the plays of Livius and Naevius as *written* texts (he rejects Livius' *fabulae* as 'not sufficiently worthy of being read a second time'); and, if we assume that the Romans were accustomed to read aloud, as many scholars do, then it is possible that Cicero had at least some appreciation of how the metre of the texts translated into rhythmical patterns.[19] However, it is very unlikely that Cicero, in contrasting the old and new *modi*, was thinking specifically of metre.[20] It is also unlikely that he was thinking of rhythm, since in Roman drama, 'rhythm must have been to a great extent determined by metre'.[21] Indeed, there is no evidence to suggest that the music of Cicero's time was more rhythmically complex than the music of the third century, when Livius and Naevius were writing. Thus, *modi* here is probably best taken as

---

[15] Moore 2012: 140.

[16] Cf. Cic. *Orat.* 10, praising Plato as *dicendi gravissimus auctor et magister*. For Cicero's engagement with Plato in general, see Long 1995.

[17] Aristox. frag. 24 = Athen. 14.632b (trans. Barker). At *Tusc.* 1.19, Cicero refers to Aristoxenus as *musicus idemque philosophus* and goes on to describe him as 'learned' (*doctus*; *Tusc.* 1.41).

[18] Moore 2008: 39. On revivals of old tragedy, see Beacham 1991: 154–98; Goldberg 1995: 24–5; Prauscello 2006: 61–3.

[19] Cic. *Brut.* 18. For the idea that the Romans read aloud, see Starr 1991. The debate is helpfully summarised by Johnson (2010: 4–9).

[20] In the case of Roman comedy, we find a reduction of metrical variety over time as the genre develops; the same was probably true of tragedy as well: see Moore 2016.

[21] Moore 2012: 146.

a generic term for 'musical accompaniment', without a clear distinction being drawn between rhythm and melody.[22]

Flexiones, the word which qualifies *modi* in Cicero's description (*modorum flexionibus*), may offer more precise insights. Moore explains that '*flexiones* may refer specifically to modulation between keys, or it may describe ornamentation of the melody or similar features'.[23] In Greek critiques of the 'New Music', *kampai* (bends, or turns) are associated primarily with modulations between *harmoniai* (i.e. between different tuning systems).[24] Cicero's use of *flexiones* may reflect this original technical sense of *kampai*. In my view, however, the term probably refers to melodic ornamentation in a more general sense. Certainly, we should not place too much faith in the idea that Roman musicians of the first century employed more modulations than their third-century predecessors. As we have seen, the language of 'bending' and 'modulating' appears in many Roman descriptions of music and is often couched in a similar moralising rhetoric. Nevertheless, as Moore emphasises, Cicero's depiction of contemporary music would not have made sense to Roman readers if it did not resonate with their own experience of theatrical spectacles.[25]

Our understanding of the passage would no doubt be greatly improved if the text itself had been preserved more securely. Of the five books of the *De Legibus* known in antiquity, only the first three have survived in a more-or-less complete state.[26] Moreover, within the extant manuscripts there are a number of textual corruptions. It is most unfortunate that we encounter one such corruption at precisely the point when Cicero turns his attention to the music of Rome (the sentence beginning *illud quidem*). The basic meaning is clear enough: in contrast with the simplicity of the old music, the modern music twists and turns (*modorum flexionibus*), provoking its listeners to twist their necks and eyes (*cervices oculosque ... torqueant*).

---

[22] This meaning of *modi* is specifically associated with the plural form: cf., e.g., Cic. *De Orat.* 1.187 (*in musicis numeri et voces et modi*); Prop. 2.22.6 (*varios incinit ore modos*); Liv. 7.2.4 (*ludiones ... ad tibicinis modos saltantes*); Tac. *Ann.* 14.15 (*ad gestus modosque haud virilis*); *TLL* s.v. 'modus', Vol. VIII, 0, 1252, 4–1321, 73 (Brandt).

[23] Moore 2016: 356.

[24] See Barker 1984: 94; Csapo 2004; D'Angour 2011: 201–2; Franklin 2013: 229–31. Timotheus of Miletus, the musician singled out as a historical exemplum in the *De Legibus* passage, was noted for his extreme use of *kampai* – a practice which the Spartans sought to keep in check by reducing the number of strings on his lyre (thereby limiting the range of notes available to him): cf. Pherecrates *ap.* [Plut.] *Mus.* 1141f–1142a, accusing Timotheus of ruining *mousike* with his 'perverted ant-crawlings'.

[25] Moore 2016: 356.

[26] On the textual tradition of *De Legibus*, see Dyck 2004; Lintott 2008: 436–8.

However, the subject of the verbs *exsultent* and *torqueant* cannot be clearly ascertained from any of the surviving manuscripts.[27] Is Cicero describing the movements of musicians and/or dancers on the stage? Or is he referring to the animated gesticulations of spectators in the *cavea*? In support of the former idea, one could point to several literary texts which allude to musicians using exaggerated movements of the eyes and face to heighten the drama of their performances.[28] However, I concur with the majority of scholars in favouring the latter interpretation. A fragment of Varro's satire *Onos Lyras* – a work to which we shall return later in this chapter – describes how 'the minds of the whole theatre are often moved by the *tibiae*, with their frequent bending (*crebro flectendo*), and their spirits are aroused'.[29] We can also refer to a passage in Philodemus' treatise *On Music*, commenting on how an overabundance of music can 'set in motion an entire theatre' (συμβαίν[ειν ...] σύνολον θέατ[ρον]).[30] The emphasis in both of these passages is on the effect of music on audience members, and it seems likely that Cicero had a similar idea in mind with the verbs *exsultent* and *torqueant*.

In light of the various difficulties surrounding the text, one could be forgiven for approaching the commentary on music in the *De Legibus* with a healthy dose of caution. And yet, it would be foolish to dismiss the value of Cicero's testimony solely on that basis. Instead of chastising the author for his lack of originality or for his failure to engage with the technicalities of performance in terms intelligible to modern musicologists, we should ask *why* Cicero made a point of addressing the subject of music in the first place. In particular, how do we account for his statement that the corruption of music 'should neither be feared so greatly, nor completely overlooked' (*nec tam valde id timendum nec plane contemnendum*)? Scholars have tended to view this apparent equivocation as the result of an underlying tension between Greek and Roman musical ethics. Cicero, it has been claimed, felt little personal connection to music, and yet he nonetheless felt

---

[27] Most editors insert a noun such as *cavea* (feminine singular) or *theatra* (neuter plural), emending *exsulte<n>t* and *torquea<n>t* as necessary.

[28] The Theban aulete Pronomus 'afforded an excess of pleasure to the theatres by means of his facial expression (τοῦ προσώπου τῷ σχήματι) and the movement of his entire body (τῇ τοῦ παντὸς κινήσει σώματος)': Paus. 9.12.5–6. Interestingly, Cicero's exemplar Timotheus of Miletus supposedly pioneered the application of mimesis to the practice of lyre-playing: Athen. 8.338a, 8.352a. Further sources cited by Power 2010: 136–43.

[29] Var. *Sat.* fr. 365: *saepe totius theatri tibiis, crebro flectendo, conmutari mentes, erigi animos eorum*. References to the *Menippean Satires* in this chapter follow the numeration of Krenkel 2002.

[30] Phld. *Mus.* 4 col. 37.16–17 Delattre.

obliged to pay lip service to it given its fundamental role in Plato's philosophy.[31] Before jumping to such conclusions, however, we would do well to consider the words of the Italian scholar Nevio Zorzetti. In his classic article 'Poetry and the Ancient City: the Case of Rome', published in 1991, Zorzetti offers a brief, yet highly perceptive, assessment of the significance of music in Cicero's philosophical worldview: 'in Cicero's time, as for that matter in Plato's, one did not argue about music for merely abstract reasons. And above all, when we look at the remarks on musical *ludi* in the *De Legibus*, what Cicero has to say about stage-music looks less like pure philosophical theory than, more than anything else, a concretely lived preoccupation of the politician'.[32] Zorzetti goes on to suggest that the discussion of music serves specifically to delineate the role of the aedile in his capacity as organiser of the games. While I believe this focus on the aedileship to be overly narrow (for reasons which will become clear), Zorzetti's comments raise an important point, as Habinek acknowledges: 'the fact that Cicero has adapted Plato's suggestions to the specifics of the Roman situation makes it clear we are dealing with Cicero's considered judgment and not just with reliance on Greek precedent'.[33] What is primarily at stake in Cicero's discussion of music, then, is not whether the narrative of decline is historically 'accurate', but why, for an educated Roman statesman of the first century BCE, this kind of narrative was 'good to think with' (to borrow Lévi-Strauss's phrase). Put simply, why was music a useful tool for analysing the social and political issues of the day?

We can begin to pursue this question by examining a passage in Book 3 of the *De Legibus*. This passage has largely escaped the notice of modern commentators, but it is helpful for situating the arguments of the previous book in a broader perspective:

> nam licet videre, si velis replicare memoriam temporum, qualescumque summi civitatis viri fuerint, talem civitatem fuisse; quaecumque mutatio morum in principibus extiterit, eandem in populo secutam. idque haud paulo est verius, quam quod Platoni nostro placet, qui musicorum cantibus ait mutatis mutari civitatum status. ego autem nobilium vita victuque mutato mores mutari civitatum puto. quo perniciosius de re publica merentur vitiosi principes, quod non solum vitia concipiunt ipsi, sed ea infundunt in civitatem, neque solum obsunt, quod ipsi corrumpuntur, sed etiam quod corrumpunt, plusque exemplo quam peccato nocent. atque haec lex dilatata in ordinem cunctum coangustari etiam potest; pauci enim atque admodum pauci honore et gloria amplificati vel corrumpere mores

[31] See Delattre 1998: 229–30.   [32] Zorzetti 1991: 325.   [33] Habinek 2005: 200.

civitatis vel corrigere possunt. sed haec et nunc satis et in illis libris tractata sunt diligentius. (Cic. Leg. 3.31–32)

> For, if you will turn your thoughts back to our early history, you will see that the character of our most prominent men has been reproduced in the whole state; whatever change took place in the lives of the prominent men has also taken place in the whole people. And we can be much more confident about the soundness of this theory than that of our beloved Plato. For he thought that the characteristics of a state could be changed by changing the character of its music. But I believe that a transformation takes place in a state's character when the habits and mode of living of its aristocracy are changed. For that reason men of the upper class who do wrong are especially dangerous to the Republic, because they not only indulge in vicious practices themselves, but also infect the whole state with their vices; and not only because they are corrupt, but also because they corrupt others, and do more harm by their bad examples than by their sins. But this law, which applies to the whole senatorial order, could be made even narrower in its application. For a few men – very few, in fact – on account of their high official position and great reputation, have the power either to corrupt the morals of the state or to reform them. But I have said enough on this subject, which is treated even more completely in my former books. (Trans. adapted from Keyes 1928)

The main driver of moral change in society, Cicero claims, is not music, as Plato professed, but rather the conduct of the leading citizens (*principes*). For a state (*civitas*) to remain prosperous, the *principes* must aspire to lead a virtuous and dignified lifestyle that befits their elevated social rank. Conversely, immoral leaders 'act especially destructively toward the republic' (*perniciosius de re publica merentur*) because they set a bad example for the rest of the population. Here we encounter an apparent inconsistency: how can Cicero speak of music as a potential danger to society in Book 2, only then to dismiss its importance altogether in Book 3? In fact, we need not see a contradiction in the two passages. Even if music was not as fundamental to Cicero's political philosophy as it was to Plato's, it mattered insofar as it factored into the larger moral responsibilities of the *principes*. It was precisely the upper classes who were tasked with keeping the potentially destructive power of music in check. To abuse this power was to risk unleashing the base passions of the music-loving *plebs*. This argument makes sense in the context of a society where musical entertainers, and stage-performers generally, were of extremely low standing. They belonged, as Cicero affirms elsewhere, to a category of men who 'are willing not only to be deprived of the privileges of other citizens, but even to be removed from their tribes by the judgment of the censors'.[34] How, then, could the musicians themselves be deemed responsible for destroying the state when they had no direct stake in it? The performers who appeared at the *ludi* did so at the behest of the presiding magistrate; it was he who employed their services, and it was he who therefore determined the quality of the spectacle. This was in stark contrast to the situation in Plato's Athens, where musicians were typically of citizen status and played an active role in the civic life of the *polis*.[35]

Cicero brings his discussion of the moral exemplarity of the *principes* to an abrupt close, stating that he has treated this subject more fully elsewhere (*haec ... in illis libris tractata sunt diligentius*). The 'books' to which he refers must belong to the *De Re Publica*, since we know that this work was originally envisioned as a companion to the *De Legibus*.[36] Might the concise treatment of music in the *De Legibus* be explained by the fact that Cicero had already provided a fuller critique of Platonic musical theory in the *De Re Publica*? Support for this idea can be found in an intriguing source. In the second book of his treatise on music, Aristides Quintilianus reveals that 'the *De Re Publica* of Cicero the Roman' contained 'words spoken against music'.[37] Aristides proceeds to note how certain critics had taken these words as an indication that Cicero was thoroughly opposed to music of all forms. He attempts to rebut this argument in two ways. First, he points out that Cicero does not actually appear as a character in the *De Re Publica*, since the dialogue is set during the mid-second century BCE long before Cicero's birth; therefore, the words in question may have been spoken by a character whose views did not necessarily align with those of the author himself. Second, Aristides draws attention to the fact that Cicero lavished praise on the actor Roscius, despite the fact that Roscius 'performed in rhythms alone, second-rate and vulgar ones at that' (ῥυθμοῖς μόνοις καὶ τούτοις ἀγεννέσι καὶ φαύλοις ἐπιδεικνύμενον).[38] The immorality of theatrical music, Aristides concludes, does not detract from the overall

---

[34] Cic. *Rep.* 4.10 (= August. *de Civ. Dei* 2.14.ext.): *cum [sc. Romani] artem ludicram scaenamque totam in probro ducerent, genus id hominum non modo honore civium reliquorum carere, sed etiam tribu moveri notatione censoria voluerunt*.

[35] Cf. Nep. *Praef.* 5: *in scaenam vero prodire ac populo esse spectaculo nemini in eisdem gentibus fuit turpitudini* (indeed, among the same nations [the Greeks], it was never regarded as a source of disgrace to appear on the stage and to exhibit oneself to the people). On the status of musicians in Classical Athens, see Hall 2002; Stewart 2020.

[36] See Lintott 2008: 436–8.

[37] Aristid. Quint. 2.61: ἐν τοῖς Κικέρωνος τοῦ Ῥωμαίου Πολιτικοῖς τὰ κατὰ μουσικῆς ῥηθέντα. The word ῥηθέντα is daggered in some editions, but the general sense is clear enough.

[38] Aristides is probably alluding here to a lost speech *Pro Quinto Roscio*; see Barker 1989: 465.

value of *mousike*: 'if some artists perform despicable melodies because these please the crowd, it is not the art that is to blame' (οὕτω δὴ καί, εἴ τινες τῶν τεχνιτῶν διὰ τὸ τοῖς πολλοῖς ἀρέσκειν τὰ ἀγεννῆ μελῳδοῦσιν, οὐ τῆς τέχνης τὸ αἰτίαμα).

So, what exactly *were* the 'words spoken against music' in the *De Re Publica*? Like the *De Legibus*, the *De Re Publica* is only partially preserved: if the work did in fact contain an extended diatribe against music, it sadly does not survive. It should be noted, however, that there is nothing in the extant text which implies an aversion to music *in general*. For example, the famous 'Dream of Scipio' episode in Book 6 contains a detailed exposition of the Pythagorean concept of the harmony of the spheres. While staying at the court of king Massinissa in Africa, the protagonist Scipio Aemilianus is visited in a dream by his deceased grandfather Scipio Africanus, who reveals to him the hidden secrets of the universe. As he looks in wonder upon the movements of the celestial bodies, Scipio hears a 'great and pleasant sound' (*tantus et tam dulcis sonus*) ringing through his ears. 'That', his grandfather explains, 'is a concord of tones separated by unequal but nevertheless carefully proportioned intervals (*intervallis disiunctus imparibus, sed tamen pro rata parte distinctis*), caused by the rapid motion of the spheres themselves'. 'Learned men', the Elder Scipio continues, have sought to imitate this system of harmonic ratios on stringed instruments and in singing (*nervis imitati atque cantibus*), recognising that it holds 'almost the key to the entire universe' (*rerum omnium fere nodus*).[39]

Furthermore, in Book 2 Cicero draws an analogy between musical harmony and political concord:

> *ut enim in fidibus aut tibiis atque ut in cantu ipso ac vocibus concentus est quidam tenendus ex distinctis sonis, quem inmutatum aut discrepantem aures eruditae ferre non possunt, isque concentus ex dissimillimarum vocum moderatione concors tamen efficitur et congruens, sic ex summis et infimis et mediis interiectis ordinibus ut sonis moderata ratione civitas consensus dissimillimorum concinit; et quae harmonia a musicis dicitur in cantu, ea est in civitate concordia, artissimum atque optimum omni in re publica vinculum incolumitatis, eaque sine iustitia nullo pacto esse potest.*
> (Cic. *Rep.* 2.69 = August. *De Civ. Dei* 2.21)

> For just as in the music of lyres and pipes or in the voices of singers a certain harmony of the different tones must be preserved, the interruption or violation of which is intolerable to trained ears, and as this perfect

---

[39] Cic. *Rep.* 6.18 (trans. Stahl 1990). On the musicological aspects of this passage, see Coleman-Norton 1950.

agreement and harmony is produced by the proportionate blending of discrete tones, so also is a state made harmonious by agreement among dissimilar elements, brought about by a fair and reasonable blending together of the upper, middle and lower classes, just as if they were musical tones. What the musicians call harmony in song is concord in a state, the strongest and best bond of permanent union in any commonwealth; and such concord can never be brought about without the aid of justice. (Trans. Keyes 1928, with slight adaptations.)

This idealisation of a republic 'harmonised' by the mutual consensus of its citizens represents a striking counterpoint to the image of political discord in *De Legibus* 2.39. Cicero's point here is not that music itself was essential to the realisation of civic harmony, but rather that musical consonance and political consonance were both achieved through the same process – namely, the blending of discrete elements into a unified whole.

All of this evidence points firmly to the conclusion that Cicero's polemic in the *De Re Publica* focused not on music as such, but on a particular *kind* of music: the popular music of the theatre or, to quote Aristoxenus, ἡ πάνδημος μουσική. This is, after all, precisely the line of attack taken in the *De Legibus*, and a correspondence in this regard would certainly not be surprising given the strong thematic overlap between the two works. At the same time, we should not assume that, in criticising the music of the theatre, Cicero was merely aping the views of Plato and other Greek thinkers without reflecting on his own lived experience. Indeed, if we examine what Cicero has to say about theatre audiences in his other writings, it becomes clear that his comments on music reflect a broader set of concerns about the role of the theatre in facilitating and legitimising popular participation in Roman politics.

The nature of popular participation in the late Republic has been the subject of heated scholarly debate in recent decades. The 'democratic' model proposed by Fergus Millar in the 1990s has come under attack from scholars such as Henrik Mouritsen, who argue that political power was wielded almost exclusively by a small clique of senatorial elites.[40] However, Millar's arguments have been vindicated by Peter Wiseman in a series of characteristically probing publications.[41] Focusing on the contemporary evidence for crowd participation at the games, Wiseman convincingly argues that the Roman people had an active stake in the everyday business of politics. Cicero provides ample testimony for the importance of the

---

[40] Millar 1995, 1998; *contra* Mouritsen 2001, 2017. [41] Wiseman 2009, 2015, 2017.

theatre 'as a sounding board for political opinion'.[42] For example, in the *Pro Sestio*, he points to the *ludi* as one of the three settings, along with *contiones* (public meetings) and *comitia* (political assemblies), at which the will of the people was most manifest.[43] He makes the same point in a letter to Atticus: 'The feelings of the people are revealed especially at the theatre and at spectacles' (*populi sensus maxime theatro et spectaculis perspectus est*).[44] Like his fellow senators, Cicero monitored the behaviour of spectators – their chants, shouts, gestures and applause – as a barometer of his popularity with the urban populace. Writing again to Atticus after the *Ludi Apollinares* in July 59 BCE, he cheerfully recalls the absence of 'shepherd-style whistling' (*pastoricia fistula*) when he entered the theatre – a mark of the people's deference towards him and his ally Pompey.[45] Mouritsen questions whether these remarks might be better understood as referring only to citizens of a higher social standing, who had both the time and the inclination to engage seriously in political matters.[46] But, following Wiseman, it seems simpler to take Cicero's words at face value: theatrical spectacles were one of the primary ways in which 'ordinary Romans expressed their views on current affairs, applauding those they approved of and whistling at those they didn't'.[47]

Cicero's comments on theatre music, then, should not be regarded as philosophically detached from the mundane concerns of a Roman politician of the mid-first century BCE. On the contrary, they are deeply implicated in contemporary debates concerning the involvement of the people in the political institutions of the Republic. It is important to remember that Cicero formulated his views on music at a time when the people's participation in the political arena was becoming an increasingly contentious issue. The tumultuous decade of the 50s was patterned by

---

[42] Wiseman 2017: 30. On the political dynamics of the theatre in the late Republic, see further Nicolet 1980: 361–73; Purcell 2013: 451–2; Flower 2014: 393–6.

[43] Cic. *Sest.* 106: *etenim tribus locis significari maxime de re publica populi Romani iudicium ac voluntas potest, contione, comitiis, ludorum gladiatorumque consessu*.

[44] Cic. *Att.* 2.19.3.

[45] Cic. *Att.* 1.16.11. The choice of this unusual musical image may be inspired by the description of Athenian theatre-goers at Pl. *Leg.* 700c: οὐ σύριγξ ἦν οὐδέ τινες ἄμουσοι βοαὶ πλήθους, καθάπερ τὰ νῦν ([the authority for judging music] was not the whistling or the unmusical shouts of the mob, as it is now ...).

[46] Mouritsen 2001: 40–1.

[47] Wiseman 2017: 20. For other Ciceronian references to the noisy outbursts of Roman theatre-goers, cf. *De Orat.* 3.196 (*theatra tota reclamat*); *Orat.* 173 (*theatra tota exclamat*); *Att.* 2.19.2 (*totius theatri clamore*); *De Am.* 24 (*qui clamores tota cavea nuper in hospitis et amici mei M. Pacuvi nova fabula*); *Rosc. Com.* 30 (*e scaena non modo sibilis sed etiam convicio explodebatur*); *Parad.* 26 (*exsibilatur, exploditur*).

recurrent bouts of mob violence, stirred up by the rival supporters of the *optimates* and the *populares*. Tensions came to a head in 52 BCE, when the Roman people avenged the murder of their hero Publius Clodius by burning down the Senate-house (*Curia*) in broad daylight. In the context of these events, it is not hard to see why Cicero expressed a desire for a return to a more austere kind of theatrical music – a music which soothed and uplifted the urban masses rather than making them more agitated and thus more inclined towards political unrest.

The Musical Experience of Pompey's Theatre

During Cicero's lifetime, the city of Rome experienced something of a theatrical revolution. In 55 BCE, Pompey the Great dedicated a monumental stone theatre on the Campus Martius, financed by his campaigns in the East (Figs. 2.1 and 2.2). It was both the first and largest building of its kind ever to be constructed in the capital. With its semi-circular rows of seats, its imposing stage-building and its sumptuous collection of sculptures by Greek masters, the monument paid homage to the great theatre complexes of Classical and Hellenistic Greece.[48] Such an impressive structure was bound to raise eyebrows at Rome, and Pompey knew it: several men before him had sought the honour of being the first to erect a permanent theatre within the city, only to be thwarted by opposition from hard-line conservatives within the Senate.[49] Never one to be outshone, Pompey devised an ingenious way of deflecting potential criticism: he crowned his theatre with a temple to Venus Victrix, positioned above the uppermost tiers of the *cavea* in such a way that it towered over the performance area below. This novel design feature allowed Pompey to present the complex as a *templum* rather than a *theatrum*, in a manner wholly consistent with traditional Roman building practices.[50]

---

[48] On the artworks, cf. Plin. *HN* 7.34, 35.39, 35.114, 35.132; discussion in Fuchs 1982; Beard 2007: 24–6; Russell 2016: 176–8; Beacham 2016: 546–8. According to Plutarch (*Pomp.* 42.4), the plan for Pompey's theatre was based on the theatre of Mitylene on the island of Lesbos, which Pompey visited in 62 BCE. Parts of the theatre are visible on the Severan Marble Plan, although the interpretation of the fragments has been debated: see Russell 2016: 159–60, with additional references.

[49] See Manuwald 2011: 57–61.

[50] Tert. *De spect.* 10: *non theatrum, sed Veneris templum nuncupavit*; cf. Gell. *NA* 10.1.7; Plin. *HN* 8.20; Beard 2007: 23.

Figure 2.1 3-D model of the Theatre of Pompey, general view, looking southeast by James E. Packer and John Burge (2002). Reproduced by permission of James E. Packer.

And yet, despite Pompey's show of religious piety, the primary function of the new complex was never in doubt: this was, above all else, a space for entertainment. That fact must have been readily apparent to anyone who attended the inaugural games of September 55, held to commemorate Pompey's victories against the Cilician pirates and King Mithridates.[51] Audiences were treated to an action-packed programme of musical and athletic events extending over several days.[52] There were lavish revivals of *Clytemnestra* and the *Trojan Horse*, each production involving a cast of several hundred actors and live animals, not to mention a prop collection numbering well over a thousand items.[53] Veteran actors came out of retirement specially to make an appearance at this once-in-a-lifetime

---

[51] Cic. *Pis.* 65, with Ascon. 1 Clark; Nisbet 1961: 199. Gellius' claim (*NA* 10.17) that the complex was dedicated during Pompey's third consulship in 52 cannot be accepted (Russell 2016: 164–5).

[52] Plut. *Pomp.* 52.4; Dio 39.38.1 (ἀγῶνας ... γυμνικοὺς καὶ μουσικούς).

[53] Cic. *Fam.* 7.1.3. The *Clytemnestra* was written by Accius, the *Trojan Horse* by either Livius Andronicus or Naevius. The props had been exhibited previously as spoils at Pompey's triumph in 61 BCE: cf. App. *Mith.* 16; Plin. *HN* 37.14; Russell 2016: 163.

Figure 2.2 3-D model of the Theatre of Pompey, view of stage and *cavea* by James E. Packer and John Burge (2002). Reproduced by permission of James E. Packer.

celebration. There were also mimes, Oscan and Greek plays, athletic contests and wild-beast hunts. Pompey ensured that nothing was omitted, no expense spared. In a public speech delivered not long before the dedication of the theatre, Cicero gushed at the prospect of witnessing 'the most elaborate and splendid games in living memory'; what 'delight of the eyes and ears' (*oculorum et aurium delectationi*) could be sweeter than that which Pompey had in store?[54]

In actual fact, the games left Cicero profoundly disappointed. Writing to a friend a few weeks after the event, he relates how one of the star actors lost his voice in the middle of a monologue; he complains of his boredom at having to sit through day after day of senseless fighting and killing; as for the other shows, they were 'mediocre' (*mediocres*) at best; people were watching the mimes 'half-asleep' (*semisomni*).[55] The whole spectacle was, in short, a lesson in style over substance. The general public marvelled at all the razzmatazz, of course; they knew no better, as far as Cicero was

[54] Cic. *Pis.* 65–66.   [55] Cic. *Fam.* 7.1.1–3.

concerned. But for a man of Cicero's refined tastes, Pompey's games failed to hit the right notes.

It is generally agreed that Cicero began working on the *De Legibus* in the late 50s BCE – that is, in the years immediately following the completion of Pompey's theatre. Might we read his commentary on the popular music of the stage as somehow overshadowed by this historic occasion? It could be argued, perhaps, that he was overstating his disappointment as a consolatory gesture to his friend Marcus Marius, who evidently regretted having been absent from Rome during the games. However, we have good reason to suspect that Cicero's disapproval was genuine. There can be no doubt that the music produced in Pompey's theatre would have been considerably louder and showier than what Roman audiences had been used to. Based on traces of the original ground-plan in the modern topography of Rome, it has been estimated that the stage of the theatre was about seventy metres wide. Filling this huge stage, as Wiseman points out, would have 'demanded music and dance, not just words'.[56] We might reasonably wonder, therefore, whether the lingering impression of Pompey's tiresomely 'overblown spectacle' (*apparatus ... spectatio*) prompted in some way Cicero's nostalgia for the simple music of the past. Flamboyance was evidently not a trait that Cicero admired in contemporary musicians. Writing in the mid-50s, he expresses his dislike of citharodes who expended all their energies on attention-grabbing preludes, only then to rush through the remainder of the performance 'in such a way that they seem not to want to be listened to'.[57] The musical accompaniments of the mime also lacked the dignified restraint that Cicero demanded in the *ludi scaenici*. In the *Pro Caelio*, he comments on the fact that mimes typically concluded with the playing of noisy *scabella* (foot clappers) and the raising of the stage curtain – these were qualities of a vulgar farce, not of a proper play (*non fabulae*).[58] Amidst the current craze for amplification, both architectural and sonic, the old-fashioned Roman predilection for *severitas iucunda* must have seemed increasingly like a relic of the distant past.

---

[56] Wiseman 2015: 89; echoed by Goldberg 2018: 142: 'the very monumentality of Pompey's theatre, not to mention the stage effects it encouraged, seems antithetical to a purely dramatic art'. The reference at Cic. *Fam.* 7.1.2 to the actor Aesopus' voice failing during the opening games may indicate that he could not fill the big theatre (Moore 2012: 77, n. 28). The large *scaenae frons* would have assisted the acoustics of the theatre, but this may have been a later Augustan addition (Wiles 2019: 80).
[57] Cic. *De Orat.* 2.325: *sic ad reliqua transeunt ut audientiam fieri sibi non velle videantur*. On the *citharoedi prooemium*, see Power 2010: 187–200.
[58] Cic. *Cael.* 65. The evidence for the musical accompaniment of the mime is compiled and analysed by Skulimowska 1966 and Wootton 2004.

Equally concerning was the impact of Pompey's theatre on the political dynamics of the games. Pompey used the spoils of his victories to create for the Roman people a public forum in which they could come together and make their voices heard. It is true that Roman audiences had long been accustomed to express themselves vocally in the theatre, and often in large numbers.[59] But Pompey's theatre represented an entirely new breed of entertainment venue. Ancient sources suggest that the theatre could hold anywhere between 17,580 and 40,000 spectators; modern estimates suggest a capacity closer to 25,000.[60] In simple terms, therefore, Pompey made it possible for larger numbers of people to congregate within a single space, thereby increasing their visibility (and audibility) within the urban environment. Moreover, unlike earlier Roman theatres, which were largely exposed to the elements, Pompey's theatre was 'an enclosed space, sealed off from the surrounding city by high walls on all sides, allowing no sense of interconnection with the sordid and unruly world of the street'.[61] This served to 'join actors and audience in a shared commitment to the performance', directing the attention of spectators inwards, towards the performers on the stage and towards each other, and so removing the potential for external distractions.[62] For a VIP spectator like Cicero, seated at ground level in the *orchestra* with his fellow senators and wedged in between the *cavea* and the stage, the experience of watching a performance must have been unlike anything else: in front, the performers raised aloft on the stage projecting a dizzying array of sights and sounds into the crowd; behind, tiers of seats descending from the lofty entrance of Venus' temple, filled with hordes of people gesticulating, shouting, chanting and hissing. Pompey's theatre was a true assault on the senses, and that would only have contributed to the politically charged atmosphere of the performances staged within it.

In a two-line epigram written almost 150 years after the building's completion, Martial links the behaviour of audiences in Pompey's theatre with the famous myth of Orpheus and the lyre: 'the *cithara*, the instrument which uprooted forests and kept wild animals in check, has often been thrown out of Pompey's theatre'.[63] Martial's words powerfully encapsulate the importance of the *theatrum Pompeianum* as a space where musical

---

[59] The temporary theatres that were erected for the games during the late Republic could be exceedingly large and elaborate; see Manuwald 2011: 63.
[60] Pliny *HN* 36: 115; Beacham and Denard 2003: 129.   [61] Wiles 2019: 78.
[62] Goldberg 2018: 145.
[63] Mart. *Ep.* 14.166: *[cithara] de Pompeiano saepe est eiecta theatro | quae duxit silvas detinuitque feras.*

culture was routinely consumed and contested by Roman audiences. The image of the *cithara* stripped of its harmonising potential, silenced by the braying masses, provides a striking metaphor for the political power of the *vox populi*. Martial's vision of Pompey's theatre would certainly have been recognisable to a Roman spectator of the late Republic. Writing in the mid-50s, Cicero describes how 'the whole theatre' (*theatra tota*) would erupt whenever an actor misspoke or got out of time with the music, despite the fact that the people protesting had no formal training in the art of rhythm and melody (*ars numerorum ac modorum*).[64] The actor's vocalisation was scrutinised particularly closely: 'how much more effeminate and luxurious (*molliores ... et delicatiores*) are ornamentations (*flexiones*) and falsetto notes (*falsae voculae*) in singing than plain notes firmly held! And yet, the former are criticised not only by persons of good taste (*austeri*) but, if used too often, even by the masses'.[65] The masses were equally sensitive to the nuances of instrumental performance. Cicero comments on the ability of Roman audiences to recognise 'Antiope' or 'Andromache' from the very first note played by the *tibicen*.[66] The author of the anonymous *Rhetorica ad Herennium*, dated to the late 80s BCE, speaks of citharodes being ejected from the stage for singing with an unpleasant voice or for employing unseemly body movements.[67] Elite prejudices aside, these testimonies clearly speak to the fact that Roman theatre-goers were engaged and discerning listeners, and were willing and able to voice their dissent when they felt that the quality of the musical accompaniment was not up to scratch.[68]

---

[64] Cic. *De Orat.* 3.196: *quotus enim quisque est qui teneat artem numerorum ac modorum? at in eis si paulum modo offensum est, ut aut contractione brevius fieret aut productione longius, theatra tota reclamant*; cf. *Parad.* 26: *histrio si paulum se movit extra numerum, aut si versus pronuntiatus est syllaba una brevior aut longior, exsibilatur, exploditur*. It should be noted that in at least one of these passages Cicero refers to movement, so it is not always clear whether the audience is responding to the actor's vocalisation or to his dance moves (or both).

[65] Cic. *De Orat.* 3.98: *quanto molliores sunt et delicatiores in cantu flexiones et falsae voculae quam certae et severae! quibus tamen non modo austeri, sed, si saepius fiunt, multitudo ipsa reclamat.*

[66] Cic. *Acad.* 2.20, 2.86. Jocelyn (1967: 253–4) argues persuasively that these are not titles of plays, as generally assumed, but names of characters who are about to sing. On the relationship between music and memory in Roman comedy, see Moore 2021.

[67] *Rhet. Her.* 4.60: *uti citharoedus ... si, cum magnam populo commorit iis rebus expectationem, repente, silentio facto, vocem mittat acerbissimam cum turpissimo corporis motu, quo melius ornatus et magis fuerit expectatus, eo magis derisus et contemptus eicitur*; cf. Cic. *Off.* 1.146: *itaque ut in fidibus musicorum aures vel minima sentiunt, sic nos, si acres ac diligentes iudices esse volumus animadversoresque vitiorum, magna saepe intellegemus ex parvis*; Hor. *Ars P.* 355–6: *citharoedus | ridetur, chorda qui semper oberrat eadem.*

[68] For similarly discerning audiences at Alexandria, cf. Dio Chrys. *Orat.* 32.46; Athen. *Deipn.* 4.176e. See also Smith 2006 on the behaviour of theatre audiences in Early Modern England.

In summary, the advent of Pompey's theatre provides an important historical backdrop against which to situate Cicero's philosophical reflections on music. Cicero believed that the moral character of all people – educated or not – was conditioned for better or for worse by the kind of music they were exposed to. This is the view put forward in the *De Legibus*, and it is reiterated in several other works.[69] He also believed that the urban masses were fickle and volatile, their passions easily aroused.[70] For these reasons, it mattered what forms music took and in what spaces it was heard. However, this was not simply an abstract philosophical concern. At a time of increasing political instability in Rome, Cicero believed strongly that philosophy could solve present-day crises.[71] Music had the potential to heal political divisions as well as to exacerbate them. And that is why it was essential that Roman politicians were aware of its 'extraordinary power' and were able to harness that power in ways that were beneficial to the wider civic community.

The Role of Music in Late-Republican Oratory and Rhetorical Invective

Musical culture impinged on the political activities of Roman elites in various ways. As Zorzetti emphasises, one of the chief responsibilities of aediles was to recruit artists for performances during public festivals.[72] Many high-ranking senators counted musicians and other theatrical personnel among their clients and *familiares*.[73] Perhaps the most important way in which Roman politicians engaged with music, however, was through the art of rhetoric. The vocations of orator and musician were closely associated in the Roman imagination by virtue of the fact that both were engaged in the art of charming listeners. According to Cicero, the skill of orator and lyre-player alike could be assessed by the 'intelligent listener' on the basis of how they moved their audience.[74] In the *De Oratore*, Cicero likens the appearance and voice of the orator to the strings of a lyre: 'for the

---

[69] At *De Orat.* 3.197, for instance, Cicero speaks of the 'extraordinary power' (*summa vis*) of rhythm and melody to arouse feelings of excitement, indolence, joy and sorrow.

[70] Cf. Cic. *Att.* 1.16.11 (*illa contionalis hirudo aerari, misera ac ieiuna plebecula*); *De Orat.* 1.118 (*haec turba et barbaria forensis*); *Dom.* 89 (*multitudinem hominum ex servis, ex conductis, ex facinerosis, ex egentibus congregatam*).

[71] On Cicero's conception of the purpose of philosophy, see Long 1995 and 2003: 73–5.

[72] Zorzetti 1991: 326.

[73] For example, Julius Caesar and the singer Tigellius (Porph. *ad* Hor. *Sat.* 1.2.2) or Mark Antony and the citharode Anaxenor (Plut. *Ant.* 24.1–2; Strabo 14.1.41; *Syll.*³ 766).

[74] Cic. *Brut.* 199.

tones of the voice are keyed up like the strings of an instrument, so as to answer to every touch, high, low, fast, slow, loud, soft'.[75] Even the audience itself could be imagined as a kind of musical instrument. 'The ears of the people', Cicero states, are 'a kind of pipes' (*tamquam tibiae*), which the orator must learn to master.[76] An orator's words played upon the emotions of listeners just as the lyre-player's hand played upon the strings (*tamquam fidibus manum*).[77]

The value of music for the Roman orator was not simply confined to the realm of metaphor and simile. Music had a practical utility as well. Among the ancient Greeks, Dionysius of Halicarnassus explains, 'the science of oratory was a kind of music' (μουσική γάρ τις ἦν καὶ ἡ τῶν πολιτικῶν λόγων ἐπιστήμη): 'in oratory, as in music, the phrases possess melody, rhythm, variety and appropriateness; so that here too the ear delights in the melodies, is stirred by the rhythms, welcomes the variations, and all the time desires what is appropriate to the occasion'.[78] Cicero makes a similar point with regard to Roman rhetoric: 'there are two qualities which please the ear – namely, sound and rhythm' (*duae sunt igitur res quae permulceant auris, sonus et numerus*); 'there is even in speech a more concealed sort of singing (*est autem etiam in dicendo quidam cantus obscurior*)'.[79] In crafting his style of delivery, then, an orator was expected to pay close attention to the musical intonations of his voice. That meant cultivating not only the correct vocal tone, but also the correct volume and stability. Politicians at Rome were routinely called upon to deliver lengthy speeches in front of large crowds in the Forum and other open-air spaces. In the face of such physically demanding work, relying on one's innate ability was not always enough. Consequently, many orators sought guidance from professional voice trainers (*phonasci*), adopting a strict regimen of vocal exercises of the sort commonly undertaken by singers and actors.[80]

---

[75] Cic. *De Orat.* 3.216: *totumque corpus hominis et eius omnis vultus omnesque voces, ut nervi in fidibus, ita sonant ut a motu animi quoque sunt pulsae. nam voces ut chordae sunt intentae, quae ad quemque tactum respondeant, acuta gravis, cita tarda, magna parva.*

[76] Cic. *Brut.* 192.

[77] Cic. *Brut.* 200. Cf. *De leg. agr.* 2.68, comparing the self-serving tribune Rullus to a musician who 'sings inwardly to himself', i.e. so that only he and those closest to him could hear (for the expression *intus canere*, cf. also *Verr.* 2.1.53).

[78] Dion. Hal. *Comp.* 11: καὶ γὰρ ἐν ταύτῃ καὶ μέλος ἔχουσιν αἱ λέξεις καὶ ῥυθμὸν καὶ μεταβολὴν καὶ πρέπον, ὥστε καὶ ἐπὶ ταύτης ἡ ἀκοὴ τέρπεται μὲν τοῖς μέλεσιν, ἄγεται δὲ τοῖς ῥυθμοῖς, ἀσπάζεται δὲ τὰς μεταβολάς, ποθεῖ δ' ἐπὶ πάντων τὸ οἰκεῖον; cf. *Comp.* 25 on the poetic and lyrical qualities of speech.

[79] Cic. *Orat.* 163, 57. It was a great badge of honour for an orator to possess a 'melodious voice' (*vox canora*): cf. Cic. *Brut.* 268 on Lucius Lentulus; *Brut.* 303 on Hortensius.

[80] Cf. *Rhet. Her.* 3.11; Sen. *Ep.* 15.7; Quint. *Inst.* 11.3.19; Suet. *Nero* 12; Barker 2010. Cicero is somewhat sceptical of this practice (cf. *De Orat.* 1.251).

Engaging with the *ars musica* therefore provided tangible benefits to the practising orator. But it also entailed serious risks. There was a perceived danger that orators might strive to emulate the techniques of professional musicians to such an extent that their speech could be confused with actual singing. Hence, Dionysius of Halicarnassus is careful to distinguish between speech that is *eumeles* (tuneful) and speech that is *emmeles* (literally, in tune).[81] In a similar vein, Cicero criticises orators from Phrygia and Caria for performing epilogues that sounded almost like musical show-tunes (*paene canticum*).[82] Inflections of the voice, if taken to such extremes, were not only unappealing to the ear; they also signalled the speaker's lack of self-control and, by extension, his failure to conform to proper standards of Roman masculinity. The ideal orator, in Cicero's view, should exercise the utmost care in regulating both his body and his voice: he should stand upright at all times, performing 'with manly bend of the body' (*virili laterum flexione*); he should display 'no softness in his neck' (*nulla mollitia cervicum*); and, above all, he should avoid 'the kind of musical delivery' (*in dicendo quidam cantus*) achieved through 'contortions of the voice' (*vocis inflexiones*).[83] The young Julius Caesar apparently expressed a similar concern about the encroachment of song on modes of aristocratic vocal performance. Quintilian attributes to him the following witticism: 'If you are singing, you are singing badly; if you are reading, you are singing' (*si cantas, male cantas; si legis, cantas*).[84] As Habinek points out, 'the assignment of this saying to Julius Caesar while still in *toga praetexta* ... fits a pattern whereby observation (or not) of the boundary between oratory and song becomes an indicator of one's success at mastering the conventions of Roman manliness'.[85]

As well as recognising the influence of music on Roman oratorical technique, it is also important to consider how musical themes were exploited by late-republican orators for polemical effect. I will discuss some specific examples later in the chapter, but for now it may be helpful to make some general observations. Three kinds of musical activities are singled out for criticism in Roman rhetorical discourse: dancing, singing

---

[81] Dion. Hal. *Comp.* 11.   [82] Cic. *Orat.* 57.   [83] Cic. *De Orat.* 1.231; cf. Cic. *Orat.* 59.
[84] Quint. *Inst.* 1.8.2. Quintilian's point in citing Caesar's *bon mot* is to emphasise the distinction between the 'manly' kind of poetic recitation (*lectio virilis*), which is song-*like*, and the 'effeminate' kind (*effeminata*), which is virtually indistinguishable from a *canticum* heard in the theatre.
[85] Habinek 2005: 101. This idea recurs frequently in Latin literature of the imperial period: cf. Plin. *Ep.* 2.14.13; Quint. *Inst.* 11.3.58; Tac. *Dial.* 26.3, *Ann.* 4.61. On the connection between oratory and masculinity, see further Graf 1991: 44–5; Gleason 1995; Gunderson 2000; Corbeill 2004: 107–39; Habinek 2005.

and attendance at private musical concerts (*symphoniae*). Scholarly attention has focused mostly on dancing, although dancing and music-making are very often associated.[86] For example, Anthony Corbeill has highlighted how dancing is heavily bound up in Roman moral strictures relating to sexual practice, alcoholic consumption and private expenditure.[87] Cicero often uses the image of the 'dancer' (*saltator*) to encapsulate what Corbeill calls the 'immoderate feast': Clodius, Verres, Catiline and others are associated with dancers or given the epithet *saltator* themselves (or, worse still, *saltatrix*); some are censured specifically for dancing naked at banquets.[88] Alternatively, the charge of dancing could be levelled against orators whose performances were deemed excessively flamboyant. Sextus Titius, tribune of the *plebs* in 99 BCE, was so notorious for his oratorical gestures that he even had a dance named after him (the Titius), while L. Afranius, the consul of 60 BCE, is alleged by Cassius Dio to have been 'a better dancer than a politician'.[89] Not even the most respected orator was immune from such slander. At the trial of Sulla in 62, Lucius Torquatus attacked the great Hortensius by addressing him mockingly as 'a posturer and a Dionysia' (Dionysia was the name of a famous dancer of the time). Interestingly, Hortensius embraced this accusation with gleeful sarcasm, replying 'in a soft and gentle voice' (*voce molli atque demissa*): 'I would rather be a Dionysia, Torquatus, yes, a Dionysia, than like you, a stranger to the Muses, to Venus and to Dionysus'.[90] Even Cicero himself was allegedly accused late on in his career of dressing like a dancer and adopting a dancer's poses while speaking.[91]

---

[86] On the role of dance in Roman rhetorical discourse, see Corbeill 1996: 135–9; Naerebout 2007; Laurence 2009: 115–7; Alonso Fernández 2015; Schlapbach 2018; Schlapbach 2020.

[87] Corbeill 1996: 135–9.

[88] Cf. Cic. *In Clod.* 22, *Sest.* 116 (Clodius); *Cat.* 2.23 (Catiline); *Ver.* 2.3.23 (Verres). Conversely, Cicero defends the consul Murena and king Deiotarus from the accusation of dancing, claiming (disingenuously, it would seem) that attacks of this nature were slanderous, undignified and unwarranted: *Mur.* 13; *Deiot.* 26–28.

[89] Cic. *Brut.* 225; Dio Cass. 37.49.

[90] Gel. *NA* 1.5.2-3: '*Dionysia malo equidem esse quam quod tu, Torquate*, ἄμουσος, ἀναφρόδιτος, ἀπροσδιόνυσος'. On the significance of this passage, see Gleason 1995: 75; Gunderson 2000: 128–30. At Cic. *Rosc. Com.* 23, the dancer Dionysia is said to command huge sums of money for her performances.

[91] Dio Cass. 46.18.2 (Calenus' speech against Cicero): ὥσπερ οἱ ὀρχησταὶ οἱ τὰς ποικιλίας τῶν ἐνθυμημάτων διδάσκοντές σε τοῖς σχήμασιν (like the dancers who teach you the subtleties of rhetorical argumentation by their poses). Dio's source is disputed: Calenus' speech may be modelled on anti-Ciceronian literature of the first century BCE, such as the lost polemics of Asinius Pollio or the pseudo-Sallustian *Invectiva in Ciceronem* (*pace* Gabba 1957: 318–21; Millar 1964: 52–55); or he may have fabricated the speech by inverting the rhetorical arguments of Cicero's *Philippics* (*pace* Burden-Stevens 2018: 130).

Figure 2.3 Wall painting depicting a musical concert. The band comprises a singer or reciter, who holds a text in her hand, a *tibicen*, wearing a *phorbeia*, and a female *cithara*-player. Two reclining banqueters watch the performance. From the Insula Orientalis (II.4,19), Herculaneum, Italy, ca. 1–79 CE. Museo Archeologico Nazionale, Naples, inv. no. 9021. Credit: Azoor Photo / Alamy Stock Photo.

Accusations of dancing in Roman invective often go hand in hand with accusations of singing. This tendency is clearly illustrated in the *Second Catilinarian*, where Cicero characterises Catiline's followers as having learned 'not only to love and be loved, to dance and sing (*saltare et cantare*), but also to brandish daggers and infuse poison'.[92] The speeches of Scipio Aemilianus and Cato the Elder also combine the charges of singing and dancing (as discussed in Chapter 1). Again, a common theme of such attacks is the association of musical proficiency with passive, and thus unmanly, sexual proclivities.

The third category – attendance at musical concerts – may seem a less obvious target, given that it is not directly concerned with active performance. However, in the eyes of many Romans (and Greeks), convivial music-making evoked ideas of decadence and exotic pleasure (see Figs. 2.3 and 2.4).[93] In several of his speeches, Cicero vilifies his opponents for

---

[92] Cic. *Cat.* 2.23.
[93] In addition to the examples cited below, cf. Cic. *Verr.* 2.3.105, 2.5.31, 2.5.92; *Cael.* 35; *Pro Gallio* fr. 1 Crawford.

Figure 2.4 Wall painting depicting Pygmies at an outdoor banquet. A seated *tibicen* playing a Phrygian pipe accompanies scenes of sex and drinking. From the House of the Doctor, Pompeii, ca. 59–79 CE. Museo Archeologico Nazionale, Naples, inv. no. 113196. Credit: Azoor Photo / Alamy Stock Photo.

obsessively collecting slave musicians (*symphoniaci*) for use as private entertainers. For example, Verres, while governor of Sicily, is accused of taking possession of half-a-dozen *symphoniaci homines* from a captured pirate vessel and having them shipped off to Rome as a gift for a friend.[94] As I have discussed elsewhere, we should not necessarily conclude from such passages that Cicero was opposed to the ownership of *symphoniaci* as such.[95] What he takes exception to are the specific circumstances in which the slaves in question exchanged hands – through bribery, duplicity and misappropriation. Nevertheless, the *symphonia* was a potent rhetorical symbol because it came with a distinct cultural baggage. It conjured thoughts of the degenerate Hellenistic kings, with their lavish symposia and hordes of effete musicians. It is no coincidence, then, that we often find references to convivial music-making in texts attacking the abuses of Roman magistrates who had served in the Greek East.[96]

---

[94] Cic. *Ver.* 2.5.64, 2.5.73.   [95] Morgan 2019: 263–4.
[96] Cf. Plut. *Luc.* 40.1, on the choruses and musical performances (χοροῖς καὶ ἀκροάμασιν) employed by L. Licinius Lucullus at his daily banquets.

To summarise: music influenced the rhetorical and political activities of late-republican elites in ways that were perceived as both positive and negative. On the one hand, music was a vital part of the orator's toolkit, aiding in the pursuit of balanced and melodious delivery. The relationship between the musician and his audience also served as a useful analogy for the relationship between the orator and his audience. On the other hand, because of its associations with the world of showbusiness, music remained a deeply ambivalent and problematic aspect of the rhetorical art. The critique of 'sing-song' oratory was born out of an elitist concern that the 'vulgar' and 'effeminate' music of the stage would infiltrate the channels of public political discourse, disrupting the mechanisms by which Roman aristocrats asserted their *auctoritas* in the eyes of their fellow citizens. It would be easy to view this critique as simply the product of conservative fearmongering. And yet, music played an important role in defining how Roman elites cultivated and maintained their public image. For all Cicero's warnings of the dangers of imitating professional musicians, there were plenty of high-ranking politicians who looked to the practice of *tibicines* and *fidicines* in search of inspiration – including one of the greatest orators the Republic ever produced, Gaius Sempronius Gracchus.

Gaius Gracchus and the *Fistula*

The career of Gaius Gracchus provides a revealing case study for examining how Roman politicians used music to curry popular favour. At the end of Cicero's *De Oratore*, the interlocutor Crassus relates a curious anecdote concerning the controversial tribune of the 120s BCE. Gaius Gracchus, so the story goes, while addressing the people, used to have a piper (*fistulator*) stationed in a well-concealed location nearby, whose role was to feed him certain musical cues as he spoke. In this way, the piper was able to moderate the tone of his rhetoric, ensuring that he maintained the appropriate level of intensity throughout:

> '*quid, ad aures nostras et actionis suavitatem quid est vicissitudine et varietate et commutatione aptius? itaque idem Gracchus (quod potes audire, Catule, ex Licinio cliente tuo, litterato homine, quem servum sibi ille habuit ad manum) cum eburneola solitus est habere fistula qui staret occulte post ipsum cum contionaretur peritum hominem qui inflaret celeriter eum sonum quo illum aut remissum excitaret aut a contentione revocaret.*' '*audivi mehercule*', inquit Catulus, '*et saepe sum admiratus hominis cum diligentiam, tum etiam doctrinam et scientiam.*' (Cic. De Orat. 3.225)

'What is better suited to delight the ear and to produce agreeableness of delivery than change, variety and modulation? Accordingly, Gaius Gracchus (as you may hear, Catulus, from your client Licinius, a man of letters, who was a slave of Gracchus and acted as his amanuensis) used to employ a skilful fellow with an ivory pipe to stand concealed behind him whenever he addressed the people, and who was promptly to sound such a note as might either rouse him when he had become relaxed, or restrain him when he was overexerting himself.' 'Indeed, I have heard this before', said Catulus, 'and have often admired the industriousness of the man, as well as his learning and knowledge.'

The story of Gracchus and his *fistulator* generated a remarkable level of interest among later writers. Aside from Cicero, the anecdote is reported by no fewer than six ancient authors, some as late as the third or fourth century CE.[97] While the gist of their accounts is broadly similar, they construe the relationship between orator and musician in different ways. Cicero maintains that the music of the *fistulator* served as both a stimulant and a sedative to Gracchus. This view is echoed by Valerius Maximus and Quintilian. However, Aulus Gellius offers a different opinion:

> *sed nequaquam sic est, ut a vulgo dicitur, canere tibia solitum qui pone eum loquentem staret, et variis modis tum demulcere animum actionemque eius, tum intendere. quid enim foret ista re ineptius, si, ut planipedi saltanti, ita Graccho contionanti numeros et modos et frequentamenta quaedam varia tibicen incineret? sed qui hoc compertius memoriae tradiderunt, stetisse in circumstantibus dicunt occultius, qui fistula brevi sensim graviusculum sonum inspiraret ad reprimendum sedandumque inpetus vocis eius effervescentes; namque inpulsu et instinctu extraneo naturalis illa Gracchi vehementia indiguisse, non, opinor, existimanda est.* (Gell. NA 1.11.11–14)

> But it is not at all the case, as is generally stated, that someone would stand behind him as he spoke, playing a *tibia*, and by varying the pitch of his music calmed his emotions and his delivery at one moment, and intensified them the next. For what could be more absurd than if a piper played rhythms and tunes and certain varied ornamentations to Gracchus as he addressed the assembly, as if for a dancing mime performer? But more reliable authorities state that the musician took his place unobserved in the audience and, from time to time, sounded on a short *fistula* quite a deep note, in order to restrain and calm the exuberant energy of his voice. For it is unthinkable in my view that Gracchus' innate vehemence required any external impulse or incentive.

---

[97] Val. Max. 8.10.praef.1; Quint. *Inst.* 1.11.27; Plut. *Mor.* 456a, *Ti. Gracch.* 2.5–6; Gell. *NA* 1.11.10–15; Dio Cas. 25.82.2; Amm. Marc. 30.4.19.

This idea that the piper acted merely as a check on the naturally hot-headed Gracchus is supported by both Plutarch and Cassius Dio.

Further uncertainty surrounds the nature of Gracchus' pipe itself. In the sources, the instrument is variously described as a *fistula*, *tibia*, *tonarion* and *phonaskikon organon*. The Latin term *fistula* generally refers to a single pipe without a reed, but it is sometimes used for several of those pipes bound together (i.e. panpipes).[98] There appears to be some confusion in the sources as to whether the Gracchan instrument produced more than one pitch. Quintilian asserts that the *fistulator* played a range of notes or tones (*modi*), which in turn dictated how Gracchus pitched his voice.[99] However, Cicero's description indicates that the playing of a single note (*eum sonum*) was sufficient for Gracchus to regain his composure whenever his speech became too vehement or too lax. Gellius, likewise, dismisses the idea that the piper played multiple 'rhythms and tunes and certain varied ornamentations' (*numeros et modos et frequentamenta quaedam varia*), suggesting that a single 'quite deep sound' (*graviusculum sonum*) was all that was required. On this basis, scholars have argued that Gracchus' *fistula* was probably not a panpipe but rather a single-reed pipe or pitch pipe, analogous to the Greek *syrinx monokalamos* or *monaulos*.[100]

There are, however, two complicating factors to consider here. First, why does Gellius refer to the pipe as both a *tibia* and a *fistula*? *Tibia* could mean a single-reed pipe, but it is more commonly used to describe a pair of pipes with double reeds, of the kind played in the theatre. It is important to note that Gellius uses the terms *tibia* and *tibicen* specifically in connection with the idea that Gracchus' speeches resembled a kind of mime performance. The identification of the pipe as a *tibia* makes sense in this context, since the *tibia* was the theatrical instrument par excellence. In Gellius' opinion, however, this was an 'absurd' (*ineptius*) notion: the piper merely sounded a single note; and a short *fistula* was more suitable for this role than the *tibia*, with its large melodic range. Secondly, why do Plutarch and Quintilian give different Greek terms for the instrument? Plutarch uses the periphrastic expression φωνασκικὸν ὄργανον (literally, sounding instrument), while

---

[98] Cf. *TLL* s.v. 'fistula', Vol. VI, 1, 828, 73–830, 69 (Bacherler).
[99] Quint. *Inst.* 1.11.27: *cui* (sc. Graccho) *contionanti consistens post eum musicus fistula, quam tonarion vocant, modos quibus deberet intendi ministrabat.*
[100] David 1983: 106; Jory 1995: 150; Schulz 2020: 371; cf. Athen. 4.184a (*syrinx monokalamos*); Plin. *NH* 7.204; Mart. 14.64.2; Athen. 14.175f–176c (*monaulos*). The reference at Val. Max. 8.10.praef.1 to Gracchus' *fistula* being made of ivory (*eburnea*) is not especially revealing, since ivory was commonly used for the manufacturing of both panpipes and single pipes in antiquity.

Quintilian opts for the obscure *tonarion* (from *tonos*, pitch).[101] *Tonarion* appears nowhere else in Latin or Greek, and it is hard to see why Quintilian would have favoured this term over *syrinx* unless he had in mind some kind of technical instrument in use among rhetorical specialists.[102] In general, it seems that the lack of consistency in our sources regarding the name and function of the pipe reflects a divergence of opinion about whether Gracchus' 'music' was inspired by the Roman stage or by Greek rhetorical practice.

How, then, might we explain the enduring fascination with Gracchus' *fistula*? One explanation is that the story reflected and reinforced the posthumous reputation of Gaius Gracchus as an oratorical maverick. In the *De Oratore*, Crassus uses the example of the pipe-player to illustrate Gracchus' unrivalled *diligentia*, *doctrina* and *scientia*. Other writers express a similar admiration for Gracchus' ingenuity and eloquence (Quintilian, for example, calls Gracchus 'the leading orator of his age'). However, in another sense, the story also served as a cautionary tale about the dangers of mixing music and politics. In Cicero's dialogue, Crassus urges the other interlocutors not to take Gracchus' technique as a literal example of how an orator should act, but rather as a lesson in the importance of *moderatio*: 'You should leave the piper at home, but take down to the forum the understanding that comes from this practice.'[103] In an ideal world, Cicero implies, public speakers would be able to moderate their own speech without the need for extraneous musical support. Gracchus' reliance on the slave piper signalled a dangerous precedent, in that it threatened to collapse the boundary between the theatrical stage and the political stage. It is precisely on these grounds that Gellius questions the credibility of Cicero's version of the anecdote. Ammianus Marcellinus, likewise, emphasises the theatrical nature of Gracchus' oratory, commenting on how the histrionic orators of the age seemed only 'to lack the *contionaria fistula* of Gracchus behind them'.[104]

---

[101] The term φωνασκός (adj. φωνασκικός) refers to a professional voice-trainer: *LSJ*, s.v. φωνασκός; for the Latin *phonascus*, cf. Quint. 2.8.1, 11.3.19, 11.3.22; Tac. *Ann.* 14.15; Suet. *Aug.* 84.2, *Nero* 25.3; Barker 2010.

[102] West (1992: 113–4) cites a Byzantine lexical source in which it is stated that a chorus-trainer might give his choir their starting note 'by piping on the so-called *epitonion*'. According to West, 'this is likely to have been a reedless pipe, since the pitch of a reed pipe would be more liable to inconstancy'. However, this source is unique and can hardly be used as evidence for choral conventions in the time of Gracchus.

[103] Cic. *De Orat.* 3.227.   [104] Amm. Marc. 30.4.19.

The story of Gaius Gracchus and the *fistula* therefore encapsulates the fraught relationship between music and oratory in Roman culture. Not without reason did Gracchus ensure that his musical accompanist remained out of sight of his audience; if the illusion of decorum was to be maintained, it was essential that the musician was visible, and the music audible, to him alone.[105] But the fact remained that Gracchus depended on that music to perform at his best. Without his trusty assistant standing by and supplying him with the necessary musical prompts, his rhetoric would have become utterly unhinged, his fearsome powers reduced to naught.[106] That in turn raised serious questions about the interdependence of orator and musician. Who was controlling whom in this scenario? Was Gracchus in command of the piper, or was it actually the piper himself who was manipulating Gracchus from behind the scenes? In a society which required of its political leaders the utmost self-discipline and *gravitas*, the thought of a mere slave playing pied piper to an elected magistrate of the Roman People was deeply troubling, if not entirely unconscionable (*non ... existimanda est*, as Gellius puts it).

But Gaius Gracchus was not just any magistrate. He was a tribune of the *plebs*, and a radical one at that. To Valerius Maximus, as indeed to Cicero and his fellow *optimates*, it was a source of deep regret that a man of such considerable rhetorical talents 'preferred to be an impious revolutionary when he could have been a splendid defender of the republic' (*cum optime rem publicam tueri posset, perturbare impie maluit*).[107] Our sources repeatedly underline the fact that Gracchus employed the services of the musician precisely when he was addressing an assembly of the people (*cum contionaretur* in Cicero; *quotiens apud populum contionatus est* in Valerius Maximus; *contionanti* in Quintilian; *cum populo agente* in Gellius). Such was the strength of this association, in fact, that the Gracchan pipe even acquired the epithet *contionaria* (*tibia contionaria* in Gellius; *fistula*

---

[105] Gellius' assertion that the piper was 'among the audience' seems at odds with the idea that he was discreet (*stetisse in circumstantibus dicunt occultius*; NA 1.11.13). A possible explanation is that Gellius was trying to distinguish Gracchus' performances from those of professional actors, since in the Roman theatre musicians stood on the stage and thus were visually conspicuous: see Moore 2012: 27–8.

[106] Valerius Maximus (8.10.praef.1) articulates this point most explicitly: *ipsum calor atque impetus actionis attentum huiusce temperamenti aestimatorem esse non patiebatur* (the heatedness and vehemence of his delivery prevented him from being an attentive judge of this balance).

[107] Val. Max. 8.10.praef.1; cf. Cic. *De Orat.* 3.226, contrasting the brilliance of Gracchus' oratory with his fraudulence as a politician.

contionaria in Ammianus).¹⁰⁸ According to Quintilian, Gracchus paid particularly close attention to the *fistulator* when he was 'in the midst of his most turbulent speeches, whether he was terrifying the *optimates* or was already in fear of them' (*inter turbidissimas actiones vel terrenti optimates vel iam timenti fuit*).¹⁰⁹ In this sense, Gracchus' *fistula* was tied strongly to his reputation as a demagogue, whose populist agenda sowed the seeds of political discord at Rome. The story can be situated alongside a larger cluster of anecdotes relating to Gracchus' innovative methods of appealing directly to the people through his speeches – for example, walking around on the Rostra and speaking in the opposite direction to the *comitium*, or pulling the toga off his shoulder as he spoke.¹¹⁰

By harnessing the affective power of music for his own political gain, the tribune was playing with dangerous forces. Ironically, the moderation that Gaius Gracchus was able to cultivate through the *fistulator* was the very thing that enabled him to rile up the masses and to mobilise them against the optimate cause. Out of the pipe's melody came civic dissonance. As Dionysius of Halicarnassus wrote in the aftermath of the Civil Wars: 'From the time that Gaius Gracchus, while holding the tribunician power, destroyed the harmony of the state, [the Romans] have been perpetually murdering and banishing one another from the city and refraining from no irrevocable acts in order to gain the upper hand.'¹¹¹ In the eyes of some, it seems, Gracchus' pipe did more harm than good.

Publius Clodius: Harpist, Chorus-Leader, Entertainer Extraordinaire

In 62 BCE, a young patrician by the name of Publius Clodius Pulcher became embroiled in a public scandal. Motivated allegedly by a desire to seduce (or, worse still, to rape) Julius Caesar's wife Pompeia, Clodius had attempted to infiltrate the secret rites of the Bona Dea, at which Pompeia, as the wife of the *pontifex maximus*, was officiating. The rites were strictly closed to men, and, knowing that they were celebrated with much music

---

¹⁰⁸ The adjective *contionarius* (belonging to the *contio*) appears elsewhere only at Cic. *Q. fr.* 2.3.4 (*contionario illo populo*). Its association with a musical instrument is almost jarring: music traditionally had no place in the *contio*.
¹⁰⁹ Quint. *Inst.* 1.10.38.   ¹¹⁰ Cf. Plut. *Tib Gracch.* 2.2, *C. Gracch.* 5.3.
¹¹¹ Dion. Hal. *Ant. Rom.* 2.11.3: ἐξ οὗ δὲ Γάιος Γράκχος ἐπὶ τῆς δημαρχικῆς ἐξουσίας γενόμενος διέφθειρε τὴν τοῦ πολιτεύματος ἁρμονίαν, οὐκέτι πέπαυνται σφάττοντες ἀλλήλους καὶ φυγάδας ἐλαύνοντες ἐκ τῆς πόλεως καὶ οὐδενὸς τῶν ἀνηκέστων ἀπεχόμενοι παρὰ τὸ νικᾶν.

(μουσικῆς ἅμα πολλῆς παρούσης), Clodius had cunningly disguised himself as a female harp-player (ψαλτρία), not only sporting the correct costume (ἐσθῆτα) but even bringing his own equipment (σκευή).[112] His disguise was foiled when one of the female attendants approached him in the darkness and 'asked him to play with her, as one woman would another, and when he refused, she dragged him forward and asked who he was and where he came from'.[113] Faced with the alternative of feigning musical expertise or responding to the woman's interrogation, Clodius chose the latter. He replied that he was waiting for one of Pompeia's maids, and 'his voice betrayed him'. The impostor was angrily evicted and put on trial for sacrilege the following year.[114]

A Roman nobleman disguised as a low-born female harpist: what role-reversal could be more outlandish, more demeaning, than this? The irony was certainly not lost on Cicero. Speaking for the prosecution at Clodius' trial, the former consul painted Clodius as the antithesis of a proper Roman *paterfamilias*. Clodius wore 'womanly dress' (*muliebris ornatus*); he had 'a harp-girl's walk' (*incessus psaltriae*); he adopted an effeminate expression and spoke in a high-pitched voice (*effeminare vultum, attenuare vocem*).[115] Much to Cicero's chagrin, Clodius managed to secure his acquittal (allegedly after bribing the jury), and while his reputation was badly tarnished by the scandal, his political career was far from buried. On the contrary, his appearances in the spotlight seemed only to endear him further to the Roman masses, who admired his youthful bravado and charismatic personality. In 59, Clodius effected the highly controversial manoeuvre of having himself adopted into a plebeian family, allowing him to run for the tribunate. As tribune in 58, he put forward a swathe of populist legislation that resulted in Cicero's year-long exile from Rome. But the image of Clodius decked out in the costume of an exotic harpist still lingered in people's minds. In 56, speaking out against Clodius' actions as tribune, Cicero made a point of reminding his audience of what had happened six years earlier, when the former patrician had donned 'a saffron-coloured robe, a headdress, woman's sandals, purple stockings, brassiere and harp'. The experience of dressing up as a musician, Cicero argued, had merely prepared the ground for Clodius' latest charade: no

---

[112] Plut. *Caes.* 9.8, 10.1; cf. Juv. 6.337 (referring to Clodius as *psaltria*). On the citharodic *skeue* (comprising both equipment and attire), see Power 2010: 11. On the events surrounding the Bona Dea scandal, see Balsdon 1966; Moreau 1982; Tatum 1999: 62–86.

[113] Plut. *Caes.* 10.2.

[114] Plut. *Caes.* 10.3–6. For a different account of these events, cf. Plut. *Cic.* 28.2–4.

[115] Cic. *In Clod. et Cur.* fr. 21 Crawford.

longer Clodius the *psaltria*, but Clodius the *popularis*, the People's Champion.[116]

By 56, Clodius was at the height of his powers. Earlier that year, the Pompeian tribune T. Annius Milo was prosecuted on the charge of inciting public violence. At a *contio* held shortly before the trial was due to take place, Clodius (now aedile) orchestrated a show of force by getting his supporters to hurl insults at Pompey, who had been invited to speak on Milo's behalf.[117] The episode is vividly narrated by Plutarch:

> τέλος δέ, προελθόντος αὐτοῦ πρός τινα δίκην, ἔχων ὑφ' αὑτῷ πλῆθος ἀνθρώπων ἀσελγείας καὶ ὀλιγωρίας μεστὸν αὐτὸς μὲν εἰς ἐπιφανῆ τόπον καταστὰς ἐρωτήματα τοιαῦτα προὔβαλλε· "Τίς ἐστιν αὐτοκράτωρ ἀκόλαστος; τίς ἀνὴρ ἄνδρα ζητεῖ; τίς ἑνὶ δακτύλῳ κνᾶται τὴν κεφαλήν;" οἱ δέ, ὥσπερ χορὸς εἰς ἀμοιβαῖα συγκεκροτημένος, ἐκείνου τὴν τήβεννον ἀνασείοντος ἐφ' ἑκάστῳ μέγα βοῶντες ἀπεκρίναντο· "Πομπήϊος." (Plut. *Pomp.* 48.7)

> And finally, when Pompey made an appearance at a public trial, Clodius, accompanied by a mob of rude and insolent villains, stationed himself in a conspicuous place and put to them questions such as these: 'Who is the general with no self-control?', 'Who is the man who runs after other men?', 'Who scratches his head with one finger?' And they, like a chorus trained to sing in alternate verses, would answer each question, as he shook his toga, by shouting out 'Pompey'.

'Like a chorus trained to sing in alternate verses' (ὥσπερ χορὸς εἰς ἀμοιβαῖα συγκεκροτημένος) is how Plutarch describes the coordinated chanting of the *Clodiani*. Meanwhile, Clodius himself, cast in the role of chorus-leader, conducts the assembled choir from the Rostra with the shaking of his toga.[118] The participle συγκεκροτημένος, from the verb συγκροτέω (strike together), has appropriately musical connotations: it is almost as if the *psaltria*-turned-aedile is playing his audience 'like a hand upon the strings of a lyre' (to quote Cicero).[119] By choreographing his

---

[116] Cic. *Har. Resp.* 44: *P. Clodius a crocota, a mitra, a muliebribus soleis purpureisque fasceolis, a strophio, a psalterio, a flagitio, a stupro est factus repente popularis*. On Cicero's use of the term *popularis*, see Seager 1972; Mackie 1992.

[117] The meeting took place in the Forum on 2 February 56 BCE. Due to the ensuing violence, Milo's trial was postponed to May, but, contrary to Plutarch's suggestion, it never actually took place (Gruen 1974: 299).

[118] Waving the toga was a gesture typically used to show support for performers at the games: see Jory 1988: 73 n. 6.

[119] Cic. *Brut.* 200 (quoted above). For *krotos* associated with lyre-playing, cf. Soph. fr. 241; Posidonius fr. 62 E.-K.

supporters to respond in a certain way to his vocal cues, Clodius created the impression that the Roman people were almost literally singing from the same song sheet. Morstein-Marx aptly describes this process as a kind of 'political theatre ... characterised by highly developed methods of audience creation and response solicitation that activated a kind of ventriloquism'.[120] Plutarch's comparison of the *Clodiani* to a theatrical chorus is more than just a rhetorical conceit; the *operae Clodianae* bore a genuine resemblance to the *operae theatrales*, the professional theatrical claques hired to drum up applause and chants at the games.[121]

The events leading up to Milo's trial scarred Cicero as well as Pompey. Having returned from exile just a few months earlier, Cicero was still wary of Clodius' power and was desperate for an opportunity to cut his rival down to size. Fortunately, an opportunity presented itself a few weeks after the *contio*, when Cicero was called to speak on behalf of the tribune Publius Sestius (like Milo, Sestius had been indicted on a charge of illegally inciting violence). The speech contains some of the most devastating passages of political invective in the entire Ciceronian corpus. Clodius, unsurprisingly, emerges as the target of the fiercest criticism. A particularly memorable moment occurs near the end of the speech, when Cicero mocks Clodius for failing to attend the theatre during his tribunate out of fear of being booed by the audience. For someone so fond of theatrics, his absence from the games given by the aedile M. Scaurus was most peculiar:

> *ipse ille maxime ludius, non solum spectator, sed actor et acroama, qui omnia sororis embolia novit, qui in coetum mulierum pro psaltria adducitur, nec tuos ludos aspexit in illo ardenti tribunatu suo nec ullos alios nisi eos, a quibus vix vivus effugit.* (Cic. *Sest.* 116)

> That entertainer extraordinaire, not only a spectator, but an actor and artiste, who knows all of his sister's musical interludes and who trespassed upon a gathering of women in the guise of a harp-girl, never visited your [i.e. Scaurus'] shows during that fiery tribunate of his, nor any others except once when he scarcely escaped alive.

The theatrical language – normally out of place in a courtroom setting – emphasises Clodius' disreputable association with the stage, while hinting at his reputation for effeminacy and sexual deviance (the phrase 'knows all

---

[120] Morstein-Marx 2004: 158. On Clodius' tactics at the *contio*, see also Tan 2013.

[121] Cf. Cic. *Q. fr.* 2.3.2; *Dom.* 14. On *operae* as theatre claques, cf. Tac. *Ann.* 1.16.3: *Percennius quidam, dux olim theatralium operarum.* Theatre claques are attested already in Plautus' day: cf. *Amph.* 65–85; their role is also highlighted by Cicero at *Sest.* 115. See further Aldrete 1999: 135–8; Morstein-Marx 2004: 128–36.

of his sister's musical interludes' is a not-so-subtle allusion to Clodius' rumoured incest with his sister Clodia).[122]

Cicero goes on to describe the events that unfolded during Clodius' only visit to the theatre in 58. The *Ludi Apollinares* were being celebrated, and during one of the performances the actors all turned towards Clodius and sang the words in unison, 'These, Titus, are the results and ends of your wicked life!'.[123] This incident generated such a commotion in the audience that Clodius was actually driven out of the theatre to the sound of hissing and jeering. How ironic, Cicero observes, that 'the man who was previously accustomed to celebrate his *contiones* with an insulting outcry of singers (*cantorum convicio*), was thrown out by the voices of actual singers (*cantorum ipsorum vocibus eiciebatur*)'.[124] This is a neat turn of phrase. On the one hand, Clodius is alleged to have undermined the dignity of the *contio* by turning it into an occasion for boisterous singing and general rowdiness. On the other hand, Clodius' ejection from the theatre recalls the similar fate suffered by many musicians and actors, whose error-prone performances could easily incur the wrath of Roman audiences.[125]

It is interesting to note that Cicero uses the word *convicium* to characterise the noisy chants of Clodius' supporters (he does so again in his letter to Quintus reporting on the *contio* before Milo's trial).[126] A *convicium* technically referred to any noise produced by a concatenation of voices.[127] But the grammarian Festus, paraphrasing the late-republican author Verrius Flaccus, relates the meaning of *convicium* to the archaic word *occentare* (to sing against), suggesting a particular connection to the world of song:

> *occentassint antiqui dicebant quod nunc convicium fecerint dicimus, quod id clare et cum quodam canore fit, ut procul exaudiri possit. quod turpe*

---

[122] '*Embolia* were balletic interludes, performed between the acts or while the next play was being prepared.' (Wiseman 1985: 27, with Schol. Bob. 136 Stangl, *pertinent ad gestus saltatorios*). For Clodia's dancing, see Schol. Bob. 135 Stangl: *veteres litterae tradunt studiosam fuisse saltandi profusius et inmoderatius quam matronam deceret* (perhaps confusing Clodia with Sallust's Sempronia); cf. also Cic. *Cael.* 35, on Clodia's musical entertainments at Baiae.

[123] The play was Afranius' *Simulans* (The Pretender): CRF Afranius 304/5. The play's protagonist, Titus, provides an obvious foil for the 'pretender' Clodius.

[124] Cic. *Sest.* 118. An 'association of Greek singers' (*societas cantorum Graecorum*) is attested in late-republican Rome; its origin and function are obscure: *CIL* I² 2519 = *ILLRP* 771; Jory 1970: 243; Giovagnoli 2014.

[125] Cf. Cic. *Rosc. Com.* 30; *Parad.* 26.   [126] Cic. *Q. fr.* 2.3.2.

[127] Cf. *Dig.* 47.10.15.7 (Ulpian): *convicium autem dicitur vel a concitatione vel a conventu, hoc est a collatione vocum. cum enim in unum complures voces conferuntur, convicium appellatur quasi convocium.*

habetur, quia non sine causa fieri putatur. inde cantilenam dici †querellam, non cantus† iucunditatem, puto. (Festus 190–192L)

The ancients used to say *occentassint* [they sang against] to describe what we now would call *convicium fecerint* [they made an insulting outcry], because this is done loudly and with a certain melodic quality, so that it can be heard from far off. It is considered shameful, because it is thought to happen not without cause. Hence I think the [grievance?] is so called [because it takes the form of?] a refrain, [not for the] pleasantness [of the song?].[128]

The custom of *occentatio* had a long history at Rome, originating in the early republican period as a private remedy for airing grievances with one's neighbour.[129] According to Cicero, a law of the Twelve Tables (ca. 450 BCE) prescribed the death penalty for anyone who 'sang or composed a song which contained a slander or insult to anyone else' (*si quis occentavisset, sive carmen condidisset, quod infamiam faceret flagitiumve alteri*); Cicero considered this an 'excellent' ruling (*praeclare*).[130] The practice of *occentatio* is frequently attested in the plays of Plautus, where it typically involves a group of amorous men turning up at the house of a female slave and chanting in front of the doors, bringing shame upon the woman's owners.[131] By the late Republic, *occentatio* had entered the political sphere, allowing disgruntled citizens to call magistrates to account by verbally abusing them from outside their houses. A notable occurrence of this kind of *occentatio* took place in 57 BCE, when, at Clodius' instigation, an angry mob descended upon Cicero's house and demanded grain.[132] As Andrew Lintott remarks, the actions of the *Clodiani* on this occasion must have involved 'a recital of chants composed by Clodius to abuse Cicero'.[133]

The evidence for *occentatio/convicium* highlights how Clodius' political tactics at the *contio* exploited the musicality of the Roman *plebs*. Whether the chants of the *operae Clodianae* really did resemble the songs sung by

---

[128] Translation slightly adapted from Richlin 2017: 179. The text of the last sentence is corrupt (hence the obeli in Lindsay's edition), but the important word is *cantilenam*, which suggests 'singsong and repetition' (Richlin 2017: 179 n. 54). For the association of *convicium* with song, cf. [Verg.] *Culex* 209 (*cecinit convicia*); Sen. *Ep.* 51.12 (*canentium nocturna convicia*). Note also Cic. *Pro Gallio* fr. 1 Crawford: *fit clamor, fit convicium mulierum, fit symphoniae cantus* (a possible allusion to Ter. *Hec.* 35: *comitum conventus, strepitus, clamor mulierum*).

[129] See Lintott 1999: 8–10; Hartnett 2016: 169–71.

[130] Cic. *Rep.* 4.12. The precise meaning of *carmen* here is disputed (it could be translated as either 'slanderous song' or 'magical incantation'): see Rives 2002: 279–88, for an overview of the debate.

[131] Cf. Plaut. *Curc.* 145, *Merc.* 408, *Per.* 569; Richlin 2017: 178–81. [132] Cic. *Q. fr.* 2.3.2.

[133] Lintott 1999: 10.

professional *cantores* is ultimately impossible to say. Modern research suggests that crowd acclamations in the Roman world could range from single words or phrases repeated in unison to full-blown choruses involving complex rhythms and melodies.[134] However, as the musicologist James Garratt observes, 'even the most banal unpitched rhythmic chant ... does more than simply transmit a message, gaining rhetorical force and collective significance through its musical dimension'.[135] One of the keys to Clodius' success, therefore, was his ability to mould popular song into a political weapon. *Occentatio* offered an effective medium of resistance because it allowed those who participated in it to impose themselves audibly on their physical surroundings, in a way that drew the attention of those nearby while maintaining the anonymity of the individual protesters.[136] At the same time, Clodius was able to capitalise on the aptitude of ordinary Romans for memorising and reperforming songs. In his book *The Culture of the Roman Plebs*, Nicolas Horsfall identifies the relationship between song and memory as one of the lynchpins of Roman popular culture.[137] Horsfall enlists support for this theory from a variety of literary sources. In the *Fasti*, for example, Ovid gives an account of the celebrations of the Anna Perenna festival, in which he notes how the Roman people would gather on the Campus Martius and 'sing songs learned at the theatres' (*cantant quicquid didicere theatris*), while clapping and dancing along with the music (*iactant ... manus; ducunt ... choreas*).[138] Lucretius describes in evocative terms how the sights and sounds of a theatrical production linger in people's minds long after the performance has ended, 'so that even while awake they seem to perceive dancers swaying their supple limbs and to hear in their ears the lyre's rippling tune and its speaking strings'.[139] The polemical writings of early Christian authors provide ample testimony for the memorability of music in later

---

[134] See Aldrete 1999; Roueché 1984; Fagan 2011: 139–40.   [135] Garratt 2019: 11–12.

[136] See Hartnett 2017: 129; cf. Suet. *Aug.* 70 on the *notissimi versus sine auctore* chanted in the aftermath of the notorious Feast of the Twelve Gods.

[137] Horsfall 2003: 11–19.

[138] Ov. *Fast.* 3.535–537. At *Ars* 3.317, Ovid encourages girls to repeat 'songs heard in the theatres' (*referant audita theatris*) as a strategy for attracting potential lovers. Ovid's own works were apparently adapted for performance in the theatre, perhaps in the form of a choreographed mime with musical accompaniment: Ov. *Tr.* 5.7.25 (*carmina quod pleno saltari nostra theatro*), 2.519-20 (*et mea sunt populo saltata poemata saepe*); Currie 1981; Wiseman 2002.

[139] Lucr. 4.979–982: *etiam vigilantes ut videantur | cernere saltantis et mollia membra moventis | et citharae liquidum carmen chordasque loquentis | auribus accipere*. Cf. also Artem. 1.76, commenting on the recollection of songs in dreams.

centuries.¹⁴⁰ By tapping into this musical culture and channelling it through the rituals of the *contio*, Clodius succeeded in creating a public platform which promoted his own political agenda while giving voice to popular dissent.

'Entertainer extraordinaire', 'actor', 'artiste', 'harpist': these were no run-of-the-mill insults. Connecting the scandal of the Bona Dea festival with the recent events of Milo's trial and the *Ludi Apollinares* of the previous year, Cicero's words in the *Pro Sestio* issued a stark reminder of the dangerous affinity between the *proscenium*, the *cavea* and the *contio* as sites where politically charged songs were composed and disseminated. Spectators in one venue could easily become performers in another. And that blurred the notional distinctions between the *humiliores* (upper classes) and *honestiores* (lower classes) upon which the Roman social hierarchy was built. Six years after that fateful night in the house of Julius Caesar, the spectre of the cross-dressing Clodius prancing about with his harp still haunted many Roman citizens.

Nec Tam Musicus: Piso, Philodemus and the Epicureans

So far in this chapter, I have focused on how Cicero and other Roman writers use musical ideas and images to problematise the networks of dependency which existed between political elites and the theatre-going *plebs*. This critique was directed especially at demagogues like Gaius Gracchus and Clodius. While Cicero and other conservatives advocated for a traditional kind of musical culture, which kept the populace under control, the so-called *populares* utilised melody and rhythm as a powerful tool of political manipulation, which in turn allowed them to rally the urban mob behind their cause. In the next part of this chapter, I turn my attention to a different kind of musical conflict – namely, the conflict between Cicero and the Epicureans. Examining attitudes to music in the surviving Epicurean literature of the period – most notably, Lucretius' *On the Nature of Things* (*De Rerum Natura*) and Philodemus' *On Music* – reveals an interesting set of tensions with the arguments put forward by

---

¹⁴⁰ For example, Tertullian (*Ad uxorem* 2.6) complains about husbands who sang to wives (or wives to husbands) songs learned from the stage or from the tavern. Prominent clerics such as Augustine, Arius and Ambrose of Milan even composed catchy hymns as a way of attracting nonbelievers to the faith and attacking heretical opponents; see especially Shaw 2011: 475–83, on Augustine's *Psalm Against the Donatists* ('the Western world's first known pop song').

Cicero. By focusing more closely on these tensions, I hope to demonstrate further that Roman musical culture in the late Republic was considerably more dynamic and more divisive than modern scholars have appreciated.

The Romans were well aware that the *ars musica* was characterised by divergent opinions. Varro states this fact plainly: 'in music ... writers disagree' (*in musica ... discrepant scriptores*).[141] Although this disagreement was not limited to any single point, perhaps the most contested topic of musicological debate in antiquity was the question of music's practical utility. On the one hand, there were those who subscribed to the teachings of the Stoic, Academic and Pythagorean schools, and so put their faith in music's affective power over human beings and its role in ordering the cosmos. On the other hand, there were those who upheld the teachings of the fourth-century philosopher Epicurus, and so assigned music a much more limited role in human and divine affairs. Epicureanism underwent a dramatic surge in popularity during the late Republic. At the core of Epicurean philosophy was the idea that the study of music, both in theory and in practice, was essentially 'useless' (*asumphoros*) and unnecessary for attaining the spiritual tranquillity (*ataraxia*) that was the ultimate goal of human existence.[142] Music was still of benefit to mankind, however, insofar as it constituted a source of pleasure, which the Epicureans defined as the highest good; it was therefore analogous to other sensual pleasures, such as food or sex. Since Epicureans viewed music as *asumphoros*, philosophical arguments about the decline of music over time, or the effects of music on the character of political states, carried little weight. Consequently, with a few notable exceptions, the question of music's impact on political and social life does not figure prominently in Epicurean sources.

If we wish to gain a better understanding of Epicurean attitudes to music in the late Republic, we might start by looking at what the most famous Epicurean of the period has to say on the subject. Music, admittedly, does not play a particularly major role in the poetry of Lucretius. Nevertheless, he still refers to it at several points in the *De Rerum Natura*. In Book 5, he advances the theory that music was not bestowed by the gods, as commonly thought, but rather was invented by mankind and perfected over time through experimentation. In the beginning, he explains, man learnt to sing by imitating birdsong; then he invented the pipes (*tibiae*); and finally,

---

[141] Varro, *Ling.* 9.111.
[142] Epicurus' treatise *On Music* no longer survives, but his views on music can be deduced from later sources. For an accessible overview, see Asmis 1995.

he introduced music and dance to the banquet.[143] Similarly, at 5.334 Lucretius speaks of musical tunes as having been 'only recently' (*modo*) discovered, again attributing the agency to the *organici* (musicians or instrument-makers) rather than to some divine progenitor. This rejection of the divine or mythological origins of music is also reflected in the account of the Magna Mater cult in Book 2, where the music-making of the human worshippers is contrasted with the goddess's silence.[144] Lucretius also reaffirms the traditional Epicurean emphasis on music as a source of pleasure: music 'delights the ears' (*aurisque iuvare*; 5.1381); melodies 'soothe minds and give pleasure' (*mulcebant atque iuvabant*; 5.1390); the lyre's sound lingers in the memory (4.979–982) and brings comfort to those who cannot sleep (5.1405). It is not the case, however, that more refined music leads to greater pleasure: the people of today 'have no more profit in enjoying [music] than the woodland people had who were born of the earth'.[145] Lucretius' stance on music can thus be summarised as follows: firstly, he implicitly rejects the metaphorical application of musical harmony to an understanding of the cosmos; secondly, he refutes the divine origins of music, describing it as a human invention; and thirdly, he speaks primarily of music as a pleasurable sensation, while stressing the ideal of simplicity.

For a more polemical articulation of the Epicurean stance on music, we can turn to Philodemus of Gadara. Philodemus made his name as the protégé of Zeno of Sidon, the head of the Epicurean school at Athens (ca. 150–ca. 75 BCE), before moving to Italy probably in the 70s BCE, where he seems to have spent most of his time in the environs of Naples.[146] Of the various philosophical and poetic works attributed to Philodemus, perhaps the most important is his treatise *On Music*. This text has come down to us on a set of papyrus bookrolls discovered in the mid-eighteenth century during the excavations of an opulent villa in the town of Herculaneum. However, it was not until the end of the twentieth century, with the advent of microscopy and infrared imaging, that the extremely fragile papyri could be fully deciphered. In his edition of the fragments, published in 2007,

---

[143] Lucr. 5.1379–404.
[144] Lucr. 2.618–25: *tympana tenta tonant palmis et cymbala circum | concava, rauci sonoque minantur cornua cantu, | et Phrygio stimulat numero cava tibia mentis | . . .* [sc. Magna Mater] *munificat tacita mortalis muta salute*.
[145] Lucr. 5.1409–11. See also Fowler 2002: 100, commenting on Lucr. 2.28 as an example of 'the Epicurean scepticism of [music's] value in the face of the high claims made by the Academy and Peripatos especially'.
[146] Janko 2000: 5–7; Gigante 1995: 79–90; Sider 1997: 3–12.

Daniel Delattre convincingly demonstrated that the extant portion of the work, which centres on a refutation of the teachings of the Stoic philosopher Diogenes of Babylon (ca. 240–152 BCE), derives exclusively from the fourth book.[147] The text has received most attention for its controversial rejection of the theory of musical *ethos*. Like Lucretius, Philodemus denies music a pedagogical or moral utility, regarding it as a human invention rather than a divine gift. The pleasures of music, for Philodemus, were not to be feared: music is 'useful for pleasure'; it distracts from what is needful and brings happiness.[148] At the same time, Philodemus emphasises the limits of music for the pursuit of *ataraxia*: 'the pleasure which comes from music is not necessary, while learning and practising music in order to amuse oneself is toilsome (*epiponon*) and excludes one from the things which are most important for our well-being'.[149] The ears will tolerate music only for so long: 'It is typical of small-minded people with nothing worthwhile to which they can dedicate themselves, let alone which would make them happy, to toil over learning (to play music) in order to amuse themselves now and again, people who do not see the abundance of public performances or the possibility of partaking in them all the time around the city, if they want to do so, and who do not consider that our nature refuses (to listen to music) for too long and quickly tires of it.'[150] In Philodemus' opinion, therefore, while music provided a pleasant distraction from life's burdens, it lacked the capacity to affect human emotions, to mould the character of the young or to alter the condition of political states.

To what extent do Philodemus' views on music cohere with those of Cicero? In his essay, 'The Dialogue of Greece and Rome about Music and Ethics in Philodemus of Gadara', Delattre argues that the treatise *On Music* can be read as a kind of philosophical manifesto for a Roman culture which privileged the passive consumption of musical entertainment over the intellectual or practical pursuit of music for its own sake. Furthermore, Delattre speculates that Cicero was not only familiar with Philodemus' *On Music*, but was 'deeply shaken' by his arguments to such an extent that he was 'inclined to be far less categorical than Plato, his master, about the risk to the balance of the State as a result of innovation in musical matters'.[151]

---

[147] There were probably four books in total. On the background and contents of the *On Music*, see the introduction to Delattre's edition. Ferguson 2003 provides a helpful summary of the work in English.

[148] Phld. *Mus.* 4, col. 132.5–7 Delattre (πρὸς τὴν ἡδονήν ... χρησιμεύειν); cf. *Mus.* 4, col. 62.38–42 Delattre.

[149] Phld. *Mus.* 4, col. 151.29–39 Delattre (trans. Blank 2009).

[150] Phld. *Mus.* 4, col. 151.8–25 Delattre (trans. Blank 2009).   [151] Delattre 1998: 230–1.

Delattre dates *On Music* to the early phase of Philodemus' literary activity (ca. 75–50 BCE), citing the influential work of the Italian papyrologist Marcello Gigante.[152] If this is correct, then we cannot rule out the possibility that Cicero had read Philodemus' work. He was certainly familiar with Philodemus' poems and praises the philosopher's *doctrina* in his treatise *On Moral Ends*.[153] Scholars have also noted a correspondence between the last part of Philodemus' *On Piety* and the first book of Cicero's *On the Nature of the Gods* (although this may simply indicate that the two authors had a common source, perhaps Zeno of Sidon).[154]

However, the intellectual affinity between Cicero and Philodemus should not be overstated. Delattre's argument rests upon the dubious assumption that Cicero's apparent lack of interest in music theory equates to a particular inclination towards Epicureanism. On the contrary, in several of his works Cicero in fact speaks quite negatively of Epicurean views on music. For example, in the *Tusculan Disputations*, he challenges the Epicurean belief that music (and other pleasurable sensations) could be used to alleviate feelings of grief: if you were confronted by someone who was mourning the loss of a relative, Cicero asks, 'would you encourage him to listen to the sound of a water-organ rather than to a dialogue of Plato?' (*hydrauli hortabere ut audiat voces potius quam Platonis?*).[155] Similarly, in *On Moral Ends*, Cicero contrasts Platonic and Epicurean views on the liberal arts, noting that unlike Plato, Epicurus did not regard music, geometry, arithmetic and astronomy as useful subjects of study, on the grounds that they contributed nothing to happiness.[156] On balance, Cicero's modification of Plato's arguments in the *De Legibus* and elsewhere does not amount to a full rejection of those arguments. Indeed, if Cicero was truly swayed by Philodemus' way of thinking, it is hard to explain why he would emphasise music's affective power and its importance in the education of the young, articulating a Stoic view that is fundamentally at odds with that of Philodemus and Lucretius.

One adherent of Epicureanism whose behaviour Cicero certainly did not endorse was L. Calpurnius Piso Caesoninus. The most illustrious of Philodemus' Roman patrons, Piso is the subject of a famous invective delivered by Cicero in 55 BCE. The *In Pisonem* purports to be a reproduction of a speech that Cicero delivered shortly before the inauguration of Pompey's theatre, during a Senate debate concerning Piso's conduct as

---

[152] Gigante 1987: 47.   [153] Cic. *Pis.* 70; *Fin.* 2.119.
[154] On the relationship between Cicero and Philodemus, see Auvray-Assayas and Delattre 2001.
[155] Cic. *Tusc. Disp.* 3.43.   [156] Cic. *Fin.* 1.72.

governor of Macedonia from 57 to 55. In fact, the invective was actually composed and circulated several months after this debate, following an attempt by Piso to defend himself against the charges raised against him on that occasion.[157] The speech represented the culmination of several years of hostility between the two senators: Piso had been one of the most vociferous opponents of Cicero's consulship in 63, and in retaliation Cicero had campaigned successfully for Piso's early recall from his province, using the *In Pisonem* to invite a formal prosecution of the proconsul. In the speech, Cicero contrasts Piso's dishonourable conduct in Macedonia with his own exemplary political career. A particularly significant passage appears in the middle of the speech, where Cicero criticises Piso's association with the disreputable Aulus Gabinius, his consular colleague in 58:

> *cum conlegae tui domus cantu et cymbalis personaret, cumque ipse nudus in convivio saltaret; in quo cum illum saltatorium versaret orbem, ne tum quidem fortunae rotam pertimescebat. hic autem non tam concinnus helluo nec tam musicus iacebat in suorum Graecorum foetore et caeno; quod quidem istius in illis rei publicae luctibus quasi aliquod Lapitharum aut Centaurorum convivium ferebatur; in quo nemo potest dicere utrum iste plus biberit an vomuerit an effuderit.* (Cic. *Pis.* 22)

> When the house of your colleague resounded with singing and cymbals, and when he himself [i.e. Gabinius] danced naked at a banquet at which he did not fear the wheel of Fortune, even then he was performing his own whirling gyrations.[158] Piso, meanwhile, neither so elegant nor so musical a debauchee, lay in the filthy stench of his Greek companions. Indeed, this banquet of his, in the midst of the Republic's struggles, was spoken of as if it were some feast of Lapiths and Centaurs, a feast at which it is impossible to say whether that villain spent more time drinking or vomiting.

Cicero's attack on Piso relies on tried-and-tested rhetorical tropes. In section 18, the speaker conjures an image of Piso emerging from a shadowy drinking den accompanied by Gabinius, whom he refers to simply as 'that dancing girl' (*illa saltatrix tonsa*).[159] In section 20, Cicero hints again at Gabinius' effeminacy by likening him to a female percussionist (he speaks of Gabinius' *cymbala*). He also makes much of Piso's fondness for exotic

---

[157] On the circumstances surrounding the speech, see Nisbet 1961; Lintott 2008: 210–11.
[158] The phrase *saltatorius orbis* is most unusual: Nisbet 1961 *ad loc.* suggests that it is 'possibly a sort of hoop used by dancing-girls', but it makes better sense as a reference to a circular motion of the body (perhaps similar to the twisting movements described in the *De Legibus*?).
[159] For Gabinius' dancing, cf. also Cic. *Sen.* 13, *Dom.* 60, *Planc.* 87; Macr. *Sat.* 3.14.15.

musicians and dancers. In section 83, Piso is said to have accepted a group of slave musicians (*servi symphoniaci*) during his travels in Greece as a token of good faith from a man he was at that very moment conspiring to murder. And in section 89, we hear of how Piso, unable to contain his grief at having been recalled from his beloved province, found solace in his retinue of effeminate Greek dancers (*tuis teneris saltatoribus*). This is all standard Ciceronian vituperation. Close parallels can be found in the *Pro Roscio Amerino*, attacking Sulla's freedman Chrysogonus, and in the *In Verrem*, attacking the corrupt governor of Sicily, Gaius Verres. Cicero claims that Chrysogonus, when entertaining guests at his mansion on the Palatine Hill, employed so many musicians that 'the whole neighbourhood resounded with the daily music of singers and strings and pipes and with nightly banquets'. Verres, similarly, is accused of hosting debauched parties on the beaches of Sicily, filled with music and sex, while the forum stood silent.[160]

What makes the speech against Piso unusual is that it connects the subject's excessive consumption of music with his devotion to Epicureanism. One of Cicero's central claims in the *In Pisonem* is that Piso aligned himself with Philodemus as a way of cloaking his hedonistic impulses under the respectable guise of philosophy. And yet, the version of Epicureanism he embraced was not authentic, but a grossly distorted version of his own devising, which essentially gave free rein to his own rampant desires.[161] This background is important for understanding the characterisation of Piso in the passage quoted above: 'This man meanwhile, neither so elegant nor so musical (*nec tam musicus*) a debauchee, lay in the filthy stench of his Greek companions'. This sentence features the only appearance of the word *musicus* in a Ciceronian speech. The sarcastic use of the term here, immediately following the reference to Gabinius' dancing, has the effect of undermining Piso's philhellenic pretensions. By portraying Piso as the antithesis of an enlightened *musicus*, Cicero was attacking not only the man himself but also the bogus and harmful philosophy which he

---

[160] Cic. *Rosc. Am.* 134: *cotidiano cantu vocum et nervorum et tibiarum nocturnisque conviviis tota vicinitas personet*; *Verr.* 2.5.31: *locum illum litoris percrepare totum mulierum vocibus cantuque symphoniae, in foro silentium esse summum causarum atque iuris*. This image of 'resounding' music can be traced back to Cicero's teacher Posidonius: cf. Posidonius, *FGrH* 87 F 10 (τὰς πόλεις ὅλας τοῖς τοιούτοις κελάδοις συνηχεῖσθαι).

[161] On Cicero's portrayal of Epicureanism in the *In Pisonem*, see Griffin 2001: 95–7. In section 20, Piso is described as *barbarus Epicurus*, a 'foreign Epicurus'; and at *Pis.* 37, *Epicure noster,* 'our Epicurus'. For Piso's association with Greek intellectuals, cf. also Cic. *Prov. cons.* 14; *Red. Sen.* 15.

used to justify his immoral behaviour. A person who revelled in 'singing and cymbals' was not truly 'musical', Cicero claims; on the contrary, he was someone who lacked a proper understanding of moral good. To paraphrase Seneca the Younger's description of the stereotypical Epicurean, Piso was 'like a strong man in a woman's dress' (*quale vir fortis stolam indutus*): whatever good qualities he may have possessed on the inside were masked by the fact that he appeared at banquets with a drum in his hand (*in manu tympanum est*).[162]

Cicero's comments on Piso and the Epicureans provide a salient reminder that the Roman aristocracy did not share a unified vision of what music was or how it should be used. The existence of such disagreement is a testament to the lively and often polemical intellectual milieu of the late Republic.[163] Indeed, the debate gained a particular moral urgency with the rise of the *symphonia* as a vehicle for elite leisure and self-display. The struggle for primacy between the adherents of Stoicism and Epicureanism created a stark ideological divide between those who thought that music was a harmless pleasure to be taken at liberty and those who thought that music was a potentially harmful force, which should be enjoyed only in moderation and, preferably, as an abstract theoretical pursuit. At a time when Epicureanism was gaining traction among intellectual circles at Rome (Cicero, writing in the 40s, claimed that Epicureans 'have taken over the whole of Italy'), not everyone was willing to embrace a philosophical creed which forced them to question their own musical proclivities.[164]

The *Onos Lyras*: Varro's Satire on Music

A little-known work by Marcus Terentius Varro helps us to situate this debate in a broader context. Contained within the larger corpus of texts known as the *Menippean Satires*, the *Onos Lyras* – or, translated into English, *Donkey* [*Hears*] *The Lyre* – has escaped the notice of all but a handful of scholars, owing both to its poor state of preservation and its apparently esoteric subject matter.[165] However, this intriguing work merits close attention, since it constitutes one of the few known texts by a Roman

---

[162] Sen. *Dial.* 7.13.3.   [163] See here the recent work of Volk 2021.
[164] Cic. *Tusc. Disp.* 4.7 (*Italiam totam occupaverunt*). On the popularity of Epicureanism in the late Republic, see Sedley 2009.
[165] The fullest discussion of the *Onos Lyras* can be found in Shanzer 1986a. However, Shanzer uses the work mainly to argue for Varronian influence on Martianus Capella. See also the brief treatment in Hahn 1905: 14–15.

author prior to the late-antique period devoted specifically to music. In the final part of this chapter, therefore, I will piece together the extant fragments of the *Onos Lyras* in the hope of shedding light on both its content and context. My analysis will focus on two key issues. First, where does the *Onos Lyras* position itself in relation to contemporary philosophical and ethical debates about music? Does it align more closely with the Stoic or the Epicurean view, or does it espouse ideas from both schools? Second, who was the intended audience of the *Onos Lyras*? Was the work composed exclusively or primarily for well-educated elites, or did it reach a broader segment of the Roman population? I will suggest that the satire does not necessarily adhere to a single viewpoint, but rather aims to place different perspectives in dialogue with one another. Furthermore, the *Onos Lyras* was probably not intended solely for the upper-class intelligentsia. In fact, we have reason to believe that the work may have been presented in the Roman theatre and thus would have appealed to a socially mixed audience. In that case, the *Onos Lyras* may provide evidence for a much stronger popular engagement with musical debates than previously acknowledged.

All that survives of the *Onos Lyras* are twenty-two fragments of one or two lines in length, quoted by the fourth-century lexicographer Nonius Marcellus.[166] Reconstructing an entire satire based on such scanty remains is, of course, an impossible task. To add to the difficulty, the truncated nature of the fragments prevents us from establishing their placement within the overall text, as well as obfuscating in some cases the syntactical function of certain words and phrases. These problems are familiar to any student of the *Menippean Satires*. The surviving titles of the *Menippeans* – 93 out of an original 150 – make for an amusing, if somewhat perplexing, miscellany (the list includes *Dog Historian*, *Double Marcus*, *Fighting Goats (On Pleasure)*, *A Husband's Duty*, *The Magic Wand*, *Perfume on the Lentils (On Good Timing)*, *A Piss-Pot Only Holds So Much (On Drunkenness)* and *Ulysses and a Half*). In many cases we have only a sentence or two from each work.[167] There are, however, roughly 600 surviving fragments in total, and examining these fragments collectively reveals some significant trends. Particularly noticeable is the preference for verse over prose (some three-quarters of the fragments are in verse), the predilection for archaisms,

---

[166] Of the nearly 400 fragments of Varro's satires which survive, the vast majority appear in Nonius' encyclopaedic dictionary. Quotations below follow the text and numeration of Krenkel 2002. An additional Varronian fragment, found in a scholiast on Vergil and describing the aid of the *cithara* in the ascension of souls, has been attributed to the *Onos Lyras*, although this is disputed: see Nock 1927 and 1929.

[167] The translations are drawn from Wiseman 2009: 139–42.

colloquial expressions and Greek loanwords, the irreverent, often self-mocking, tone, and the encyclopedic subject matter.[168] But the fact remains that, in dealing with individual satires, one must rely to a large extent on educated guesswork.

Onos Lyras is a curious title. It derives from the Greek proverb ὄνος λύρας (literally, a donkey to a lyre). First attested in the Athenian comic poets Cratinus (519–422 BCE) and Menander (ca. 341–290 BCE), the proverb remained current throughout antiquity and grew again in popularity during the Middle Ages.[169] Phaedrus, the Roman writer of fables, provides a narrative context for the proverb:

> *Asinus iacentem vidit in prato lyram;*
> *accessit et temptavit chordas ungula,*
> *sonuere tactae. 'bella res mehercules*
> *male cessit,' inquit, 'artis quia sum nescius.*
> *si reperisset aliquis hanc prudentior,*
> *divinis aures oblectasset cantibus.'*
> *sic saepe ingenia calamitate intercidunt.*
> (Phaedrus, 'Perotti's Appendix', no. 14, ed. Perry 1965)

> A donkey spotted a lyre lying in a meadow. He went up to it and tried the strings with his hoof; they sounded at his touch. 'A beautiful thing, indeed,' he said, 'but it has ended badly, because I am ignorant of the art. If only someone of greater skill had found this, he might have charmed ears with divine music.' Thus genius often goes to waste through misfortune.

---

[168] Quintilian (*Inst.* 10.1.95) describes Varro's satires as 'mixed from a variety not only of poems [sc. but of prose as well]' (*non sola carminum varietate mixtum*). On the general character of the *Menippeans*, see Horsfall 1982: 288–9. Varro is thought to have composed the *Menippeans* between roughly 85 and 60 BCE; the *Onos Lyras* cannot be dated precisely within this range.

[169] For ancient references to the proverb, cf. Cratin. fr. 247 (PCG = 229 FCG): ὄνοι δ' ἀπωτέρω κάθηνται τῆς λύρας; Men. *Mis.* 295: ὄνος λύρας; *Psophodees* fr. 527 Kock: ὄνος λύρας ἤκουσε καὶ σάλπιγγος ὗς; Phanias *Anth. Pal.* 6.307: ἔνθα λύρας ἤκουεν ὅπως ὄνος; Gell. *NA* 3.16.13: *ii si erunt ὄνοι λύρας*; Luc. *Ind.* 4: ὄνος λύρας ἀκούεις κινῶν τὰ ὦτα; *De merc. cond.* 25: "τί γὰρ κοινόν," φασί, "λύρᾳ καὶ ὄνῳ;"; *Pseudol.* 7: ὁ δέ, τοῦτο δὴ τὸ τοῦ λόγου, ὄνον κιθαρίζειν πειρώμενον ὁρῶν ἀνεκάγχασε μάλα ἡδύ; *Dial. meret.* 14.4: ὄνος αὐτολυρίζων; Athen. 8.349d: ὄνος λύρας ἐλέγετο, νῦν δὲ Βοῦς λύρας; Jer. *Ep.* 27.1: *asino quippe lyra superflue canit*; 61.4: *verum est illud apud Graecos proverbium*: ὄνῳ λύρα; Mart. Cap. 8.807: *saltem Prieneiae ausculta nihilum gravate sententiae et ni* ὄνος λύρᾳ, *καιρὸν γνῶθι*; cf. also Ael. *NA* 10.28: λέγουσι δὲ οἱ Πυθαγόρειοι ὑπὲρ τοῦ ὄνου καὶ ἐκεῖνο, μόνον τοῦτον τῶν ζῴων μὴ γεγονέναι κατὰ ἁρμονίαν· ταύτῃ τοι καὶ πρὸς τὸν ἦχον τὸν τῆς λύρας εἶναι κωφότατον; Plu. *Mor.* 150d8–f10 (the use of asses' bones to make *auloi*); Boeth. *Cons.* 1.4.1. For the history of the proverb in antiquity and the Middle Ages, see Ziolkowski 2007: 216–17; Adolf 1950.

Like many proverbs, the story of the donkey and the lyre was open to multiple interpretations. The moral of Phaedrus' fable emphasises the precariousness of *ingenium* (genius, or talent): just as the finest lyre, if placed in the hands of a donkey, could be rendered useless, so could the brightest *ingenium* be squandered by an unfortunate twist of fate.[170] In most ancient citations of the proverb, however, the hapless donkey represents something quite different – namely, a person who lacks artistic appreciation or who claims expertise in a topic about which they are ignorant.[171] Varro himself is the source of two such citations. A quotation from the satire *The Will* refers to sons being disinherited 'if they are donkeys to the lyre' (*ii si erunt ὄνοι λύρας, exheredes sunto*); here the proverb seems to describe people who are unteachable or unmanageable.[172] And in the *Onos Lyras* itself, we find the saying applied to those who reject music for the 'uncultured' pursuits of the forum (as discussed later in this section).[173] So why choose *Onos Lyras* as the title of a satire? Obviously, the title signals that this is a satire about music. But it also suggests a subtler point – that when it comes to *mousike*, it is not always obvious who are the real experts and who are the donkeys.

The *Onos Lyras* seems to have taken the form of a dispute between a *musicus* and an *amousos*. The preponderance of first-person verbs and pronouns among the fragments confirms that there was (at least) one character who spoke in his own voice, while the presence of second-person verbs and pronouns indicates a dialogue of some sort.[174] One fragment invokes the traditional exit line of a comic drama (*valete | et me palmulis producite*, farewell, and send me away with applause), but changes the customary *nos* (us) to the singular *me* (me).[175] This is unique and suggests a single speaker. However, we cannot necessarily assign all the first-person statements to the same speaker. This leaves us with two possibilities: either the satire was written as a monologue, with a single character (the

---

[170] Varro makes a similar point about citharodes in the *De Re Rustica* (2.1.3): *non omnes, qui habent citharam, sunt citharoedi* (not all those who have a cithara are citharodes).

[171] Cf., e.g., Luc. *Ind.* 4, *Pseud.* 7; Jer. *Ep.* 27.1; Athen. 8.349d.   [172] Gell. *NA* 3.16.13.

[173] Var. *Sat.* fr. 349.

[174] Var. *Sat.* fr. 359: *iurgare coepit dicens: | 'quae scis, atque in vulgum vulgas artemque | expromis inertem*; fr. 360: *tuus autem ipse frater cibarius fuit Aristoxenus*; fr. 361: *nempe suis silvaticos in montibus sectaris venabulo | aut cervos, qui tibi mali nihil fecerunt, verutis. | a artem praeclaram*; fr. 364: *non vidisti simulacrum leonis ad Idam eo loco, ubi | quondam subito eum cum vidissent quadrupedem galli | tympanis adeo fecerunt mansuem, ut tractarent manibus?*; fr. 367: *voces Amphionem; tragoedum iubeas Amphionis agere | partis; infantiorem quam meus est mulio*; fr. 369: *si non plus testiculorum offenderis quam in castrato | pecore in Apulia, vincor: non esse masculum ad rem.*

[175] Var. *Sat.* fr. 355. For occurrences of this formula in comic drama, cf. Plaut. *Epid.* 733, *Menaech.* 1162, *Truc.* 968; Ter. *Heauton Timorumenos* 1067, *Eun.* 1094, *Phormio* 1055.

musicus?) articulating both sides of a debate, or it was structured as a dialogue between two or more interlocutors, who voiced opposing views.

An important question to consider here is to what extent the first-person speaker (or speakers) of the *Onos Lyras* represented the opinions of the author himself. We know that several of the *Menippean Satires* had a self-reflexive dimension. For example, Varro's *praenomen* features in the titles of *Marcopolis (On Political Power), Marcus' Boy* and *Double Marcus*, while his *cognomen* appears in a line from *Triple Phallus (On Virility)*.[176] Although there is no mention of a 'Marcus' or a 'Varro' in the surviving excerpts of the *Onos Lyras*, it would not be unreasonable to suppose that the *musicus* persona projected in some way the attitudes of the real Marcus Terentius Varro. In support of this idea, Peter Wiseman has drawn attention to a reference in the *Onos Lyras* to the musical rites of the lion-taming Galli at Mount Ida.[177] Wiseman claims that this passage may have been inspired by Varro's scholarly explorations in Phrygia while stationed there on military service: the scholiast Pseudo-Acro informs us that Varro had written about *tibiae* with four apertures which he had observed in the temple of Marsyas (likely the one at Kelainai in Phrygia), and so it would appear that Varro had spent time in Phrygia 'thinking about musical instruments'.[178] This theory is hard to credit. Varro may simply have learnt about the Galli from a written source or through word of mouth. Indeed, as the author of a fully fledged treatise on music, he was better informed about musical arcana than most. Like the *De Musica*, the *Onos Lyras* was doubtless a work of considerable scholarship and, in this sense, can be seen as a typically Varronian product.

The content of the satire, insofar as it can be reconstructed, certainly seems to align with what we might expect a Roman student of the *ars musica* to have been interested in. This was not a work about 'music' in the modern sense, but about *mousike*, broadly conceived.[179] The satire evidently dealt with poetry, as well as song and dance:

> *Pacuvi discipulus dicor. porro is fuit <Enni>,*
> *Ennius Musarum. Pompilius clueor.*
> (Var. *Sat.* fr. 356)

---

[176] Var. *Sat.* fr. 562: *ego nihil, Varro, video*; Wiseman 2009: 144–7.   [177] Var. *Sat.* fr. 364.
[178] Wiseman 2009: 145; Var. fr. 44 Funaioli = ps.Acro on Horace, *Ars P.* 202 (*Varro ait ... quattuor foraminum fuisse tibias apud antiquos, et se ipsum ait in Marsyae templo vidisse tibias quattuor foraminum*). On the temple of Marsyas at Kelainai, cf. Hdt. 7.26.3; Xen. *An.* 1.2.8.
[179] The author's debt to Hellenic culture is evidenced by the many references to Greek places and people (both real and legendary) in the extant fragments: Var. *Sat.* fr. 357 (Achilles, Ionia), 364 (Mt. Ida), 367 (Amphion), 368 (Briseis), 360 (Aristoxenus).

Student of Pacuvius – so I will be called, and he was the student of
Ennius, Ennius the student of the Muses. I myself am called Pompilius.

The context of this epigram is obscure, but we know of a Roman tragedian named Pompilius whose works were familiar to Varro; perhaps this Pompilius was the inspiration behind the *musicus* character in the *Onos Lyras* (his connection to the Muses via Pacuvius and Ennius is certainly suggestive in this regard).[180]

Other fragments are clearly situated in the world of Greek musical theory. Most informative are the references to the science of harmonics and the 'harmony of the spheres':

scientia doceat, quemadmodum in psalterio extendamus
nervias.
(Var. *Sat.* fr. 366)

... that knowledge teaches us how to tighten the strings on the lyre.

quam mobilem divum lyram sol harmoge
quadam gubernans motibus diis veget.
(Var. *Sat.* fr. 351)

The sun guides the moving Lyre of the gods in harmony and keeps it moving forever.

Finally, there are several allusions to the theatre and its personnel. We encounter mentions of comic actors (*comici*) and stage-players (*scenatici*), the writers or compilers of dramatic prologues (*qui fabularum conlocant exordia*), tragic actors (*tragoedum*), pipe-players in the theatre (*theatri tibiis*) and professional singers (*cantantiumque*).[181]

In dealing with this diverse subject matter, Varro was clearly engaging with the same kinds of questions about the value of music invoked by Cicero and other contemporary thinkers. The affective power of music appears to have been a particular area of focus. The fragment about the Phrygian Galli taming a lion at Mount Ida speaks of how the priests 'made [the lion] so tame with their drums that they could stroke him with their hands' (*tympanis adeo fecerunt mansuem, ut tractarent minibus*).[182]

---

[180] The only extant verse of Pompilius appears in Var. *Ling.* 7.93; see discussion in Manuwald 2011: 211, 278; Feeney 2016: 166–7.
[181] Var. *Sat.* fr. 353, 354, 348, 365. Rawson (1985: 168) surmises on this basis that the *Onos Lyras* was 'largely about music in the theatre'. Though impossible to prove, this theory becomes especially attractive if one accepts that the work was intended for theatrical performance (see later in this section).
[182] Var. *Sat.* fr. 364.

Another fragment highlights the influence of music on theatre audiences: 'Often the minds of the whole theatre are affected by the *tibiae*, with their frequent bending, and their spirits are aroused' (*saepe totius theatri tibiis, crebro flectendo, | conmutari mentes, erigi animos eorum*).[183] Both of these passages probably appeared in the context of a discussion of *ethos*. Moreover, the *Onos Lyras* seems to adopt a nostalgic and conservative attitude towards music that is very much in line with Cicero's.[184] Music is described in one fragment as 'belonging to nature, since it is innate, like the voice itself, its basis' (*primum eam esse* φυσικήν, *quod siet* ἔμφυτος, *ut | ipsa vox, basis eius*).[185] The use of Greek terminology here grounds the text in the thought world of Plato, Aristotle and Aristoxenus, all of whom stressed the importance of preserving the natural order of *mousike*. This emphasis on musical simplicity is also borne out by another fragment, discussing different kinds of work songs: 'Countryfolk sing simple songs at the grape harvest, the dressmakers [at their work, the millers] at their mills' (*homines rusticos in vindemia incondita cantare, | sarcinatricis <in opere, pistricis> in machinis*).[186]

Conversely, the music of the theatre seems to have been a target of criticism or mockery. This is suggested not only by the depiction of professional *tibicines* quoted in the previous paragraph, recalling Cicero's remarks in the *De Legibus*, but also by the following excerpt:

> *iurgare coepit dicens: quae scis atque in vulgum vulgas artemque expromis inertem.*[187]
>
> He started to get nasty, saying: 'The things you know and publicise to the masses, and that art without art you're putting out.'

In another passage, we are told that some people actually take pride in their own *amousia*, being blinded by a vain desire for glory (*quibus suam delectet ipse amusiam | et aviditatem speribus lactet suis*).[188] This may be a criticism of musicians who pander to the masses rather than respecting the integrity of their art. Alternatively, as Danuta Shanzer points out, it is possible that Varro here is referring to members of the Roman aristocracy who dismissed the *ars musica* as an unnecessary distraction from

---

[183] Var. *Sat.* fr. 365. As mentioned by Augustine (*De quantitate animae* 19.33), Varro alluded in one of his works to a *tibicen* who 'so charmed the hearts of the people that they made him king' (*ita populum delectavit ut rex fieret*). Augustine does not say where he found this quote, but it could have been from either the *De Musica* or the *Onos Lyras*.

[184] On nostalgia as a key theme within the *Menippean Satires*, see Wiseman 2009: 146–51.

[185] Var. *Sat.* fr. 362.   [186] Var. *Sat.* fr. 363.   [187] Var. *Sat.* fr. 359   [188] Var. *Sat.* fr. 350.

politics.[189] One fragment seems to single out frequenters of the forum as the kind of people prone to *amousia*:

> *si quis* μελῳδεῖν *est* ὄνος λύρας
> *praesepibus se retineat forensibus*
> (Var. *Sat.* fr. 349)
>
> Whoever sings like a donkey to the lyre, let him stay in his stables at the forum.

Shanzer makes a convincing case for interpreting the adjective *forensis* literally as 'pertaining to the forum', arguing that the 'donkeys' in this case are 'advocates or holders of public office'.[190] It is worth noting that the corruption of the political class is a recurrent theme in the *Menippean Satires* and in other Varronian writings.[191] However, one could also read the fragment as a xenophobic attack against Greek musicians, instructing them to keep to their 'foreign barnyards' (i.e. away from Rome).[192]

There are a few basic facts about the *Onos Lyras* which can be established on the basis of the preceding discussion. The satire evidently dealt with an extremely diverse range of themes relating to *mousike* in both Greek and Roman contexts, synthesizing elements of myth, history and philosophy. It also engaged dialectically with a set of questions concerning the distinction between 'good' and 'bad' *mousike*. Finally, it made repeated references to Pythagorean and Stoic theory – most notably, the concepts of *ethos* and *harmonia* – thereby perhaps refuting Epicurean views on music.

What, then, can we deduce about the intended audience of the text? In a thought-provoking discussion of the *Menippean Satires*, Wiseman hypothesises that the *Menippean Satires* (including the *Onos Lyras*) were not consumed solely as written texts, but also were adapted for performance on the stage. Wiseman bases this hypothesis largely on internal evidence within the *Menippeans* themselves. We noted before that several fragments of the *Onos Lyras* allude to the world of the theatre, with one passage featuring a variation on the traditional exit line of a Roman comic

---

[189] Shanzer 1986a: 279.   [190] Shanzer 1986b: 40.
[191] Cf. Var. *De vita populi Romani* fr. 121 Riposati: *tanta porro invasit cupiditas honorum plerisque ut vel caelum ruere, dummodo magistratum adipiscantur, exoptent* (besides, most of them have been infected by so great a lust for honours that they'd even long for the sky to fall, provided they get their magistracy; trans. Wiseman 2009: 150); *Sat.* fr. 512 speaks of wrongdoers 'melting away' whatever is owed to the people in the middle of the forum (*hodie, si possumus quod debemus populo in foro medio luci claro decoquere*).
[192] Cf. *TLL* 6.1.1054.53 (Vollmer), taking the phrase *praesepibus ... forensibus* as a neutral use of the adjective *forensis* to mean *alienus* or 'foreign'.

drama ('farewell, and send me away with applause'). Most tellingly, the satire *Glory (on Envy)* addresses an audience *in theatro* and calls on listeners to 'take literature home from the theatre' (*domum ... feratis ex theatro litteras*).[193] For Wiseman, these passages provide compelling evidence that Varro wrote with a popular audience in mind: 'the *satura* was indeed a "mixed dish", not only a showpiece for a versatile performer but also a wonderfully entertaining medium for an author who wanted to reach the Roman People'.[194] Moreover, given the multi-metric character of the fragments (especially the use of iambic senarii), it is possible that performances of the *Onos Lyras* incorporated traditional elements of a Roman comedy or mime, including both sung and spoken dialogue, dancing and perhaps even musical accompaniment.

Is it too far-fetched to imagine that the Roman people would have been interested in a staged debate about music? It is true that ancient writers on music like to present their subject as highly technical and obscure. Philodemus, for instance, states unequivocally that 'musical theory is incomprehensible in the eyes of most people', while Vitruvius, writing a generation later, describes music theory as *obscura et difficilis*, especially for those unfamiliar with the Greek language.[195] However, one does not need to possess a knowledge of music theory in order to engage critically with music. We have already seen that the Roman people were discerning and engaged listeners. There are also signs that some non-elite Romans were familiar with the basic philosophical positions on music. Jerry Toner has argued that philosophy was by no means the exclusive preserve of educated elites. Drawing insights from a collection of 'popular' texts (including fables, proverbs and jokebooks), Toner shows how non-elite Romans built up a store of practical wisdom which helped them to navigate the travails of everyday life.[196] Obviously, this tradition of 'popular philosophy' represents quite a different vein of philosophical thinking from the abstract teachings of Platonism and Stoicism. However, there is evidence that some aspects of Greek philosophy filtered down to the lower classes. The famous 'Tavern of the Seven Sages' in Ostia contains paintings of the Seven Sages of the seventh century BCE paired with images of ordinary men in the act

---

[193] Var. *Sat.* fr. 218. Cf. also the reference to the 'stagey mode/measure' (*modus scenatilis*) in fr. 304. On the links between Varronian satire and Roman comedy (especially Plautus), see Freudenburg 2013.
[194] Wiseman 2009: 143.
[195] Phld. *Mus.* col. 152.19–21 Delattre (τὸ δὲ θεωρητικὸν πρὸς τῶν πλείστων οὐ συνιέμενον); Vitr. 5.4.1.
[196] Toner 2017.

of defecating. The transposition of the Sages, symbols of venerable Greek wisdom, into the scatological realm is obviously intended to 'mock the grandiose rhetoric of intellectuals in general and the Sages in particular'.[197] Another vector of philosophical ideas was the theatre. As Nicholas Horsfall points out, Roman dramatic productions were 'full of allusions to philosophical ideas, at least in simple formulation, with a definite vein of curiosity about Pythagoreanism'.[198] In a fragment from his lost speech *On Behalf of Gallio*, Cicero refers to a mime play (or plays), involving banquets attended by famous poets and philosophers. He scoffs at the blatant anachronism of watching Euripides converse with Menander and Socrates with Epicurus, and the gullibility of the 'uneducated' masses, who applauded regardless.[199] But Cicero's outrage may be misdirected: perhaps the audience knowingly delighted in the incongruity of a play which pitted poets and philosophers from different centuries against one another. A short quotation attributed to the Augustan poet and tragedian Varius Rufus provides an additional testimony. In the passage, the speaker (unidentified in the quotation) makes an oblique reference to the Pythagorean concept of the harmony of the spheres: '[Mercury] was the first to stretch the lyre with seven strings, and to fit on it the different intervals of sound, in harmony with which the tuneful Universe re-echoes as it revolves backwards over its own path'.[200] The philosophical reference may well have been lost on some members of the audience. However, the playwright surely would not have used this imagery unless he thought that it would resonate with a broad cross-section of the Roman public.

The prospect of a dramatised debate about music staged before a Roman audience is tantalising indeed. But we should not get carried away. For all its ingenuity, Wiseman's hypothesis is purely conjectural; and even if the satire *was* performed in the theatre, we cannot assume that all audience members would have appreciated its philosophical nuances. Nevertheless, the content of the *Onos Lyras*, insofar as it can be reconstructed, does

---

[197] Clarke 2003: 170–80, especially 173. For the idea of popular philosophy as a rejection or mockery of elite philosophy, see also Toner 2017: 176–7.
[198] Horsfall 2003: 54–5. Dutsch (2014: 10–15) discusses Pythagorean intertexts in the works of Plautus.
[199] Cic. *Pro Gall.* fr. 4 Crawford.
[200] Varius Rufus fr. 157 Hollis: *primum huic | nervis septem est intenta fides | variique apti vocum moduli | ad quos mundi resonat canor in | sua se vestigia volventis* (trans. Hollis 2007: 258). Since the original context of this fragment is obscure, it is uncertain whether these lines were intended for theatrical performance or for private recitation. However, Moore (2016: 358) argues persuasively that the passage was composed for performance; the fragment may derive from Varius' *Thyestes*, in which case we can pinpoint a performance date in 29/28 BCE.

indicate a widespread interest in the *ars musica* among Varro's contemporaries, which may (if Wiseman's theory is correct) have penetrated beyond the schools and libraries of the elite and taken hold among the wider populace. That would contradict the argument made by Rawson that the Romans drew a sharp conceptual distinction between the theory of music and its practical application, resulting in the 'impoverishment' of musical culture as a whole. If the *Onos Lyras* tells us anything, it is that the *ars musica* was far from impoverished.

Conclusion

Cicero's comments on music have long been neglected by historians and musicologists. It has been assumed that Cicero, like most educated Romans, was largely uninterested in music theory. What is more, the scattered references to music in his treatises have been criticised for their dependence on Plato and other Greek musical theorists. However, Cicero wrote about the *ars musica* for a reason. He shared with many of his contemporaries a firm belief in the power of music to seduce and corrupt, to educate and enlighten. While this conviction was certainly grounded in the teachings of Stoic, Platonic and Pythagorean philosophy, it was not aloof from the concerns of the modern-day Roman statesman. On the contrary, Cicero believed strongly that good philosophers made good politicians, and in writing about music he sought to edify his peers in how to become upstanding leaders of society.

The *De Legibus*, despite its manifold difficulties, highlights the social and political tensions caused by the popular music of the theatre. Unlike Plato, Cicero did not view music as a critical driver of societal change. And yet, he lived in an age in which the intervention of the people in political life was an urgent issue. He believed, moreover, that the moral standing of the Roman people was conditioned in part by the kinds of music to which they were exposed. It was imperative, therefore, that the music of the theatre reflected the purest traditions of Roman culture and remained in the hands of *principes* who were morally good. The construction of Pompey's theatre represented a dangerous inflection point, since it encouraged a shift towards louder and more ostentatious forms of musical entertainment which appealed directly to the tastes of ordinary Romans. From Cicero's oligarchic perspective, this kind of populism set a worrying precedent:

> *an tibicines ique, qui fidibus utuntur, suo, non multitudinis arbitrio cantus numerosque moderantur, vir sapiens multo arte maiore praeditus non*

quid verissimum sit, sed quid velit vulgus, exquiret? an quicquam stultius quam, quos singulos sicut operarios barbarosque contemnas, eos aliquid putare esse universos? (Cic. Tusc. Disp. 5.104)

Are pipe-players and lyre-players to follow their own tastes, not the tastes of the multitude, in regulating melody and rhythm, and shall the wise man, gifted as he is with a far higher art [i.e. philosophy], seek out not what is truest, but what is the pleasure of the masses? Can anything be more foolish than to suppose that those, whom individually one despises as uncultured labourers, are worth anything collectively?

Despite Cicero's anxieties about the spread of popular music, there were many politicians in the late Republic who used melody and rhythm as a tool to advance their own interests. As we have seen, music impinged on the political activities of Roman elites primarily because of its relationship to the art of oratory. By employing a piper to accompany his speeches, Gaius Gracchus was able to harness the affective power of music, thereby ensuring that his rhetoric achieved maximum impact. A few decades later, Publius Clodius exploited the medium of song as a way of uniting the Roman people against his political enemies. The ability for song to function as a kind of social leveller, breaking down hierarchies of order and status, meant that the co-option of musical culture by Roman elites naturally lent itself to a demagogic style of politics. But it is vital that we situate the rhetorical tactics of Gaius Gracchus and Clodius in the broader context of Roman elite engagements with music in this period, especially the growing interest in musical theory and the rise of the *symphonia*.

Although much of this chapter has focused on explicating the comments of one man (albeit a man of exceptional clout), examining the testimony of Cicero in conjunction with other literary sources from the period has highlighted the diversity of Roman elite attitudes to music. Naturally, many questions remain unanswered; we would doubtless have a much clearer picture if Varro's writings had survived fully intact. However, it is simply not the case that Roman thinkers were uninterested in, or uninformed about, musical issues. The speech against Piso illustrates how debates about musical *ethos* were coloured by the private lives of Roman elites. Furthermore, Varro's neglected satire *Onos Lyras*, though difficult to reconstruct, hints at the possibility that musical debates gained traction outside upper-class circles, even perhaps influencing the subject matter of theatrical performances.

During his lifetime, Cicero had seen a succession of demagogues seize power by giving a voice – a musical voice – to the *plebs*. He had seen the rich and famous seduced by the pleasures of song, the Senate browbeaten by dancing consuls and harp-wielding tribunes, the Palatine populated by effete men whose houses echoed with the deafening sound of orchestras and choirs, and the popular assemblies – once synonymous with honour and dignity – overwhelmed by the coarse chanting of rival factions. From Cicero's perspective, the Romans had lost touch with their musical roots. He wanted the music of the theatre to be restored to its former austerity, and the music of the *convivium* to be stripped of its Greek trappings. Only in this way could there be a return to ancestral norms, to social cohesion and political stability.

In the end, it would take the implosion of the entire republican system for Cicero's dream of a 'harmonious' Rome to be realised.

3 | Augustus, Apollo's Lyre and the Harmony of the Principate

in Actiaco litore mare citharam sonat.

Along the shore at Actium the sea has a sound like that of a lyre.
Martianus Capella, *On the Seven Disciplines* 9.929

One of the most striking features of the Augustan Principate is the special relationship which the *princeps* cultivated with the god Apollo. Promoted initially by Octavian in his capacity as triumvir, this relationship assumed a pivotal role in the aftermath of the victory over Mark Antony and Cleopatra at the Battle of Actium in 31 BCE and culminated a few years later with the dedication of the magnificent Temple of Apollo on the Palatine Hill in Rome. Visitors to the new temple were greeted by imposing statues of the god himself, brought stunningly to life in marble and gold.[1] Beyond the Palatine, Apollo's image was ever-present. Coins bore his likeness. Poets sang of him in their verses. Public festivals were celebrated in his honour. To his worshippers Apollo appeared in various guises – as prophet, archer, healer, sun-god. Yet there was one particular incarnation of Apollo which came to personify the spirit of the Augustan Age. The deity chosen to embody the hopes of the fledgling Principate was none other than Apollo Citharoedus, god of music.

The significance of Apollo as a political totem for the Augustan regime has not gone unnoticed by historians of the period.[2] Octavian, so it is said, sought initially to exploit Apollo's dual identity as archer and musician as a means of negotiating the paradoxical nature of his own self-presentation as both conqueror and pacifist. Subsequently, in the wake of Antony's defeat, the victor wrote Apollo into the mythology of Actium by locating him at the centre of an eye-catching monumental programme, which conspicuously downplayed Apollo's martial aspect and emphasised instead his association with the musical arts. By populating his city with images of the lyre-playing deity, the *princeps* promoted a model of autocratic rule

---

[1] Prop. 2.31.5–6, 15–6, discussed in the section 'Apollo Citharoedus on the Palatine'.
[2] The classic study of the Augustan Apollo is Gagé 1955: esp. 523–81. See also Zanker 1988: 48–53, 85–9; Gurval 1995: 87–136; Miller 2009; Lange 2009; Wiseman 2019.

based on the Apolline ideals of peace, harmony and rationality. In doing so, he laid the foundations of a new world order. The significance of this message was not lost on contemporary poets. 'I have sung enough of war', writes Propertius in his fourth book of *Elegies*; 'Apollo the victor now demands the *cithara* and has laid aside his arms for peaceful dances'.[3]

The connection between Apollo, music and peace seems logical enough. But the matter is not quite as simple as Propertius' poem suggests. It is generally agreed that Apollo occupied a relatively minor status in the Roman pantheon prior to his elevation by Octavian.[4] If that is true, what exactly was the *princeps* trying to achieve by aligning himself with this particular deity? Why did he choose to dedicate one of his first major public buildings in Rome to the god of music, when other divine personifications of 'peace' and 'victory' were available to him (one thinks, for instance, of Concordia or Victoria, both well-established cults by this period)? How did Octavian's cultivation of Apollo relate to Mark Antony's cultivation of Dionysus, a god with his own (contrasting) musical associations? And to what extent did the Augustan promotion of Apollo inspire new developments in Roman musical thought and/or practice in this period? Was there a 'golden age' of Roman music under Augustus?

This chapter re-examines Augustus' interactions with Apollo with a view to shedding light on the intersections between musical and political culture at the end of the first century BCE. My central focus will be on how the *princeps* used musical imagery, both literally and figuratively, as a way of representing and embodying a restorative political message. Our search for Apolline imagery will require us to traverse well-trodden and sometimes challenging terrain. The representations of Apollo on Augustan coins and in Augustan texts have generated heated debate in modern scholarship. The archaeology of the Augustan Palatine has been a particular point of contention in recent years, especially surrounding the identification of the so-called House of Augustus and its topographical relationship to the temple of Apollo. The material relating to Augustus and Apollo Citharoedus must therefore be gone over with a fine-tooth comb if fresh insights are to be gleaned. The chapter also reassesses Augustus' relationship with Apollo by placing it in dialogue with Mark Antony's use of

---

[3] Prop. 4.6.69–70: *bella satis cecini: citharam iam poscit Apollo | victor et ad placidos exuit arma choros.* For other references to Apollo as a lyre-player in Augustan texts, cf. Hor. *Od.* 2.10.18–20, 3.3.72, 4.6.25–6, 4.15.1–2; Prop. 2.34.79–80, 4.1.73–4; 4.6.31–2; Ov. *Am.* 1.1.11–12, *Ars* 2.493–4, 3.141–2, *Met.* 2.601–2, 11.165–9; Virg. *Aen.* 12.393–4; *Eleg. Maec.* 1.51.

[4] Beard, North and Price 1998: 199: 'Previously his main role had been as a healing god, of no particular prominence; now he was to be central to Augustus' new Rome.'

Dionysiac music. I argue that Augustus' promotion of Apolline *kitharoidia* represented a rejection of Antony's 'foreign' musicality and an attempt to return music to its older, more foundational Roman setting. By foregrounding these themes, I hope to offer a new context for discussing the political, social and cultural reforms of the Augustan Principate.

Apollo Citharoedus on the Palatine

In 36 BCE, following the defeat of Sextus Pompey at Naulochus in Sicily, Octavian unveiled plans to erect a temple to Apollo on the south-west corner of the Palatine Hill.[5] The announcement was most likely made in an address to the Senate and people upon his return to Rome in November.[6] According to Cassius Dio, the decision to dedicate the temple was made when a bolt of lightning struck an area of land which Octavian had recently procured for his private residence.[7] After duly consulting the haruspices – and taking full advantage of the opportunity for a show of reverence – Octavian declared that this land would be made public property, and that a sanctuary would be built on the very site where the lightning had struck.

It was not until 9 October 28 BCE, nearly eight years later, that the new complex was finally opened to the public. With its elevated position on the Palatine Hill and its expansive portico, adorned with a rich array of artworks, the Temple of Apollo quickly gained a reputation as one of Rome's most spectacular landmarks.[8] It also came to play an important role in the political life of the city.[9] The temple's poor state of preservation

---

[5] Vell. Pat. 2.81.3: [*Octavianus*] *templumque Apollinis et circa porticus facturum promisit, quod ab eo singulari exstructum munificentia est.*

[6] Appian (*BC* 5.130-1) notes that, on the day after his return, Octavian 'addressed both the Senate and the people, giving a detailed account of his achievements and his administration from the beginning to the present time' (ἐβουληγόρησέ τε καὶ ἐδημηγόρησε, τὰ ἔργα καὶ τὴν πολιτείαν ἑαυτοῦ τὴν ἀπ' ἀρχῆς ἐς τότε καταλέγων). On the chronology, see Hekster and Rich 2006.

[7] Dio Cass. 49.15.5: τὸν γὰρ τόπον ὃν ἐν τῷ Παλατίῳ, ὥστ' οἰκοδομῆσαί τινα, ἐώνητο, ἐδημοσίωσε καὶ τῷ Ἀπόλλωνι ἱέρωσεν, ἐπειδὴ κεραυνὸς ἐς αὐτὸν ἐγκατέσκηψε. Octavian had acquired the former house of Hortensius 'probably in late 43 or 42 BC' (Wiseman 2013: 255), and subsequently purchased several neighbouring properties (Suet. *Aug.* 72.1; Vell. 2.81.3).

[8] The construction of the temple is recorded in the *Res Gestae* (*RG* 19). Later visitors marvelled at its size and splendour: cf. Joseph. *BJ* 2.81; Asconius on Cic. *Tog. Cand.* 90; Suet. *Aug.* 90. In addition to the statues of Apollo, there were four bulls by Myron around the altar (Prop. 2.31.5-8) and the pediments of the temple contained works by the archaic masters Bupalos and Athenis (Plin. *HN* 36.11-14). Augustus himself was a discerning art critic: Suet. *Aug.* 89.1; Plin. *HN* 35.91.

[9] The Senate often met in the temple: Suet. *Aug.* 29.3; *Tab. Hebana* ll. 1-4 (Crawford and Cloud 1996: 519); *SC Larinum* l. 2 (Rawson 1983: 98).

in the archaeological record gives only a faint impression of its former grandeur. Excavation of the site has been ongoing since the 1960s but has failed to produce conclusive evidence concerning the temple's architectural design and topographical orientation.[10]

We are, however, reasonably well-informed about the decoration of the temple thanks to the poems of Propertius. In an elegy composed shortly after the inauguration of the Palatine sanctuary, Propertius writes to his girlfriend Cynthia apologising for his lateness to a recent rendezvous:

> *quaeris, cur veniam tibi tardior? aurea Phoebi*
> *porticus a magno Caesare aperta fuit.*
> *tantam erat in speciem Poenis digesta columnis,*
> *inter quas Danai femina turba senis.*
> *hic equidem Phoebo visus mihi pulchrior ipso*
> *marmoreus tacita carmen hiare lyra ...*
> *deinde inter matrem deus ipse interque sororem*
> *Pythius in longa carmina veste sonat.*
> (Prop. 2.31.1–6, 15–16)

> You ask why I come to you a little late? The golden sanctuary of Apollo was opened by great Caesar. It was arranged in remarkable splendour with Punic columns, between which were statues of the female brood of aged Danaus. Here I saw one who seemed to me even more beautiful than Phoebus himself, a marble figure with parted lips as if singing to his silent lyre ... Then inside the Pythian god himself, standing between his mother and his sister and dressed in a long robe, performs his songs.

Propertius pictures the Palatine temple from the perspective of an approaching visitor, focusing initially on the outer portico and then moving sequentially towards the altar, the temple doors and, finally, to the cult objects within. We seem to be confronted with not one but two statues of Apollo, the first made of marble (*marmoreus*) and situated in the golden portico in front of the temple (ll. 4–5), and the second (of unspecified material) located within the temple itself (ll. 15–16).[11] Both statues

---

[10] Zink (2012) argues on the basis of archaeological evidence that the temple was oriented to the south-west, overlooking the Circus Maximus, whereas Claridge (2010) and Wiseman (2012) argue for a north-east orientation, relying primarily on textual evidence. It was long believed that the temple was connected directly to the lower residential quarters of Augustus' house via a ramp: see Carettoni 1983: 7–16; Zanker 1988: 51. However, this theory has since been refuted: Iacopi and Tedone 2005–2006: 351–78; Wiseman 2013 and 2019. On the architecture of the temple, see further Marchetti 2001; Zink 2008.

[11] Butler and Barber (1933: 247–8) make a case for transposing lines 5–8 to follow line 16, assuming that the same statue is referred to in both cases. However, this is an unnecessary

represent the god in the guise of *citharoedus*, chanting songs to the accompaniment of the lyre.[12] The first Apollo appears as a lone figure, while the second is accompanied by his mother Latona and his sister Diana (*inter matrem ... interque sororem*).

Modern analyses of Propertius 2.31 have rightly underlined the dangers of reading the poem as a realistic eyewitness account.[13] Not only do we lack sufficient archaeological evidence to corroborate Propertius' narrative, but we must also remember that the process of ekphrastic composition called for a certain creativity on the part of the poet, which may have resulted in the distortion, elaboration or omission of certain details. The description of an inanimate statue as being 'more beautiful than Phoebus himself' (*Phoebo visus mihi pulchrior ipso*), even appearing to 'sing' (*carmen hiare*; *sonat*), is as much a testament to Propertius' powers of imagination as it is a comment on the beauty of a real statue (although, of course, these two ideas are not mutually exclusive).[14] Nonetheless, the existence of the statues is beyond dispute. Other Augustan writers also allude to a lyre-playing Apollo in poems mentioning the Palatine temple. In an elegy commemorating the promotion of his patron's son to the priestly office of *quindecimvir*, Tibullus evokes the image of Apollo greeting him at the threshold of his temple 'with lyre and with songs' (*cum cithara carminibusque*).[15] Horace, similarly, marks the occasion of the temple's dedication with a prayer that in his old age he may not 'lack the lyre' (*nec turpem senectam ... cithara carentem*).[16] It is highly likely that both poets wrote these words with the Palatine statues in mind.[17]

The name of the sculptor responsible for creating one of the statues is helpfully disclosed by Pliny the Elder in his *Natural History*. In a passage discussing the works of famous sculptors, Pliny refers to a 'Palatine Apollo' by Scopas of Paros, who was active during the fourth century BCE.[18]

---

emendation (*pace* Last 1953: 27–9; Roccos 1989: 572). Among other factors, the inclusion of the temporal marker *deinde* at the start of l. 15 (cf. *tum*, 2.31.9) implies a clear 'sequence of viewing' which disassociates the statue of Apollo with *tacita ... lyra* (l. 6) from the one *in longa ... veste* (l. 16); Welch 2005: 91.

[12] *Lyra* in line 6 is a poetic synonym for *cithara* (cf. Martial 8.6.6: *muros struxit Apollo lyra*). The citharodic aspect of the second statue is suggested by the reference in line 16 to Apollo's 'long robe' (the quintessential costume of the citharode) and by the use of *sonat*, which implies instrumental performance (cf. Hor. *Epod.* 9.5: *sonante mixtum tibiis carmen lyra*).

[13] Isager 1998: 405–6; Welch 2005: 89–96; Miller 2009: 196–206.

[14] See here Miller 2009: 202–4, noting the influence of Callimachus' *Hymn to Apollo* on Propertius' description of the statues.

[15] Tib. 2.5.2.   [16] Hor. *Od.* 1.31.20.   [17] Cairns 1984: 153.

[18] Plin. *HN* 36.25: *Scopae laus cum his certat. is fecit ... Apollinem Palatinum*. Some scholars state that Octavian acquired Scopas' statue from a sanctuary of Apollo at Rhamnous near Athens

Pliny also refers in the same passage to a statue of Latona by the third-century Athenian sculptor Cephisodotus and a statue of Diana by Timotheus of Epidaurus (a contemporary of Scopas), both of which were displayed in the Palatine temple.[19] If we associate this pair with the 'mother' and 'sister' of Propertius' poem (*inter matrem ... interque sororem*), then the Apollo of Scopas is probably better identified with the statue inside the *cella* ('the god himself' in Propertius' description) than the one in the outer portico.[20] Parallels for the triadic grouping of Apollo, Diana and Latona can be found elsewhere in Augustan and Julio-Claudian art. A set of painted terracotta plaques, unearthed in 1968 during the excavations of the Palatine temple, represents Apollo and Diana adorning a sacred pillar with their respective instruments – Apollo the lyre and Diana the bow and quiver. The plaques (now in the Palatine Museum) are thought to have originally decorated the walls of the *cella* (Fig. 3.1).[21] In addition, a relief from the Villa Albani represents Apollo Citharoedus, trailed by his sister and mother, processing in stately formation towards the goddess Victoria, who welcomes them to her sacred precinct on the Palatine (Fig. 3.2).[22] Similar imagery can be seen on an Augustan relief from Italy, now in the Cleveland Museum of Art, as well as on the so-called Sorrento Base, usually dated to the late Augustan or early Tiberian period (Fig. 3.3).[23]

How the cult statues were displayed within the Palatine temple remains a mystery. Suetonius tells us that in 12 BCE Augustus made the decision to relocate the Sibylline Books from the Temple of Jupiter Capitolinus to the

---

(see, e.g., Claridge 2010: 143). This is inferred from a reference to the Palatine temple as *aedis Apollinis Ramnusii* in two regionary catalogues from the 350s CE. However, no direct evidence exists for a sanctuary of Apollo at Rhamnous. Wiseman (2013: 250) instead links the epithet *Ramnusius* to Apollo's role as an avenging deity, but this idea is equally speculative. The significance of *Ramnusius* remains unclear.

[19] Plin. *HN* 36.24 (*Latona in Palatii delubro*), 36.32 (*Diana Romae est in Palatio Apollinis delubro*).
[20] Last (1953) makes the opposite case, citing evidence in the *Tabula Hebana* for a *simulacrum Apollinis* covered by a 'roof' (*fastigium*). However, the word *fastigium* is a restoration, and, even if correct, it is possible that the word refers to an *aedicula* within the *cella* and not, as Last suggests, to a kind of 'canopy', physically detached from the temple building itself. It would make sense for the *Apollo Palatinus* to have resided inside the *cella*, given that this was normally where the most sacred cult images were displayed: see Miller 2009: 188–9.
[21] See additional illustrations in Tomei and Gasparri 2014: 154.
[22] The temple shown in the relief may be the temple of Victoria on the Palatine, built in the early third century BCE (Livy 10.33.9).
[23] On the 'Sorrento Base', see Roccos 1989. Additionally, archaising figures of Apollo, Diana and Leto appear on a three-sided Neo-Attic candelabrum base from the early Augustan period, found in 1848 at the via della Conciliazone and now in the collections of the Musei Capitolini (inv. 2271). For representations of Apollo Citharoedus and Diana in Roman villa contexts, see Roccos 2002.

Figure 3.1 Terracotta plaque from the sanctuary of Apollo on the Palatine, showing Apollo and Diana adorning a sacred pillar; ca. 30 BCE. Antiquario del Palatino, Rome, inv. 379051. Photo: Werner Forman / Universal Images Group / Getty Images.

Temple of Apollo, where he housed them 'in two golden bookshelves beneath the base of the Palatine Apollo' (*duobus forulis auratis sub Palatini Apollinis basi*).[24] This comment has been taken to imply that the

---

[24] Suet. *Aug.* 31.1; cf. Serv. *ad Aen.* 6.72.

Figure 3.2 Apollo, Diana and Latona received by Victoria on the Palatine; Augustan marble relief. Villa Albani, Rome, inv. 1014. © Staatliche Mussen zu Berlin, Antikensammlung, Photo: Universität zu Köln, Archäologisches Institut, CoDArchLab, 109909_FA-SPerg003568-01_Gisela Geng.

cult statue was mounted above a kind of ornamental bookcase, although in the absence of reliable archaeological evidence we cannot be sure whether this arrangement existed prior to 12 BCE.[25]

Scholarly interest in the Temple of Apollo was piqued in 1950 by a sensational discovery. Archaeologists excavating in the vicinity of the temple stumbled upon a large fragment of a wall-painting depicting the lone figure of Apollo, rendered in stunning detail with fine drapery, laurel wreath and quiver (Fig. 3.4).[26] The god holds in his hands a seven-stringed *cithara*, his mouth agape as though in the midst of song. The painting's find spot would prove significant, since it lay within the confines of a late-republican house soon to be identified by Gianfilippo Carettoni as belonging to none other than Augustus himself.[27] This connection

---

[25] Claridge 2010: 142; Wardle 2014: 248–9; *contra* Zink 2012.
[26] Originally published by Romanelli and Carettoni 1955: 208–14. Miller (2009: 1) raises the interesting possibility that the fragment was part of a larger mythological panel, perhaps representing Apollo and the Muses or Apollo competing against the satyr Marsyas.
[27] Carettoni 1956.

Figure 3.3 Apollo, Diana and Latona on the Sorrento Base; Augustan/early imperial period. Apollo stands in the centre and holds a lyre in his left hand. Museo Correale, Sorrento. Photo: German Archaeological Institute, Rome 1965.1255.

inevitably gave rise to much speculation: what if Augustus commissioned a painting of his patron god to be displayed proudly in his palace, thereby creating a symbolic link with the adjacent temple?[28] However, subsequent research has indicated that the complex known as the 'House of Augustus' was in fact largely demolished to make room for the temple and its surrounding portico.[29] In this case, the residence – including the painting of Apollo – may not have belonged to Augustus at all. The real house of Augustus is likely to have been considerably smaller than previously supposed – not a palace as such, but something more akin to an old-fashioned republican *domus*.[30] As Suetonius explains in his *Life*, Augustus'

---

[28] The idea that Augustus aspired to create a unified palace-sanctuary complex on the model of the great Hellenistic centres of Pergamum and Alexandria was influentially argued by Zanker (1988: 51–3).

[29] Iacopi and Tedone 2005–2006: 351–78.   [30] See Wiseman 2013 and 2019.

Figure 3.4 Apollo with cithara and quiver depicted on a fragment of a wall painting from the House of Augustus. Antiquario del Palatino, Rome, inv. 379982. Photo by Werner Forman / Universal Images Group / Getty Images.

house was 'remarkable neither for size nor elegance' (*neque laxitate neque cultu conspicuis*), having 'rooms without any marble or decorated pavement' (*sine marmore ullo aut insigni pavimento conclavia*).[31]

Nevertheless, the fact that the *princeps* chose to live on the Palatine next to his patron god undoubtedly represented a powerful statement of intent. Never before had a living Roman fostered such a deep personal connection with a particular deity.[32] Not only was the *princeps*' affinity with Apollo writ large on the monumental landscape of the Palatine, as we have seen, but it was also rendered visible through the medium of sculpture. Alessandro Barchiesi has suggested that the statue in the portico of the temple of Apollo, described by Propertius as being 'more beautiful than Phoebus himself', may actually have imitated the likeness of the *princeps*.[33]

---

[31] Suet. *Aug.* 72.1.
[32] As Ovid famously remarked, a single house held three gods: Apollo, Vesta and Augustus (*stet domus! aeternos tres habet una deos*; *Fast.* 4.954). In 12 BCE, Augustus installed a shrine to Vesta within the Palatine precinct, perhaps combined with his household shrine to the Penates: see Capelli, *LTUR V*, s.v. Vesta, Ara, Signum, Aedes (in Palatio), 128–9.
[33] Barchiesi 2005: 284.

Figure 3.5 Marble statue of Augustus from Prima Porta; after a bronze original, ca. 20 BCE. Vatican Museums, Rome, inv. 2290. Photo by Prisma / UIG / Getty Images.

This hypothesis is not as far-fetched as one might think. It is certainly not hard to see how the idealised classicism of Augustus' official portraiture, the serene expression and ageless beauty, could evoke comparisons with the eternally youthful Apollo. To appreciate the resemblance, we need only compare the features of Augustus on the famous statue from Prima Porta with those of the lyre-playing Apollo, whose image adorns the right flank of Augustus' breastplate (Fig. 3.5).[34] In Athens, where the divinisation of living rulers was less taboo, Augustus was honoured in inscriptions as 'the New Apollo' and probably represented in this guise on statues too.[35]

---

[34] The statue was modelled on a bronze original from around 20 BCE (Zanker 1988: 188–9).

[35] *SEG* 29, 167 (21/20 BCE): [Σεβαστὸ]ν Καίσ[αρα Νέον Ἀ]πόλλωνα | Ποσ[ειδώνι]ος Δημη[τρίου] Φλυεὺς | ἀγωνοθέτης ἐν ἐφήβ[οι]ς αὐτοῦ; Peppas-Delmousou 1979; Hoff 1992. An Athenian

Most importantly, the public library which stood next to the Palatine temple is said to have contained a statue of Augustus 'with the garb and stance of Apollo' (*habitu ac statura Apollinis*).³⁶ Servius may be referring to the same statue when he speaks of a *simulacrum* depicting Augustus 'with all the attributes of Apollo' (*cum Apollinis cunctis insignibus*).³⁷ Although we cannot be certain, there is a strong possibility that the *princeps* was made to resemble a citharodic Apollo, as would be appropriate for a statue displayed in a library devoted to Greek and Latin literature (literature being the domain of the Muses).³⁸

Apollo Citharoedus and the Commemoration of Actium

When did the connection between Octavian and Apollo first manifest itself publicly? Was it prior to Octavian's assumption of autocratic power, and, if so, how did the Romans' perception of that relationship change after the victory at Actium? The traditional view, espoused by Jean Gagé in his book *Apollon romain*, is that Octavian began to cultivate Apollo as his patron deity while serving as triumvir during the 40s.³⁹ This argument hinges effectively on three literary testimonies: (1) the episode in Suetonius' biography known as the Feast of the Twelve Gods, in which the young Caesar is reprimanded by the famine-stricken *populus* for attending a banquet dressed as Apollo; (2) the rumour reported by Cassius Dio that Octavian's mother was impregnated by Apollo in the form of a snake; and (3) Valerius Maximus' reference to 'Apollo' being chosen by Octavian and Antony as the watchword at the Battle of Philippi.⁴⁰ However, Gagé's interpretation of these texts has rightly been called into question: the Suetonian anecdote has the ring of apocryphal Antonian propaganda; the rumour of Atia being impregnated by Apollo could only have gained currency after Augustus' supremacy was assured; and, according to Plutarch, it was Brutus who chose 'Apollo' at Philippi, not the triumvirs

---

decree from around the same time mentions the foundation of an annual festival in honour of Augustus on Boedromion 12 (the emperor's *dies natalis*), shortly after the annual celebration of Apollo's 'birthday' in Athens on Boedromion 7: *IG* II² 1071 = *SEG* 16 (1960) no. 34, with commentary by Stamires 1957: 260–85.

³⁶ Ps.-Acro ad Hor. *Ep.* 1.3.17: [*Augustus*] *sibi posuerat effigiem habitu ac statura Apollinis.*
³⁷ Serv. *ad* Verg. *Ecl.* 4.10.
³⁸ Suet. *Aug.* 29: *addidit porticus cum bibliotheca Latina Graecaque*. Champlin (2003a: 142) favours an identification with Apollo Citharoedus on the basis of a comparison with Nero's statues in *citharoedicus habitus* (cf. Suet. *Nero* 25.2).
³⁹ Gagé 1955: 479–94.   ⁴⁰ Suet. *Aug.* 70; Dio Cass. 45.1.2; Val. Max. 1.5.7.

(and even if Valerius is correct, the watchword was used jointly by Octavian *and* Antony).[41] A fourth piece of evidence – namely, Vergil's *Fourth Eclogue* – has also been adduced by some scholars in support of an early connection between Octavian and Apollo. The poem, composed in 40 BCE, speaks of a 'child' who will bring an end to civil war and restore the reign of Apollo and the kingdom of Saturn.[42] But criticisms can be raised here too: upon closer examination, the identification of Vergil's *puer* as Octavian seems exceedingly unlikely.[43] It is safest, then, to place the turning point in the year 36 BCE, with the defeat of Sextus Pompey's fleet at Naulochus and the vow of the Palatine temple. The lightning-bolt struck, the haruspices declared that Apollo required a temple inside the *pomerium*, and Octavian seized the moment. With his colleague Lepidus now out of the picture and Mark Antony preoccupied in the East, the young Caesar began to make his mark on Rome's cityscape by publicly honouring the god who had guaranteed his victory over Sextus Pompey.

By the time that the temple was finally dedicated in 28 BCE, the situation had changed. Octavian's triumph at Actium had elevated him into a position of unrivalled pre-eminence. It had also handed him a golden opportunity to strengthen ties with the god who had ensured his rise to power. By a fateful coincidence, the gulf of Actium was overlooked by an ancient sanctuary of Apollo. Taking the initiative once again, Octavian ordered a new, larger temple of Apollo to be built on the hill where the ancient sanctuary had stood. Next to it he constructed an imposing victory monument consisting of a network of 'boathouses' containing ten ships captured during the battle.[44] Across the Actian gulf, Octavian founded the new city of Nicopolis through a synoecism of neighbouring communities. In its northern suburb, he laid out an expansive precinct with a stadium and gymnasium purpose-built for the celebration of quinquennial games in honour of Apollo.[45] On a site to the north of the city ('the spot where he had had his tent', according to Cassius Dio) he erected an open-air shrine to Apollo, in addition to another, even larger, naval monument dedicated

---

[41] Plut. *Brut.* 24.7; Gurval 1995: 94–102; Hekster and Rich 2006: 160–1; Levick 2010: 203–4.
[42] Verg. *Ecl.* 4.8–10: *tuus iam regnat Apollo.*   [43] See Lange 2009: 46.
[44] The literary evidence for Octavian's Actian monuments comes from Strabo 7.7.6, Dio Cass. 51.1.3 and Suet. *Aug.* 18.2. Archaeological excavation has yielded invaluable information about the structural and topographical aspects of the campsite memorial at Actium: see Zachos 2003 and 2007, building on the findings of Murray and Petsas 1989. The precise dating of the Actian monuments remains contested; the chronology in Dio is very vague (ταῦτα μὲν ὕστερον ἐγένετο; 51.1.4), while Strabo says nothing about it at all.
[45] Strabo 7.7.6; Dio Cass. 51.1.2; Suet. *Aug.* 18.2; Schäfer 1993: 247. On the foundation of Nicopolis, see Purcell 1987; Lange 2009: 99–106.

to Neptune and Mars. Those who looked upon these impressive structures could have been left in no doubt that Octavian's elevation had been divinely ordained.

As news of Antony's defeat in sight of Apollo's ancient sanctuary reached Rome, the temple of Apollo taking shape on the Palatine must have assumed a very different aspect: no longer just a symbol of the victory at Naulochus, but a token of something greater, the total cessation of civil war. Cassius Dio informs us that, following the announcement of the victory at Actium, the Senate decreed 'that a festival [in Rome] should be held every four years in honour of Octavian'. The first edition of these 'Actian' games, as they were known, is likely to have coincided with the dedication of the Palatine temple in 28.[46] Although the 'Actian' Apollo is often portrayed in Augustan poetry in military guise – as a fearsome archer and marshal of the battlefield – he was also conflated with the citharodic god who presided over the Palatine.[47] We find this assimilation expressed, for instance, in the anonymous *Elegies on Maecenas*, in which *Apollo Actius* is pictured plucking his lyre with the ivory plectrum after the trumpets of victory have fallen silent.[48] In one of the Medinaceli reliefs, a set of panels decorated with major events from the life of Augustus, Apollo is shown holding a *cithara* while looking down on the ships fighting at Actium (Fig. 3.6).[49] The reliefs date from after Augustus' death (perhaps from the reign of Claudius), but they capture an idea that would surely have been recognisable to Romans of an earlier period: the god who guaranteed Octavian's triumph in the historic battle was the same god who resided beside him on the Palatine.

The conflation of the 'Actian' and 'Palatine' Apollos is further underscored by a series of Augustan coins issued a decade or so after the inauguration of the Palatine temple. Of particular interest is a denarius minted in Lugdunum in 16 BCE by the moneyer C. Antistius Vetus (Fig. 3.7). A profile of Augustus appears on the obverse of the coin, with his titles emblazoned around the edge. The reverse shows Apollo, wearing a laurel wreath and dressed in a long *chiton* (tunic). He carries a *cithara* in

---

[46] Dio 51.19.2: πανήγυρίν οἱ πεντετηρίδα ἄγεσθαι. Additional celebrations are recorded in 16 BCE and 9 CE: Dio Cass. 53.1.4–5, 54.19.8; Plin. *HN* 7.158; *CIL* 6.877a; Hekster and Rich 2006: 165; Lange 2009: 168.
[47] See Miller 2009: 54–94; Pelling 1997.
[48] *Eleg. in Maec.* 1.51-2: *Actius ipse lyram plectro percussit eburno, | postquam victrices conticuere tubae.*
[49] For illustrations of the full set of reliefs, see Schäfer 2013: 321–3; see also discussion in Castaldo 2018: 97–100.

156 Augustus, Apollo's Lyre and the Harmony

Figure 3.6 Apollo Citharoedus overlooking the Battle of Actium; Medinaceli Reliefs, detail of panel; second quarter of first century CE. Museum of Fine Arts, Budapest, inv. 4817.1. © László Mátyus, Museum of Fine Arts, Budapest.

his left hand and a *patera* (libation bowl) in his right, from which he pours a libation into a burning altar situated directly beside him. The accompanying legend reads: C ANTISTI VETVS IIIVIR APOLLINI ACTIO (C. Antistius Vetus *triumvir* to Actian Apollo). We have here, therefore, an explicit allusion to the role of Apollo Citharoedus as Augustus' divine protector at Actium. An image of Apollo playing the lyre is also coupled with an allusion to Actium in two other coin types, dating from 15–13 and 11–10 BCE respectively. In the first type, Apollo faces forward and holds a plectrum (Fig. 3.8); in the second, Apollo faces right and holds a *patera*, just as we see on the denarius of Antistius Vetus (Fig. 3.9).

Although Apollo and the lyre had been appearing on Roman coins prior to the Battle of Actium, the Augustan coinage is the first to represent Apollo specifically in the guise of *citharoedus*.[50] The interpretation of these

---

[50] A denarius minted by Brutus in 42 BCE shows on the obverse a personification of Libertas and on the reverse a plectrum, a rectangular lyre and a laurel wreath (all attributes of Apollo): *RRC* 501; *BMCRR* East, 471 n. 38. The head of Apollo is juxtaposed with an image of a lyre on another denarius from the same year: *RRC* 504; *BMCRR* East, 476 n. 55. An image of a god playing the *cithara* appears on an Italian denarius from ca. 32–29 BCE (*RIC* I^2 257). However, the god in question is not Apollo but Mercury, the mythical inventor of the *cithara*, as is made clear by the fact that he is represented with a *petasus* (broad-brimmed hat) slung behind his back (for the idea of Mercury as the inventor of the *cithara*, cf. Hor. *Od.* 1.10.6, 1.21.12,

Figure 3.7 Denarius struck by C. Antistius Vetus, 16 BCE, Rome mint. Obverse: head of Augustus. Reverse: Apollo with lyre in left hand and *patera* in right hand, pouring a libation over an altar. The deity and altar are situated on a base ornamented with prows and anchors. The legend reads APOLLINI ACTIO (for Actian Apollo). *RIC* I² 365–66 + Pl. 7; BMCRE 95. © The Trustees of the British Museum. 1846,0910.177.

coins has sparked a great deal of controversy in recent decades. The debate has centred mostly on the meaning of the Antistius Vetus coin. Why is Apollo shown standing atop a rostra adorned with *navalia spolia* (the outlines of two anchors and three rams are clearly visible)? Might the imagery of the coin reflect the appearance of an actual naval monument erected by Augustus in Rome or elsewhere? In Paul Zanker's view, the two Apollo coin types (Apollo with plectrum and Apollo with *patera*) are deliberately modelled on the iconography of the Palatine statues: the Apollo with plectrum corresponds with the cult statue inside the *cella* (the work of Scopas), while the Apollo with *patera* corresponds with the Apollo in the *porticus* (which Zanker labels the 'Apollo of Actium'). Based on this correspondence, Zanker deduces that the statue in front of the temple must have stood on a platform adorned with the rams and anchors of ships captured at Actium.[51] An alternative explanation has been

---

3.11.3–4; Diod. Sic. 1.16.1). *Citharae* alone appear on Roman coins from the late second century BCE onwards: *RRC* 320, 410.1–10b, 416.1, 417, 472.4a, 501; *RIC* I² 293.

[51] Zanker 1983: 31–2 and 1988: 88. See, more recently, Tomei 2017, arguing on the basis of the numismatic evidence for the existence of a (now lost) commemorative monument of Actium on

Figure 3.8 Aureus of Augustus, 15–13 BCE, Lugdunum mint. Observe: head of Augustus. Reverse: Apollo with plectrum in right hand and lyre in left hand. *RIC* I² 170. © The Trustees of the British Museum. R.5997.

proposed by Hans Jucker. Jucker postulates that the image on the coin of Antistius Vetus alludes not to the Palatine statues in Rome but to an otherwise unknown statue of Apollo which decorated Augustus' campsite memorial at Actium.⁵² Given the presence of a temple of Apollo on this site, it is highly likely that the god was represented sculpturally in some form. Since the publication of Jucker's article in 1982, important new evidence has emerged from the archaeological excavations at Actium. We now know that the upper terrace of the naval monument supported a large altar, which may have been decorated with a statue of Apollo. A semicircular base was also discovered in the vicinity (its original location is unknown), which represents Apollo, accompanied by eleven other gods, holding a lyre in his left hand and a plectrum in his right hand.⁵³

In my opinion, however, neither Zanker nor Jucker make a convincing case for pinning the numismatic iconography onto a particular monument.

---

the Palatine. Gagé (1955: 545) and Sutherland (*RIC*² I, 365) misinterpret the rostra on the Antistius Vetus coin as a statue base, citing Suetonius' description of the cult statue inside the Palatine temple ('two golden bookshelves beneath the base of the Palatine Apollo').

⁵² Jucker 1982.
⁵³ Zachos 2003: 89–90 (with illustration) and 2007: 414; see also Lange 2009: 107–8, 177–80.

Figure 3.9 Aureus of Augustus, 11–10 BCE, Lugdunum mint. Observe: head of Augustus, laureate. Reverse: Apollo with *patera* in right hand and lyre in left hand. The legend on the exergue reads ACT (Actium). *RIC* I² 192A. © The Trustees of the British Museum. BNK,R.3.

Propertius makes no mention of a rostra in his description of the Apollo statues, and it is hard to see why he should have omitted such a conspicuous detail if it was indeed part of the sculptural display. The reappearance of Apollo Citharoedus on later coins issued under Antoninus Pius, Commodus and Septimius Severus complicates matters further. The legends inscribed on these coins (either APOLLINI AVGVSTO or APOLLINI PALATINO) hark back to the first *princeps* and his role in the building of the Palatine temple. However, the iconography varies considerably from that of the earlier Augustan coins: in the Commodan examples, Apollo's lyre is shown resting on a column.[54] It is hardly plausible that these coins were modelled on a single cult statue – indeed, it is debatable whether the original cult statues still stood by the time the coins were issued.[55]

---

[54] Commodus: *RIC* III 197, 197a, 206, 218, 578, 588. Antoninus Pius: *RIC* III 63A–C, 126, 598A–B. Severus: IV 40, 345, 682, 699.

[55] It is possible that the great fire of 64 CE damaged parts of the Palatine temple (Champlin 2003a: 124–5). Another fire in 192 CE destroyed large swathes of the Augustan Palatine (Dio Cass. 72.24; Hdn. 1.14.2–6); the destruction caused by this fire might have prompted the reissuing of the 'Apollo Citharoedus' series under Septimius Severus.

Taking stock of the evidence, then, it seems that there was indeed a recognised association between the 'Palatine' and 'Actian' Apollos in the early decades of the Augustan Principate. This association must have been apparent already by the time Apollo Citharoedus first appeared on Augustan coins. However, the depiction of *navalia spolia* on the denarius from 16 BCE need not be interpreted as a literal representation of a real statue or monument. Rather, it should be understood as a composite design which could equally have evoked several different Augustan monuments, whether in Rome, Actium or Nicopolis.[56] Instead of trying to match each Apollo 'type' to a physical counterpart, we should emphasise the political resonances of the musical Apollo in the wake of Octavian's victory over Mark Antony and Cleopatra.

Antony, Cleopatra and the Triumph over Dionysian Music

A fruitful way of contextualising Augustus' association with Apollo is to place it in dialogue with, and in opposition to, the Dionysian self-fashioning of his rival Mark Antony. Plutarch suggests that Antony was already styling himself as 'New Dionysus' in 41; other sources indicate a date closer to 39.[57] It seems clear, at any rate, that the divine alter egos of Antony and Octavian were understood by contemporaries as being in competition with one another.[58] Significantly, the historical sources pertaining to the life of Antony are full of references to music. Largely neglected by modern scholars, these references provide revealing clues about how Antony presented himself as a leader, especially while consorting with Cleopatra in the East. More specifically, I will contend in this section that Antony's engagement with Dionysian music can be seen as a key part of a project to present himself through the language of Hellenistic kingship. This provided a model against which Octavian in turn defined his Apolline 'programme'.

Our conception of the Apollo/Dionysus polarity owes much to the legacy of Friedrich Nietzsche. In his essay *The Birth of Tragedy* (1872), Nietzsche developed the notion of a binary opposition between the 'Apollonian' and the 'Dionysian', arguing that the struggle between these two elements constituted the intellectual foundation of Greek civilization: Apollo stood for order, clarity, harmony and logic, Dionysus for disorder,

---

[56] See Gurval 1995: 286–7.   [57] Pelling 1988: 179; Lange 2009: 42.
[58] On the rival images of Antony and Octavian, see Zanker 1988: 44–53; Miller 2009: 18, 26–8.

intoxication, emotionality and excess. The ancients themselves, however, do not seem to have recognised such a polarising distinction. After all, Apollo and Dionysus were both sons of Zeus and eternally young. They also occupied overlapping cultural spheres, as patrons of music and the arts.[59] Nevertheless, the anthesis between the Apolline and the Dionysian was not purely Nietzsche's invention. The idea that the two gods fulfilled different *musical* roles was deeply engrained in Greek and Roman thought. Apollo's instrument, the *cithara*, was serene and subtle; Dionysus' instrument, the *aulos/tibia*, was strident and chaotic, often featuring in ritual contexts along with drums and cymbals.[60] In this sense, the relationship between the two gods was both complementary and oppositional. Much like Antony and Octavian, erstwhile allies-turned-rivals, Apollo and Dionysus were bound together by an awkward affinity which made them apt to be viewed side by side.

The tension between Apollo and Dionysus was manifested most strikingly in the myth of Marsyas. A devoted follower of Dionysus, the satyr Marsyas took up the *aulos* after the goddess Athena rejected it as unseemly. Growing overconfident in his ability, Marsyas challenged Apollo to a musical contest, and as punishment for his hubris he was skinned alive (Fig. 3.10). The story was retold over the centuries as an allegory of the triumph of order over chaos, civilization over barbarism. For Plato, the flaying of Marsyas enshrined the moral and aesthetic superiority of the Apolline *cithara* over the Dionysian *aulos*.[61] Augustan texts convey a similar message. As has been noted by Piers Rawson, Augustan depictions of the myth place a marked emphasis on Marsyas' hubris, laying the blame solely with the upstart satyr and denying any brutality or duplicity on the

---

[59] On the similarities between Apollo and Dionysus, see Graf 2009: 139.
[60] The role of orgiastic music in Dionysian cult is evident in sixth-century BCE Athenian vase painting and tragedies such as Euripides' *Bacchae* (Ieranò 2020). For the association of the *aulos* with Dionysus, cf. also Arist. *Pol.* 8.1342b: πᾶσα γὰρ βακχεία καὶ πᾶσα ἡ τοιαύτη κίνησις μάλιστα τῶν ὀργάνων ἐστὶν ἐν τοῖς αὐλοῖς. Bacchic satyrs playing pipes appear on bronze *cistae* from Latium dating from the fourth century BCE (Wiseman 2008). Although in late-republican and Augustan Rome strings and pipes were often played together in public and private settings (cf. Cic. *Tusc. Disp.* 4.4; Hor. *Od.* 3.11.5–6), the conceptual distinction between the Apolline *cithara* and the Dionysian *aulos/tibia* was strongly entrenched: cf. Lucr. 2.505–6: *Phoebeaque daedala chordis | carmina*; contrasted with Cat. 64.261–4: *plangebant aliae proceris tympana palmis, | aut tereti tenues tinnitus aere ciebant; | multis raucisonos efflabant cornua bombos, | barbaraque horribili stridebat tibia cantu*. For the distinction between strings and pipes in Athenian culture, see Wilson 2004.
[61] In the *Republic* (399d–e), Plato expresses a preference for 'the instruments of Apollo over Marsyas and his instruments' (τὰ τοῦ Ἀπόλλωνος ὄργανα πρὸ Μαρσύου τε καὶ τῶν ἐκείνου ὀργάνων), on the grounds that the *kithara* possessed superior ethical qualities to the *aulos*.

Figure 3.10 Wall painting illustrating the musical contest between Apollo and Marsyas. On the right, a knife-wielding Scythian prepares to flay Marsyas, who is tied to a tree. The satyr's pipes lie on the ground in front of him. On the left, the victorious Apollo sits on a chair, holding a lyre and plectrum; a muse stands next to him. Olympus, Marsyas' student, kneels at Apollo's feet, begging for mercy. From Herculaneum, 60–79 CE. Museo Archeologico Nazionale, Naples, inv. no. 9539. Credits: Album / Alamy Stock Photo.

part of Apollo.[62] It would be tempting, therefore, to imagine a kind of Augustan rewriting of the myth in line with the peaceful image of Apollo promoted by the imperial regime. However, the argument should not be pushed too far. Read from a different perspective, the flaying of Marsyas cast a rather more sinister shadow on the *princeps*' relationship with the god of music. In some versions of the story – most notably, in Ovid's *Metamorphoses* – the satyr is presented as a tragic and even sympathetic figure, who suffered at the hands of a cruel and vindictive Apollo.[63] The statue of Marsyas which stood proudly in the Roman Forum showed the satyr in a pose of triumphant liberation, his right arm raised aloft, his left shoulder supporting a large wine-skin, and with broken shackles on his ankles.[64] It was at this very statue, in fact, that Augustus' daughter Julia was allegedly caught in the act of committing adultery with Iulius Antonius, the son of Mark Antony, in 2 BCE and subsequently sent into exile.[65] Was the 'New Apollo' really the harbinger of peace and harmony, as his public

---

[62] Rawson 1987: 4–11; cf., e.g., Ov. *Fast.* 6.706–7; further discussion in James 2004 and Wiseman 2000: 273–4.

[63] Ov. *Met.* 6.382–400.

[64] According to Servius (*ad Aen.* 3.20, 4.58), the statue represented 'a sign of freedom' (*indicium libertatis*). No physical traces of the statue survive. However, the statue is illustrated on the reverse of a coin struck in 82 BCE, with an image of Apollo on the obverse: Small 1982: 68–92, 127–42; Rawson 1987: 11–12, 224–5; Newby 2016: 71–8.

[65] Sen. *De Benef.* 6.32.1; Plin. *HN* 21.8. Antonius was summarily executed on a charge of treason: Vel. Pat. 2.100.4, Tac. *Ann.* 4.44.3, Dio Cass. 55.10.15.

images proclaimed? Or was he in fact Apollo the Tormentor, the authoritarian commander-in-chief whose obsession with order and discipline stood in the way of true civic liberty? Having acquired a reputation during the civil war as someone inclined to dispatch his rivals by ruthless means, Octavian was no doubt conscious of the risks of being associated with Marsyas' torturer; the Roman people had made that connection already once before, following the infamous Feast of the Twelve Gods.[66] To defeat Antony, Octavian also had to defeat the ideology that he stood for, and that meant ensuring the symbolic victory of Apolline harmony over the liberating musicality of the Bacchanalian revel.

Mark Antony's devotion to music is a leitmotif of Plutarch's biography. His penchant for entertainment is first mentioned in connection with his tenure as Caesar's *magister equitum* at Rome, when he is said to have 'used the houses of respectable men and women as quarters for common prostitutes and harp-girls' (σωφρόνων ἀνδρῶν καὶ γυναικῶν οἰκίαι χαμαιτύπαις καὶ σαμβυκιστρίαις ἐπισταθμευόμεναι).[67] Musicians later accompanied Antony on his tour of Asia Minor in 41:

ἐν Ῥώμῃ δὲ Καίσαρος στάσεσι καὶ πολέμοις ἀποτρυχομένου πολλὴν αὐτὸς ἄγων σχολὴν καὶ εἰρήνην ἀνεκυκλεῖτο τοῖς πάθεσιν εἰς τὸν συνήθη βίον, Ἀναξήνορες δὲ κιθαρῳδοὶ καὶ Ξοῦθοι χοραῦλαι καὶ Μητρόδωρός τις ὀρχηστὴς καὶ τοιοῦτος ἄλλος Ἀσιανῶν ἀκροαμάτων θίασος, ὑπερβαλλομένων λαμυρίᾳ καὶ βωμολοχίᾳ τὰς ἀπὸ τῆς Ἰταλίας κῆρας, εἰσερρύη καὶ διῴκει τὴν αὐλήν, οὐδὲν ἦν ἀνεκτόν, εἰς ταῦτα φορουμένων ἁπάντων ... εἰς γοῦν Ἔφεσον εἰσιόντος αὐτοῦ γυναῖκες μὲν εἰς Βάκχας, ἄνδρες δὲ καὶ παῖδες εἰς Σατύρους καὶ Πᾶνας ἡγοῦντο διεσκευασμένοι, κιττοῦ δὲ καὶ θύρσων καὶ ψαλτηρίων καὶ συρίγγων καὶ αὐλῶν ἡ πόλις ἦν πλέα, Διόνυσον αὐτὸν ἀνακαλουμένων χαριδότην καὶ μειλίχιον. (Plut. *Ant.* 24.1–3)

While in Rome Caesar was being worn out by civil strife and foreign wars, Antony himself was basking in ample leisure and tranquillity and, stirred by his passions, reverted to his accustomed lifestyle. Citharodes like Anaxenor, choral pipe-players like Xouthos, a certain dancer called Metrodorus, and the rest of that troupe of Asiatic performers, who surpassed in lasciviousness and vulgarity the pests from Italy, flooded into his court and held sway there – it was completely intolerable that everything reached such a point ... Indeed, when Antony made his entry into Ephesus, he was led by women dressed as Bacchae, and men and

---

[66] Cf. Suet. *Aug.* 70: *Caesarem esse plane Apollinem, sed Tortorem*. On Octavian's ruthlessness during the proscriptions, cf. Suet. *Aug.* 27.
[67] Plut. *Ant.* 9.5. For Antony's links with other performers (especially *mimoi* and *gelotopoioi*), cf. Plut. *Ant.* 9.4, *Brut.* 45.6–9; Phld. *De Signis* col. 2.15–18 De Lacy, with discussion in Last 1922.

children dressed as Satyrs and Pans. The whole city was filled with ivy, thyrsus wands, harps, panpipes and *auloi*; and Antony was invoked repeatedly as Dionysus Giver of Joy, the Gracious One.

Subsequently, while preparing for war with Octavian, Antony summoned all the Artists of Dionysus to his camp on the island of Samos and had them take part in an uproarious festival:

> καὶ τῆς ἐν κύκλῳ σχεδὸν ἁπάσης οἰκουμένης περιθρηνουμένης καὶ περιστεναζομένης, μία νῆσος ἐφ' ἡμέρας πολλὰς κατηυλεῖτο καὶ κατεψάλλετο πληρουμένων θεάτρων καὶ χορῶν ἀγωνιζομένων. (Plut. *Ant.* 56.4)

> And while almost the entire world echoed around with cries of mourning and lamentation, this single island resounded for days on end with the music of pipes and harps; theatres were filled, and choruses performed in competitions.

Following the festivities, Antony gifted the city of Priene to the Artists of Dionysus, before sailing to Athens and continuing his theatrical escapades there.[68]

These snapshots from Plutarch's biography highlight the shocking extent of Antony's debauchery and depravity, his Asiatic affectations and, worst of all, his pretensions to divine status. In true Bacchic fashion, Antony surrounds himself with loud music wherever he goes. Theatres and entire cities are filled with the noise of his musicians. His entourage is even likened to a *thiasos*, a word typically used to describe the followers of Dionysus. Music, then, is more than just a source of pleasure for Antony; it is central to the way in which he *performs* himself as Dionysus incarnate.

It would be easy to dismiss Plutarch's colourful narrative as the stuff of fiction, fabricated in order to blacken the memory of Augustus' arch-nemesis long after it had been formally consigned to ignominy. However, the evidence tells a different story. In composing his *Life of Antony*, Plutarch drew from a number of first-hand accounts, not all of which were overtly hostile.[69] Strabo, for example, writing towards the end of the first century BCE, provides confirmation of Antony's relationship with the citharode Anaxenor:

> Ἀναξήνορα δὲ τὸν κιθαρῳδὸν ἐξῆρε μὲν καὶ τὰ θέατρα, ἀλλ' ὅτι μάλιστα Ἀντώνιος, ὅς γε καὶ τεττάρων πόλεων ἀπέδειξε φορολόγον στρατιώτας αὐτῷ συστήσας. καὶ ἡ πατρὶς δ' ἱκανῶς αὐτὸν ηὔξησε, πορφύραν ἐνδύσασα, ἱερωμένον τοῦ Σωσιπόλιδος Διός, καθάπερ καὶ ἡ γραπτὴ εἰκὼν ἐμφανίζει ἡ ἐν τῇ ἀγορᾷ. ἔστι δὲ καὶ χαλκῆ εἰκὼν ἐν τῷ θεάτρῳ, ἐπιγραφὴν ἔχουσα·

---

[68] Plut. *Ant.* 75.1.   [69] On Plutarch's sources for the *Life of Antony*, see Pelling 1979.

ἤτοι μὲν τόδε καλὸν ἀκουέμεν ἐστὶν ἀοιδοῦ
τοιοῦδ', οἷος ὅδ' ἐστί, θεοῖς ἐναλίγκιος αὐδῇ.
(Strabo 14.1.41)

The theatres exalted Anaxenor the citharode, but Antony exalted him most of all, since he even appointed him as the revenue collector of four cities, arranging a bodyguard of soldiers for him. In addition, his native land greatly increased his honours, clothing him in purple and appointing him priest of Zeus Sosipolis, as his painted image in the marketplace illustrates. There is also a bronze statue of him in the theatre, which is inscribed as follows:
'Surely this is a beautiful thing, to listen to a singer
Such as this man is, like unto the gods in voice.'

Remarkably, an honorific inscription set up by the *boule* (council) and *demos* (people) of Magnesia to Anaxenor has actually survived, bearing the same Homeric quotation that is recorded by Strabo.[70] Clearly, Anaxenor was no ordinary musician. His renown brought him to the attention of the de facto ruler of Asia, who elevated him to a position of considerable political influence.

Antony's interactions with the Artists of Dionysus at Samos are also corroborated by a contemporary source. A letter sent by Mark Antony to the *koinon* (federation) of Asia, preserved on a papyrus copy, records a series of legal privileges conferred on 'the worldwide association of victors in the festival games'. These privileges included exemption from military service, immunity from all liturgies, freedom from billeting, personal inviolability and the right to wear purple robes (traditionally granted only to kings).[71] The document states that the meeting between Antony and the envoys of the Artists of Dionysus took place at Ephesus. From this we can deduce that the privileges were granted in either 42–41 or 33–32 BCE, that is, on one of the two occasions when Antony is known to have visited the city.[72]

Plutarch's suggestion that Antony was already cavorting with musicians in Italy during the 40s finds support in Cicero's *Fifth Philippic*, delivered on 1 January 43 BCE. In the course of attacking Antony's recent judiciary law, Cicero mocks his opponent for extending membership of juries to 'dancers, lyre-players, in short, the whole chorus of the Antonian *comissatio*'.[73] The

---

[70] *Syll.*³ 766. The quoted verses are from Hom. *Od.* 9.3–4.
[71] *EJ*², no. 300 (trans. Sherk, *RGE*, no. 85).
[72] For the first visit, cf. Plut. *Ant.* 24; App. *BC* 5.4.5; Dio Cass. 48.24; for the second, Plut. *Ant.* 56, 58. Pelling (1988: 177–8) favours 42/1 BCE as the likely date of the letter.
[73] Cic. *Phil.* 5.15: *saltatores, citharistas, totum denique comissationis Antonianae chorum.*

term *comissatio* roughly translates as 'drinking party', but, like the Greek word *thiasos*, it is closely associated with the cult of Bacchus.[74] Of course, Antony had not actually co-opted dancers and lyre-players onto Roman juries; they appear here simply as rhetorical targets, designating the kinds of lowlifes that would be shown favour if Antony were given the reins to the state. Nevertheless, Cicero's words speak to an obvious pattern of theatricality in Antony's behaviour. As Lauren Curtis comments, 'In addition to tarring Antony with a general smear of Hellenism, through the language of Greek performance culture, Cicero's words evoke more specifically Antony's suspiciously flamboyant incorporation of Greek spectacle into his public persona.'[75]

For an additional testimony, we can turn to the Augustan historian Socrates of Rhodes, whose history of the Civil War may have been used as a source by Plutarch:

> ἱστορεῖ δὲ καὶ αὐτὸν τὸν Ἀντώνιον ἐν Ἀθήναις μετὰ ταῦτα διατρίψαντα περίοπτον ὑπὲρ τὸ θέατρον κατασκευάσαντα σχεδίαν χλωρᾷ πεπυκασμένην ὕλῃ, ὥσπερ ἐπὶ τῶν Βακχικῶν ἄντρων γίνεται, ταύτης τύμπανα καὶ νεβρίδας καὶ παντοδαπὰ ἄλλ' ἀθύρματα Διονυσιακὰ ἐξαρτήσαντα μετὰ τῶν φίλων ἐξ ἑωθινοῦ κατακλινόμενον μεθύσκεσθαι, λειτουργούντων αὐτῷ τῶν ἐξ Ἰταλίας μεταπεμφθέντων ἀκροαμάτων συνηθροισμένων ἐπὶ τὴν θέαν τῶν Πανελλήνων. μετέβαινε δ' ἐνίοτε, φησίν, καὶ ἐπὶ τὴν ἀκρόπολιν ἀπὸ τῶν τεγῶν λαμπάσι δᾳδουχουμένης πάσης τῆς Ἀθηναίων πόλεως. καὶ ἔκτοτε ἐκέλευσεν ἑαυτὸν Διόνυσον ἀνακηρύττεσθαι κατὰ τὰς ἀπόλεις ἁπάσας. (Socrates *FGrH* 192 F2 = Athen. 4.29b-c)

> He [Socrates] also reports that when Antony himself spent some time in Athens after this, he had a roughly framed hut built in a conspicuous spot above the Theatre and covered with green brushwood, as they do with Bacchic "caves"; and he hung drums, fawn skins, and other Dionysiac paraphernalia of all sorts in it. He lay inside with his friends, beginning at dawn, and got drunk; musicians summoned from Italy entertained him, and the whole Greek world gathered to watch. Sometimes, he says, Antony moved up onto the Acropolis, and the entire city of Athens was illuminated by the lamps that hung from the ceilings. He also gave orders that from then on he was to be proclaimed as Dionysus throughout all the cities. (Trans. Olson 2007)

---

[74] For the Bacchic associations of *comissatio*, cf. Cic. *Mur.* 13; Liv. 40.13; Suet. *Calig.* 55; Mart. 12.48; Manuwald 2007: 608. On the *Philippics* as a model for Plutarch's *Lives*, cf. Plut. *Cic.* 48.3-4; Pelling 1979: 89-90.

[75] Curtis 2017: 9.

Like Plutarch, Socrates presents Antony's musical followers as an extension of his quasi-divine persona. As with the episodes at Ephesus and Samos, private entertainment and public ceremonial merge into one: the home of the Great Dionysia is transformed into a Bacchic grotto and repurposed as a venue for symposia. What makes this spectacle especially perverse is the fact that it is performed in front of 'all of the Greeks'. The implication is that Antony subverted the traditions of a panhellenic festival by using the musicians as a vehicle for his own self-promotion.

However, from the perspective of Antony, a Roman interloper in the East, being seen as a patron of the musical arts brought tangible political benefits. Music was part of the pageantry of Hellenistic kingship. It gave rulers a charismatic, even godlike, authority in the eyes of the people over whom they exercised power. In around 40 BCE, while Antony was managing affairs in the East, King Antiochus I of Commagene issued a proclamation which contained detailed instructions concerning the celebration of his ruler cult. The inscribed decree stipulated that the festival held in the king's honour should be celebrated with 'a multitude of musicians' (πλῆθος ... μουσικῶν), whose status he guaranteed to protect.[76] Far from being incidental, then, musicians were central to the performance of Hellenistic autocracy. They could exert influence not only as entertainers, but also as courtiers, who enjoyed close relations with their royal patrons. When Alexandra, daughter of the Hasmonean dynast John Hyrcanus II, wrote to Cleopatra in Egypt asking for Antony to appoint her son to the high priesthood of Jerusalem, she enlisted the help of a certain musician (μουσουργοῦ τινος) to deliver the letter.[77] She no doubt felt confident that the messenger would be warmly received. Cassius Dio reports that, after the decisive conflict at Actium, the fleeing Cleopatra 'crowned her prows with garlands as if she had actually won a victory, and had songs of triumph chanted to the accompaniment of pipe-players' (τάς τε πρώρας ὡς καὶ κεκρατηκυῖα κατέστεψε καὶ ᾠδάς τινας ἐπινικίους ὑπ' αὐλητῶν ᾖδεν), hoping thereby to allay fears of her defeat upon reaching Egypt.[78] The presence of large numbers of musicians in the Ptolemaic court is also suggested by Plutarch's account of Cleopatra's first encounter with Antony at Tarsus. The rowers on board the Egyptian royal yacht, we are told, were accompanied by the sound of pipes, panpipes and lyres (πρὸς αὐλὸν ἅμα σύριγξι καὶ κιθάραις).[79] This spectacle of regal opulence provided

---

[76] OGIS 1.383.   [77] Joseph. AJ 15.24.   [78] Dio Cass. 51.5.4.   [79] Plut. Ant. 26.1.

a model for Antony when it came to orchestrating his own *adventus* ceremony at Ephesus a few years later.

Antony could claim, therefore, that his patronage of musicians made shrewd political sense. The association of the Artists of Dionysus was an extremely influential organisation in the first century BCE, boasting a number of regional branches throughout the Greek world. These branches, known as *koina* or *synodoi*, were powerful enough to organise and take part in their own festivals, often in collaboration with local rulers or benefactors.[80] Members of the association benefited from legal, social and economic privileges.[81] In Ptolemaic Egypt, where the assimilation of the *basileus* with Osiris/Dionysus was firmly rooted in historical tradition, the Artists of Dionysus ranked among the most important officials in the kingdom.[82] There was certainly something to be gained from championing the cause of musicians like Anaxenor, who possessed a large popular following and thus could be usefully exploited as political pawns. Anaxenor's rise from entertainer to tax-collector was exceptional, but he was certainly not the first musician of his kind to be commemorated with statues and civic honours.[83] Nor was he the first to be entrusted with administrative or diplomatic powers on behalf of the state. In around 170 BCE, a citharode from the island of Teos was invited to serve as an ambassador to Crete and was subsequently honoured by his hosts with an honorific inscription listing his accomplishments.[84] Later on, during the period of the Sullan dictatorship, the Asiatic guild of Dionysiac Artists, whose headquarters were situated in the Ionian town of Lebedus, sent a certain lyre-player by the name of Alexander, a citizen of Laodicea, to Rome to act as its representative. There Alexander succeeded in obtaining

---

[80] Cf., e.g., *IG* II² 1330 (Le Guen 2001, I. 67–74, no. 5); further discussion in Aneziri 2003 and 2007.

[81] On these privileges, which included immunity from taxation (*ateleia*) and priority in litigation (*prodikia*), see Aneziri 2009: 230–2. The guild maintained its privileged status under Augustus: see *BGU* 4.1074; Viereck 1908: 413–26.

[82] On the conflation of Osiris/Dionysus, cf. Hdt. 2.42.2, 2.144.2. The presence of Dionysiac *technitai* in Egypt can be traced back to the third century BCE: *OGIS* 50–1; Le Guen 2001, II. 7–9, 34–6.

[83] Alexander the Great commemorated the citharode Aristonicus with a bronze statue and included both male and female pipe-players in his army: Plut. *De Alex. fort.* 334d–335a; Athen. 12.539a. Cicero (*Verr.* 2.1.53) mentions a famous statue of a lyre-player from the town of Aspendus in Pamphylia which was appropriated by Verres while he was serving there as a legate in 80 BCE.

[84] *I.Cret.* I.viii.11; *I.Cret.* V.xxiv.1; Barker 2011.

permission from Sulla and the Roman Senate for the guild to erect a stele at Cos recording the privileges formerly granted to it.[85] Antony's decision to summon to Samos all of the Artists of Dionysus at once (πᾶσι τοῖς περὶ τὸν Διόνυσον τεχνίταις) thus could be seen as an acknowledgement of the guild's long-standing involvement in Greek political affairs. Despite Plutarch's moral outrage, the gift of Priene was as much a symbol of Antony's beneficence as an act of reckless profligacy. Antony need only have looked to the dissension on nearby Cos, where a fierce struggle for power was being fought out between the tyrant Nicias and his rival Theomnestos, a harp-player (*psaltes*) by trade, to appreciate the importance of having the *technitai* on his side.[86]

Naturally, those on the side of Octavian saw things differently. In their eyes, Antony's devotion to music was the mark of a man who had abandoned his duties as a Roman statesman and surrendered himself to a life of eastern luxury, succumbing more and more as his infatuation with Cleopatra grew ever stronger. One of the more curious aspects of Cleopatra's portrayal in the literary sources is the way she is assimilated with the archetypical figure of the Hellenistic musician-concubine. As Christopher Pelling points out, Plutarch uses the same word, *lamuria* (charm, or flirtatiousness), to describe both Cleopatra and the musicians in Antony's retinue.[87] What is more, the queen's voice is actually likened to a musical instrument:

> ἡδονὴ δὲ καὶ φθεγγομένης ἐπῆν τῷ ἤχῳ· καὶ τὴν γλῶτταν, ὥσπερ ὄργανόν τι πολύχορδον, εὐπετῶς τρέπουσα καθ' ἣν βούλοιτο διάλεκτον.
> (Plut. *Ant.* 28.3)
>
> There was sweetness also in the tones of her voice; and her tongue, like an instrument of many strings, she could readily turn to whatever language she pleased.

Later on, as Octavian's prisoner, Cleopatra sought to use her vocal talents to win over her captor's affections. In the words of Cassius Dio, 'She kept turning her eyes toward Caesar and bewailing her fate in melodic inflections (ἐμμελῶς ἀνωλοφύρετο).'[88] Octavian, Odysseus-like, turned a

---

[85] Iscr. di Kos ED 7 = Sherk, *RGE*, no. 62 (84/81 BCE); see also discussion in Sherk 1966. Sulla's penchant for music is variously attested: cf. Macr. *Sat.* 3.14.10; Plut. *Sull.* 2.2–3, 36; Val. Max. 6.9.6. It evidently suited him to be seen as an enthusiastic patron of musicians.

[86] Strabo 14.2.19. Nicias' tyranny should be dated between ca. 40 and 31 BCE: *BNP*, s.v. 'Nicias' [8].

[87] Plut. *Caes.* 49.2 (λαμυρᾶς φανείσης); Pelling 1988: 178.   [88] Dio Cass. 51.12.4.

deaf ear to the call of this Egyptian Siren; Antony, the weaker man, showed no such resolve.

Cassius Dio's account of the conflict at Actium provides a particularly acute insight into how Antony's association with music was turned against him both by his contemporary detractors and by later historians. In his speech to the troops before the battle, Octavian taunts his rival for having become 'one of the cymbal-players from Canopus' (εἷς τῶν ἀπὸ Κανώβου κυμβαλιστῶν).[89] This insult is damning in more ways than one. In antiquity, the 'Canopic life' was a byword for hedonism; it was synonymous with *lamuria*, the very quality that Cleopatra exuded.[90] According to Strabo, who visited the pleasure town not long after Antony, revellers would sail down to Canopus from Alexandria to enjoy licentious music and dance.[91] Canopus was also a favourite destination of the royal lovers. Plutarch describes how 'Antony ... was often disarmed by Cleopatra, subdued by her spells and persuaded to drop from his hands great undertakings and necessary campaigns, only to roam about and play with her on the sea-shores by Canopus and Taphosiris'.[92]

By identifying Antony as a Canopic percussionist, Dio's Octavian not only ridicules his opponent's effete lifestyle, but also hints suggestively at his claims to the Ptolemaic throne. The rulers of Egypt were notoriously passionate about musical instruments. Ptolemy IV Philopator, who reigned from 221 to 204 BCE, was allegedly 'so corrupted in his soul by women and wine' that he would roam around the palace liked a crazed worshipper, 'drum in hand' (τύμπανον ἔχων), leaving charge of the state to his mistress and his mother.[93] Cleopatra's father, Ptolemy XII, was known disparagingly as 'Auletes' on account of his penchant for performing on the *aulos*

---

[89] Dio Cass. 50.27.2; cf. Pet. *Sat.* 22, linking the *cymbalistria* with the Bacchanalian *comissatio*.
[90] Strabo 17.1.16: ἀρχή τις Κανωβισμοῦ καὶ τῆς ἐκεῖ λαμυρίας; cf. Sil. *Pun.* 11.425–31, associating Canopus with exotic flutes; Stat. *Silv.* 3.2.111; Ov. *Am.* 2.13.6–7; Juv. 6.84, 15.44–6; Sen. *Ep.* 51.3.
[91] Strabo 17.1.17.
[92] Plut. *Ant. and Dem.* 23: Ἀντώνιον ... πολλάκις Κλεοπάτρα παροπλίσασα καὶ καταθέλξασα συνέπεισεν ἀφέντα μεγάλας πράξεις ἐκ τῶν χειρῶν καὶ στρατείας ἀναγκαίας ἐν ταῖς περὶ Κάνωβον καὶ Ταφόσιριν ἀκταῖς ἀλύειν καὶ παίζειν μετ' αὐτῆς. Propertius (3.11.39) calls Cleopatra *incesti meretrix regina Canopi*.
[93] Plut. *Agis and Cleomenes* 54.2; cf. Plut. *Cleom.* 35.2, on Ptolemy IV's devotion to *sambucistriae*. Justin (*Epitome of Pompeius Trogus* 30.1.8–9) depicts Ptolemy IV as a lyre-player: *adduntur instrumenta luxuriae, tympana et crepundia; nec iam spectator rex, sed magister nequitiae nervorum oblectamenta modulatur* (there are added the instruments of debauchery, drums and rattles; and the king, no longer a spectator, but a master of depravity, modulates the charms of the lyre strings).

in the palace at Alexandria.⁹⁴ Significantly, both Ptolemy IV Philopator and Ptolemy XII Auletes were worshipped during their lifetime as 'New Dionysus'.⁹⁵ The three figures – Ptolemy IV, Mark Antony and Ptolemy XII – are in fact directly compared by Plutarch as men who learned through the flattery of their courtiers to confuse vice with virtue: Ptolemy IV ruined Egypt by his 'effeminacy' (θηλύτητα), his 'religious mania' (θεοληψίαν), and his 'clashing of drums' (τυμπάνων ἐγχαράξεις); Antony perverted Roman morals through his 'luxury' (τρυφάς), 'excess' (ἀκολασίας) and 'ostentation' (πανηγυρισμούς); and Ptolemy XII brought shame upon his people by taking up 'the *phorbeia* and the pipes' (φορβειὰν καὶ αὐλούς).⁹⁶

In summary, the rival image-making of Octavian and Antony reflects in many ways a clash between two opposing musical ideologies: the Apolline versus the Dionysian. The tacit symbolism of the Palatine Apollo (recall Propertius' mention of his *tacita lyra*) stands in marked contrast to the noisy excess which characterises the Dionysian music of Antony. Whereas Augustus' *cithara* serves as a metaphor for the harmonising of the Roman state, elevated above the banalities of performance, Antony's *aulos* is firmly rooted in the sensual world of the Hellenistic court. The call for music in the Augustan elegists is a call for celebration after the conclusion of war (*bella satis cecini*, in the words of Propertius).⁹⁷ Antony's passion for music, on the other hand, is at its most all-consuming when the war is in its critical phase, when the fate of the Republic still hangs in the balance. It is notable that both Vergil and Propertius in their depictions of Actium frame the contrast between Octavianic virtue and Antonian vice in terms of a clash between the Roman *tuba* and the Egyptian *sistrum* (the former traditional, martial and virile, the latter exotic, feeble and

---

⁹⁴ Cf. Strabo 17.1.11; Dio Chrys. *Orat.* 3.135, 32.70; Plut. *Mor.* 56f; Luc. *Cal.* 16 alludes to cymbal-playing in the court of an unspecified Ptolemy (probably Auletes).

⁹⁵ Ptolemy IV: Powell 1925: 176; Clement of Alexandria *Protrep.* 4.54.2. Ptolemy XII: *OGIS* 186.9–10, 191.1, 741.1; *SEG* 8.408; Porph. *ap.* Eus. *Chron.* = FGrH 260.2 [12] and [15]. Mithridates was also worshipped as 'New Dionysus': Cic. *Flacc.* 60; Athen. 5.49.

⁹⁶ Plut. *Mor.* 56e–f. The *phorbeia* was a leather strap which went around the head of the *aulos*-player and was used to restrain the player's cheeks and to help him or her maintain a secure oral grip on the instrument: see Wilson 1999: 70–2.

⁹⁷ Cf. *Eleg. Maec.* 1.51–2: 'The Actian god himself struck the lyre with his ivory plectrum after the trumpets of victory fell silent' (*Actius ipse lyram plectro percussit eburno, | postquam victrices conticuere tubae*). Note also Hor. *Epod.* 1.9.5–6, describing a celebration at Maecenas' villa immediately after the battle of Actium: the guests are entertained by 'the lyre making music mixed with the pipes, the former Doric, the latter barbarian' (*sonante mixtum tibiis carmen lyra, | hac Dorium, illis barbarum*). 'Barbarian' in this context implies 'Dionysiac' (cf. Catull. 64.264); the Doric mode was the quintessential warlike mode (Wiseman 2016: 141 n. 46).

effeminate).⁹⁸ The poet Prudentius, writing some three centuries later, substitutes the *sistrum* for the *symphonia*: 'On the waves of Actium a *symphonia* gave Egypt the signal for war, while on the other side a horn rang out.'⁹⁹ Musical imagery of this kind reinforces the negative characterisation of Antony in the sources as a thoroughly despotic and corrupt figurehead. While Antony's regal aspirations are played up at every turn, Cleopatra, as his consort, is effectively demoted from the status of queen to that of concubine. She is rather like the hapless piper Lamia, who, after serving as the mistress of Ptolemy I for many years, was captured by Demetrius Poliorcetes, Antony's counterpart in Plutarch's *Parallel Lives*, only then to take *him* captive as her lover.¹⁰⁰ Hellenistic history abounds with similar stories of powerful rulers being seduced by female musicians: other examples include Alexander the Great and the *auletris* Thais, Ptolemy II Philadelphus and the citharode Glauce of Chios, and Mithridates of Pontus and the harp-player Stratonice.¹⁰¹

I conclude this section by returning briefly to Plutarch's *Life of Antony*. Plutarch closes his narrative of Antony's life with a haunting vignette. On the eve of Antony's death, the citizens of Alexandria experienced a strange portent:

> αἰφνίδιον ὀργάνων τε παντοδαπῶν ἐμμελεῖς τινας φωνὰς ἀκουσθῆναι καὶ βοὴν ὄχλου μετὰ εὐασμῶν καὶ πηδήσεων σατυρικῶν, ὥσπερ θιάσου τινὸς οὐκ ἀθορύβως ἐξελαύνοντος· εἶναι δὲ τὴν ὁρμὴν ὁμοῦ τι διὰ τῆς πόλεως μέσης ἐπὶ τὴν πύλην ἔξω τὴν τετραμμένην πρὸς τοὺς πολεμίους, καὶ ταύτῃ τὸν θόρυβον ἐκπεσεῖν πλεῖστον γενόμενον. ἐδόκει δὲ τοῖς ἀναλογιζομένοις τὸ σημεῖον ἀπολείπειν ὁ θεὸς Ἀντώνιον, ᾧ μάλιστα συνεξομοιῶν καὶ συνοικειῶν ἑαυτὸν διετέλεσεν. (Plut. *Ant.* 75.3–4)

Suddenly certain harmonious sounds from all sorts of instruments were

---

⁹⁸ Prop. 3.11.43: *Romanamque tubam crepitanti pellere sistro*; Verg. *Aen.* 8.696: *regina in mediis patrio vocat agmina sistro*.
⁹⁹ Prudent. *C. Symm.* 528–9: *fluctibus Actiacis signum symphonia belli | Aegypto dederat, clangebat bucina contra.*
¹⁰⁰ Plut. *Dem.* 16.3–4; cf. *Dem.* 27.3–6.
¹⁰¹ Alexander: Plut. *Alex.* 38, *Peric.* 1.5–6. Ptolemy II: Theoc. *Id.* 4.31; Plin. *HN* 10.51; Athen. 4.176c–d; Ael. *NA* 1.6, 5.29, 8.11. Mithridates: Plut. *Pomp.* 36.3. We also hear of a Samian pipe-player and dancer named Aristonica, who emigrated to Alexandria to work at the Ptolemaic court, probably during the reign of Ptolemy IV: Plut. *Mor.* 753d. These examples are helpfully contextualised by Loman 2004 in light of the Hellenistic phenomenon of travelling female entertainers. The relationship between the cithara-player Panthea of Smyrna and the Emperor Lucius Verus offers a comparable example from the imperial period (Lucian, *Imag.* 13; *SHA Ver.* 7.10). Male musicians were sexually desirable too: cf., e.g., Athen. 8.603e, on the Macedonian king Antigonus II Gonatas' infatuation with the citharode Aristocles.

heard, and the shouting of a crowd, accompanied by cries of Bacchic revelry and the ecstatic leaping of satyrs, as if a troop of revellers, making a great clamour, were leaving the city; and their procession seemed to follow a course through the middle of the city towards the outer gate which faced the enemy, at which point the noise became loudest and then died down. Those who tried to discover the meaning of the sign came to the conclusion that the god to whom Antony always most likened and attached himself was now abandoning him.

Why does Antony's music suddenly become 'harmonious', when until now it has been so stridently dissonant? The answer may be tied to the meaning of the portent itself. Dissonance gives way to harmony at the precise moment at which the balance of power swings irrevocably in Octavian's favour. Antony's impending death effectively marks the start of Octavian's triumphant return to Rome. It is only fitting that Plutarch marks this long-awaited climax by guiding Dionysus' marching band in the direction of the Roman camp, and towards a brighter, more harmonious future.[102]

Tuning the World

Octavian's decision to build a temple to Apollo on the Palatine carried a deep prophetic resonance. The Palatine was the place where 'according to legend the city of Rome was first settled'.[103] It was from the summit of this hill that Romulus used to address his citizens, and the 'hut' which he had originally used for taking the auspices could still be seen from the forecourt of Octavian's residence.[104] Indeed, the very name 'Augustus', adopted by Octavian in 27 BCE, called to mind the immortal line of Ennius' *Annales*

---

[102] Similarly, Cassius Dio (51.17.4) comments on the sound of musical instruments as a portent of Egypt's enslavement after the capture of Alexandria by Octavian: κτυπήματά τέ τινα ἑτέρωθι καὶ τυμπάνων καὶ κυμβάλων καὶ βοήματα καὶ αὐλῶν καὶ σαλπίγγων ἐγίγνετο (elsewhere there was the clashing of drums and cymbals and the noise of pipes and trumpets). Compare Dio's account (41.61.3) of the omen of Pompey's defeat before the Battle of Pharsalus: ἔν τε Περγάμῳ τυμπάνων τέ τινα καὶ κυμβάλων ψόφον ἐκ τοῦ Διονυσίου ἀρθέντα διὰ πάσης τῆς πόλεως χωρῆσαι (in Pergamum a noise of drums and cymbals rose from the temple of Dionysus and spread throughout the city). See also Pelling 1988: 303–4 and Hekster 2010: 610–13, who interpret the Antony episode as a kind of *evocatio* (summoning out) ritual, whereby the conquered god of the enemy was assimilated into the Roman pantheon.
[103] Joseph. *AJ* 19.223.
[104] For myths locating Romulus on the Palatine, cf. Dion. Hal. *Ant. Rom.* 2.5.1–2, 14.2.2. For the 'hut of Romulus' and its relationship to Augustus' house, see Wiseman 2012: 384–5.

on Rome's foundation 'by august augury' (*augusto augurio*).¹⁰⁵ By assuming this title, Octavian announced himself as Romulus' successor, the man who had founded the city anew. What better way to celebrate this act of refoundation than by invoking the god whose music brought cosmic unity to the realm of gods and men? When Propertius and his contemporaries visited the sanctuary of Apollo and encountered 'the Pythian god himself' (*deus ipse ... Pythius*) with his *cithara*, they could imagine him singing prophetically of the golden age to come as well as contemplating the ages that had passed.¹⁰⁶

The Palatine was symbolically important not only as the site of Rome's foundation, but also as the place where – according to one Augustan writer at least – the first seeds of Rome's musical culture were sown. In his *Roman Antiquities*, Dionysius of Halicarnassus puts forward the argument that Rome was originally established as a Greek city. To support this argument, he provides information about the cultural history of Latium prior to Rome's foundation. The Palatine, he explains, was originally settled by colonists from Arcadia, who brought with them to Italy 'music played on instruments which are called lyres (λύραι), *trigona* (τρίγωνα) and pipes (αὐλοί), the previous people having used no musical devices apart from pastoral panpipes (σύριγξι ποιμενικαῖς)'.¹⁰⁷ Later on in the narrative, Dionysius describes the upbringing of the twins Romulus and Remus: 'The story goes that after the children were weaned they were sent by those who had reared them to Gabii, a town not far from the Palatine Hill, to be given a Greek education (Ἑλλάδα παιδείαν). There they were brought up by some personal friends of Faustulus, being taught letters, music (μουσικήν), and the use of Greek arms until they grew to manhood.'¹⁰⁸ So not only was Rome founded by a man steeped in *mousike*, according to Dionysius, but the first traces of this *mousike* in Italy were to be found precisely in the area where Augustus built his temple to the patron deity of music. The significance would surely not have been lost on Dionysius' readers.

---

[105] Suet. *Aug.* 7.2; cf. Varro, *Rust.* 3.1.2, Ov. *Fast.* 1.587–616, Livy *Epit.* 134. There were some who claimed that Octavian had actually desired to be called 'Romulus', but was deterred by its kingly associations: Dio Cass. 53.16.7.

[106] For *carmina* as 'prophecies', cf. Verg. *Ecl.* 4.4; Ov. *Met.* 6.582; Liv. 1.45.5, 23.11.4; Sen. *Apocol.* 4.15.

[107] Dion. Hal. *Ant. Rom.* 1.33.4–5. On the Arcadian settlement of the Palatine, cf. Polyb. 4.20.5–21.9; Dion. Hal. *Ant. Rom.* 1.33.5, 1.89.2; Solinus 1.14.

[108] Dion. Hal. *Ant. Rom.* 1.84.5. This image of Romulus as *mousikos* is unparalleled in the sources. However, Cicero (*Rep.* 2.18) writes that Romulus' lifetime coincided with a rich period of Greek music. Plutarch (*Rom.* 6) may have music in mind when he speaks of Romulus' curriculum including 'letters ... and the other subjects which are necessary for those of good birth' (γράμματα ... καὶ τἆλλα, ὅσα χρὴ τοὺς εὖ γεγονότας).

By locating Apollo at the centre of his regenerative monumental programme, and by representing himself alongside (and perhaps in the very likeness of) the citharodic god, Augustus announced himself as the restorer of Roman *harmonia*. The strings of Apollo's lyre served, in effect, as a metaphor for the sounding of world peace, of *pax Augusta restituta*, imbuing the actions of the *princeps* with a powerful cosmic meaning.[109] To some Romans, even the very word 'lyre' – *fides* in Latin – called to mind lofty notions of loyalty and civility. The grammarian Verrius Flaccus, who acted as tutor to Augustus' grandsons Lucius and Gaius, observed in his treatise *De verborum significatu* that the word *fides* referred both to 'a type of *cithara*' (*genus citharae*) and to the abstract concept of 'trustworthiness'. More than just a coincidental homonym, the two meanings were in his view intrinsically linked: the instrument got its name because 'its strings resonate together to the same extent that *fides* resonates among men' (*tantum inter se chordae eius, quantum inter homines fides concordet*).[110]

Etymological subtleties of this kind might not have meant much to Romans outside the upper-class intelligentsia. But we should not imagine that the civic and cosmic associations of the lyre were something that one could appreciate only with the benefit of a formal education. As discussed in Chapter 2, the theatre served as a vehicle for the public dissemination of philosophical ideas about music. An intriguing fragment attributed to the Augustan playwright Varius Rufus alludes to Mercury as the mythical inventor of the lyre and draws on the Pythagorean concept of the harmony of the spheres:

> *primum huic*
> *nervis septem est intenta fides*
> *variique apti vocum moduli*
> *ad quos mundi resonat canor in*
> *sua se vestigia volventis.*
> (Varius Rufus fr. 157 Hollis)

---

[109] For the cosmic symbolism of Apollo's statues, cf. Cornutus, *De Natura Deorum*, Lang p. 67: 'He [Apollo] has been depicted as a musician and lyre-player because he plucks every part of the cosmos harmoniously and causes it to be in tune with all the other parts, and there is no disharmony observed among the things which exist' (trans. Hays 1983).

[110] Verrius Flaccus *ap.* Festus 89L; *TLL* s.v. 'fides' (2), Vol. VI, 1, 691, 69–693, 37 (Klee); Conte 1994: 386–7. We happen to know that the temple of Fides Publica, erected on the Capitoline Hill in the mid-third century BCE, contained a painting by Aristides of Thebes of an old man teaching a child to play the lyre (Plin. *HN* 35.100: *spectata est et in aede Fidei in Capitolio senis cum lyra puerum docentis*; possibly playing on the double meaning of *fides*, *pace* Freyburger 1986: 262).

> He was the first to stretch the lyre with seven strings, and to fit on it the different intervals of sound, in harmony with which the tuneful Universe re-echoes as it revolves backwards over its own path.
> (Trans. Hollis 2007: 258)

If, as Moore surmises, these lines derive from Varius' famous tragedy, the *Thyestes*, it is possible that they were sung at the games held to mark the dedication of the temple of Apollo Palatinus in 28 BCE.[111]

The figure of the divine citharode, harmonising the universe with his music, provided writers of the Augustan age with a powerful mythological paradigm for praising the achievements of their leader. A poem by the Augustan epigrammatist Crinagoras casts the *princeps* in the mythical role of Orpheus, the son of Apollo, tuning the natural world to the sound of his *cithara*: 'Orpheus made the beasts obey him in the hills, and now every bird tunes its voice for you, Caesar, unbidden.'[112] The metaphor of *harmonia* also figures prominently in an encomium of Augustus written by the Jewish author Philo some thirty years after the *princeps*' death:

> οὗτος ὁ τὰς πόλεις ἁπάσας εἰς ἐλευθερίαν ἐξελόμενος, ὁ τὴν ἀταξίαν εἰς τάξιν ἀγαγών, ὁ τὰ ἄμικτα ἔθνη καὶ θηριώδη πάντα ἡμερώσας καὶ ἁρμοσάμενος, ὁ τὴν μὲν Ἑλλάδα Ἑλλάσι πολλαῖς παραυξήσας, τὴν δὲ βάρβαρον ἐν τοῖς ἀναγκαιοτάτοις τμήμασιν ἀφελληνίσας, ὁ εἰρηνοφύλαξ. (Philo *Leg.* 147)

> This was the man who reclaimed every state to liberty, who led disorder into order and brought gentle manners and harmony to all unsociable and brutish nations, who enlarged Hellas by many a new Hellas and hellenised the outside world in its most important sectors, the guardian of the peace.

Of particular interest here is Philo's use of the verb ἁρμοσάμενος. From ἁρμόζω, it means 'to set in order', 'to regulate' or 'to govern': hence, Augustus 'brought order to unsociable and brutish nations'. But ἁρμονία is also, of course, the technical term for a musical 'scale', and in fact the

---

[111] A note contained in two Italian codices, dating from the eighth and ninth centuries respectively, states that Varius' *Thyestes* was performed *post Actiacam victoriam Augusti ludis*. I follow Jocelyn (1978: 70) in taking these *ludi* to refer to the games performed at the dedication of the Palatine temple; Leigh (1996: 171) and Hollis (2007: 261) associate them with the games performed by Octavian after his triple triumph in 29 BCE. For the attribution of this fragment to the *Thyestes*, see Moore (2016: 358), noting that the anapaestic metre suggests 'a lively and elaborate dance on stage'.

[112] *Anth. Pal.* 9.562.7-8: Ὀρφεὺς θῆρας ἔπεισεν ἐν οὔρεσι· καὶ δὲ σέ, Καῖσαρ, νῦν ἀκέλευστος ἅπας ὄρνις ἀνακρέκεται.

primary sense of ἁρμόζω is 'to tune a lyre'.¹¹³ Philo was certainly aware of the musical connotations of the word, as his characterisation of the Jewish patriarch Moses reveals: 'He relaxed the overstrained and tightened the lax, and as on a musical instrument blended the very high and the very low at each end of the scale with the middle chord, thus producing a life of harmony and concord (ἁρμονίαν βίου καὶ συμφωνίαν) which none can blame.'¹¹⁴ So Augustus was the man who 'restored *harmonia* to nations that were out of tune with one another' – just as King Numa was remembered for 'having harmonised (ἁρμοσάμενος) the whole people like an instrument'.¹¹⁵

This conception of the *princeps* as musician and conductor was not associated exclusively with Augustus. When Tiberius delivered the eulogy at Augustus' funeral, he described himself as being 'like the leader of a chorus', in that his role was 'to give out the leading words, while you [i.e. the people] join in and chant the rest'.¹¹⁶ Some two centuries later, Septimius Severus is said to have dreamt that 'he was escorted by someone to a place which commanded a wide view, and as he gazed down from there upon all the land and sea he laid his fingers on them as one might on an instrument capable of playing all modes (ὥσπερ παναρμονίου τινὸς ὀργάνου), and they all sang together (συνεφθέγγετο)'; this dream caused him to harbour ambitions for the imperial throne.¹¹⁷ The biographer of the *Historia Augusta*, narrating the same dream, speaks of 'the provinces singing together to the accompaniment of the lyre or pipe (*concinentibus provinciis lyra, voce vel tibia*)'.¹¹⁸ Finally, in the 150s CE, the orator Aelius Aristides extolled the achievements of Antoninus Pius by proclaiming that 'the whole world sings as one in celebration with tighter harmony than a chorus (ἅπασα ἡ οἰκουμένη χοροῦ ἀκριβέστερον ἐν φθέγγεται), praying together that this empire shall survive through eternity, so wonderfully is it directed by this chorus-leader ruler (τοῦ κορυφαίου ἡγεμόνος)!'¹¹⁹ The choral metaphor powerfully encapsulates the Augustan ideal of a diverse community of citizens united under a just and benevolent figurehead. It

---

¹¹³ Cf. *LSJ*, s.v. ἁρμόζω. In the *Orphic Hymn to Apollo*, Apollo is said to 'harmonise' the poles of the universe with his 'much-sounding *kithara*' (πάντα πόλον κιθάρηι πολυκρέκτωι | ἁρμόζεις; no. 34 Fayant, ll. 16–7).
¹¹⁴ Philo *Spec. leg.* 4.102; cf. *Spec. leg.* 2.157, *Virt.* 145, *Mos.* 2.7. On Philo's conception of music, see Feldman 1986–1987; Levarie 1991; Ferguson 2003.
¹¹⁵ Dion. Hal. *Ant. Rom.* 2.46.2. For ἄμικτος in the sense of 'difficult to blend or harmonise', cf. *LSJ*, s.v.; Aesch. *Ag.* 321 (βοὴν ἄμεικτον).
¹¹⁶ Dio Cass. 56.35.4–5: ἐμοῦ τε ὥσπερ ἐν χορῷ τινὶ τὰ κεφάλαια ἀποσημαίνοντος, καὶ ὑμῶν τὰ λοιπὰ συνεπηχούντων.
¹¹⁷ Dio Cass. 74(75).3.   ¹¹⁸ *SHA Sev.* 3.   ¹¹⁹ Aristid. *Or.* 26.29 Keil.

also invokes the emperor's unquestionable authority and his ability to bend others to his will. With Augustus Caesar as *koryphaios* (chorus leader), one felt part of an ordered and peaceful world. But there was always the veiled threat of punishment – a warning of what could happen to those who sounded the wrong note.

Sound, Ritual and the Citharodic Experience

Thus far, I have suggested that the accession of Augustus inspired a complex set of Roman (and Greek) reflections on the nature of music and its role in society. By adopting the citharodic god as his divine mascot, Augustus promoted a vision of Rome as the epicentre of a politically ordered universe. In the following section, I want to take this line of argument a step further. My aim is to demonstrate that the harmony of Apollo's lyre was evoked not only through literary and artistic allusion and metaphor, but also through carefully controlled sounds and rituals which gained performative meaning through the temporal and spatial contexts of their production. In pursuing this line of argument, I am particularly interested in exploring how Apollo's divinity was mediated through the sensory environment, including the musical soundscapes that accompanied public sacrifices and festivals like the *Ludi Saeculares*.

The temple on the Palatine was not the first cult site in Rome to be devoted to Apollo. The Roman cult of Apollo had a long history, dating back as far as the sixth century BCE.[120] In 431 BCE, the consul Cn. Julius dedicated a temple to Apollo Medicus (the Healer) in the Campus Martius.[121] This temple was refurbished several times during the republican period and served for a long time as a venue for meetings of the Senate outside the *pomerium*.[122] Sometime between 34 and 32 BCE, the Antonian partisan C. Sosius undertook another major refurbishment of the temple, perhaps in response to Octavian's project on the Palatine.[123] It was probably not until after the Civil War that the final renovations were completed. Augustus not only allowed Sosius' monument to remain intact –

---

[120] On the origins of the Roman cult of Apollo, see Gagé 1955: 155–220.
[121] Livy 4.29.7, 40.51.6; cf. Ascon. on Cic. *Tog. Cand.* 90. The temple was vowed in 433 BCE in expiation of a plague (Livy 4.25.3). On the temple and its early development, see Platner-Ashby 1929: 15–16; Viscogliosi 1993a: 49–50.
[122] For example, the temple was refurbished in 353 BCE following the Gallic fire (Livy 7.20.9). Senate-meetings in the temple: Livy 39.4, 41.17; Cic. *QFr.* 2.3.2, *Fam.* 8.4, 8.5.6; Lucan 3.103.
[123] See Hinard 1992: 57–72; Viscogliosi 1993a: 50–3; Rutledge 2012: 244.

a gesture of magnanimity after Sosius' appeal for amnesty – but incorporated it into his own large-scale monumental complex at the north-eastern end of the Circus Flaminius, which included the Portico of Philippus (dedicated ca. 28 BCE), the Portico of Octavia (dedicated ca. 27 BCE) and the Theatre of Marcellus (dedicated in 13 or 11 BCE).[124]

Pliny the Elder provides information about the temple's sculptural programme in his *Natural History*. The temple contained, in total, no fewer than four statues of Apollo, all of Greek origin. The first, made of cedar wood, had been imported to Rome from Seleucia (Pliny gives it the epithet *Sosianus*, suggesting that Sosius acquired it during his governorship of Syria from 38 to 36 BCE).[125] There were, in addition, two Apollos by the second-century sculptor Philiscus of Rhodes – one of unknown type, the other naked and accompanied by Latona, Diana and the Muses. Lastly, there was a colossal statue of Apollo 'holding a lyre' by Timarchides of Athens.[126] The origin of these statues is disputed. Filippo Coarelli has proposed that the statue by Timarchides was installed in 179 BCE by the Roman censors on the occasion of their restoration of the temple.[127] However, the exact nature of the censors' activities is itself disputed, and according to some experts Timarchides was not active until the *latter* half of the second century. Another possibility is that the statues were brought over by Sosius as triumphal booty or perhaps later at the behest of Augustus himself. The important point, in any case, is that the decorative programme of the temple at the Circus Flaminius aligned closely with that

---

[124] A sculptural frieze discovered during the modern excavations of the temple represents scenes from Octavian's triple triumph of 29 BCE: Musei Capitolini inv. no. MC 2776 (currently displayed at Centrale Montemartini); Steinby *LTUR*, s.v. "Apollo, Aedes in Circo", 49–54.

[125] Plin. *HN* 13.53: *cedrinus est Romae in delubro Apollo Sosianus Seleucia advectus*.

[126] Plin. *HN* 36.34–5: *ad Octaviae vero porticum Apollo Philisci Rhodii in delubro suo, item Latona et Diana et Musae novem et alter Apollo nudus. eum, qui citharam in eodem templo tenet, Timarchides fecit*. The Apollo *qui . . . citharam tenit* has been identified on chronological and stylistic grounds as the model for the Apollo of Cyrene, a late Hellenistic work of neoclassical style now displayed in the British Museum (Becatti 1935; La Rocca 1977). Vitruvius (10.2.13) reports that the *colossici Apollinis in fano basis* underwent repairs sometime 'in living memory' (*nostra . . . memoria*). Some have identified this colossus with the citharodic statue by Timarchides, others with the cedar-wood statue from Seleucia. Other artworks in the temple included a Niobid group by Scopas or Praxiteles and paintings by Aristides of Thebes (Plin. *HN* 36.28 and 36.99). The pediments, which represent the battle between the Greeks and the Amazons, might have been taken by Sosius from the late Archaic Temple of Apollo Daphnophorus at Eretria: see La Rocca 1985: 76–7.

[127] Coarelli 1970–1971: 77–8, 86–7. Livy (40.51.1–5, 52.1) mentions only a *theatrum et proscenium ad Apollinis* and a *porticus <ad> aedem Apollinis*, but archaeological investigation has revealed traces of building work on the temple itself during the first quarter of the second century BCE (Viscogliosi 1993a: 49–50).

of the temple on the Palatine. In both spaces, the dominant image was that of Apollo the Citharode, 'Leader of the Muses', brother of Diana and son of Latona.

Is it possible that the appearance of real citharodes in the Theatre of Marcellus somehow enhanced the religious aura of the citharodic god whose colossal statue stood inside the temple immediately adjacent to it? Augustus in the *Res Gestae* refers to the theatre as being 'next to the temple of Apollo', and it has been argued persuasively by Amanda Claridge that the theatre of Marcellus was built precisely 'to serve the temple'.[128] It is certainly not inconceivable that the sight and sound of lyre-players on the stage evoked comparisons with Apollo himself. Professional citharodes in Greece and Rome are often represented as human embodiments of Apollo, reflecting the god's status as the prototypical *citharoedus*.[129] According to Tacitus, the emperor Nero sought justification for his own performances on the grounds that *kitharoidia* was 'sacred to Apollo', and that 'this outstanding and prescient deity was represented in the guise of *citharoedus* not only in Greek cities but also in Roman temples'.[130]

The nearby Portico of Philippus was invested with its own citharodic symbolism. Erected by Augustus' stepbrother and uncle L. Marcius Philippus, this monument extended the pre-existing temple to Hercules Musarum which had stood on the site since 187 BCE.[131] There is no reason to believe that the original cult statues were replaced or removed during Philippus' renovations. Ovid devotes a passage at the end of his *Fasti* to the *clari monumenta Philippi*, in which he makes reference to a lyre-playing Hercules accompanied by the nine Muses.[132] The juxtaposition of Hercules and Apollo, each with their respective lyres and Muses, would have further underscored the 'musical' associations of this area of the Circus Flaminius, symbolising the harmonious incorporation of Greek cult (and culture) into Roman society.

The cult of Apollo was associated with a particular category of public ritual known by the Romans as the *ritus Graecus*, or 'Greek rite'. According to Livy, the sacrifices at the *Ludi Apollinares*, the games celebrated in honour of Apollo every July, were made 'according to the Greek

---

[128] *RGDA* 21.1 (*theatrum ad aedem Apollinis*); Claridge 2010: 227. Vitruvius, in his treatise addressed to Augustus, maintains that temples to Apollo and Liber should be built 'next to the theatre' (*secundum theatrum*; 1.7.1).
[129] Power 2010: 28–31.   [130] Tac. *Ann.* 14.14.1.
[131] On the Porticus Philippi and its relation to the Temple of Hercules Musarum, see Richardson 1977; Martina 1981; Hardie 2007; Heslin 2015.
[132] Ov. *Fast.* 6.811–12: *doctae assensere sorores; | adnuit Alcides increpuitque lyram.*

rite'.[133] The *ritus Graecus* appears to have originated during the third or second century BCE as an official way of recognising 'certain new religious customs or certain old Roman cults whose Greek origins were now discovered or emphasised, such as the cult of Hercules'.[134] In practice, the distinction between the *ritus Graecus* and the *ritus Romanus* was somewhat blurry. Nevertheless, there are two features particular to the *ritus Graecus* which can be identified on the basis of the extant sources. Firstly, during the Greek rite the celebrants crowned themselves with laurel wreaths, instead of covering their heads with the toga (as in the Roman rite). Secondly, and most significantly for our purposes, the Greek rite involved 'a particular kind of musical accompaniment'.[135] Whereas sacrifices conducted in the *ritus Romanus* traditionally featured the music of *tibiae* only, the *ritus Graecus* seems to have been accompanied by both pipes and lyres, and perhaps choral singers as well.[136] In Roman artistic representations of sacrifices, in fact, lyre-players appear almost exclusively in scenes invoking the performance of the *ritus Graecus*. Lyre-players certainly took part in religious ceremonies of other kinds (Cicero and Horace testify to the use of lyres at ceremonial banquets, for instance).[137] However, the use of the lyre in religious contexts seems to have been interpreted by the Romans as a marker of 'Greekness'.

Apollo and the *ritus Graecus* played an especially important role in the *Ludi Saeculares* of 17 BCE. The inscribed record of the festival mentions, on the night of 31 May, sacrifices to the Moirai (Fates) conducted 'in the Greek rite', followed by games held 'on a stage without the additional construction of a theatre and without the erection of seating'.[138] On the following day, there were 'Latin games in a wooden theatre which had been erected on the Campus Martius next to the Tiber'. On the third day, the Roman people watched the *princeps* take part in sacrifices and prayers to Apollo in front of his temple on the Palatine. It was at this point that Horace's *Carmen Saeculare* was performed by a choir of twenty-seven boys

---

[133] Livy 25.12.10: *decemviri Graeco ritu hostiis sacra faciant*. On the history of the *ludi Apollinares*, cf. Livy 25.12.2–15; Scullard 1981: 159–60. According to Varro (*Ling.* 7.88), the *sacra* of the Sibylline Books were also conducted *Graeco ritu*.

[134] Scheid 2003: 37; see also Scheid 1995.   [135] Scheid 2003: 37.

[136] The *societas cantorum Graecorum*, attested on a late-republican inscription, is sometimes connected with the *ritus Graecus*: see, e.g., Rüpke and Gordon 2007: 95.

[137] Cic. *Tusc. Disp.* 4.4: *et deorum pulvinaribus et epulis magistratuum fides praecinunt*; Hor. *Od.* 3.11.5–6: *nunc et divitum mensis et amica templis*; cf. Porph. *ad Hor. Od.* 1.36: *fidicines hodieque Romae ad sacrificia adhiberi sicut tibicines nemo est qui nesciat*. Note also the pairing of musicians on the Altar of Domitius Ahenobarbus: Vincent 2016: 162–6; Vendries 2004: 407.

[138] *CIL* 6.32323 = *ILS* 5050; Schnegg-Köhler 2002.

and twenty-seven girls, first on the Palatine and then again on the Capitoline.[139] The song paid tribute to Apollo in his triple role as prophet, archer and musician (*augur et fulgente decorus arcu / Phoebus acceptusque novem Camenis*, ll. 61–62), the phrase *acceptusque novem Camenis* invoking his traditional Greek epithet *Musagetes* (Leader of the Muses). Apollo is also addressed in his capacity as the guardian of the Palatine (*si Palatinas videt aequus aras*, l. 65). The festivities concluded with seven additional days of *ludi scaenici*, including 'Latin plays (*ludi Latini*) in the wooden theatre which is next to the Tiber at the second hour, Greek choral performances (*ludi thymelici*) in the theatre of Pompey at the third hour, and Greek city-games (*ludi astici*) in the theatre which is in the Circus Flaminius at the fourth hour'.[140]

It is likely that the sacrifices at the *Ludi Saeculares* featured musical accompaniments characteristic of the *ritus Graecus*. A *fidicen* and a *tibicen* appear together in the commemorative coinage from Domitian's *Ludi Saeculares* of 88 CE (Fig. 3.11).[141] The two musicians wear togas and stand behind an altar facing the emperor, who holds a *patera* and performs a sacrifice. Although we lack a direct Augustan parallel for this coin, it is generally agreed that the Domitianic sacrifices followed an Augustan model. Thus, we can fairly assume that the sacrifices which Augustus himself performed on 3 June in front of the Palatine temple were accompanied by both a *tibicen* and a *fidicen*.[142] Might the sight of Augustus

---

[139] *CIL* 6.32323 = *ILS* 5050, ll. 148–9: *[X]XVII quibus denuntiatum erat patrimi et matrimi et puellae totidem carmen cecinerunt; eo[de]m modo in Capitolio. carmen composuit Q. Hor[at]ius Flaccus*. The meaning of *carmen composuit* has generated much debate. Horace refers to himself in his poetry as *Romanae fidicen lyrae* (*Od.* 4.3.23; cf. *Epist.* 2.2.84–86, 143), and some have taken this as a sign that he was directly involved in the composition of the music, in the manner of Greek lyric poets: see Lyons 2010; *contra* Thomas 2011: 57 ('only H.'s words were part of the performance'). Little credence should be given to the notion that Horace actually accompanied the singers on the lyre himself (*pace* Wille 1967: 253; Bonavia-Hunt 1969: 7–14). But we should not discount the possibility that the performance of the *Carmen Saeculare* involved instrumentalists as well as singers (Scheid 1995: 26; Barchiesi 2002: 112–18; Vendries 2004: 405). For a discussion of the history of scholarship on this issue, see Lowrie 2009: 81–97. On the choral aspects of the *Carmen Saeculare*, see Curtis 2017: 149–57.

[140] *CIL* 6.32323 = *ILS* 5050. *Ludi astici* were dramatic performances, modelled on the City Dionysia at Athens: Manuwald 2011: 21 n. 28. There were also *ludi astici* at the games held in honour of Augustus' triumph in 29 (cf. Suet. *Tib.* 6.4). For the significance of *ludi thymelici*, cf. *LSJ*, s.v. θυμελικός; *IG* II² 1350, VII 2712, *et al.*; Virtuv. 5.7.2; Ulp. *Dig.* 3.2.4; Isid. *Orig.* 18.47; Lightfoot 2002: 210; Rocconi 2006: 74–5.

[141] See discussion in Sobocinski 2006: 586–91.

[142] As suggested by Baudot 1973: 112; Vendries 1999: 203; Vincent 2016: 213–6. The inscribed *acta* for the *Ludi Saeculares* of Septimius Severus in 204 may include a reference to lyre-players accompanying the procession from the Palatine to the Capitoline: see *AE* 1932, 70 = *AE* 1935, 26 (*fidicinum* restored by Pighi 1941: 293). We have, in addition, a Severan coin from 204

Figure 3.11 Bronze as of Domitian, 88 CE. Rome mint. Observe: head of Domitian, laureate. Reverse: Domitian sacrifices over an altar in front of a temple, accompanied by a *tibicen* and *fidicen*. RIC II 623, BMCRE II 434.
Courtesy of the American Numismatic Society 1944.100.42607.

holding a *patera* and standing next to a lyre-player (or lyre-players) have prompted comparisons with the statue of the divine citharode in the nearby portico, perhaps equipped with a *patera* of his own?

By reducing the symbolic currency of Apollo Citharoedus to the level of banal abstractions, we lose something of its vitality in the lived experience of contemporary Romans. To be sure, Apollo's lyre stood for everything that Romans valued about Greek culture – rationality, harmony, order, civilization – but what gave it meaning was its physical embeddedness within the Augustan cityscape. Apollo's lyre created an interface between the visual and the aural, the imagined and the experienced. The message of Apolline *kitharoidia* was communicated not only through gold and marble, through the written and spoken word, but also through rituals and sounds, concentrated at certain places and at certain times where the god's presence was most strongly felt: the Palatine sanctuary; the temple of Apollo at the Circus Flaminius and its adjoining theatre; the *Ludi Apollinares*; and the *Ludi Saeculares*.

Art, architecture, literature and performance merged to create a dynamic 'musical' idiom. Although this idiom exploited the Romans' nostalgia for ancient Greek culture, it was couched in a way that appealed to traditional Roman values and customs. Hence, the *Ludi Saeculares*

which, like the Domitianic issue, shows a *tibicen* and a *fidicen* accompanying a sacrifice at the *Ludi Saeculares*: BMCRE 5, p. 325, no. 810.

incorporated aspects of a Greek festival (*ludi thymelici, ludi astici*, sacrifices 'in the Greek rite') while retaining a quintessentially Roman modality. Similarly, as John Scheid has emphasised, the *ritus Graecus* served as a means of enhancing the prestige and legitimacy of Roman culture by stressing the assimilation of Greek (i.e. foreign) peoples and customs. Its importance lay not in 'the content of the celebration itself, but in the way of celebrating the ceremonies' – that is, the *Roman* way.[143] Apollo's presence in the Augustan city therefore signified the realisation of a new symbiotic relationship between Greek and Roman cultures, paving the way for a more ordered and harmonious society.

A 'Golden Age' of Music?

In the conclusion of his book, *Musiciens romains de l'antiquité*, Alain Baudot argues that Roman music underwent 'un enrichissement général' in the period from the end of the Republic to the start of the reign of Tiberius.[144] Baudot bases this argument on two suppositions: firstly, that the Augustan period witnessed significant progress in the manufacture of instruments and in performance techniques; and, secondly, that the advent of pantomime in the early Augustan period brought new sounds and rhythms to the Roman stage, resulting in a more 'refined' and 'elevated' musical experience. Baudot goes on to situate these developments in the broader context of what he calls the 'apollinisation' of Roman society under Augustus.[145] This raises an important question: did Roman musical culture undergo a transformation during the Augustan Principate, and if so, to what extent was this transformation attributed by contemporaries to the Augustan cult of Apollo?

The evidence for a 'revolution' of Roman music in the time of Augustus is in fact extremely tenuous. The scattered remnants of musical instruments from across the Roman world preclude generalising interpretations. It is true that the *tibiae* discovered in Pompeii possess a greater number of finger-holes (between ten and fifteen) than our earlier examples of Greek *auloi*, which have between five and nine holes.[146] It is also true that advances in the manufacture of reed-pipes probably facilitated a more virtuosic style of performance over time. Fragmentary *tibiae* have been excavated in Sudan and Israel, dating from the first century BCE, which

---

[143] Scheid 1995: 18.   [144] Baudot 1973: 130.   [145] Baudot 1973: 131.
[146] Creese 2006: 419.

originally possessed a rotating metal collar that allowed the player to switch between different harmonic modes in a single performance.[147] *Tibiae* of this kind were certainly capable of producing complex music. However, rotating collars were not a Roman invention; they are attested as early as the fifth century BCE.[148] So although we may be able to detect signs of gradual change over a number of centuries, the idea that instrumental technologies dramatically evolved during the Augustan period is unsubstantiated.

The same problems apply to the study of musical notation. Musical papyri from the imperial period have been shown to indicate a more 'florid and dramatic style' than is apparent in the musical papyri of the Hellenistic period.[149] However, the documents in question (which pertain to texts written exclusively in Greek) are far too fragmentary and few in number to allow us to pinpoint any precise change over time. In any case, most of the Roman-era papyri date from long after the Augustan period (mainly the second and third centuries CE). It is simply impossible to make the disparate evidence fit a single model of historical change. To the extent that any measurable 'progress' can be detected around the time of the late Republic and early Principate, such progress can hardly be ascribed to an Apolline ideology.

The pantomime is one area where we definitely can detect innovation. This popular form of theatrical entertainment revolved around a solo masked dancer known as a *pantomimus*. Through the use of mimetic gestures alone, the *pantomimus* acted out famous scenes from mythology to the accompaniment of musicians and singers. The pantomime was first introduced to Rome in 23 or 22 BCE by two dancers named Pylades and Bathyllus, who hailed from Cilicia and Alexandria respectively.[150] Macrobius describes a (likely fictional) encounter between Pylades and Augustus, in which the pantomime is asked by the emperor to explain his contribution to the dance and replies, quoting Homer's *Iliad*, 'the sound of pipes and flutes and the din of men'.[151] Suetonius provides a context for

---

[147] Braun 2002: 223.   [148] West 1992: 87; Landels 1999: 36–7.   [149] Johnson 2000a: 58.
[150] Jer. *Chron.* 2.143 (Helm) assigns the introduction of the pantomime to the year 22 BCE. However, Jory (1981) suggests plausibly that the pantomime made its debut in Rome during the games staged by Augustus' son-in-law Marcellus in 23 BCE. Cf. Athen. 1.20d–e (Bathyllus as the inventor of 'comic' dance, and Pylades the 'tragic' dance); Zosimus, *Historia Nova* 6.1; Suda s.v. 'Alexandria', 'pantomimos', and 'Bathyllos'. For the Augustan origins of pantomime, cf. Luc. *Salt.* 348; Hunt 2008.
[151] Macr. *Sat.* 2.7.18; the quotation is Hom. *Il.* 10.13: αὐλῶν συρίγγων τ' ἐνοπὴν, ὁμαδόν τ' ἀνθρώπων.

this anecdote: 'Whereas the ancients used to dance and sing themselves, Pylades the Cilician pantomime was the first at Rome to have a chorus and pipe music accompany him.'[152] Music, then, was undoubtedly responsible for much of the pantomime's popularity.[153] The pantomimes themselves may have been the stars of the show, but their accompanists were much more than just supporting artists. Phaedrus dedicates one of his fables to a celebrated pipe-player called Princeps, who was 'accustomed to ply his trade on the stage with Bathyllus'. He clearly boasted a large following, judging from how the Roman public reacted to an injury which he sustained after falling off a stage machine during a performance: 'They began to long for the man whose breath inspired the dancers with energy.'[154] Another musician who starred alongside Bathyllus was the singer Philonides. A Greek epigram by the poet Crinagoras addresses Philonides directly and calls upon him to 'write a piece composed for four parts or even more; for neither your singing nor the motions of Bathyllus' hands shall be lacking in grace'.[155] It would not be unreasonable, therefore, to associate the advent of pantomime with a 'general enrichment' of Roman musical culture in the age of Augustus, at least within the realm of public spectacle. However, the idea that the pantomime helped to embed a culture of 'apollinisation' is misleading. It makes much better sense in my opinion to view the introduction of pantomime as a reflection of Augustus' desire to appeal to the cultural interests of ordinary Romans. Tacitus explicitly associates the *princeps*' patronage of pantomime dancers with his willingness 'to mingle in the pleasures of the people' (*misceri voluptatibus vulgi*).[156] Investing in this new art form was a way for him to show that he had his finger on the pulse of popular entertainment.

Stories of Augustus delighting in musicians at his dinner-parties are somewhat harder to interpret. Suetonius comments that Augustus used to entertain his dinner guests with musical performances (*acroamata*), as well as actors (*histriones*) and itinerant players from the Circus (*triviales ex circo*

---

[152] Suet. *De Poetis* fr. 3 (Rostagni p. 65) = Jer. *Chron.* 2.143 (Helm): *Pylades Cilex pantomimus, cum veteres ipsi canerent atque saltarent, primus Romae chorum et fistulam sibi praecinere fecit.*
[153] Lucian, in his second-century treatise *On the Dance*, speaks of the *aulos* and the *kithara* as 'parts of the dancer's paraphernalia' (μέρη ... τῆς τοῦ ὀρχηστοῦ ὑπηρεσίας; *Salt.* 26); cf. Cassiodorus, *Variae* 4.51.9: *pantomimo igitur, cui a multifaria imitatione nomen est, cum primum in scaenam plausibus invitatus advenerit, assistunt consoni chori diversis organis eruditi.* On the role of percussion (especially the *scabellum*) in pantomime, cf. Lib. *Or.* 64.97.
[154] Phaedrus 5.7 (citations from ll. 5, 14–15). [155] Crinagoras 39 = *Anth. Pal.* IX 542.
[156] Tac. *Hist.* 1.54. On the role of public spectacle in Augustan politics, see Beacham 1999: 92–154.

ludii).¹⁵⁷ As Christopher Jones points out, 'The implication is that this is modest fare: we may suspect that contemporaries of Augustus, not to mention hosts under his immediate successors, would have offered very much more.'¹⁵⁸ In reality, however, the musical offerings of the *domus Caesaris* were probably just as extravagant as those of any other aristocratic household. In Macrobius' *Saturnalia*, we read of how Augustus was so greatly enamoured with the *symphoniaci* of the slave-dealer Toronius Flaccus that he wished to award them with a grain ration. When he requested the musicians' presence at another banquet, he was told that they were 'at the mills' (i.e. as slaves undergoing punishment).¹⁵⁹ We happen to possess epitaphs belonging to two *symphoniacae* who served in the household of Augustus' sister Octavia.¹⁶⁰ Moreover, the Sardinian singer Hermogenes Tigellius, the favourite of Julius Caesar and Cleopatra and later nemesis of Horace, is said to have been welcomed into Augustus' *familiares domestici*.¹⁶¹ This evidence suggests that musicians were conspicuous members of the *familia Caesaris* and in a few cases even formed personal relationships with both the *princeps* and his extended circle of friends and family. Still, there is no sign that Augustus sought to overhaul Roman musical culture to make it align with an Apolline programme.

Before we conclude our exploration of Augustan musical culture, there is one final category of evidence to be taken into consideration – namely, the epigraphic testimonies for musicians' guilds in Rome. In his article 'Auguste et les tibicines', published in 2008, Alexandre Vincent pinpoints a significant development in the nomenclature of the guild of Roman pipe-players during the early imperial period. Whereas in republican inscriptions the guild is designated simply as the *collegium tibicinum Romanorum*, from the start of the first century CE the title is always extended to *collegium tibicinum Romanorum qui sacris publicis praesto*

---

[157] Suet. *Aug.* 74. On the *triviales ex circo ludii*, see Wiseman 1980: 13: 'the sort of "strolling players" who might perform at a street-corner, among the beggars, parasites and gossiping loungers'. The term *ludius* technically referred to someone who performed in the *ars ludicra*, but it became associated generally with vulgar kinds of dance: *TLL* s.v. 'ludius', vol. VII, 2, 1768–9 (Beikircher). The reference to the *circus* may also hint at an association with the category of street entertainers known as *circulatores*, on whom see O'Neill 2003.
[158] Jones 1991: 193.   [159] Macr. *Sat.* 2.4.28.   [160] *CIL* 6.33372, 6.33373.
[161] Porph. ad Hor. *Sat.* 1.2.2: *Marcus Tigellius Hermogenes musicae artis scientia praeditus Gaio Caesari dictatori fuit familiaris, postea Cleopatrae, quia dulciter cantabat et iocabatur urbane. Augusto quoque ita placuit, ut inter familiaris domesticos haberetur*; cf. Hor. *Sat.* 1.3.4–8, on Tigellius' refusal to sing at Augustus' request; *PIR*² T 202. It is unclear whether this is the same Tigellius whose funeral is mentioned at Hor. *Sat.* 1.2.3 (*pace* Freudenburg 1993: 115–7) as opposed to a separate individual of the same name (*pace* DuQuesnay 1984: 56; Nisbet 1995: 97).

sunt.¹⁶² Vincent suggests that this new emphasis on the guild's participation in public religious rites reflects a desire on the part of the Augustan authorities to revive traditional state religion. Suetonius tells us that Augustus disbanded all *collegia* except those that were *antiqua et legitima*.¹⁶³ According to Vincent, the *collegium tibicinum* was likely exempt from this ban, in view of its ancient association with King Numa, who supposedly authorised its original foundation.¹⁶⁴ In that case, the *collegium* must have been given authorisation to reconstitute itself with immediate effect, taking on the new extended title.

The *collegium tibicinum* was not the only musicians' guild active in Augustan Rome. An inscription, discovered in 1847 in one of the columbaria at Vigna Codini on the Via Appia, attests to the creation of a *collegium symphoniacorum* under the terms of a Julian law. The text also states that the Senate permitted the *collegium* to be founded 'on the authority of Augustus for the sake of the games'.¹⁶⁵ The *symphoniaci* who belonged to this guild evidently performed at the behest of the public authorities rather than private patrons, as indicated by their involvement in the *ludi*. Vincent argues that the *collegium symphoniacorum* was not an entirely new foundation, but rather superseded the pre-existing *collegium tibicinum et fidicinum*, which is known from earlier inscriptions.¹⁶⁶ The *collegium tibicinum Romanorum* and the *collegium symphoniacorum* should thus be regarded as distinct but similar organisations, each with a clearly prescribed civic function.

Taken as a whole, the evidence for musical *collegia* indicates two things. First, the Augustan reforms of the *collegium tibicinum Romanorum* and the *collegium symphoniacorum* seem to have resulted in a more formal division between musicians involved in stage performances and musicians involved in the more strictly religious aspects of the *ludi*. The mandate of these *collegia* was not primarily to provide entertainment, but to accompany the solemn sacrifices and processions that took place in conjunction with the *ludi scaenici*.¹⁶⁷ Their members were privileged by their association with public cult and had the rights afforded to free-born citizens or freedmen

---

¹⁶² *Collegium tibicinum Romanorum*: *CIL* 1.989; *AE* 1991, 120; *CIL* 1.2, 2984b (from Rome); *CIL* 14.3564 (from Tibur). *Collegium tibicinum Romanorum qui s. p. p. s.*: *CIL* 6.240, 3.877a.
¹⁶³ Suet. *Aug.* 32.   ¹⁶⁴ Plut. *Num.* 17.2–3.
¹⁶⁵ *CIL* 6.2193: *Dis Manibus collegio symphoniacorum qui sacris publicis praestu sunt quibus senatus c(oire) c(onvenire) c(ollegi) permisit e lege Iulia ex auctoritate Aug(usti) ludorum causa.*
¹⁶⁶ *CIL* 6.2919; Vincent 2008: 431–2.
¹⁶⁷ Vincent (2008: 440) suggests that stage performers might have been incorporated into a separate *collegium scabillariorum*.

(slaves, it should be noted, were generally excluded from *collegia*). By contrast, those who performed on the stage continued to be subject to harsh legal penalties, in accordance with their status as *infames*. For example, the Julian law on adultery passed by Augustus in 18 BCE specified that a married man was entitled to kill an adulterer 'if he was a pimp or if he was previously an actor or performed on the stage as a singer or dancer'.[168] One recalcitrant dancer by the name of Stephanio, who appeared at the *Ludi Saeculares* of 17 BCE, was beaten with rods in each of Rome's theatres and banished for engaging in an improper association with a Roman matron.[169] The *princeps* was willing to support theatrical performers, but only so long as they avoided any kind of scandal.

My second point has to do more specifically with the cult of Apollo. One of the major consequences of the new *collegium symphoniacorum* was that it afforded greater visibility to lyre-players acting in the service of public religion. This development may have been a corollary of Augustus' promotion of the *ritus Graecus*, which emphasised collaboration between *tibicines* and *fidicines*. The foundation of the *collegium symphoniacorum* could thus be seen as contributing to the 'ambience apollinienne' of rituals such as the *Ludi Saeculares*.[170] While the reforms of the *collegia* did not necessarily amount to a 'golden age' of Roman music, they may have amplified the resonance of Apolline *kitharoidia* by highlighting the indispensable role of musicians in the civic community.

Conclusion

When Octavian returned to Rome in 30 BCE, following his decisive victory over Antony and Cleopatra, he faced the unenviable task of restoring order to a society torn apart by decades of civil war. The ruthless image that Octavian had crafted as triumvir was incompatible with the image he now wished to propagate as *princeps*. The Roman people cried out for a leader who would bring lasting peace and prosperity, and the victor of Actium responded by giving them a divine champion to rally behind. That champion was Apollo Citharoedus.

---

[168] *Digest* 48.5.25[24] pr. Macer.   [169] Suet. *Aug.* 45.3–4; Plin. *HN* 7.159.
[170] See Vincent 2008: 433: 'L'on pourrait même se demander si la mention "*ludorum causa*" dans l'inscription des *symphoniaci* n'est pas un rappel plus précis de la présence du couple *tibicen-fidicen* lors des Jeux Séculaires célébrés quelques années auparavant par Auguste.'

The texts, images and monuments discussed in this chapter mainly cluster around the first twenty years of Augustus' principate. By the end of the first century, Apollo largely disappears from the emperor's public imagery, eventually to be supplanted by the no less imposing figure of Mars Ultor (the Avenger), whose temple crowned the new Forum Augustum, completed in 2 BCE. Various explanations for this disappearance might be posited: perhaps the persona of the youthful Apollo was deemed unsuitable for an aging *princeps*; perhaps the outbreak of foreign wars created an opportunity for the emperor to align himself with a more martial deity; perhaps the Apollo motif was simply getting tired. In any case, the times had changed. The foundations of lasting autocracy had been laid.

But in the climate of uncertainty which pervaded the early years of Augustan rule, the talismanic presence of Apollo Citharoedus was all-important. It provided a sense of permanence, anchoring the fledgling regime in a powerful ideological and cosmological narrative. The *harmonia* of the *cithara* was distilled into a metaphor for the new world order. Transcending text and image, the symbolism of *kitharoidia* was writ large on Rome's monumental landscape and embedded in its public rituals, spectacles and institutions. In this way, the cult of Apollo harmonised with the cultural and moral aims of the Augustan restoration, banishing once and for all the spectre of Antonian Bacchanalia. The sound of Apollo's lyre would be heard echoing along the shores of Actium for centuries to come.

4 | Nero and the Age of Musomania

Ἀλέξανδρος δὲ ὁ πολίτης μου (οὗτος δ' οὐ πρὸ πολλοῦ τετελεύτηκε) δημοσίᾳ ἐπιδειξάμενος ἐν τῷ τριγώνῳ ἐπικαλουμένῳ ὀργάνῳ οὕτως ἐποίησε πάντας Ῥωμαίους μουσομανεῖν ὡς τοὺς πολλοὺς καὶ ἀπομνημονεύειν αὐτοῦ τὰ κρούσματα.

My fellow-citizen Alexander (he died not long ago) gave a public concert on the instrument called the trigonon and made all the Romans so mad about music that many of them have even memorised his tunes.

Athenaeus, *Deipnosophistae* 4.184e

Ἡ φωνὴ δέ, Μουσώνιε, δι' ἣν μουσομανεῖ ... πῶς ἔχει τῷ τυράννῳ;

And that voice of [Nero's], Musonius, which makes him mad about music ... what is the tyrant's voice like?

[Lucian], *Nero or on the Digging of the Isthmus* 6

The verb *mousomanein* (to be mad about music) is attested only twice in the entire corpus of extant Greek literature; I have chosen both instances as my pair of epigraphs to this chapter.[1] The first time we come across this word is in Athenaeus' *Deipnosophistae*. The interlocutor Alceides tells the story of a musician from Alexandria who migrates to Rome at the turn of the third century CE and bewitches audiences with his triangular harp, known to his Greek-speaking compatriots as a *trigonon*.[2] The second attestation of *mousomanein* occurs in a short dialogue entitled *Nero or on the Digging of the Isthmus*, preserved in the manuscripts of Lucian but normally attributed to the writer and sophist Philostratus of Athens (active during the early third century).[3] In the dialogue, a character named Menecrates enters into a debate with the Stoic philosopher Musonius

---

[1] *LSJ*, s.v. μουσομανέω; μουσομανεῖ appears in a fragment of Sophocles (fr. 245 Pearson) but is best interpreted as a dative of the adjective μουσομανής; for μουσομανής attested elsewhere, cf. Plut. *Mor.* 706c; *Anth. Pal.* 10.16.
[2] On the *trigonon*, cf. Athen. 4.175d.   [3] See Whitmarsh 1999: 143–4.

Rufus about the emperor Nero's exploits during his infamous tour of Greece in 66–67 CE.[4] The main topic of discussion is Nero's abortive attempt to cut a canal through the Isthmus of Corinth, but the two speakers also have much to say about Nero's accomplishments as a musician. What, Menecrates wonders, is the voice of this tyrant really like?

We all know Nero as the emperor who 'fiddled while Rome burned'. The story owes as much to the imagination of early modern playwrights as it does to the annals of ancient history, yet it has become enshrined during the last century as a moral axiom, endlessly repeated in satirical cartoons and Hollywood films (see Fig. 4.1).[5] Whether the *princeps* really did ascend to the summit of the Palatine in 64 CE and sing a poetic lamentation on the Fall of Troy will forever remain a mystery (doubts were expressed even in antiquity), but the insinuation alone speaks to an extraordinary commitment to the performing arts.[6] In a city of musomaniacs, Nero stood out.

'Fiddle' he most certainly did not, but the emperor's enthusiasm for the *cithara* was all too real and knew no bounds. That, at least, is the impression conveyed by the three main chroniclers of his reign – Tacitus, Suetonius and Cassius Dio – not to mention the satirist Juvenal, in whose verses Nero is simply *citharoedus princeps* (the emperor who sang to the lyre).[7] Nero's passion for music was sparked at an early age. As a boy, he took lessons in singing, as well as sculpture, painting and horse-riding.[8] Thus imbued with a rudimentary knowledge of music, he proceeded upon his accession to the throne at the age of seventeen to undertake specialist training as a citharode. He summoned to his court the famous maestro Terpnus and, under his tutelage, began practising all the usual exercises 'for preserving or strengthening the voice' (*vel conservandae vocis causa vel augendae*).[9] Initially, the young ruler confined himself to a private stage in

---

[4] Menecrates may be related to the Neronian citharode of the same name: cf. Petr. *Sat.* 73.19; Suet. *Nero* 30.2; Dio Cass. 63.1; Whitmarsh 1999: 142 n. 4.

[5] The ancient narratives are Tac. *Ann.* 15.39, Suet. *Nero* 38, Dio Cass. 62.18.1. The first documented reference to Nero's 'fiddle' appears in an anonymous play called *The Tragedy of Nero*, published in 1624; in Shakespeare's *Henry IV*, Nero plays the 'lute': see Gyles 1947. For Nero's 'fiddling' in modern political satire, see Mitchell 2013: 324–32; Perrin 2018. For cinematic depictions of Nero, see Wyke 1994; Pucci 2011; Winkler 2017.

[6] The reference to τό Παλάτιον in Cassius Dio (62.18.1) is open to interpretation. Suetonius, by contrast, states that Nero watched the fire from the Tower of Maecenas – that is, in the *Horti Maecenatiani* (*Nero* 38.2). Tacitus is the most sceptical of the three, reporting a 'rumour' that Nero sang the Fall of Troy on a private stage (*domesticam scaenam*; *Ann.* 15.39). On the discrepancy between the ancient narratives, see Champlin 2003a: 48–9; Wiseman 2016: 146–7.

[7] Juv. 8.198. Pliny's nickname for Nero, *imperator scaenicus* (*Paneg.* 46.4), encompasses his performances as both *citharoedus* and *tragoedus*.

[8] Tac. *Ann.* 13.3.7 (*caelare pingere, cantus aut regimen equorum exercere*).   [9] Suet. *Nero* 20.1.

Figure 4.1 Poster for the silent motion picture *Quo Vadis* (1913) showing Nero fiddling while Rome burns. Photo by VCG Wilson / Corbis via Getty Images.

his gardens across the Tiber.[10] It was here, in 59, that he celebrated the Juvenile Games (*Ludi Iuvenalium* or *Iuvenalia*), a festival marking the first shaving of his beard, during which he gave a concert on the lyre.[11] From that moment on, Nero started to dream of a career as a professional citharode.[12] The turning point came in 64, when the *princeps* made his long-awaited public debut in the 'quasi-Greek city' of Naples.[13] This was followed in 65 by a star turn at the Neronian Games (*Neronia*), a quinquennial festival of music, drama and athletics held in Rome. Having declined the opportunity to perform in the inaugural contests of 60, Nero now entered – and duly won – the prize for *kitharoidia*. He also recited one of his own compositions to great popular acclaim.[14] This success emboldened him, in 66, to embark on a 'grand tour' of Greece, encompassing all the main panhellenic festivals (the calendars were synchronised in order to allow him to compete).[15] Nero departed in late summer and would be gone for over a year. His return at the end of 67 was celebrated in typically grandiose fashion, with a great triumphal procession through the streets of Rome. Relations with the Senate were already strained, and this latest bout of public exhibitionism only made things worse. The revolt of Julius Vindex, the governor of Gallia Lugdunensis, in 68 triggered a succession of mutinies across the frontiers. Nero fled Rome in ignominy and committed suicide on 9 June 68 CE.

Singing to the lyre was Nero's earliest and greatest passion. But his musical ambitions did not end there. The young emperor also took a liking to *tragoidia* – the art of singing arias on tragic themes.[16] We first encounter Nero as a *tragoedus* in 67, during the tour of Greece. His roles, as reported by Suetonius, included *Canace in Childbirth*, *Orestes the Matricide*, *Oedipus Blinded* and *Hercules Insane*; Dio adds Thyestes and Alcmaeon to the list.[17] To be sure, the art of *tragoidia* had much in common with that of *kitharoidia*, combining displays of vocal pyrotechnics and mythological role play; it is not hard to see why the genre appealed to the stagestruck

---

[10] Plin. *HN* 15.33 (*theatrum peculiare trans Tiberim in hortis*).

[11] Tac. *Ann.* 14.15; cf. *Ann.* 15.33.1.

[12] Among friends he would quote the Greek proverb, 'there is no respect for hidden music' (*occultae musicae nullum esse respectum*, Suet. *Nero* 20.1); cf. Gell. *NA* 13.31.3; Luc. *Harm.* 1.

[13] Tac. *Ann.* 15.44 (*quasi Graeca urbs*); Suet. *Nero* 20.2–3. On Roman Naples as a centre of Greek cultural activity, see Taylor 2021: 291–346.

[14] Tac. *Ann.* 16.4.2–4; Dio Cass. 62.29.1.   [15] Suet. *Nero* 23.1; Philostr. *VA* 5.7.

[16] On Nero as *tragoedus*, see especially Kelly 1979; Bartsch 1994: 36–62.

[17] Suet. *Nero* 21.3; Dio Cass. 63.9.4–5; cf. Philostr. *VA* 5.7; Juv. 8.228. Tacitus does not represent Nero as a *tragoedus* in the extant portions of the *Annals*, which further suggests that Nero's tragic career was limited to the final years of his reign. Dio (62.8.2) notes that Nero went to Greece partly in order to 'perform tragic songs' (τραγῳδίας ὑποκρίσει).

emperor.[18] But it also afforded a different set of creative opportunities: unlike citharodes, tragic singers wore a variety of costumes, which matched the individual features of the character they were impersonating; they used props; and they wore masks.[19]

By the end of his reign, Nero's musical interests had shifted yet again. In 68, a few months before his death, we find Nero putting on private exhibitions of water-organs (*organa hydraulica*) in the imperial palace and promising public games in which he would appear as an organist (*hydraules*), a pipe-player (*choraules*) and a bagpiper (*utricularius*).[20] He also apparently had ambitions as a pantomime dancer. Suetonius comments, with more than a hint of irony, that he had desired to play the role of Turnus, the doomed antagonist of Vergil's *Aeneid*.[21] Whether the emperor's late-career obsession with wind-instruments and pantomime dancing ever materialised in actual performances is unknown, but it is notable that Dio Chrysostom, writing not long after Nero's death, could imagine him playing the pipes both 'with his mouth' (τῷ τε στόματι) and 'by tucking a bag beneath his armpits' (ταῖς μασχάλαις ἀσκὸν ὑποβάλλοντα)'.[22]

In plotting the trajectory of Nero's musical career, subsequent generations of writers found an effective vehicle for mapping out the tensions and ambiguities of his reign. Suetonius, in his biography of Nero, introduces the section on the emperor's vices with a discussion of his musical pursuits.[23] Tacitus, similarly, associates Nero's moral degeneration in the aftermath of Agrippina's murder with his 'disgraceful enthusiasm' (*foedum studium*) for singing to the lyre 'in the stage manner' (*ludicum in modum*).[24] Indeed, for Dio Chrysostom, Nero's singing – or, more precisely, his 'tongue' – was to be blamed for the collapse of the entire Julio-Claudian dynasty (οἰκίαν συντριβεῖσαν ... διὰ γλῶτταν).[25]

Nero's music-making, then, played a formative role in shaping the historical memory of his principate. Negative reviews of his performances provide telling glimpses into the man behind the music, revealing his delusions and obsessions, his tyrannical whims and desires. Indeed, as

---

[18] On the affinity between *tragoedus* and *citharoedus*, see Power 2010: 143.
[19] Nero's masks either bore the emperor's own likeness or the likeness of his wife Poppaea Sabina: Dio Cass. 63.9.4–5; Suet. *Nero* 21.3. His prop collection included gold chains and a sceptre: Suet. *Nero* 24.1, 21.3; Dio Cass. 63.9.6.
[20] Suet. *Nero* 54, 41.2; Dio Cass. 63.26.4–5.   [21] Suet. *Nero* 54; Dio Cass. 63.18.1.
[22] Dio Chrys. *Or*. 71.9, alluding to the *auloi* and bagpipes respectively.
[23] Suet. *Nero* 19.3–20.1.   [24] Tac. *Ann*. 14.14.1.
[25] Dio Chrys. *Or*. 66.6. In *Or*. 32.60, Dio likens the emperor's infatuation with music to a 'disease' (νόσος), which drove him insane.

one traces Nero's reception over the centuries, it becomes increasingly difficult to dissociate the musician from the monster. Jewish and Christian writers, from Josephus to Orosius, ranked singing and acting among the worst of Nero's sins.[26] In the Fifth Sibylline Oracle, composed at the turn of the second century, a striking connection is formulated between Nero's musical accomplishments and his crimes of homicide and matricide: 'Playing at theatricals with honey-sweet songs rendered with melodious voice, he will destroy many men, along with his wretched mother'.[27]

Modern scholars, confronted with this mass of hostile testimony, have tended to dismiss Nero's musomania as the symptom of a defective personality. Twentieth-century assessments of Nero look remarkably Tacitean in their fixation on the emperor's psychopathology. Miriam Griffin, in her influential biography, cites a 'weak character and intellect', a 'love of applause' and a 'natural exhibitionism' as the key factors which precipitated his political demise.[28] However, a radical new direction was signalled in 1994 with the publication of the volume *Reflections of Nero*, edited by Jaś Elsner and Jamie Masters. In her chapter on 'theatre and the subversion of imperial identity', Catharine Edwards recast Nero as a highly self-conscious actor, who exploited the transgressive power of theatricality in order to 'find new discursive strategies for representing imperial power'.[29] Edwards' emphasis on the representational aspects of Neronian stagecraft (and statecraft) found an even more powerful expression in Edward Champlin's monograph of 2003, entitled simply *Nero*. Far from being a maniacal tyrant, Champlin's Nero comes across as a consummate showman, a 'very serious' performer endowed with a 'ferocious energy', 'passionate determination' and a 'fecund imagination'.[30] Above all, the young emperor is portrayed as an expert manipulator of his own self-image, successfully turning popular opinion in his favour by imbuing his political actions with a kind of mythological symbolism. Admittedly, Champlin's revisionism has not won universal acceptance. But the 'performative turn' in Neronian scholarship has undoubtedly helped to facilitate a more nuanced understanding of the emperor's musicianship. The picture that emerges is no longer of a mindless fanatic hell-bent on the

---

[26] Cf. Joseph. *BJ* 2.251; Aur. Vict. *Caes.* 5.5; Eutr. 7.14; Sid. *Carm.* 5.1.322; Oros. 7.7. On Nero's reception in the Judaeo-Christian tradition, see Klauck 2001; Champlin 2003a: 17–24; Maier 2013.

[27] *Oracula Sibyllina* 5.141–2, ed. Geffcken 1902 (trans. Collins 1983): ὅστις παμμούσῳ φθόγγῳ μελιηδέας ὕμνους / θεατροκοπῶν ἀπολεῖ πολλοὺς σὺν μητρὶ ταλαίνῃ.

[28] Griffin 1984: 187, 233; cf. Warmington 1969: 113, alluding to Nero's 'addiction' and 'craving for applause'.

[29] Edwards 1994: 87. [30] Champlin 2003a: 82.

stage, but rather of a rational and even talented leader who used music as a way of projecting his political agenda and personality onto the world around him.[31]

The most significant breakthrough in understanding the musical dimensions of Nero's principate came in 2010 with the publication of Timothy Power's monograph, *The Culture of Kitharôidia*. The first part of the book consists of an impressively detailed study of Neronian citharodic politics. Power rightly emphasises that previous discussions have lumped Nero's artistic endeavours together under the umbrella of 'acting' or 'performance'. The problem with this broad-brush approach is that it risks eliding the complex cultural semiotics which distinguished *kitharoidia* from other types of musical entertainment in the Greco-Roman world.[32] By reframing Nero's performances through the lens of *kitharoidia*, Power opens up fascinating new perspectives on the emperor's reign, stressing in particular his 'complex relationship to Greek culture'.[33] Nero's lyre-playing, Power argues, was not simply motivated by a desire to transgress Roman mores, but was born from 'a profound understanding of the political resonances of the art in Greek history and myth'.[34] At the same time, Power credits Nero with significantly elevating the profile of *kitharoidia* at Rome: 'As patron and performer, he was the prime instigator of a process of cultural, musical, even political and ideological translation, a kind of mass-market *paideia* – making the Hellenic language of *kitharoidia* legible and lovable to Romans.'[35]

The lack of interest that Power's book has garnered in recent scholarship on Nero is disappointing.[36] Clearly, there are benefits to be gained from approaching the self-fashioning of the *citharoedus princeps* in the context of broader developments in the musical culture of the Greco-Roman world. Above all, Power's study highlights the dangers of viewing Roman musical culture as a static and monolithic phenomenon. It will not suffice to see

---

[31] On the 'performative turn' and its impact on Neronian studies, see Bartsch, Freudenburg, and Littlewood 2017: 2–3. On Nero's musical and theatrical performances specifically, see Rea 2011; Pausch 2013; Deppmeyer 2016. The revisionist trend in Neronian studies continues to gather steam, as evidenced by the selection of essays in Tomei and Rea 2011 and Walde 2013.

[32] Power 2010: 8–9.

[33] Power 2010: 148. On Nero's philhellenism, see Perrin 1990; Mratschek 2013. Alcock (1994) takes three key moments from the tour of Greece in 66–67 CE – namely, the participation at Olympia, the cutting of the canal through the Isthmus and the liberation of Achaea – in order to show how Nero used his influence as both artist and ruler to effect a cultural rapprochement between Greece and Rome.

[34] Power 2010: 148.   [35] Power 2010: 101.

[36] It does not appear in the bibliographies of the two *Companion* volumes on Nero: Buckley and Dinter 2013; Bartsch, Freudenburg and Littlewood 2017.

Nero's music-making solely as a reaction against the conservative and repressive impulses of a small clique of hard-line elites. As we have seen in the previous chapters, many Romans, both elite and non-elite, adopted a much more liberal stance on music. Building on the arguments of Champlin and others, Power makes a persuasive case for seeing Nero as the harbinger of lasting change in Roman musical culture. But how exactly was he able to enact this change? Which groups in Roman society did he appeal to, and why?

My approach in this chapter differs from that of Power and other scholars in two important respects. Firstly, my primary focus will be not on Nero's appearances as *citharoedus* and *tragoedus* as such, but on his role behind the scenes as producer, composer and choreographer. In many ways, I suggest, Nero's actions off the stage reveal more about his impact on musical culture than his actions on the stage. Secondly, I push back against the idea that Nero's music-making was driven primarily by a desire to introduce Romans to new forms of Greek culture. While I certainly do not wish to downplay the novelty of his performances, scholars have underestimated the extent to which Nero modelled his behaviour on the pre-existing musical interests and practices of his Roman subjects. Aside from his actual performances, Nero shaped Roman musical culture by contributing a new musical repertoire (*cantica Neroniana*), by popularising instruments like the water-organ and bagpipes, and by encouraging the musical passions of young Roman aristocrats of a similar age and upbringing to himself. It is also important to consider the range of spaces in which Nero's music was heard – not only the theatres of Rome, Naples and the Greek East, but also the arenas, circuses, taverns and houses of Rome and other cities throughout the empire. Of course, we cannot escape the fact that Nero's musical forays proved fatally misjudged: his success at winning over the *plebs* and more liberally minded elites came at the cost of the support of the senatorial majority and the military – the ultimate source of the emperor's power. But, for all his narcissism and naïvety, there remained even at the end a method to his musical 'madness'.

'O Apollo, O Augustus': Making Sense of a Musical Emperor

In his first address to the Senate as *princeps*, Nero announced his intention to rule 'according to the example of Augustus' (*ex Augusti praescripto*).[37]

---

[37] Suet. *Nero* 10.1.

This was, in a sense, a perfunctory declaration, expected of any successor at the start of his reign. As the years wore on, however, Nero's *imitatio Augusti* looked increasingly hollow. Certainly, by the end of the reign, any hope of a restored Augustan Golden Age had long since evaporated. Hindsight created the impression of a sharp gulf between the first and last of the Julio-Claudians which rendered them useful as contrasting archetypes. Nowhere was this dichotomy more starkly revealed than in the emperors' respective attitudes towards public performance. Cassius Dio makes the point that, whereas Augustus visited Greece strictly on official business, Nero travelled there 'for the purpose of driving chariots, performing as a citharode, making proclamations and acting in tragedies' (ἐπί τε ἡνιοχήσει καὶ κιθαρῳδήσει κηρύξει τε καὶ τραγῳδίας ὑποκρίσει).[38] In Dio's view, the dignity of the imperial office was gravely undermined by the appearance of an emperor – a 'Caesar' and an 'Augustus' – treading the boards while clad in a citharode's robe.[39]

Nero's dress forms the basis of a similar antithesis in Philostratus' biography of the philosopher Apollonius of Tyana (ca. 3 BCE – ca. 97 CE). In a scene from Book 5, the protagonist discourses with his young follower Menippus on the ethical implications of Nero's stage performances. Menippus launches into a tirade against the former *princeps*, in which he chastises him for 'casting aside the costume of Augustus and Julius in exchange for that of Amoebeus and Terpnus' (τὴν Αὐγούστου τε καὶ Ἰουλίου σκευὴν ῥίψαντα μεταμφιέννυσθαι νῦν τὴν Ἀμοιβέως καὶ Τερπνοῦ).[40] The 'costume' of the Caesars is, of course, the toga – that sacrosanct symbol of *Romanitas* – which Nero substitutes for the effeminate garb of the professional citharode. Menippus goes on to accuse Nero of confusing the roles of emperor and musician, inserting a clever pun on the Greek word *nomos* (both 'law' and 'musical composition'): 'Instead of making *nomoi*, he sings them' (ἀντὶ τοῦ νομοθετεῖν νόμους ᾄδειν). Later in the narrative, Apollonius is approached by the newly crowned Vespasian and invited to share his opinion of the deceased Nero. 'Nero may have understood how to tune a lyre', Apollonius replies, 'but he disgraced his

---

[38] Dio Cass. 62.8.2.
[39] Dio Cass. 62.10.1–2: ἔστη τε ἐπὶ τῆς σκηνῆς ὁ Καῖσαρ τὴν κιθαρῳδικὴν σκευὴν ἐνδεδυκώς, καὶ "κύριοί μου, εὐμενῶς μου ἀκούσατε" εἶπεν ὁ αὐτοκράτωρ, ἐκιθαρῴδησέ τε Ἄττιν τινὰ ἢ Βάκχας ὁ Αὔγουστος (The Caesar stood on the stage decked out in the garb of a lyre-player. And this emperor said: 'My lords, lend me a favourable ear', and the Augustus sang to the cithara some piece called Attis or Bacchus.); cf. Dio Cass. 62.9.3: Nero's participation in citharodic contests guaranteed his defeat in the 'contest of the Caesars' (κιθαρῳδῶν ... ἀγῶνα νικήσας ἡττήθη τὸν τῶν Καισάρων).
[40] Philostr. *VA* 5.7.2. Amoebeus and Terpnus were famous citharodes; the former was active during the third century BCE, the latter during the reign of Nero.

reign/the empire by letting the strings go too slack and by drawing them too tight' (Νέρων ... κιθάραν μὲν ἴσως ᾔδει ἁρμόττεσθαι, τὴν δὲ ἀρχὴν ᾔσχυνεν ἀνέσει καὶ ἐπιτάσει).[41] The insinuation is clear: good rulers knew how to 'tune' peoples, not lyres.[42]

In fact, Nero's relationship with Augustus was rather more complex than these indictments would lead us to believe. Recent scholarship has highlighted how Nero exploited Augustus' special relationship with Apollo Citharoedus as a means of legitimising his own musical endeavours. Three episodes have been singled out in particular. Firstly, at the Juvenalia, Nero is said to have hired a corps of cheerleaders, roughly 5000 in number, and assigned them the duty of orchestrating the applause during his performance. He referred to them as his 'Augustiani' (or Αὐγούστειοι). Their chants, as recorded by Dio, likened the emperor to Apollo, while recalling his dynastic ties to Augustus: 'Fair Caesar! Apollo! Augustus! Another Pythian!' (ὁ καλὸς Καῖσαρ, ὁ Ἀπόλλων, ὁ Αὔγουστος, εἷς ὡς Πύθιος). Following the show's conclusion, the populace reconvened for a moonlit party at the artificial lake built by Augustus in 2 BCE as the backdrop for his *naumachia* (staged naval battle).[43]

The second noteworthy episode is linked to the festivities of the First Neronia. Suetonius comments that when Nero was awarded honorary first place in the contest for lyre-playing (honorary because he had not actually competed), he 'knelt before the trophy and ordered that it be laid at the feet of Augustus' statue' (*adoravit ferrique ad Augusti statuam iussit*).[44] It is unclear which statue Suetonius is referring to, if indeed he had a particular statue in mind, but the one of Augustus 'with the garb and stance of Apollo' in the Palatine Library might be a possible candidate.[45]

The third Augustan moment coincided with Nero's return to Rome in December 67, following the tour of Greece.[46] Nero took the opportunity to stage a grand triumphal spectacle to celebrate his artistic and athletic victories. He allegedly rode into the city on the same chariot that had borne Augustus (then Octavian) during his triple triumph of 29.[47] By his

---

[41] Philostr. *VA* 5.28.1.
[42] Augustus was one such ruler (cf. Philo *Leg.* 147); so was Numa (Dion. Hal. *Ant.* 2.6.25).
[43] Dio Cass. 62.20.4–5.   [44] Suet. *Nero* 12.3–4.
[45] For this suggestion, see Champlin 2003a: 142. Power (2010: 156) argues for the statue of Apollo Citharoedus in the *porticus*, on the premise that this statue bore a physical resemblance to Augustus. There is no evidence, however, that such a resemblance existed.
[46] On the chronology, see Bradley 1978a.
[47] Suet. *Nero* 25.1; cf. Dio Cass. 62.20.3: αὐτὸς ἐφ' ἅρματος ἐπινικίου, ἐν ᾧ ποτε ὁ Αὔγουστος τὰ πολλὰ ἐκεῖνα νικητήρια ἐπεπόμφει.

side stood the 'captive' citharode Diodorus, occupying a position of prominence normally reserved for the *triumphator*'s son.[48] Instead of the customary escort of soldiers, Nero was followed by a large entourage of supporters – the same supporters who had accompanied him on his travels in the East. At the departure of the tour the emperor had equipped them with lyres and plectrums, and we might imagine that they carried the same paraphernalia upon their return.[49] As they marched joyously through the streets, they proudly announced themselves as 'Augustiani and the soldiers of Nero's triumph' (*Augustianos militesque se triumphi eius clamitantibus*).[50] Dio has the whole population join in the chanting, 'the senators themselves most of all'. When the imperial convoy passed by, the crowds proclaimed in unison:

> Ὀλυμπιονῖκα οὐᾶ, Πυθιονῖκα οὐᾶ, Αὔγουστε Αὔγουστε. Νέρωνι τῷ Ἡρακλεῖ, Νέρωνι τῷ Ἀπόλλωνι. ὡς εἷς περιοδονίκης, εἷς ἀπ' αἰῶνος, Αὔγουστε Αὔγουστε. ἱερὰ φωνή· μακάριοι οἵ σου ἀκούοντες. (Dio Cass. 62.20.5)
>
> Olympian victor, bravo! Pythian victor, bravo! Augustus! Augustus! Hail to Nero, our Hercules! Hail to Nero, our Apollo! The only victor of the agonistic circuit, the only one from the beginning of time! Augustus! Augustus! O Sacred Voice! Blessed are those who hear you![51]

The parade culminated, fittingly, at the Temple of Apollo on the Palatine.[52] This was another pointed departure from 'triumphal' convention: rather than heading for the Temple of Jupiter Capitolinus (the usual endpoint of the triumph), Nero chose as his final destination the temple built by Augustus to celebrate the Greek god of music. The significance of

---

[48] Dio Cass. 62.20.3: καὶ αὐτῷ ὁ Διόδωρος ὁ κιθαρῳδὸς παρωχεῖτο; Miller 2000: 416. Alternatively, Diodorus may have stood in place of the servile *comes*: see Beard 2007: 85–92, discussing problems of evidence.

[49] Cf. Dio Cass. 62.8.4.

[50] Suet. *Nero* 25.1. Miller (2000: 418) suggests that the shouting of the Augustiani was scripted in advance as a way of 'commenting on Nero's Augustan imitation'.

[51] Dio claims to be reporting 'the very words spoken' (αὐτὰ τὰ λεχθέντα, 62.20.6); 'the acclamations themselves ... clearly were recorded' (Roueché 1984: 184). Germanicus was greeted with shouts of οὐᾶ when he visited Alexandria in 13 CE: *P.Oxy.* 25.2435 *recto*, ll. 4–5. Further parallels are noted by Aldrete 1999: 111, 143. However, it is possible that Dio was drawing inspiration from imperial acclamations in his own time. On the significance of περιοδονίκης (victor of the agonistic circuit) in the context of Nero's Greek tour, see Kennell 1988.

[52] Suet. *Nero* 25.2 (*Palatium et Apollinem*); Dio (62.20.4) states simply τὸ Παλάτιον. On the route of the procession, see Miller 2000: 414–15. Dio (62.21.1) adds that Nero proceeded from the Palatine to the Circus Maximus, where he dedicated his racing trophies around the Egyptian obelisk in the *spina* imported to Rome by Augustus in 10 BCE.

that choice could hardly have been lost on Nero's contemporaries. According to Tacitus, Nero had sought justification for his citharodic performances by claiming that 'songs [were] sacred to Apollo (*cantus Apollini sacros*), and that this pre-eminent and prescient deity stood with such adornment not only in Greek cities, but in Roman temples too'.[53] There were two *templa* in Rome which contained statues of Apollo Citharoedus, and both had direct ties to Augustus.[54]

What these three episodes show clearly is that Nero saw his musical persona as being in dialogue with, or inspired by, the memory of the first *princeps*. Assessing the intent behind this emulation is far from straightforward, given the hostile nature of the sources. Was Nero earnestly declaring his affinity with Augustus as a fellow patron of *kitharoidia*? Or was he subversively refashioning Augustus' legacy by promoting the primacy of his own artistic achievements over the political and military achievements of his predecessor? Power offers a nuanced discussion of this issue in his book. He argues that Nero invested the Augustan imagery of Apollo Citharoedus with a kind of flawed realism. There was, in his view, a glaring disconnect between the 'purely symbolic' music embodied by the Augustan Apollo and the 'audible' *kitharoidia* which Nero broadcast through his own interactions with the god: Nero was 'passive-aggressively remaking the lyric Augustus in his own image, literalizing, and so vulgarizing, making a travesty of, his purely symbolic musicality'.[55] That is certainly what Suetonius and Cassius Dio imply; but would Nero's contemporaries have regarded his actions in the same way? As discussed in Chapter 3, the Augustan Apollo already had a strong performative dimension, being mediated through the physical and sonic environment of Roman temples and theatres. Thus, to speak of the 'lyric Augustus' as a 'purely symbolic' concept may be misleading. Rather than viewing Nero as a kind of misguided interpreter of Augustan culture, perhaps a better approach would be to emphasise the novel perspectives which Nero brought to bear on this particular aspect of Augustus' legacy.[56] As John Miller points out, it was common throughout the Principate for emperors to appropriate elements

---

[53] Tac. *Ann.* 14.14.1.
[54] Power 2010: 362. On the colossal statue by Timarchides that adorned the Temple of Apollo Sosianus, cf. Plin. *HN* 36.34–5 (discussed in Chapter 3).
[55] Power 2010: 157.
[56] It is important to bear in mind that the legacy of Augustus was multi-faceted and open to divergent interpretations: see Levick 2010: 297–302; Goodman 2018: 3–6. See also Green 2018 on Seneca's construction of Augustus as an ambivalent model, and Drinkwater 2012 on Nero as a victim of the institutional problems created by Augustus.

of triumphal ritual in marking novel situations.[57] It could be argued, then, that Nero's self-conscious evocations of Augustus were not necessarily subversive in intent, but rather served to validate his performances by situating them in the physical and cultural landscape of Augustan Rome.[58]

While Suetonius and Cassius Dio represent Nero's *imitatio Augusti* as an outrage and a sham, there are signs in the contemporary sources of a more positive perception of Nero's Apolline self-fashioning. Most notably, Seneca's *Apocolocyntosis* includes a scene in which Apollo prophesies the future greatness of Nero Caesar with explicit reference to his beauty and musical talents:

> *'Ne demite, Parcae'*
> *Phoebus ait 'vincat mortalis tempora vitae*
> *ille mihi similis vultu similisque decore*
> *nec cantu nec voce minor ...*
> *Caesar adest, talem iam Roma Neronem*
> *aspiciet. flagrat nitidus fulgore remisso*
> *vultus et adfuso cervix formosa capillo.'*
> (Sen. *Apocol.* 4, ll. 20–3, 30–3)

> 'Don't make it shorter, Fates,' Apollo says.
> 'Let him live beyond the span of mortal years,
> That man so similar to me in grace
> And beauty, and no less skilled at singing ...
> ... such a Caesar now
> Approaches. Such a Nero, now, all Rome
> Will gaze upon. His radiant face blazes
> With gentle brilliance; his lovely neck
> Displays the beauty of his flowing hair.'
> (Trans. Nussbaum 2010)

One could argue, of course, that this is not a heartfelt expression of approval, but a sycophantic panegyric in praise of a tyrant. It was long believed that Seneca wrote the *Apocolocyntosis* during the formative early years of Nero's reign, channelling the spirit of optimism that typically accompanied the accession of a new emperor. However, this idea was disputed by Champlin in an article published in 2003. A version of the

---

[57] Miller 2000: 417, citing Bradley 1978b: 149. Cf. Caligula's triumph over the Ocean: Suet. *Cal.* 47. The ceremony held to mark Tiridates' arrival into Rome in 66 CE provides another instance of a Neronian 'reinvention' of the triumph: Suet. *Nero* 13, Dio Cass. 63.4.

[58] On the creativity of Nero's *imitatio Augusti*, see Champlin 2003a: 139–44.

Figure 4.2 Bronze as of Nero, 62–68 CE. Rome mint. Observe: head of Nero, radiate. Reverse: (Nero as?) Apollo Citharoedus, singing and playing *cithara*. *RIC* I² 211. © Numismatica Ars Classica NAC AG, Auction 59, 2011, Lot 1872.

Apocolocyntosis must have been in circulation shortly after Claudius' death, but Champlin shows that the passage in question makes better sense as a later interpolation of the 60s.[59] Not all scholars have agreed with this assessment. And yet, even if we allow the original date to stand, the bulk of the evidence supports the view that Nero's identification as 'New Apollo' coincided with his 'coming out' as a performer. The references to Nero's association with Apollo in the works of Suetonius, Tacitus and Dio all postdate his return from Campania in 59, following the murder of Agrippina.[60]

The theory that Nero began to align himself with Apollo after 59 is borne out by the coins minted during his reign. A well-known coin type, minted in Rome and Lugdunum between 62 and 65, presents a bust of Nero on the obverse and an image of Apollo Citharoedus on the reverse (Fig. 4.2).[61] Suetonius was familiar with these coins, and erroneously identifies them as a commemorative issue marking Nero's victories in Greece. He also implies that the lyre-player pictured on the reverse was supposed to represent the emperor himself (*statuas suas citharoedico habitu [posuit], qua nota etiam nummum percussit*).[62] Scholars such as

---

[59] Champlin 2003b: 279–80.
[60] Champlin 2003b: 276. The poems of Calpurnius Siculus have sometimes been adduced in support of Nero's assimilation with Apollo: e.g. *Eclogue* 4.87 presents Apollo as 'Caesar's companion' (*comitatus Apolline Caesar*). However, the traditional identification of Calpurnius as a Neronian poet has been hotly contested, and in fact the weight of evidence favours the view that he was writing much later, probably under the Severans: Champlin 1978, 2003b: 280–1; Armstrong 1986; Baldwin 1995; Horsfall 1993, 1997; *contra* Townend 1980; Mayer 1980.
[61] *RIC* 73–82, 205–12, 380–1, 384–5, 414–17, 451–5.   [62] Suet. *Nero* 25.2.

Christopher Howgego have questioned the validity of this assessment: 'There is no element of iconography, facial characteristic, or inscription on the coins to indicate that Nero is intended. The coins simply show Apollo.'[63] However, it is not hard to see why Suetonius might have conflated the representation of Apollo Citharoedus with that of Nero. Unlike the Augustan coin types, which depict Apollo in a static pose, holding either a plectrum or a *patera* in his right hand, the Neronian coinage shows Apollo actively engaged in performance – the mouth agape, the body expressively contorted, the plectrum raised towards the strings. Moreover, these coins were issued during the latter part of Nero's reign, and thus coincided with the period of Nero's public performances. It is likely, then, that the representation of the citharodic Apollo on the Neronian coinage would have encouraged a strong association between emperor and god, while evoking the ideals of peace and harmony articulated by the earlier coins of Augustus.[64]

In the eastern provinces, where the worship of the *princeps* as a living god was widely accepted, the assimilation of emperor and god became even more firmly entrenched. Suetonius asserts that civic communities in Greece felt no compunction in acclaiming Nero as 'the equal of Apollo in song' (*Apollinem cantu ... aequiperare existimaretur*).[65] This statement is substantiated by three inscribed statue bases from Athens, which explicitly identify Nero as 'New Apollo'.[66] Equally revealing are the coin types minted by Greek *poleis* in conjunction with Nero's tour in 66–67. For example, a coin issued by Nicopolis commemorates 'Nero Apollo the Founder'; here the image of a lyre-playing Apollo on the reverse is obviously meant to be identified with Nero.[67] Similarly, coins minted in Patras show Nero crowned with a laurel wreath on the obverse, with 'Apollo Augustus' playing the lyre on the reverse.[68] Apollo Citharoedus also appears on coins issued by the Thessalian League, honouring 'Nero

---

[63] Howgego 1995: 79; see also Bergmann 2013: 347.
[64] Neronian coins from the same period represent the Ara Pacis, commissioned in honour of Augustus in 13 BCE, and the Temple of Janus, which Nero is supposed to have shut in 66 CE (the first emperor to do so since Augustus): *RIC* 456–61; 263–71, 283–91, 300–11, 323–8, 337–42, 347–50, 353–5, 362, 366–7, 468–72, 510–12, 537–9, 583–5; cf. Suet. *Nero* 13.2, Lucan 1.60. For a discussion of Nero's 'theomorphism', see Bergmann 2013: 346–7.
[65] Suet. *Nero* 53.
[66] *AE* 1929.75, *AE* 1971.435, *AE* 1994.1617. The statues are sadly lost, and the inscriptions cannot be dated securely to a particular period of Nero's reign; 'whether they were public or private is not clear' (Champlin 2003a: 117).
[67] *RPC* 1371; cf. 1372–7. The term *ktistes* on the coin's legend calls to mind the original founder of the city, Augustus.
[68] *RPC* 1275.

Augustus Caesar' and 'Nero of the Thessalians', and by the citizens of Perinthos in Thrace.[69] Even in the far-flung cities of Asia Minor, coins have been found showing Nero accompanied by Apollo in various citharodic guises – with lyre and *patera*, with lyre and plectrum, or with lyre alone.[70]

In summary, Nero's cultivation of Apollo provides a window onto the problems surrounding both his own self-presentation as emperor and his representation in the literary sources. Ancient writers paint a picture of a young ruler who tried fastidiously to emulate the example of Augustus. As long as his music-making remained behind closed doors, away from the prying eyes of the public, he succeeded in living up to this example.[71] The turning point came supposedly in 59 with the murder of Agrippina and the celebration of the Juvenile Games. With these developments any hopes of a new Golden Age were dashed, and a reign of terror descended just as Nero outed himself as an aspiring concert musician. The *princeps* began to style himself as 'New Apollo' in a bid to cloak his aberrant theatricality under the respectable guise of Augustanism. But now that his music was officially out in the open this gesture merely exposed his own hubris.

There is another side of the story, however. By insisting on a stark dichotomy between Nero and Augustus, the literary sources obscure real points of overlap in the two emperors' use of Apolline imagery. After all, Augustus had ordered a statue of himself to be carved with the features of Apollo and displayed on the Palatine, in the very heart of Rome. In Athens, meanwhile, he was commemorated in statues as the 'New Apollo'.[72] Nero's failure, in the eyes of his detractors, lay in the fact that he implicated Apollo in his citharodic performances; he made Apollo's symbolism literal. But that was just the perspective of his detractors. There were many contemporaries, it seems, who looked fondly upon the reign of 'Emperor Nero Caesar Augustus, New Apollo'. It is to these supporters that I now turn.

The Master's Songbook: *Neroniana Cantica* and Popular Music at Rome

During the last few decades, scholars have become increasingly fixated on Nero's relationship with the people of Rome. The extent of Nero's

---

[69] RPC 1599, 1752, 1439, 1444 (Thessaly); 1752 (Thrace).   [70] RPC 3045–6, 3059.
[71] Trajan supposedly declared that five years of Nero's reign surpassed the reigns of all other *principes*: cf. Aur. Vict. *Lib. de Caes.* 5.2–4, *Epit. de Caes.* 5.2–5, applying this comment to the start of the reign. See discussion in Lepper 1957; Murray 1965; Griffin 1984: 37–8.
[72] Ps.-Acro *ad* Hor. *Ep.* 1.3.17; Serv. ad Verg. *Ecl.* 4.10; *SEG* 29, 167; Peppas-Delmousou 1979.

popularity with lower-class Romans is underscored by numerous sources. Tacitus, for example, comments at the beginning of the *Histories* that Nero's death was mourned most fervently by the '*plebs* accustomed to the circus and the theatre' (*plebs circo ac theatris sueta*).[73] Posthumous tributes paid to Nero by the Roman people included the placing of his togate images on the Rostra (hardly the token of an emperor who had shed his imperial trappings, as Dio and Philostratus would claim!).[74] Stories of captive audiences coerced into acknowledging the emperor's 'divine voice' must be read against reports of Otho adopting Nero's name 'in the hope of winning over the common people' (*spe vulgum adliciendi*) and Vitellius honouring Nero with public sacrifices.[75] Not without reason did Suetonius write that Nero 'was carried away by a desire for popularity above all else'.[76] All good musicians needed a loyal fan base, and it seems Nero found his in the *populus Romanus*.

There is particularly compelling evidence for Nero's popularity in the East. The liberation of Achaea in 67 was evidently well-received in many parts: Pausanias refers to it as a 'gift' (δώρου), rashly revoked by Vespasian, while Philostratus describes it as an act of uncharacteristic wisdom.[77] Rumours of Nero's survival lingered in the East for decades, even centuries, after his death – not because he was feared, but because he was loved. Dio Chrysostom, who was brought up in Prusa during Nero's reign, claims in a later speech that 'everybody wishes he were still alive; and the great majority do believe that he is'.[78] Remarkably, we know of several individuals who attempted successfully to impersonate Nero (they were eventually tracked down by the Roman authorities and summarily executed).[79] One of the most curious aspects of these 'false Neros' is that they are nearly all described as possessing a special talent for music. Tacitus speaks of a

---

[73] Tac. *Hist.* 1.4.3. Cf. Suet. *Nero* 21.1 and *Vit.* 4, noting the universal demand for Nero to perform in the citharodic contests at the Neronia (*flagitantibus cunctis*).

[74] Suet. *Nero* 57.

[75] Otho: Tac. *Hist.* 1.78.2; cf. Suet. *Otho* 7.1; Plut. *Otho* 3. Vitellius: Tac. *Hist.* 2.95.1. Even the ultra-conservative Galba evoked memories of Nero by lavishing money on the famous *tibicen* Canus: Plut. *Galb.* 16.1; Suet. *Galb.* 12.3; cf. Philostr. *VA* 5.21.

[76] Suet. *Nero* 53.1: *maxime autem popularitate efferebatur*.

[77] Paus. 7.17.4; Philostr. *VA* 5.41 (σωφρονέστερόν τι ἑαυτοῦ, literally 'something wiser than he himself [was]'). Nero's speech is preserved in an inscribed decree from Acraephia in Boeotia (*SIG*³ 814): Gallivan 1973; Alcock 1994; Bergmann 2002. According to Cassius Dio (62.14.4), Nero dedicated his victories won in East to 'the Roman people and the whole world'; cf. Philostr. *VA* 5.7.

[78] Dio Chrys. *Or.* 21.10.

[79] For detailed examinations of the 'Nero *redivivus*' myth, see Klauck 2001; Hedrick 2015; Malik 2020.

mysterious pretender – 'a slave from Pontus or, as others have reported, a freedman from Italy' – who set sail with a motley crew of renegades and vagabonds and committed a spate of armed robberies in the Western Cyclades. Not only did this man bear a striking resemblance to Nero, but he was also 'skilled at playing the lyre and singing, as a result of which people were more inclined to believe his deception'.[80] A different Neronian pretender, identified by Cassius Dio as a man of Asiatic origin named Terentius Maximus, rose to prominence in Asia Minor and even found refuge with the Parthian king, Artabanus. He, too, bore a resemblance to Nero 'both in appearance and in voice (for he also sang to the lyre)'.[81] Looking like Nero was one thing; but if you really wanted to embody the emperor, you had to *sound* like him as well.[82]

The impact of Nero's music on Rome's cultural landscape is further highlighted by an episode from Book 4 of Philostratus' *Life of Apollonius*. The protagonist is travelling to Rome with eight of his most devoted students on a mission to spread the word of philosophy. Stopping at an inn close to the city gates, they stumble upon a drunken busker on the hunt for tips:

> οὐκ ἀγλευκῶς τῆς φωνῆς ἔχων, περιῄει δὲ ἄρα κύκλῳ τὴν Ῥώμην ᾄδων τὰ τοῦ Νέρωνος μέλη καὶ μεμισθωμένος τοῦτο, τὸν δὲ ἀμελῶς ἀκούσαντα, ἢ μὴ καταβαλόντα μισθὸν τῆς ἀκροάσεως, ξυνεκεχώρητο αὐτῷ καὶ ἀπάγειν ὡς ἀσεβοῦντα. ἦν δὲ αὐτῷ καὶ κιθάρα καὶ ἡ πρόσφορος τῷ κιθαρίζειν σκευὴ πᾶσα, καί τινα καὶ νευρὰν τῶν ἐφαψαμένων τε καὶ προεντεταμένων ἀποκειμένην ἐν κοιτίδι εἶχεν, ἣν ἔφασκεν ἐκ τῆς Νέρωνος ἐωνῆσθαι κιθάρας δυοῖν μναῖν, καὶ ἀποδώσεσθαι αὐτὴν οὐδενί, ἢν μὴ κιθαρῳδὸς ᾖ τῶν ἀρίστων τε καὶ ἀγωνιουμένων Πυθοῖ. (Philostr. *VA* 4.39.1)

> He had quite a pleasant voice, and went around Rome singing Nero's songs for pay and making a business out of it. If anybody listened without

---

[80] Tac. *Hist*. 2.8: *tunc servus e Ponto sive, ut alii tradidere, libertinus ex Italia, citharae et cantus peritus, unde illi super similitudinem oris propior ad fallendum fides, adiunctis desertoribus, quos inopia vagos ingentibus promissis corruperat, mare ingreditur; ac vi tempestatum Cythnum insulam detrusus et militum quosdam ex Oriente commeantium adscivit vel abnuentis interfici iussit, et spoliatis negotiatoribus mancipiorum valentissimum quemque armavit.* Cf. Suet. *Nero* 57.2, not mentioning musical accomplishments.

[81] Dio Cass. 66.19.3: ἐπὶ τούτου καὶ ὁ Ψευδονέρων ἐφάνη, ὃς Ἀσιανὸς ἦν, ἐκαλεῖτο δὲ Τερέντιος Μάξιμος, προσεοικὼς δὲ τῷ Νέρωνι καὶ τὸ εἶδος καὶ τὴν φωνήν (καὶ γὰρ καὶ ἐκιθαρῴδει).

[82] A point well made by Champlin (2003a: 12): 'To make a success of being Nero you clearly needed to look like him and to play the lyre reasonably well, as he had done.' For positive assessments of Nero's singing, cf. Suet. *Nero* 39.3; Philostr. *VA* 4.42; Ps.-Luc. *Nero* 6; Gyles 1962; Bélis 1989. It should be noted, however, that some sources suggest Nero's voice was husky and unappealing: cf., e.g. Suet. *Nero* 20.1 (*exiguae vocis et fuscae*); Juv. 8.225 (*foedo ... cantu*).

attention, or refused to pay for the performance, the man was privileged to arrest him for treason. He also had a lyre and all the paraphernalia appropriate for lyre-players. In addition, he kept stored in a box a string from a lyre that had already been strung and tightened, which he claimed was from Nero's lyre. He had bought it for two minae, he said, and would not sell it to anybody unless they were first-class lyre players and planning to compete at the Pythian games. (Trans. Jones 2005, with slight adaptations)

Despite the apparent realism of this episode, one must be careful not to lose sight of its setting within a fictionalised and sensationalistic biography. Nonetheless, Philostratus would not have written such a description if it did not seem believable to those who knew something about Nero. On first impression, the itinerant musician seems to be a caricature of an 'Augustianus', modelled on the satirical trope of the 'informer' (*delator*). He doubles as an imperial henchman, the impersonal passive construction ξυνεκεχώρητο αὐτῷ suggesting that he has received an official licence 'from the top', so to speak. Indeed, the opportunistic citharode bears an uncanny resemblance to the emperor whose musical talents he claims to vouch for. Like all good Neronian impostors, he has a decent singing voice. He shares with Nero an inflated ego and a jealous streak. Most striking of all is the objectification of the emperor's *cithara*. Nero's lyre string is both a commodity and a souvenir item, detached from his person yet still invested with his charismatic aura.[83]

The fact that the episode is set in a tavern adds an additional layer of complexity. Taverns were, notoriously, the favourite haunt of the *plebs*, but they were also a place where Nero felt very much at home. A few chapters later in Philostratus' narrative, in fact, we actually find a description of Nero singing in a tavern situated next to his newly built gymnasium in Rome, 'naked except for a loincloth, like the most shameless shopkeeper'.[84] Again, this is a fictional portrayal, but it resonates strongly with the depictions of Nero in the works of Tacitus, Suetonius and Cassius Dio. Early on in his reign, we are told, the teenaged emperor would roam around the city under cover of darkness, trailed by gangs of ruffians, and

---

[83] The genitive plural participles ἐφαψαμένων and προεντεταμένων reinforce the point that this was a *used* lyre string, since it was one of several which had been previously fitted to, and subsequently detached from, Nero's own *cithara*. It would presumably have been easier to obtain a new string than to remove one from an already strung lyre – let alone a lyre from the emperor's private collection – hence the musician's eagerness to vouch for its provenance.

[84] Philostr. *VA* 4.42.1: ᾖδε δὲ ἐν καπηλείῳ πεποιημένῳ ἐς τὸ γυμνάσιον διάζωμα ἔχων γυμνός, ὥσπερ τῶν καπήλων οἱ ἀσελγέστατοι.

wander in and out of brothels and taverns, causing mischief wherever he went.[85] Suetonius could just about condone this behaviour as 'the folly of youth' (*velut iuvenili errore*). Yet the association with the seedy underworld of the *plebs* was one which Nero failed to shake off. When, in 64, his much-maligned praetorian prefect Tigellinus staged a debauched floating banquet on the Stagnum Agrippae, he decorated the banks of the lake with *lupanaria* and populated them with women of high rank (*inlustribus feminis*). Tacitus describes the scene in lurid detail, singling out, among other things, the 'obscene gestures and dances' (*gestus motusque obsceni*) and loud music (*consonare cantu*) that emanated from these lakeside brothels.[86] That was not the only occasion during Nero's reign when aristocratic women were put to work as prostitutes. One of Nero's favourite pastimes, according to Suetonius, was to board a ship and sail along the Tiber or the gulf of Baiae. Not content with the natural landscape, he had rows of makeshift taverns (*deversoriae tabernae*) erected along the shores and banks and staffed them with matrons playing the role of barkeepers soliciting sex (*matronarum institorio copas imitantium atque hinc inde hortantium ut appelleret*).[87]

These stories of Neronian depravity tap into elite anxieties about the tavern and the brothel as spaces of disruptive popular leisure. But beneath the indignation and the snobbery lies a fundamental truth: Nero's musical interests aligned closely with, and drew energy from, the cultural enthusiasms of the Roman people. With their noisy and convivial atmosphere, taverns were one of the main places outside the theatre and arena where non-elite Romans were able to partake in musical entertainment. They were also, according to one ancient writer at least, ideal places for recruiting potential leaders of theatrical claques.[88] For a citizen of Neronian Rome, the prospect of encountering an 'Augustianus' lurking in the corners of a *taberna* was certainly not beyond the realms of possibility.

Philostratus' vignette therefore offers a vivid insight into the musical atmosphere of Neronian Rome. It highlights how Nero's music permeated the everyday lived experience of Romans and Greeks alike, inspiring a wave of Neronian copycats, who found in the repertoire of *Neroniana cantica* an

---

[85] Tac. *Ann.* 13.47; Suet. *Nero* 26; Dio Cass. 61.8.1–4, 9.24.
[86] Tac. *Ann.* 15.33–7. Cassius Dio (62.15.2–3) describes taverns and brothels being erected around a great platform positioned in the centre of the lake. For an excellent discussion of this episode as presented in Tacitus' *Annals*, see Woodman 1992; further remarks in Coleman 1993: 50–1.
[87] Suet. *Nero* 27. These *copae* may have doubled as musical performers: cf. Ps.-Verg. *Copa* 1–4; Morgan 2017: 93–4.
[88] Augustine (*De cat. Rud.* 16.25.7–8) describes 'people who sing songs in bars' (*qui in popina ... cantabant*) as the kind likely to be imprisoned for leading theatrical claques.

effective means of channelling and usurping the emperor's star power.⁸⁹ In antiquity, as in later times, it was a mark of the most popular musicians that their music lived on without them.⁹⁰ Alexander, the harp-player whom we met in the epigraph of this chapter, proved such a hit with Roman audiences that they 'even memorised his songs' (καὶ ἀπομνημονεύειν αὐτοῦ τὰ κρούσματα). In Nero's time, the compositions of the citharode Menecrates seem to have achieved similar renown: in a scene from Petronius' *Satyricon*, we find the wealthy freedman Trimalchio singing *Menecratis cantica* while relaxing in the baths; unsurprisingly, in his inebriated state, Trimalchio butchers the songs terribly.⁹¹

It would be easy to dismiss Nero's interest in composition as a vanity project – a sign of his egomania and jealousy towards rival performers.⁹² However, as the examples of Alexander and Menecrates demonstrate, there was much to be gained from popularising one's own tunes. The composers of popular hits had a remarkable ability to influence the kind of cultural messages to which ordinary Romans were exposed. Among the original works attributed to Nero is a poem on the Fall of Troy (*Troica*), which was still known at the turn of the second century.⁹³ Like other *carmina Neroniana*, this work was probably intended originally for recitation rather

---

[89] The emergence of these Nero tribute acts seems to have gone hand in hand with a craze for Neronian memorabilia, if Philostratus' narrative is to be believed: 'It is more than likely that many other Neronian strings were bought and sold in Rome and throughout the Empire at large' (Power 2010: 10). Cf. Juv. 6.383–4, for the collecting of citharodes' plectrums as keepsakes.

[90] One could cite numerous musician-composers from the Classical and Hellenistic periods who achieved such immortality. To give just one example: the third-century citharode Glauce of Chios is described in Hedylus 1883 Gow-Page (ap. Athen. 4.176d) as a maker of drinking songs reperformed by the aulete Theon; at Theocritus, *Idyll* 4.31, Corydon, a rustic singer to the syrinx, claims he can 'strike up the tunes of Glauce' (τὰ Γλαύκας ἀγκρούομαι). The scholiast on this passage calls her a *kroumatopoios*, a term which can denote any kind of instrumental composer but probably means aulete here (Power 2010: 62 n. 144).

[91] Pet. *Sat.* 73.3: *coepit Menecratis cantica lacerare*. For the identification with the Menecrates favoured by Nero, see Power 2010: 97. Menecrates' fame was no doubt bolstered by his association with the *princeps*: cf. Suet. *Nero* 30.2; Dio Cass. 63.1.1.

[92] The negative assessment of Nero's *carmina* at Tac. *Ann.* 14.16.1 would seem to support this view. However, at *Ann.* 13.3.3, Tacitus grudgingly acknowledges that Nero possessed 'the elements of learning' (*elementa doctrinae*) when it came to composing *carmina*. Suetonius was impressed by his industry and facility as a composer (*Nero* 52.1). Martial, writing under the Flavian emperors, describes Nero as *doctus* (learned) and his *carmina* as *nota* (famous) (8.70).

[93] Serv. *ad Aen.* 5.370, *ad Georg.* 3.36 (*Troica Neronia*). Juvenal (8.220–1) states that unlike Nero, Orestes 'never sang on stage and did not write on Trojan themes' (*in scaena numquam cantavit Orestes, Troica non scripsit*). According to Cassius Dio (62.29.1), on one occasion, during a popular festival, Nero descended to the *orchestra* of the theatre and 'read some Trojan poems of his own composition' (ἀνέγνω Τρωϊκά τινα ἑαυτοῦ ποιήματα); cf. Suet. *Nero* 10.2: *recitavit et carmina, non modo domi sed et in theatro*. Nero's *Troica* is generally considered to be a fully

than for musical performance. But the sources also describe Nero's *carmina* being sung through the media of *tragoedia* and *kitharoidia*.[94] The songs in question were probably not very long, and so were easily memorised and reperformed: scholars tend to speak of 'concert tragedies' or monologues as the default mode of *tragoedia*, while the citharodic *nomos* has been compared to a modern operatic aria, since they tended to be excerpted from larger dramatic works.[95] The tavern episode from the *Life of Apollonius* gives a good indication of how Nero's (apparently lengthy) citharodic recitals could be broken down into shorter musical snippets. Philostratus describes the busker's 'act' as consisting firstly of a 'customary' instrumental overture or *anabole* (ἀναβαλόμενος οὖν, ὅπως εἰώθει), followed by a short hymn in praise of (or composed by) Nero (βραχὺν ... ὕμνον τοῦ Νέρωνος), and then a medley of Nero's songs, 'some from the *Oresteia*, some from the *Antigone*, and some from other tragic plays which the emperor had performed' (ἐπῆγε μέλη τὰ μὲν ἐξ Ὀρεστείας, τὰ δὲ ἐξ Ἀντιγόνης, τὰ δ' ὁποθενοῦν τῶν τραγῳδουμένων αὐτῷ).[96] It is very hard to imagine that these songs individually lasted longer than a few minutes.

We need not suppose that the popularity of *Neroniana cantica* was confined to cities where the emperor himself had visited and performed. In another scene from Philostratus' work, we are introduced to a *tragoedus* not dissimilar to the citharode from the tavern:

> τραγῳδίας ὑποκριτὴς τῶν οὐκ ἀξιουμένων ἀνταγωνίζεσθαι τῷ Νέρωνι ἐπῄει τὰς ἑσπερίους πόλεις ἀγείρων, καὶ τῇ τέχνῃ χρώμενος ηὐδοκίμει παρὰ τοῖς ἧττον βαρβάροις, πρῶτον μὲν δι' αὐτὸ τὸ ἥκειν παρ' ἀνθρώπους, οἳ μήπω τραγῳδίας ἤκουσαν, εἶτ' ἐπειδὴ τὰς Νέρωνος μελῳδίας ἀκριβοῦν ἔφασκε. (Philostr. *VA* 5.9)

> A tragic actor who had been thought unworthy to compete with Nero was money-grubbing around the cities of the west. His exhibitions of skill brought him success among the less uncivilized, primarily because of the simple fact that he visited people who had never heard a tragedy, and also because he claimed to be a connoisseur of Nero's songs. (Trans. Jones 2005)

The opportunistic *tragoedus*, in other words, could take advantage of the cultural cachet that Nero's music had generated far and wide, among

---

fledged epic poem (see Power 2010: 151, 168), but it could also have consisted of 'a series of shorter poems on Troy', performed either in excerpts or in full (Kelly 1979: 30).

[94] For example, Cassius Dio (62.18.1) depicts Nero singing his *Capture of Troy* in citharodic costume during the Fire of 64.

[95] See Champlin 2003a: 79. [96] Philostr. *VA* 4.39.2; Power 2010: 190.

communities who had never heard him play. Having been deemed unworthy to compete *against* Nero (τῶν οὐκ ἀξιουμένων ἀνταγωνίζεσθαι τῷ Νέρωνι), he chose instead to perform *as* Nero and became an overnight celebrity. He gave the people what they wanted: the giddy sensation of witnessing the 'New Apollo' live in concert.

At Rome, and probably elsewhere, the magnetic attraction of Nero's music continued to be felt even after the emperor's demise. Suetonius recalls how, at the public banquet celebrating Vitellius' accession to the throne, a citharode performed particularly admirably. Impressed, Vitellius asked the musician to name something *de dominico*, meaning 'from the imperial patrimony'. However, the citharode deliberately mistook this as a request to play something 'by the master'. He launched into some of Nero's songs (*Neroniana cantica*) and was amply rewarded for both his skill and ingenuity.[97] The unusual word *dominico* requires clarification. It derives from the adjective *dominicus* (belonging to the master) and can be construed here either as a substantive (*dominicum*, the master's stuff) or as qualifying a noun which has been omitted (probably *liber*, the master's book). In any case, the meaning can be clearly inferred from the context: Suetonius must be describing a kind of Neronian 'songbook' – a catalogue of Nero's 'greatest hits'.[98] Exactly what this work comprised, and how it became known, remains a mystery. But its publication was likely authorised by the *princeps* during his lifetime. There are strong hints in our sources that Nero made a conscious effort to disseminate his songs, both on and off the stage. For example, upon hearing news of Galba's insurrection in Spain, Nero is said to have ridiculed the leaders of the revolt by composing 'songs set to licentious music' (*carmina lasciveque modulata*), which he 'accompanied with gestures' (*etiam gesticulatus est*). By this late stage in the reign, he was living in deep isolation; and yet, according to Suetonius, the songs 'became publicly known' (*vulgo notuerunt*).[99] This did not happen by accident: Nero must have encouraged his courtiers to

---

[97] Suet. *Vit.* 11.2.
[98] Cf. *TLL* s.v. 'dominicus', Vol. V, 1, 1887, 29–1892, 48 (I. Kapp), esp. section IIA (*ad imperatorem pertinens*); see also brief discussion in Griffin 1984: 152. David Ruhnken, the eighteenth-century Dutch commentator on Suetonius, suggested somewhat fancifully that the title originated with the slaves and freedmen in the *familia Caesaris*, who knew Nero as their 'master': *Dominicum, servi et liberti appellasse videntur canticum, quod dominus suus Nero scripsisset* (Geel 1966: 349). Another possibility is that *dominicus* refers to *domini factionum*, i.e. the leaders of theatre factions (cf. Suet. *Nero* 5.2, 22.2). Horsfall (2003: 40) speculates that the *domini factionum* were responsible for the memorisation of popular tunes. Are we meant to think of Nero as a faction leader, instructing his audiences in which songs to memorise?
[99] Suet. *Nero* 42.2.

circulate his ditties beyond the imperial court.¹⁰⁰ That they succeeded in this endeavour, despite the mounting opposition to Nero from within the ranks of the army and the Senate, is surely testament to the enduring receptivity of Roman audiences to the emperor's poetic and musical output.

Taken together, the evidence amounts to a compelling argument. Nero did more than just promote musical culture; he actively remade it in his own image. He provided a populace of Roman musomaniacs with an outlet for their passions: his pursuits became their pursuits, and vice versa. As Cassius Dio puts it, Nero was adored by the mob (ὅμιλος) because he shared his passions with them (ἐδημοσίευσεν).¹⁰¹

The intensity of emotion that musical performances aroused in Nero's subjects is easy to discern from contemporary sources. In one of the *Moral Epistles*, Seneca recalls walking past the theatre of Naples and eavesdropping on the conversations of the spectators inside: 'People are deciding, with tremendous zeal (*ingenti studio*), who is entitled to be called a good pipe-player; even the Greek trumpeter (*tubicen Graecus*) and herald draw the crowds.'¹⁰² The Roman philosopher Musonius Rufus, writing around the same time, comments on the shouting and gesticulating of an agitated crowd at the performance of a *tibicen*.¹⁰³ If ordinary musicians could generate such intense feelings of excitement, we can only imagine the crowd's reaction to a musician of Nero's calibre. Regardless of one's level of artistic appreciation, there must have been something uniquely thrilling about the spectacle of the *princeps* taking on a role normally reserved for an individual deemed *infamis* in Roman law. Tacitus implies as much in his assessment of the spectators at the Neronia of 65: 'You would think they were pleased, and perhaps they were pleased, in their lack of concern for public disgrace (*per incuriam publici flagitii*).'¹⁰⁴ As Ray Laurence explains,

---

[100] In the *Suda* we hear of a certain Didymus, a grammarian who 'spent time with Nero and conducted business; he was an exceptional musician, with a talent for singing': Δίδυμος, ὁ τοῦ Ἡρακλείδου, γραμματικός, ὃς διέτριψε παρὰ Νέρωνι καὶ ἐχρημάτισατο: μουσικός τε ἦν λίαν καὶ πρὸς μέλη ἐπιτήδειος (*Suda* δ 875). In what settings did Didymus display his musical talents? And what songs did he sing? We do not know. But it is not inconceivable that there were many *mousikoi* like Didymus in Neronian Rome who performed not only for the emperor and his guests but also for humbler clientele outside the imperial palace, and whose repertoire included songs made famous, or actually composed, by Nero himself. For interesting speculation on Didymus' background and career, see Barker 1994: 64.

[101] Dio Cass. 61.5.2.   [102] Sen. *Ep.* 76.4.

[103] Muson. fr. 49 (= Gell. *NA* 5.1): *clamitant . . . gestiunt . . . exagitantur*.

[104] Tac. *Ann.* 16.4. Philostratus, similarly, speaks of Nero 'debasing himself to please the masses' (χαριζόμενος τοῖς ὄχλοις τὴν ἑαυτοῦ αἰσχύνην; *VA* 4.36.2).

'Nero inverted the principles of *virtus* and *dignitas* and engaged with theatre audiences directly. In his performance the audience could identify themselves.'[105] We should not be deluded into thinking that Nero either coerced or intimidated his audiences to applaud him against their wishes. Many of his subjects, it seems, were willing participants. And they were perfectly happy to let their Master call the tunes.

Water-Organs, Bagpipes and the Lure of the Arena

We can gain a deeper insight into Nero's populism by examining a neglected episode from the spring of 68, just a few months before his death.[106] Nero was holidaying in his adoptive city of Naples when he received news that Julius Vindex, the governor of Gallia Lugdunensis, had revolted. At first, his response was to do nothing. But his demeanour changed drastically when he received a proclamation from Vindex heaping scorn on his family name and disparaging his ability as a lyre-player.[107] Nero hurried back to Rome in a fit of rage and immediately summoned a meeting of the imperial council in his newly built palace, the Domus Aurea.[108] The councillors nervously assembled in anticipation of a formal briefing. But, as it turned out, the emperor was in no mood to talk politics:

> *ac ne tunc quidem aut senatu aut populo coram appellato quosdam e primoribus viris domum evocavit transactaque raptim consultatione reliquam diei partem per organa hydraulica novi et ignoti generis circumduxit, ostendensque singula, de ratione et difficultate cuiusque disserens, iam se etiam prolaturum omnia in theatrum affirmauit, si per Vindicem liceat.* (Suet. *Ner.* 41.2)

> Not even then did he convene a public meeting of the Senate or the people, but called a few of the leading men to his palace and, after holding a brief conference, spent the rest of the day guiding them through some water-organs, of a new and unknown kind, showing them off one by one and lecturing on the workings and difficulty of each; he even promised that he would exhibit them all in the theatre – with Vindex's permission.

---

[105] Laurence 2009: 122.
[106] The following narrative is based on Suet. *Ner.* 40.4–41.2. The arguments in this section are developed at greater length in Morgan 2022.
[107] Suet. *Ner.* 41.1: *nihil autem aeque doluit, quam ut malum se citharoedum increpitum ac pro Nerone Ahenobarbum appellatum*; cf. Philostr. *VA* 5.10.2: ἔφη γὰρ Νέρωνα εἶναι πάντα μᾶλλον ἢ κιθαρῳδόν καὶ κιθαρῳδόν μᾶλλον ἢ βασιλέα.
[108] Bradley 1978b: 253: 'The last few days in March appear to be the most reasonable time for the date of this event.'

The epitomator of Cassius Dio preserves a different account of the same episode:

> νύκτωρ ποτὲ τοὺς πρώτους τῶν βουλευτῶν καὶ τῶν ἱππέων ἐξαπίνης σπουδῇ, ὡς καὶ περὶ τῶν παρόντων τι κοινώσων σφίσι, μεταπέμψας "ἐξεύρηκα" ἔφη "πῶς ἡ ὕδραυλις" (αὐτὸ γὰρ τὸ ῥηθὲν γραφήσεται) "καὶ μεῖζον καὶ ἐμμελέστερον φθέγξεται." τοιαῦτα μὲν καὶ τότε ἔπαιζεν. (Dio Cass. 63.26.4–5)
>
> One night he suddenly summoned the foremost senators and equestrians as a matter of urgency, as if to make some communication to them regarding the present situation, and then said to them (I quote his exact words): 'I have discovered a way by which the water-organ will produce louder and more tuneful music.' Such were the games he played even at that time.

As the days and weeks wore on, Nero's obsession with the organ showed little sign of wavering. It would be only a matter of time, Nero thought, until the renegade Vindex and his Gallic insurgents would be forced into submission. A great celebration was called for, and who better to preside over the festivities than the emperor himself?

> *sub exitu quidem vitae palam vouerat, si sibi incolumis status permansisset, proditurum se partae victoriae ludis etiam hydraulam et choraulam et utricularium ac nouissimo die histrionem saltaturumque Vergili Turnum.* (Suet. *Ner*. 54)
>
> Near the end of his life, indeed, he had publicly made a vow that, if his power remained intact, he would perform at his victory games as an organist, a pipe-player and a bagpipe-player, and that on the last day he would appear as an actor and dance 'Vergil's Turnus'.

Much to Suetonius' relief, Nero's victory games proved to be nothing more than a flight of fancy. Within a few months of Vindex's revolt, the emperor was dead, and his memory forever consigned to infamy.

Such, in short, is the surviving ancient testimony for Nero's association with the water-organ: two brief accounts of a curious incident in the Domus Aurea and an allusion to victory games which never took place. Whether Tacitus made mention of Nero's organ-playing in the relevant section of his *Annals* we do not know, since the extant narrative breaks off in the middle of 66. Here, as ever, the loss of a potentially corroborating source is regrettable. Dio's account is preserved only in the Byzantine epitome of Xiphilinus, compiled during the eleventh century. Although Xiphilinus is generally considered a reliable transmitter of Dio's text, we cannot discount the possibility that he condensed or reworked his source material in some way.¹⁰⁹ More importantly, there is considerable doubt surrounding the historicity of the ancient narratives. As scholars have noted, Nero's demonstration of the *organa hydraulica* bears an uncanny resemblance to an episode from the reign of Caligula, in which the crazed emperor summons an audience of consular advisers to his palace in the middle of the night, appears unannounced adorned in full actor's costume, and performs a lively musical number before disappearing again.¹¹⁰ There are obvious problems, therefore, in taking the story of the water-organ at face value. Indeed, according to Keith Bradley, the story is 'no more than a literary representation' of Nero's mania for the performing arts.¹¹¹ It is telling that, in the copious scholarship on the Neronian Principate, the emperor's association with the organ has received only the occasional passing comment.¹¹²

However, the episode is worth a closer look. Even if we reject the notion that Nero turned to the organ as a distraction from civil war, and even if we deny that he contemplated games to celebrate Vindex's defeat, it is very likely that his interest in the *organon hydraulicon* had some basis in reality. We can be confident, at least, that the idea of Nero as an *utricularius* did not originate with Suetonius, since Dio Chrysostom refers to Nero's interest in the bagpipes in a speech given during the Flavian period.¹¹³ While I do not wish to downplay the rhetorical aspects of the literary sources, with closer scrutiny of the evidence it is possible to reconstruct a plausible picture of why the 'historical' Nero might have cultivated an image of himself as a collector and connoisseur of esoteric wind instruments. To prepare the ground for this discussion, I will begin by briefly surveying the history of the water-organ from its origins in the Hellenistic period up to the mid-first century CE, before considering how it fits into the broader political landscape of Nero's Principate.

The invention of the water-organ was attributed in antiquity to an engineer named Ctesibius, a barber's son from Alexandria who lived

---

¹⁰⁹ On Xiphilinus' practices as an epitomator, see Mallan 2013.
¹¹⁰ Suet. *Calig.* 54; Cass. Dio 59.5.5. The story also recalls Dio's account of Domitian's nocturnal banquet: Cass. Dio 67.9.
¹¹¹ Bradley 1978b: 254.
¹¹² See, e.g., Griffin 1984: 164; Champlin 2003a: 2, 80; Fantham 2013: 20; Leigh 2017: 26; Drinkwater 2019: 123; Schulz 2019: 197, 227, 234.
¹¹³ Dio Chrys. *Or.* 71.9, referring to Nero as 'one of the monarchs of our time' (τῶν νῦν βασιλέων τις).

sometime during the third century BCE.[114] Ctesibius achieved lasting fame as a pioneer in the field of hydraulics. He was credited with the discovery of the piston-pump and water-clock, among various other *hydraulicae machinae*.[115] But the organ was arguably his most enduring creation of all, starting a trend in the manufacture of keyboard instruments that would shape the history of western music for over two millennia.[116] A product of remarkable human ingenuity, the water-organ was clearly distinguished from the *cithara* and the *auloi/tibiae*, in that it lacked a foundation in the mythological tradition. Its cultural cachet derived principally from the fact that it was a man-made invention, designed to astonish as well as to entertain.

The *hydraulis* worked by harnessing the compressed air inside a cistern filled partially with water.[117] Two cylindrical pistons on either side, worked by levers, pumped air into a hollow chamber inside the cistern, called a *pnigeus*. The incoming air displaced water into the cistern through apertures at the base of the *pnigeus*, driving the water level in the cistern upwards and thereby maintaining the high air pressure within the chamber. When a key was depressed, a spring mechanism allowed the compressed air from the *pnigeus* to escape freely through the pipe, producing a musical sound. As air escaped the pipe, the pressure in the *pnigeus* dropped, allowing water to re-enter. The constant operation of the pistons was therefore necessary to ensure that the organ was primed for playing.

Little is known about the early history of the *hydraulis*. The instrument is first attested in an honorific decree from Delphi, dating from around 90 BCE. The inscription records the achievements of a Cretan organ-player (ὕδραυλος) named Antipatros, who had been invited specially by the

---

[114] Vitr. *De arch.* 9.8.2; Athen. 4.174b. For a summary of the main arguments surrounding Ctesibius' date, see Drachmann 1948: 1–3. Extensive studies of the *hydraulis* have been undertaken by Perrot (1971) and Markovits (2003); useful surveys can also be found in West 1992: 114–18; Beschi 2009: 247–66; Creese 2009: 569–71.

[115] Vitr. *De arch.* 9.8.4; Plin. *HN* 7.125.   [116] See Williams 1980, 1993; Dessì 2008.

[117] Our knowledge of the technical workings of the *hydraulis* derives mainly from the writings of Hero of Alexandria (*Pneum.* 1.42) and Vitruvius (*De arch.* 10.8.3–6), as well as from the remains of two water-organs excavated during the twentieth century, the first from Aquincum (modern Budapest) and the second from Dion in northern Greece. On the Aquincum organ, see Hyde 1938; Kaba 1976. On the Dion organ, see Markovits 2003: 97–8; Beschi 2009: 256–7; Stroux 2009. Fragments belonging to a third water-organ, unearthed at Aventicum (modern Avenches), are discussed by Jakob *et al.* (2000). Curiously, we do not know whether the conventional nominative form in Latin was *hydraulis* (Gk. ὕδραυλις) or *hydraulus* (Gk. ὕδραυλος), since all extant references to the instrument occur in oblique cases. The *TLL* and *OCD* use *hydraulus* as the lemma. However, ὕδραυλις is the more commonly attested Greek form (cf. *LSJ*, s.v. ὕδραυλις), and thus I prefer to use the Latin transliteration here.

Delphic archons to participate in a two-day festival and was subsequently rewarded for his performance with various honours, including a bronze statue.[118] We do not know at what point, or in what setting, the Romans first encountered Ctesibius' invention. They certainly knew of the existence of the *hydraulis* by the middle of the first century BCE, since Cicero alludes to the instrument in his *Tusculan Disputations* (discussed later in this section).[119] By the time of Nero, at any rate, the organ was most familiar to audiences in Rome for its role in accompanying public spectacles of various kinds. In a scene from Petronius' *Cena Trimalchionis*, the sight of a slave carving meat is likened to 'a gladiator in a chariot fighting to the accompaniment of a water-organ' (*essedarium hydraule cantante pugnare*), while in the anonymous poem *Aetna*, usually dated to the 60s or 70s CE, the *hydraulis* is described as a 'vessel' which 'with its water-worked song makes music in large theatres' (*carmineque irriguo magnis cortina theatris ... canit*).[120]

It is also around the middle of the first century CE that the *hydraulis* starts to appear in Roman art. Of the forty or so artistic representations of the instrument which survive, the majority are associated either with gladiatorial spectacles or with performances in the theatre or the circus (see, e.g., Fig. 4.3). In several cases, the *hydraulis* is represented as part of a larger instrumental ensemble, including brass-players (*tubicines* and *cornicines*) and pipe-players (*tibicines*). Unfortunately, none of the extant iconography can be securely dated to the period before or during Nero's reign.[121] The appearance of a *hydraulis* on the reverse of a fourth-century

---

[118] *Syll.*³ 737 = *Choix Delphes* 192. There is an erasure in lines 8–9 of the text; Dittenberger, ad loc., restores the name of the games (i.e. Pythian) and the total prize money: τῶι ἀγῶν[ι τῶν Πυθίων δραχμαῖς χιλίαις καὶ πεντακοσίαις καὶ] εἰκόνι χαλκέαι. The inscription states that additional honours were conferred on a certain Cryton, the brother of Antipatros (lines 13–14), as well as a group of attendants (line 20), who may have assisted Antipatros in the operation of the instrument: see Chaniotis 2009: 88.

[119] Cic. *Tusc.* 3.43: *hydrauli hortabere ut audiat uoces potius quam Platonis?* Perrot (1971: 45–6) speculates that Cicero might have encountered the *hydraulis* at some point during his travels in Greece between 79 and 77 BCE, but there is no evidence to support this claim.

[120] Petron. *Sat.* 36; *Aetna* ll. 296–7. On the date of the *Aetna*, see Goodyear 1984: 353.

[121] A tiny engraved gem from the British Museum shows an organ-player accompanied by two assistants who operate the pistons (GR 1859.3–1.112; BM Cat Gems 1051). Markovits (2003: 39) dates it to the first century BCE but does not say on what grounds, while Perrot dates it to the third century CE on the opinion of 'experts at the British Museum' (Perrot 1971: 84–5, with Plate VIII, no. 2). The *hydraulis* is also represented in two terracotta figurines from Tarsus and Alexandria, dating from either the first century BCE or CE (Perrot 1971: 77–8, with Plate V, 99–100, with Plate XVI, no. 1; Markovits 2003: 739, Taf. 5 and 6). Also noteworthy is a small graffito of an organ from a *taberna* in Pozzuoli, found alongside a larger graffito of a gladiator's trident; usually dated to the mid-first century CE (Guarducci 1971: 219–23, with Plate 23a; not

Figure 4.3 Medallion depicting an organist and *cornicen* on amphitheatre mosaic from Roman villa at Nennig, near Trier, Germany; second or third century CE. Photo by DeAgostini / Getty Images.

contorniate medallion, coupled with an image of Nero on the obverse, may point towards an association between Nero and the organ in Late Antiquity (Fig. 4.4). However, it should be noted that the *hydraulis* also features on other contorniates of the period alongside portraits of Trajan and Caracalla.[122]

First and foremost, then, the *hydraulis* was associated by Roman audiences of the early imperial period with large public spectacles in the circus, arena and theatre; it was, by all accounts, an extremely popular instrument. In the *Tusculan Disputations*, Cicero finds fault with those of an Epicurean disposition who, in seeking to mitigate feelings of pain or suffering, preferred to listen to the sound of a *hydraulis* rather than to a dialogue of

---

mentioned by Perrot or Markovits); this dating is disputed by Creese (2009: 571 n. 41). For artistic depictions of the *hydraulis*, see also extensive references and discussion in Dunbabin 2016.

[122] See Perrot 1971: 90–1, with plate IX, nos. 1–2; Markovits 2003: Taf. 26a; Alföldi and Alföldi 1990: 2.223–4, with additional tables.

Figure 4.4 Copper alloy contorniate, minted in Rome, late fourth or fifth century CE. Observe: head of Nero, laureate, with palm-branch countermark. Reverse: *hydraulis* with a figure standing facing on the left, with legend LAVRENTI NICA (the victory of Laurentius). The iconography probably alludes to Nero's reputation as a great giver of games, rather than commemorating Nero's affinity with the *hydraulis* specifically. © The Trustees of the British Museum. R.4865.

Plato.[123] The pleasure derived from listening to the water-organ, Cicero implies, was akin to eating a fine fish (*accipenserem*), looking at a diverse array of flowers (*florida et varia*) or smelling a fragrant bouquet (*fasciculum*). This passage tells us more about the sublime sensory qualities of the organ than it does about its perceived 'elite' status. Dio's suggestion that Nero attempted to make the organ 'louder and more musical' (μεῖζον καὶ ἐμμελέστερον) accords well with its reputation as a device with supernaturally loud properties. Seneca, for example, alludes to the *hydraulis* as an instrument that 'by water pressure emits a sound louder than that which can be produced by the human voice' (*aquarum pressura maiorem sonitum formant quam qui ore reddi potest*), likening it on this basis to the horn (*cornu*) and the trumpet (*tuba*).[124] It could be argued therefore that, by presenting himself as an ardent supporter of the *hydraulis*, Nero was

---

[123] Cic. *Tusc.* 3.43.
[124] Sen. *QNat.* 2.6.5. The loudness of the *hydraulis* is also suggested by an inscription from Rhodes, dating from the third century CE, which refers to an organ-player belonging to the cult of Dionysus, whose role was to 'wake up the god' (τῷ ὑδραύλῃ τῷ ἐπεγείροντι [τὸ]ν θεὸν):

seeking to capitalise on the instrument's popular appeal in the face of the mounting political opposition to his rule. For an emperor who styled himself as both a supreme aesthete and a patron of the *plebs*, the *hydraulis* represented a potentially useful means of bridging the gap between private luxury and public leisure. It is significant in this respect that Suetonius mentions Nero's aspirations as an organist in a section of the *Life* dealing with his *popularitas*.[125]

So much for the water-organ; what about Nero's association with the bagpipes? The bagpipes probably originated as a humble folk instrument in the regions of Egypt, Syria and Asia Minor.[126] According to Martin West, the instrument may not have been known in the Mediterranean world before the second century BCE, 'and even after that it is doubtful how often it was seen.'[127] The bagpipes are attested in only a handful of examples of Greco-Roman art. The most notable example is a terracotta figurine from Alexandria, dating from the third century CE, which shows a male *syrinx*-player seated with an inflated skin bag under his left arm. A pipe attached to the bag extends to his right arm, while his right foot is fitted with a *scabellum*. He is accompanied by a cymbal-playing dwarf (Fig. 4.5). Parallels can be drawn with another figurine, also from Alexandria and dated to the first century CE, which depicts a woman playing the *hydraulis* and a macrophallic dwarf blowing into a long trumpet (Fig. 4.6).[128]

Whether or not Nero was personally responsible for bringing the bagpipes to Rome is unclear, but his intention to elevate the bagpipes to the status of a concert instrument evidently ran contrary to cultural norms. Revealingly, Martial thought it degrading for an esteemed *tibicen* like Canus to 'desire to be a bagpiper' (*concupiscat esse Canus ascaules*).[129] Nero's idea of transforming the bagpipes into a high art form evidently struck Suetonius and Dio Chrysostom as a ludicrous innovation. But seen from a different perspective, the bagpipes were a suitable tool for a political leader who wished to advertise his affinity with the *plebs*.

The anecdotes surrounding Nero's interactions with the organ and bagpipes underline how his music-making appealed directly to the cultural interests of lower-class Romans. In crafting his musical persona, Nero took

---

Reinach 1904: 206, ll. 23–4; *I.Ephesos* 1601a provides further evidence of the use of organs in noisy Dionysiac ritual.

[125] Suet. *Ner.* 53.1: *maxime autem popularitate efferebatur*.
[126] See Sachs 1940: 141; Baines 1960: 64–6; West 1992: 107–9; Calvo-Sotelo 2015.
[127] West 1992: 107.   [128] See Vendries 2013: 208.
[129] Mart. 10.3.8. *Ascaules* is the Greek word for 'bagpiper'. Canus specialized as a *choraules* and rose to fame under Nero: cf. Suet. *Galb.* 12.3.

Figure 4.5 Terracotta figurine from Alexandria, Egypt,
ca. 200 CE, showing a pair of musicians. The larger figure plays panpipes and bagpipes and has a *scabellum* attached to his right foot; he is accompanied by a dwarf who plays cymbals. Ägyptisches Museum und Papyrussammlung, Staatliche Museen zu Berlin, inv. ÄM 8798. Credit: bpk Bildagentur / Ägyptisches Museum und Papyrussammlung, SMB / Sandra Steiß / Art Resource, NY.

inspiration not only from the world of tragedy and *kitharoidia*, but also from the circus and the arena. Nero's interest in these venues is, of course, well-documented through his exploits as a charioteer.[130] Suetonius also reports a rumour that Nero had a lion prepared for him to kill in the amphitheatre before the public, so that he would be compared with Hercules.[131] It is perhaps no surprise, then, that the stagestruck emperor

---

[130] Cassius Dio (62.15) reports that Nero raced chariots in public for the first time in 64 CE. Before that, he had driven chariots in a private circus in the Vatican valley: Tac. *Ann.* 14.14.2. On Nero's chariot-racing, see Schollmeyer 2019.

[131] Suet. *Nero* 53; cf. Philostr. *VA* 4.36 on Nero living and fighting with gladiators.

Figure 4.6 Terracotta figurine from Alexandria, Egypt, first century CE, showing a female organ-player wearing a diadem and a macrophallic dwarf playing the *tuba*. The pipes of the *hydraulis* are cut away to show the head of the organist. Louvre, Paris, inv. CA 426. Credit: RMN-Grand Palais / Art Resource, NY.

was seduced by the instruments whose music filled Rome's circuses and amphitheatres, energising both competitors and spectators alike.

Musomania in a Young Man's World

Music, in the eyes of the Greeks and Romans, was a young man's game. Its patron god was a model of eternal beauty: flowing locks, radiant complexion, soft skin – Apollo was a natural mascot for the Neronian regime. Nero came to power at the tender age of seventeen. When we first encounter him in Tacitus' *Annals*, it is as a participant in the *ludus Troiae* (Troy Game), an equestrian exercise performed by young *nobiles*.[132] Nero made his debut as

---

[132] Tac. *Ann.* 11.11.2; cf. Suet. *Aug.* 43.2.

a *citharoedus* at a festival celebrating the first shaving of his beard. Wherever he went young men followed, from the Greek ephebes enfranchised at the *Ludi Maximi* of 59 to the legion of sturdy Italian recruits mustered at the emperor's behest in Achaea.[133] Nero truly lived up to his title of *princeps iuventutis*, 'leader of the youth'.[134]

Musical emperors nearly all have in common the trait of *iuventas*. The tyrannical Caligula succeeded to the throne at twenty-four and was a passionate devotee of music and the performing arts. Philo of Alexandria, who encountered him on an embassy to Rome in 40 CE, comments on his 'boyish' (μειρακιωδέστερον) predilection for dancers and musicians, to the point that he would sometimes join in the singing and dancing.[135] The same habit is noted by Suetonius: 'He pursued the theatrical arts of dancing and singing most ardently' (*scaenicas saltandi canendique artes studiosissime appeteret*); 'even at public performances he could not resist singing along with the tragic actor as he delivered his lines (*tragoedo pronuntianti concineret*), or from openly imitating his gestures, to praise or correct them.'[136] Titus, another musical emperor, received his education around the same time as Nero (he was born just two years after him) and is described by Suetonius as an excellent singer and lyre-player. Although he did not become emperor until his late thirties, Titus' musical interests are presented as having been cultivated during his childhood (*in puero*), with the implication perhaps that he grew out of them once he reached maturity.[137] Caracalla, who became co-ruler with his father aged ten in 198, was an avid student of *kitharoidia* and erected a cenotaph for the citharode Mesomedes.[138] The fourteen-year-old Elagabalus could sing and dance, and was proficient on several instruments.[139] His taste for music was inherited by his successor Severus Alexander, who came to power at the

---

[133] Suet. *Nero* 12.1, 19.2.
[134] Granted in 51 CE: Tac. *Ann*. 12.41. He renounced the title 'Pater Patriae' 'on account of his youth' (*propter aetatem*; Suet. *Nero* 8). Cf. Tac. *Hist*. 1.7, on the contrast between Nero's youth and Galba's senility. On Nero's youth as a structural motif in Tacitus' *Annals*, see Henderson 1989: 181–90.
[135] Philo, *Leg*. 42; cf. *Leg*. 44, 79, 96.
[136] Suet. *Calig*. 11, 54.1; cf. Dio Cass. 59.29; Aur. Vict. *Caes*. 3.12. On the resemblance between Caligula and Nero in this and other respects, see Elsner 1994: 118 and Edwards 1994: 87. There is little evidence that the mature emperors Tiberius and Claudius showed much interest in music: see Beacham 1999: 157–65, 186–96, for their relationship with the theatre more generally.
[137] Suet. *Tit*. 3.2 (*ne musicae quidem rudis, ut qui cantaret et psalleret iucunde scienterque*).
[138] Dio Cass. 77.13.7.
[139] *SHA Heliog*. 32.8 (*ipse cantavit, saltavit, ad tibias dixit, tuba cecinit, pandurizavit, organo modulatus est*). Herodian (5.5.9) comments on his habit of dancing during sacrifices 'to the

age of thirteen.[140] Severus could play the lyre, the pipes, the organ and even the trumpet, although he gave it up when he succeeded to the throne; he also had an excellent singing voice.[141] Hadrian – 'the most musical emperor', according to one source – stands out as a rare example of a 'good' emperor who cultivated musical interests into adulthood; Augustus, of course, was another.[142] In general, playing instruments was a juvenile pastime, acceptable for precocious youngsters but irreconcilable with the serious duties of the mature Roman citizen. Nero's problem was that he failed to outgrow his childish image. Indeed, as Emily Gowers stresses, he made a spectacle of his immaturity.[143] When Nero played music, to quote Cassius Dio, he 'acted like a child' (ἔπαιζεν).[144]

In reality, Nero's musical education was probably not unusual for a Roman boy of his age and rank. Precisely *how* unusual is difficult to say on the basis of the surviving evidence. It has been reasonably claimed that, during the mid-first century CE, 'most young aristocrats gained some knowledge of music, dance and singing as part of their general education'.[145] Suetonius certainly gives no indication that Titus' musical accomplishments were considered unsuitable or indecorous. On the contrary, singing and lyre-playing are listed among Titus' 'physical and mental gifts'

---

accompaniment of all sorts of musical instruments' (περί τε τοὺς βωμοὺς ἐχόρευεν ὑπὸ παντοδαποῖς ἤχοις ὀργάνων).

[140] *SHA Alex.* 27.5 (*ad musicam pronus*).
[141] *SHA Alex.* 27.9 (*lyra, tibia, organo cecinit, tuba etiam, quod quidem imperator numquam ostendit*); 27.7 (*cantavit nobiliter*). It is unclear whether the concessive *quod* clause refers only to the trumpet-playing or to all the instruments mentioned.
[142] Athen. 115b (μουσικώτατος βασιλεύς); cf. Aur. Vict. *Caes.* 14.2; *SHA Had.* 14.9, with a hint of censure: *iam psallendi et cantandi scientiam prae se ferebat. in voluptatibus nimius.* There is no evidence that Augustus ever played musical instruments, although he was reportedly quite fond of musicians (see Chapter 3).
[143] Gowers 1994: 134.
[144] Dio Cass. 63.26.5; cf. 62.1.1 (ἐπαίζετο). For children as composers and performers of songs, cf. Suet. *Cal.* 16: (*nobilibusque pueris ac puellis carmine modulato laudes virtutum eius canentibus*); Gell. *NA* 4.5.5 (*versus scite factus cantatusque esse a pueris urbe tota fertur*). The late-antique Syriac writer Jacob of Serugh speaks of 'melodies which attract children': see Moss 1935: 105. Cf. also Epictetus, *Encheiridion* 29.3, criticising those who throw themselves 'like children' (ὡς τὰ παιδία) from one activity to the next: 'They [i.e. children] play wrestlers, again gladiators, again they blow trumpets, and then act a play.' According to Julian (*Or.* 3.111b), the kind of people who went to the theatre to gaze at a citharode's dress and lyre tended to be either children or adults with childish tastes (παῖδας καὶ τῶν ἀνδρῶν καὶ γυναικῶν).
[145] Laurence 2009: 121. Echoed by Wallace-Hadrill 1983: 182; Eyben 1993: 87–8; Leigh 2017: 21. Hagel and Lynch (2015: 409) are more sceptical, suggesting that 'practical musical skills seem to have been regarded as an extra', but the salient point is that Nero's musical education would not itself have been a cause for scandal.

(*corporis animique dotes*).¹⁴⁶ The positive perception of musical training among Roman aristocrats of the mid-first century CE is highlighted especially in the anonymous panegyric known as the *Laus Pisonis*:

> si carmina forte
> nectere ludenti iuvit fluitantia versu,
> Aonium facilis deducit pagina carmen;
> sive chelyn digitis et eburno verbere pulsas,
> dulcis Apollinea sequitur testudine cantus,
> et te credibile est Phoebo didicisse magistro.
> ne pudeat pepulisse lyram, cum pace serena
> publica securis exultent otia terris,
> ne pudeat: Phoebea chelys sic creditur illis
> pulsari manibus, quibus et contenditur arcus.
> (*Laus Pisonis*, ll. 163–72)

> If you maybe liked to weave something easy-listening through playful verse, the page collaborates, spinning down an Aonian song; or if you pluck your lyre with your fingers and an ivory rod, a sweet song trails from the Apolline shell, and it's plausible you learned the trade from Phoebus' class. Don't be shy to strike the lyre; with peace and tranquility, let official holidays rejoice in a world without care; don't be shy. In that very way – so we think – Apollo's lyre is twanged by the very same hands that stretch the bow. (Trans. Geue 2017: 151)

Even allowing for poetic licence, the idealisation of a young Roman aristocrat as an accomplished citharode says much about the perceived value of acquiring musical skills as part of a well-rounded liberal education. The fact that the *Laus Pisonis* was probably composed in honour of the anti-Neronian conspirator Gaius Calpurnius Piso makes the resemblance with Nero all the more arresting.¹⁴⁷ We happen to know from Tacitus' *Annals* that Piso occasionally performed as a *tragoedus*, on which grounds he was likened to Nero by the tribune Subrius Flavus.¹⁴⁸ It is hardly

---

¹⁴⁶ Suet. *Tit.* 3.1.
¹⁴⁷ See Power 2010: 80 n. 195: 'The anonymous poet is careful to specify that Piso plays the amateur's tortoise-shell lyre (*testudo*, *chelys*, *lyra*) rather than the *cithara*, and that he does so "without shame" (169, 171), following the example of Achilles, whose musical interests complemented his martial glories. That so large a chunk of the panegyric is devoted to the lyre, however, suggests that Piso took seriously his lyric culture, and may even have harboured quasi-professional ambitions similar to Nero's, if not as grand.'
¹⁴⁸ Tac. *Ann.* 15.65: *quin et verba Flavi vulgabantur, non referre dedecori, si citharoedus demoveretur et tragoedus succederet, quia ut Nero cithara, ita Piso tragico ornatu canebat* (moreover, there was a saying of Flavus in circulation, that 'as far as disgrace was concerned, it

inconceivable that he also sang to the lyre from time to time, at least in private.

For a deeper insight into the musical interests and pursuits of Roman citizens in the time of Nero, we can turn to the writings of his tutor Seneca the Younger.[149] Seneca's stance on music is that of a typical Roman moralist. He often speaks disparagingly of his contemporaries' craze for singing and dancing and associates this behaviour with the decline of old-fashioned Roman values. 'The private stage resounds throughout the whole city. Both men and women dance upon it; husbands and wives contend with each other over which of the two can bare their flank more seductively.'[150] In one of the *Moral Epistles*, Seneca takes aim at 'effeminate' music teachers, who, he claims, instruct their students to perform 'effeminate movements of the body and effeminate and emasculating songs' (*molles corporis motus ... mollesque cantus et infractos*).[151] He is also critical of private musical concerts (*symphoniae*) and associates them with the vices of luxury and drunkenness.[152]

Seneca's aversion to convivial music-making and musical training stemmed not only from concerns about the spread of immorality, but also from a keen awareness of the cognitive effects of music. Catchy tunes heard at the theatre or at a banquet could easily become lodged in the listener's memory, distracting them from their daily tasks: 'those who have listened to a *symphonia* carry with them in their ears that *modulatio* and the sweetness of the songs (*dulcedinem cantuum*), which impedes their thinking and prevents them from concentrating on serious matters'.[153] For some people, music even became an addiction:

> *quid illi, qui in componendis, audiendis, discendis canticis operati sunt, dum vocem, cuius rectum cursum natura et optimum et simplicissimum fecit, in flexus modulationis inertissimae torquent, quorum digiti aliquod intra se carmen metientes semper sonant, quorum, cum ad res serias,*

made no difference if a citharode [i.e. Nero] was removed and a tragic singer [i.e. Piso] took his place'; for just as Nero sang to the cithara, so Piso sang in tragic costume).

[149] For a general discussion of the role of music in the writings of Seneca the Younger, see Luque Moreno 1997.

[150] Sen. *NQ* 7.32.3: *privatum urbe tota sonat pulpitum; in hoc mares, in hoc feminae tripudiant: mares inter se uxoresque contendunt uter det latus mollius.*

[151] Sen. *Ep.* 90.19; cf. *Ep.* 114.1 (*infracta et in morem cantici ducta*); *Tranq.* 17.4 (*molliter se infringens*).

[152] Sen. *Ep.* 51.4 (*symphoniarum cantibus strepentes lacus*), 51.12 (*canentium nocturna convicia*).

[153] Sen. *Ep.* 123.9. On the memorability of theatrical music in particular, cf. Ov. *Fast.* 3.535, Lucr. 4.973–83; Horsfall 2003: 11–17, 41–2. Cf. also Sen. *Ep.* 56.2.3, on the *insignita modulatio* of street-vendors hawking their wares.

etiam saepe tristes adhibiti sunt, exauditur tacita modulatio? non habent isti otium, sed iners negotium. (Sen. *Brev.* 12.4)

And what of those who are absorbed in composing, hearing, and learning songs, while they twist the voice, whose best and simplest movement nature designed to be straightforward, into inflections of the most feeble warbling, whose fingers are always snapping in time to some song they have stuck in their head, who are overheard humming a tune when they have been asked to attend to serious, often even unhappy, matters? These people have not leisure, but idle occupation.

Seneca here coins the phrase *iners negotium* (idle occupation) to describe the habit of wasting one's life engaged in frivolous pursuits. Music buffs constituted one of the groups of people who, in Seneca's opinion, fostered a kind of *iners negotium*. In particular, Seneca objects to the obsessive cultivation of *cantica* to the point that it caused one to stray from the path of true philosophical *otium*.[154] His targets, we must assume, are members of the educated upper classes – those who possessed the necessary skills and time for composition, those who actually had 'serious business' (*res seriae*) to attend to. The tone almost verges on satire: imagine a Senate-house echoing to the sound of foot-tapping and finger-snapping, or courtrooms disturbed by the noise of jurors humming their favourite tunes!

Such fearmongering was nothing new, of course. The use of descriptive terms like *flexus* and *modulatio* harks back to Ciceronian discussions of musical decline (compare, for example, the phrase *flexus modulationis inertissimae torquent* in the passage quoted above with *cum modorum flexionibus torqueant* in *De Legibus* 2.39). Seneca's uncle had used very similar language in passing judgement on the younger generation of his own time: 'Look at the character of idle youth ... a repulsive obsession for singing and dancing transfixes these effeminates.'[155] Nevertheless, the writings of the Younger Seneca are valuable in showing that Roman elites during the early imperial period adhered to very different criteria when it

---

[154] On the ideal of philosophical *otium* in the *De Brevitate Vitae*, see Williams 2003: 20–5; Leigh 2012.

[155] Sen. *Contr.* 1.praef.8: *ecce ingenia desidiosae iuventutis ... cantandi saltandique obscena studia effeminatos tenant.* For the Elder Seneca's opposition to dancing, cf. also *Contr.* 9.2.8: *quid ego nunc referam, iudices, ludorum genera, saltationes, et illud dedecoris certamen, praetorne se mollius moveret an meretrix?* It is interesting to note, however, that as a young man Seneca had been in the habit of memorising passages by the declaimer Fuscus and singing them aloud with his peers, each inserting his own melodic flourishes (*Suas.* 2.10: *recolo nihil fuisse me iuvene tam notum quam has explicationes Fusci, quas nemo nostrum non alius alia inclinatione vocis velut sua quisque modulatione cantabat*).

came to judging the aesthetic and ethical qualities of music. At the very least, I think we can assume the existence a subculture of leisured Roman elites, who were not only avid consumers of songs but also skilled composers and performers. In addition to the sources already discussed, we can draw on the testimony of the agricultural writer Columella, a contemporary of Seneca. Columella bemoans the fact that the students of his day, rather than seeking out teachers of agriculture, were instead flocking to experts in singing and dancing.[156] The reference in Seneca's *Natural Questions* to Roman men and women dancing on the 'private stage' (*privatum ... pulpitum*) is also corroborated by the archaeological remains of private stages found in villas at Pompeii and elsewhere. Some of these stages are impressively large. For example, the villa owned by Vedius Pollio near Naples, bequeathed to Augustus in 15 BCE, had a theatre with a 47-metre diameter which could hold around 1500 people.[157] The fact that Nero began his career by performing on a 'private stage across the Tiber' (*theatrum peculiare trans Tiberim*) is usually understood as a sign of his reluctance to cause a public scandal, but it could also be contextualised in light of the Roman elite's predilection for taking part in private theatrical performances.[158]

The *convivium* afforded another opportunity for educated Romans to cultivate their musical interests. Tacitus describes how, during the festivities of the Saturnalia in 55 CE, Nero exercised his prerogative as Saturnalian King by calling upon his stepbrother Britannicus to 'rise, advance into the centre, and strike up a song' (*exsurgeret progressusque in medium cantum aliquem inciperet*). Much to Nero's dismay, Britannicus got up and ably performed a *carmen* hinting at 'his expulsion from his father's house and throne'; he left his listeners in raptures and attracted much sympathy to his cause.[159] The wording leaves open the possibility that Britannicus was reciting a poem rather than singing a song. Given the Saturnalian context, however, it would certainly not be surprising if Tacitus had some kind of musical performance in mind. The Stoic philosopher

---

[156] Col. *Rust.* 1.*praef*.3: *vocis et cantus modulatorem nec minus corporis gesticulatorem scrupulosissime requirant saltationis ac musicae rationis studiosi*.

[157] Sear 2006: 46–7.

[158] Plin. *HN* 37.19. According to Suetonius (*Nero* 21), Nero initially promised to sing *in hortis* (i.e. in the gardens of the imperial palace) at the Second Neronia. Of course, the entertainments staged in private theatres were not exclusively provided by citizen amateurs. Tacitus (*Ann.* 1.77), for instance, states that following a pantomime riot in 15 CE senators were barred from attending the houses of pantomimes and from watching pantomimes 'except in the theatre', implying that the pantomimes were used to performing in private spaces.

[159] Tac. *Ann.* 13.15.

Figure 4.7 Wall painting of a banquet scene, from Room 15 of the House of the Triclinium, Pompeii (V.2.4). Museo Archeologico Nazionale, Naples, inv. no. 120029. Credit: Akg images.

Epictetus, who was roughly contemporary with Tacitus, says that the Saturnalian king could call on someone to 'sing' (ᾆσον) on command; the reference to singing is explicit in the Greek.[160] A pair of wall paintings from the House of the Triclinium in Pompeii offer a further glimpse into the musical world of the *convivium*. The first painting (Fig. 4.7), on the north wall of the *triclinium*, shows a banquet in full swing. Above one of the diners is written the caption, *faciatis vobis suaviter ego canto* (Make yourselves comfortable, I'm going to sing!), to which his neighbour responds, *est ita valea(s)* (That's right! To your health!). The second painting (Fig. 4.8), on the east wall, shows a continuation of the same

---

[160] Epict. *Diss.* 1.25.8.

Figure 4.8 Wall painting of a banquet scene, from Room 15 of the House of the Triclinium, Pompeii (V.2.4). Museo Archeologico Nazionale, Naples, inv. no. 120030. Credit: Museo Archeologico Nazionale di Napoli.

scene. Though this painting is badly damaged, the main details are discernible. Two *tibicines* and a naked female dancer shaking castanets have appeared at the bottom-left of the picture. The man who earlier announced that he would sing is now clapping his hands to the music. And his neighbour has collapsed in a drunken stupor.[161]

For some artistically inclined Romans, performing privately in front of one's peers was not enough; the attraction of the public stage was simply too alluring to resist. We know that Roman equestrians and noblewomen had been participating sporadically in the *ludi scaenici* since the early days

---

[161] For further discussion of these paintings, see Clarke 2003: 242–5; Fröhlich 1991: 225–6.

of the Principate, if not earlier.[162] In most cases, the specific nature of these performances cannot be determined (though mimes are occasionally mentioned). Nevertheless, it would be fair to assume that many of the aristocratic men and women who appeared on the Roman stage would have engaged in singing and dancing of some sort. That they managed to perform at all was quite some feat. Several emperors before Nero had imposed laws prohibiting the sons and daughters of senators from appearing in theatrical shows or fighting as gladiators.[163] And yet, remarkably, some elites felt such an urge to perform that they willingly forfeited their equestrian rank (usually by being convicted of a minor crime) in order to exempt themselves from this restriction. Compared to being sent into exile – the punishment inflicted upon knights and senators who defied the ban – the shame of *ignominia* was a price worth paying if it meant being able to experience the thrill of stepping onto the stage.

In marked contrast to his predecessors, Nero enthusiastically encouraged members of the upper classes to participate in his games. At the *Ludi Maximi*, staged in 59 after the death of Agrippina, aristocratic men and women featured in several events, as Dio describes:

> ἐκεῖνο δὲ δὴ καὶ αἴσχιστον καὶ δεινότατον ἅμα ἐγένετο, ὅτι καὶ ἄνδρες καὶ γυναῖκες οὐχ ὅπως τοῦ ἱππικοῦ ἀλλὰ καὶ τοῦ βουλευτικοῦ ἀξιώματος ἐς τὴν ὀρχήστραν καὶ ἐς τὸν ἱππόδρομον τό τε θέατρον τὸ κυνηγετικὸν ἐσῆλθον ὥσπερ οἱ ἀτιμότατοι, καὶ ηὔλησάν τινες αὐτῶν καὶ ὠρχήσαντο τραγῳδίας τε καὶ κωμῳδίας ὑπεκρίναντο καὶ ἐκιθαρῴδησαν, ἵππους τε ἤλασαν καὶ θηρία ἀπέκτειναν καὶ ἐμονομάχησαν, οἱ μὲν ἐθελονταὶ οἱ δὲ καὶ πάνυ ἄκοντες. (Dio Cass. 62.17.3)
>
> Something took place that was at once most shameful and most appalling: both men and women not only of equestrian but also senatorial rank appeared as performers in the *orchestra*,[164] the circus and the

---

[162] At least five such occasions are recorded between 23 and 2 BCE: cf. Dio Cass. 54.2.5 (knights and noblewomen gave exhibitions on the stage in 22 BCE, prompting an official ban); Suet. *Aug.* 43.3 (Augustus banned knights from appearing on the stage or fighting as gladiators, perhaps identical with the ban of 22); Dio Cass. 53.31.3 (a knight and a distinguished woman were brought on the stage at Marcellus' aedilician games in 23 BCE); Suet. *Nero* 4 (L. Domitius Ahenobarbus brought Roman knights and matrons onto the stage as mimes in ca. 19 and 16 BCE); Dio Cass. 55.10.11 (knights and matrons appeared on the stage at the praetorian games of Quinctius Crispinus in 2 BCE). Kleijwegt (1994) notes that the Roman men of equestrian status who appeared on the stage tended to be young.

[163] Cf. Suet. *Tib.* 35.2; *Dig.* 48.5.11(10).2 (Papinian). Discussion in Slater 1994: 140–1; see also Levick 1983: 105–8, on the *senatus consultum* from Larinum. A full list of imperial measures can be found in Bodel 2015: 31, table 1.

[164] Dio's use of ὀρχήστραν is very interesting here, given the common assumption that the orchestras of Roman theatres were filled with seats for senators (on which, see Rawson 1987).

amphitheatre like the most infamous outcasts. Some of them played the pipes and danced or acted in tragedies and comedies or sang to the lyre; they drove horses, slaughtered wild animals, and fought as gladiators, some willingly and some with great reluctance.

We also hear of elite participation at the Juvenalia:

> τεκμήριον δέ, Αἰλία Κατέλλα τοῦτο μὲν γένει καὶ πλούτῳ προήκουσα, τοῦτο δὲ καὶ ἡλικίᾳ προφέρουσα (ὀγδοηκοντοῦτις γὰρ ἦν) ὠρχήσατο, οἵ τε λοιποὶ οἱ διὰ γῆρας ἢ νόσον ἰδίᾳ μηδὲν ποιῆσαι δυνάμενοι ἐχορῴδησαν. ἤσκουν μὲν γὰρ πάντες ὅ τι τις καὶ ὁπωσοῦν οἷός τε ἦν, καὶ ἐς διδασκαλεῖα ἀποδεδειγμένα συνεφοίτων οἱ ἐλλογιμώτατοι, ἄνδρες, γυναῖκες, κόραι, μειράκια, γραῖαι, γέροντες· εἰ δέ τις μὴ ἐδύνατο ἐν ἑτέρῳ τῳ θέαν παρασχεῖν, ἐς τοὺς χοροὺς κατεχωρίζετο. (Dio Cass. 62.19.2–3)

> To give an example: Aelia Catella, a woman who was not only distinguished by virtue of her birth and wealth, but also respected on account of her advanced years (she was an octogenarian), danced in a pantomime, while others, whose old age or ill health prevented them from doing anything by themselves, sang in the chorus. For everyone rehearsed whatever talent each one possessed, as best they could, and the most illustrious attended schools set aside for this purpose – men, women, girls, boys, old women, old men; if anyone failed to provide entertainment of one kind or another, they were assigned to the chorus.

According to Tacitus, large numbers of people put their names forward for consideration, many of high-ranking status:

> ... passim nomina data. non nobilitas cuiquam, non aetas aut acti honores impedimento, quo minus Graeci Latinive histrionis artem exercerent usque ad gestus modosque haud virilis. (Tac. Ann. 14.15)

> People nominated themselves on all sides. Neither noble birth, nor age, nor an official career impeded anyone from practising the art of a Greek or Latin actor, even to the point of performing gestures and songs not fit for a man.

One possibility is that he is using the term metonymically to mean 'theatre'; however, to my knowledge, this usage of ὀρχήστρα is not otherwise attested. Alternatively, Dio may be suggesting that Nero broke with Roman custom by staging musical performances in the *orchestra* (i.e. in the Greek fashion). Dio mentions elsewhere (62.29.1) that Nero once went down to the *orchestra* of the theatre to perform one of his poems. Suetonius (*Nero* 44.1), by contrast, emphasises Nero's concern for preserving traditional seating arrangements in the theatre. He did, however, go down to the *orchestra* to receive the crown in Latin oratory and poetry during the Neronia (*Nero* 12.3) and feasted with a large crowd in the *orchestra* of the Neapolitan theatre (*Nero* 20.2). The most likely explanation, therefore, is that on certain special occasions Nero had the orchestras of his theatres cleared of seating to accommodate 'Greek-style' performances.

Whether or not there is any truth to Dio's suggestion that Nero dispatched his blue-blooded recruits to special performing arts schools (διδασκαλεῖα ἀποδεδειγμένα), the logical conclusion is that the men, women and children who starred in his shows already possessed at least a modicum of technical proficiency, especially when it came to dancing (ὠρχήσαντο), singing (ἐχορῴδησαν) and playing instruments (ηὔλησάν ... ἐκιθαρῴδησαν).

Clearly not everyone was coerced. Shadi Bartsch has emphasised the fact that, of all the references to aristocratic participation in Nero's games, only two individuals are specifically named as being negligent or resistant in their acting. These are the senators Thrasea Paetus and Vespasian.[165] Significantly, Tacitus reveals that Thrasea 'had sung in tragic costume' (*habitu tragico cecinerat*) at ancient games in his native town of Patavium.[166] Performing at a traditional local festival in one's native town was very different from performing on the great stages of Rome. But the fact remains that Thrasea still possessed the desire and the ability to sing in public. How many others shared the same inclination? Tacitus emphasises the willingness of the majority of the participants at the Neronia.[167] At the Juvenalia, people even 'put their names forward' for consideration (*nomina data*). We also hear of specific instances of senatorial support for Nero's theatrical ventures. Fabius Valens, consul in 69, had as a young man acted in mimes at the Juvenalia, 'initially out of compulsion, but soon out of desire' (*velut ex necessitate, mox sponte*).[168] Vitellius presided over the contests of the First Neronia and eagerly urged the emperor to perform in the competition for citharodes.[169] The former consul Cluvius Rufus served as Nero's herald at the Second Neronia and throughout the tour of Greece. With the partial exception of Fabius Valens, there is no suggestion that any of these individuals acted reluctantly.[170]

Another way of participating in Nero's games was to serve as an Augustianus – that is, as a member of his official cheer squad. Tacitus and Dio state that the Augustiani were initially formed at the Juvenalia.[171]

---

[165] Bartsch 1994: 6. Thrasea: Dio Cass. 61.20.4. Vespasian: Tac. *Ann.* 16.5, Suet. *Vesp.* 4.4, Dio Cass. 64.11. In Tacitus' account, Vespasian falls asleep during Nero's recital at the Second Neronia, whereas Suetonius and Dio place the incident during the tour of Greece. It is unclear which of these alternatives, if either, we should believe.

[166] Tac. *Ann.* 16.21; Dio Cass. 62.26.3–4.

[167] Tac. *Ann.* 14.21: *pluribus ipsa licentia placebat*. At least some of the performers at the *Ludi Maximi* volunteered of their own volition, according to Dio (οἱ μὲν ἐθελονταί; 62.17.3).

[168] Tac. *Hist.* 3.62.   [169] Tac. *Hist.* 2.71; cf. Suet. *Vit.* 11.2.

[170] Suet. *Nero* 21.2; Dio Cass. 62.14.3.   [171] Tac. *Ann.* 14.15; Dio Cass. 62.20.3–4.

According to Tacitus, the group consisted of Roman *equites*, who were 'conspicuous for their youthful vigour' (*aetate ac robore conspicui*). Dio says that there were 5000 members in total, but makes no reference to their social status, describing them only as 'soldiers' (στρατιῶται). Suetonius refers to the Augustiani solely in connection with Nero's debut in Naples, noting that the claques consisted of 'young men of equestrian rank' (*adulescentos equestris ordinis*), plus an additional 5000 plebeians 'of vigorous youth' (*quinque amplius milia e plebe robustissimae iuventutis*).[172] It would appear, therefore, that there were two distinct stages in the development of the organisation, centred on the two performances in 59 and 64. However, the lack of clarity in our sources is a problem. Were there 5000 Augustiani to begin with, as Dio claims, or does this number reflect the plebeian contingent that was added later on, as Suetonius suggests? And how much credence do we give to the idea that the group was originally made up exclusively of young equestrian men?[173]

One fact about the Augustiani that emerges clearly from all three sources is their age profile. These claqueurs, 'distinguished by their sleek hairstyles and outstanding appearance' (*pinguissima coma et excellentissimo cultu*), represented the very finest specimens of *Romana iuventus*.[174] Their idiosyncratic style of 'musical acclamations' (*modulatis ... laudationibus*) must have been something to behold. Young, attractive and musically gifted, these men perfectly embodied the ideals of Neronian masculinity.

The purpose of the Augustiani was not just to make Nero look good, however. They also acted as intermediaries between the *princeps* and his audience, helping ordinary spectators to make sense of and engage with the performance. Dio informs us that the Augustiani were assigned the task of instructing the general populace in the proper forms of applause (ἐξῆρχον τῶν ἐπαίνων). It is surely no accident that, when Nero took to the stage for the first time in Rome, his listeners knew exactly how to respond: in Tacitus' narrative, the chanting and clapping of the urban *plebs* exhibits all the hallmarks of a trained chorus (*personabat certis modis plausuque composito*), and stands in stark contrast to the flagging incompetence of the Italian provincials, whose hands could not keep up (*manibus nesciis fatiscerent*); 'uninitiated' (*inexperti*), they were bullied into submission by Nero's cronies, lest any moment should pass 'in unsuitable clamour or

---

[172] Suet. *Nero* 20.3.
[173] For discussion of these issues, see Bartsch 1994: 7–9; Bradley 1978b: 127–8; Mourgues 1988, 1990.
[174] Suet. *Nero* 20.3.

sluggish silence' (*inpari clamore aut silentio segni*).¹⁷⁵ In this way, as Alan Cameron points out, the Augustiani usurped the role traditionally played by theatre claques (organised groups of clappers and applauders).¹⁷⁶ Like Nero himself, the Augustiani were meant to be viewed and admired, but they also encouraged the audience at large to become participants in their own spectacle. As we have seen, the Roman people had a natural inclination for memorising and performing songs and gestures in the theatre. The Augustiani provided the means and the licence for them to indulge that inclination – all in the name of celebrating the emperor.

The ancient sources give a misleading impression of Nero's musicality as totally alien to the aristocratic society in which he was raised. In fact, many well-born Romans of Nero's generation had access to lessons in singing, dancing and instrumental performance (especially lyre-playing). Roman banqueters traded songs with one another while dining and celebrating festivals like the Saturnalia. Some members of the upper classes commissioned private theatres to be built on their estates and even contrived opportunities to perform publicly in a variety of musical and dramatic disciplines. These activities seem to have been driven especially by well-educated adolescent men of around the same age as Nero. It was to this demographic that Nero felt perhaps the greatest affinity. Like all successful demagogues before him, he collapsed the boundaries between performer and spectator. He styled himself as the champion of a Roman youth culture which had long valorised the display of artistic prowess. And by encouraging his subjects to share in his musical endeavours, he broke down the stigma associated with putting oneself on show.

Of course, in considering the phenomenon of elite participation, various motivations must be taken into account. No doubt there were many who enrolled as performers in the hope of social advancement or financial reward, or indeed out of fear of incurring the emperor's wrath, as the sources would have us believe. And yet, the disguised motivations of individual actors would hardly have affected the overall impression of the spectacle. Nero's productions enacted social conformity on a grand scale, presenting a vision of young and old, elite and non-elite, united through a shared participation in performance. The *princeps iuventutis*, 'first of all

---

[175] Tac. *Ann.* 16.4–5.
[176] Cameron 1976: 234–5. These claques were held responsible for several violent incidents in the decades prior to Nero's accession. Pantomimes were banned from appearing at the Neronia apparently because of concerns over recent outbreaks of partisan rivalry (Tac. *Ann.* 14.21). However, cf. Tac. *Ann.* 13.25, on Nero's encouragement of theatre claques (*fautores histrionum*) earlier in his reign.

Romans from the beginning of time', was the charismatic prodigy at the centre of it all.[177]

Conclusion

This chapter has offered a new perspective on the musical activities of the emperor Nero. I have argued that Nero's music-making responded to, and drew energy from, the cultural interests of the Roman people, bringing together different groups of society for whom singing and dancing provided a happy relief from the humdrum monotony of daily life. The 'New Apollo' fostered a spirit of *joie de vivre* that combined elements of traditional Augustan imagery with a novel imperial persona: youthful, larger-than-life, and, for many, excitingly transgressive. In this way, Nero succeeded in creating and disseminating an original musical language (*carmina Neronis*, the 'Master's Songbook'), which repackaged elements of Greek culture into a distinctly Roman product optimised for mass consumption. His attempt to rebrand himself as an organist and bagpiper represented a final, radical affirmation of his passionate commitment to popular music.

Although Nero's music-making was not the primary cause of his downfall, it certainly contributed to his alienation from the Senate and the army. It also played a role in creating the myth of Nero the monster. The ancient authors to whom we owe our image of the man who 'fiddled while Rome burned' were well-versed in the rhetoric of musical criticism and found in this rhetoric a rich vocabulary of contempt. Nero's music – so these authors claim – made a mockery of the principate and of Rome itself: a generation of Roman knights was corrupted by the 'sweetness' (*dulcedo*) of his singing, his 'unmanly gestures and tunes' (*gestus modosque haud virilis*) and 'emasculated sounds' (*fractos sonos*).[178] And yet, while these opinions may reflect the views of some elites, they certainly do not represent the views of *all* elites, either in Nero's time or in other periods. Thus, if we are to have any hope of recovering a faithful image of the man behind the myth, we must pay close attention to the diversity of beliefs and practices which comprised the musical world of Neronian Rome. Musomania may have hastened Nero's demise and ensured his posthumous damnation, but it also allowed him to connect with his subjects on a profound level, both in life and in death.

---

[177] During Nero's triumphal procession into Rome in 67 CE, men carried inscribed placards which referred to the *princeps* as πρῶτος πάντων τῶν ἀπὸ τοῦ αἰῶνος Ῥωμαίων (Dio Cass. 62.20.2–3).

[178] Tac. *Ann.* 14.20.

Epilogue

In his famous satire on the perils of cosmopolitanism, Juvenal bemoans the transformation of Rome into a 'Greek city' (*Graeca urbs*), inundated with filthy immigrants and littered with cultural imports from the East. Speaking through the character Umbricius, the poet conjures up the graphic image of a stream of exotic goods flowing westwards from Syria and polluting the pure waters of the Tiber. Various types of goods are listed, but special prominence is given to musical instruments: 'The Syrian Orontes has long since flowed into the Tiber, bringing its language, customs, slanted strings along with pipers (*cum tibicine chordas obliquas*), native drums (*nec non gentilia tympana*), and girls ordered to offer themselves at the Circus.'[1] Strings, pipes, drums – all had their proper place in Roman life. But these were not the instruments of traditional Roman ritual: they were symbols of oriental luxury and illicit pleasure, contaminated by their association with the Syrian musician-cum-prostitute. For the girls who stood outside the Circus Maximus offering their services to passers-by were not just sex workers, but also skilled entertainers (and they might just as often have been found performing *inside* the Circus during the games).[2] As long as these foreign starlets commanded the eyes and ears of Roman audiences, as long as the slanted strings of the *sambuca* and the tambourines beloved by the worshippers of Cybele had a place in the city, Roman vice would continue to run rampant.

Juvenal's cynical assessment of Roman musical culture at the turn of the second century CE resonates with many of the themes explored in this book. We have seen how music served as a key marker of Roman identity, distinguishing citizen and foreigner, elite and plebeian, male and female, and old and young. Music had a particularly important bearing on the performance of gender: some kinds were associated with a 'hardening'

---

[1] Juv. 3.62–5.
[2] See Fear 1991 on the *ambubaiae*, a term for a kind of Syrian showgirl-cum-prostitute deriving from the Aramaic word for pipe (*abbub* or *abbuba*); cf. Schol. Hor. *Sat.* 1.2.2: *ambubaiae dicuntur mulieres tibicinae lingua Syrorum. etenim Syris tibia sive symphonia ambubaia dicitur.* Nero enjoyed watching *ambubaiae* while dining in the Circus Maximus: Suet. *Ner.* 27.

effect on both mind and body, others with a 'softening' effect. This dichotomy is evident already in the speech of Scipio Aemilianus Africanus from 129 BCE, attacking the effeminate dancing of the *cinaeduli*. We have also seen how music helped the Romans to make sense of the present and its relation to the past, often by accentuating the moral failings of the current generation. Music thus played an important role in the formation of the Romans' historical memory.

In highlighting these themes, this book has taken a different approach from previous scholarship on ancient Roman music. Rather than attempting to characterise Roman musical culture solely on its own terms, I have focused on probing the intersections between music, politics and society. In doing so, I have promoted a more holistic and pluralistic model of Roman musical culture. As emphasised in the Introduction, the acts of singing and playing musical instruments assumed very different meanings depending on the sociological and psychological contexts in which they took place. Not everyone in Rome danced to the same tune. Furthermore, the boundaries of musical culture were never clearly defined. The Greek concept of *mousike*, encompassing song, dance, poetry and drama, continued to exert a strong influence in Roman thought and social practice. Because the Romans often encountered music in the context of the *ludi* and the *convivium*, they could also group musical activities conceptually with other types of public and private entertainment, including stage performances, chariot-racing and gladiatorial contests. The *ars musica* expanded the parameters of 'music' further still, placing the study of rhythm, harmony and metre within the broader scope of the liberal arts (including grammar, rhetoric, geometry, arithmetic and astronomy). Attempts to define *musica Romana* as an isolated phenomenon are thus doomed to failure. If we wish to comprehend the true vitality and dynamism of the Roman musical experience, we must acknowledge the myriad ways in which music was woven into the fabric of Roman society.

In this epilogue, I summarise the findings of the previous chapters and assess what I believe to be the major contributions of this book to the broader field of ancient Roman history. I will concentrate on three areas in particular: the relationship between music and social class; Roman responses to Greek music; and the use of music as a political tool.

First, what can the study of music tell us about social class at Rome? Within the field of ethnomusicology, it has often been asserted that music functions as a kind of social leveller, uniting people of disparate backgrounds, cultures and beliefs.³ Certainly, among the communities of the ancient Mediterranean world, music was a ubiquitous feature of civic life. It was a language understood by all. From the rhythmic chanting of crowds in the forum and the theatre to the boisterous songs sung by soldiers during the triumph, music had a unique power to transcend social boundaries and to generate a sense of community.

Although it is difficult to gauge precisely, there does not appear to have been a great difference in the musical tastes of upper- and lower-class Romans. The musical entertainments of the theatre always attracted a socially mixed audience. Moreover, the enslaved (or formerly enslaved) musicians who performed at the banquets of wealthy aristocrats and emperors did not remain entirely out of the public eye. Some would have been rented out or donated to the producers of public games or local festivals, thereby gaining prominence among audiences of lower social rank. Others might have belonged to a *collegium* made up of *symphoniaci*, *tibicines* or *scabillarii* (players of the *scabellum*), which are attested in large numbers in Rome and throughout Italy. An inscription found at Spoletum (about 120 kilometres north of Rome) and dated to the first half of the second century CE provides an interesting insight into the dynamics of musical patronage. The inscription commemorates an equestrian named M. Septimius Septimianus, who served as a member of the town council of Spoletum and acted as patron to a group of four *scabillarii* attached to the local theatre. Although the social status of the *scabillarii* is not clearly spelled out in the text, it is possible that these musicians were the freedmen of Septimius Septimianus himself and had been placed at the disposal of the city in an act of euergetism. The *scabillarii* may have put on private shows for Septimianus and his friends as well as performing in theatrical spectacles produced for the citizens of Spoletum.⁴

---

³ See, e.g., Nettl 2005: 42–9.
⁴ *CIL* 11.4813 = *ILS* 5272 = *AE* 2005: 161, no. 439: *M(arco) Septimio | M(arci) fil(io) Hor(atia) | Septimiano, | equo publico, IIIIvir(o) i(ure) d(icundo), | praef(ecto) fabr(um) Romae, | dec(uriae) IV scamillar(iorum) (sic) | operae veteres | a scaena, patrono ob | merita eius l(oco) d(ato) d(ecreto) d(ecurionum)*. See discussion in Peyras 2002 and Vincent 2008. Papyri from Roman Egypt provide additional evidence for the circulation of enslaved musicians. The slave(s) in question would be dispatched with the owner's permission to a nearby town or village to perform at a local festival (see Westermann 1924 for examples). We can also compare the case of the pantomimes owned by Ummidia Quadratilla, a noblewoman who lived in the time of Pliny the Younger. Ummidia enjoyed watching the pantomimes perform at home, but they also made appearances *in theatro*, where audiences would mimic their gestures *cum canticis* (along with the songs): Plin. *Ep.* 7.24, with discussion in Sick 1999: 340. Did Ummidia also own the musicians who accompanied the pantomimes' performances?

Nevertheless, we should be careful not to eradicate any distinction between highbrow and lowbrow music at Rome. Roman elites engaged in a set of exclusionary practices intended to mark out their musical culture as intellectually and morally superior to that of the masses. Some undertook training in music theory, eager to capitalise on the prestige conferred by a well-rounded education. Others advertised their status by having musicians perform at their behest, whether in the context of private events (e.g. banquets, weddings and funerals) or public events such as games and triumphs (and the more musicians one had at one's disposal, the better). Having access to musical entertainment on demand was a luxury which only the very wealthiest could attain. The *symphonia*, despite its links to the world of public spectacle, connoted a level of wealth that was unimaginable for the vast majority of Romans.

First and foremost, however, the division between elite and popular music was ideological. Throughout history, the people's music has come under assault from the gatekeepers of 'High' culture.[5] Rome was no exception in this regard. Roman aristocratic society attached a strong stigma to public performance of any kind. The outlets of mass musical culture (especially the theatre) were attacked by conservative elites as breeding grounds for immorality and lawlessness. The speeches of Cato the Elder and Scipio Aemilianus, chastising members of the Senate for singing too freely and instructing their children in the performing arts, highlight an additional concern that the music of the masses would infiltrate the corridors of power, corrupting Rome's political leaders. Anxieties surrounding the pedagogical function of music continued to flare up throughout the imperial period: young men are reprimanded for their 'repulsive obsession for singing and dancing' (*cantandi saltandique obscena studia*); and girls of respectable birth are warned against taking up musical instruments which might associate them with lower-class prostitutes.[6]

Moral arguments about music carried weight only so long as there were people who opposed them. Accounts of high-ranking men and women aspiring to quasi-professional levels of musicianship, though exaggerated, are not wholly unsubstantiated. For as much as Nero's music-making offended aristocratic sensibilities, there was no shortage of senators and

---

[5] See Marsh 2013: 59–63, 73–87, on the opposition to popular music in Early Modern England, and Godbolt 1984: 3–4, 8, 11–12, 29, on the hostile reception of jazz music in early twentieth-century Britain.

[6] Sen. *Contr.* 1.praef.8; Quint. *Inst.* 1.10.31; Jer. *Ep.* 107.8. Cf. also Ov. *Ars am.* 3.505, warning girls against taking up the *tibia* lest they should seem unattractive to potential suitors.

equestrians willing to cheer on and, indeed, to participate in the emperor's performances. Whatever their personal motivations for doing so, the important point is that these individuals were willing and able to transgress the traditional moral injunction against performance. Nero's reign was exceptional, admittedly, but it can be seen as the culmination of a long pattern of Roman musomania going back to the time of Cato and Scipio in the second century BCE. While the boundary between highbrow and lowbrow music was certainly a marked one, it was not entirely impermeable.

For the most part, elite insecurities about musical performance probably had a negligible impact on what the lower classes actually heard and thought. Varro's satire *Onos Lyras* (*Donkey [Hears] the Lyre*) does hint at the potential diffusion of elite ideas about music among a broader cross-section of Roman society, but it is a difficult source to interpret for several reasons and does not necessarily provide an accurate reflection of musical attitudes among the general population. Despite the protests of certain influential figures within the political establishment, music continued to flow freely through the conduits of popular culture. However, the Roman authorities did make sporadic attempts to police the public consumption of music. The ban on the *ludus talarius*, issued by the censors of 115 BCE, offers a particularly striking example of musical censorship: rightly or wrongly, the ban was linked by Fronto to concerns about the encroaching influence of popular music within the civic sphere (the catchy rhythms of the castanets and cymbals disturbed the censor as he went about his official business). Similarly, the Augustan and Julio-Claudian laws against public performance, though not confined strictly to music-making, prescribed stringent punishments for Roman citizens who sang and danced on the stage.

In summary, the study of music contributes to our understanding of the broad spectrum of Roman social relations. It encourages us to conceive of Roman society as a complex and diverse entity, made up of various, often conflicting, subcultures. There was no single musical culture which united all of Rome's inhabitants. Rather, music gave rise to a multiplicity of beliefs and behaviours, some of which eroded social hierarchies and some of which reinforced them. Thus, if we want to understand the full impact of music on Roman society, we cannot afford to focus exclusively on the dominant elite view represented by our literary sources; we must take account of the heterogeneous and contradictory responses which music generated among elites and non-elites alike.

The theme of social class dovetails closely with the second major theme of this book: the relationship between Greek and Roman music. This theme can be subdivided into two main categories. The first category concerns Roman responses to Greek *ideas* about music (especially Platonic ideals about harmony and musical *ethos*) and the second concerns Roman responses to Greek musical *practice*. For too long, scholars have clung onto the assumption that the Romans did not develop a musical identity of their own. This assumption is both lazy and unhelpful. Roman thinkers did not simply regurgitate Greek precepts without thought. The difficult task for the historian is to discern precisely which strands within the various Roman arguments about music derive from Plato and other Greek theorists, and which strands are intertwined with the lived experiences of a given author. There is no denying that the Romans, in formulating their conception of music, drew heavily on the teachings of Platonism, Stoicism, Pythagoreanism and Epicureanism. They also drew heavily on Greek musical terminology. Nevertheless, it would be wrong to assume on this basis that the Romans merely copied the Greeks. The salient question is not whether the Romans relied on Greek models, but rather how they adapted these models to address contemporary issues and to mould their own reality (or the reality they wished to create). After all, the Romans inhabited a very different world from that of Plato and Aristotle. As James Zetzel rightly points out, Greek culture 'achieve[d] meaning and significance' for Roman elites 'only in and for a social context'; it had to 'contribute to the reinforcement of societal values' and speak to present-day needs and concerns.[7] It is important, therefore, to pay close attention to the different ways in which Greek ideas about music were put to work in the service of Roman politics and ideology. For example, Cato the Elder, in enshrining the tradition of *carmina convivalia*, created a kind of Roman analogue to the sympotic songs of ancient Greece. And yet, in doing so, ironically, he sought to protect the integrity of Roman aristocratic culture against the perceived encroachment of Hellenic luxury. During the late Republic, Cicero used the Platonic concept of musical revolution to model the decline of Roman society under the influence of radical populism. A generation later, Augustus transformed the image of Apollo Citharoedus into a powerful symbol of Roman political *harmonia*. This subsequently inspired Nero to work Apollo into his own imperial self-fashioning. Each of these adaptations involved active engagement on the part of Roman political leaders.

---

[7] Zetzel 2003: 134, 137.

The second part of the Greek/Rome dichotomy is the Romans' response to Greek musical practice. To be sure, Greek musical styles and performers enjoyed remarkable popularity at Rome from an early date. From around the early second century BCE, Roman elites began to stage elaborate Greek-inspired theatrical productions which advertised their political influence and cultural sophistication. Around the same time, Greek musicians and music teachers were assimilated into the patronage networks and households of affluent Romans.

These developments went hand in hand with a mounting senatorial opposition to the musical cultures of the Hellenistic East. Music figures especially prominently in the anti-Hellenic discourse of the mid-to-late Republic and early Principate. Citizens who cultivated strong ties with musicians from the Greek East or who undertook practical training under their tutelage are frequently accused of overstepping the bounds of acceptability. Cornelius Nepos presents the issue most starkly in the introduction to his *Life of Epaminondas*: 'We know that, according to our customs, music is not in keeping with the personality of a leading citizen, while dancing is even counted among the vices; all these things are considered pleasing and praiseworthy among the Greeks.'[8] Nepos' comments have been cited uncritically by some scholars as evidence of the Romans' antipathy towards music in general.[9] However, what is at stake in Nepos' comparison is not the question of Roman 'musicality' as such, but rather the idea of dancing and playing instruments as disreputable activities, which incurred the same social stigma as appearing on the stage or prostituting oneself.[10]

The existence of such radically polarised attitudes to Greek musical practice is consistent with modern conceptions of 'Hellenisation'. The traditional view of the Romans as boorish imitators of Greek culture has long since been abandoned by scholars working in the fields of philology, history, archaeology and philosophy (the term 'Hellenisation' itself is a problematic label for describing the interactions between Greeks and Romans, since it implicitly privileges the notion of one-way cultural exchange). The Romans were not passive consumers of Greek music. Nor did they fall neatly into pro-music and anti-music camps. The Romans'

---

[8] Nep. *Ep.* 1.2: *scimus enim musicen nostris moribus abesse a principis persona, saltare vero etiam in vitiis poni; quae omnia apud Graecos et grata et laude digna ducuntur.*

[9] As early as the eighteenth century, the English musicologist John Hawkins (1719–1789) cited the biographer as 'the fullest testimony' to the fact that the Romans held the 'science [of music] in small estimation' (Hawkins 1776: xxvi).

[10] Cf. Nep. *Pref.* 1–5.

stance on Greek music was usually situational rather than strictly ideological. For example, an orator delivering a political or legal speech might be expected to adopt a conservative attitude to music, since the situation demanded that he should cultivate an image of himself as a man of unimpeachable moral character. And yet, in another setting – during a *convivium*, for example – that same individual might have taken a much more liberal stance, secure in the knowledge that singing and dancing were deemed socially acceptable on such occasions. In short, the study of music highlights the dynamic and often paradoxical nature of Greek and Roman cultural exchange. For this reason, it deserves a more prominent place in the ongoing scholarly debate about the nature of Hellenisation.

This brings us to the third and final major theme of the book: the role of music as a political tool. Each of the previous chapters has painted a picture of how competing political actors used music to advance their own self-interests. Chapter 1 focused on the musical games of the praetor L. Anicius Gallus in 167 BCE. Through a close analysis of Polybius' narrative, I argued that Anicius' orchestration of the spectacle was cleverly designed to magnify the importance of his military victory. I also discussed how the spread of new musical styles from the East incurred the hostility of prominent members of the senatorial class, including Cato the Elder and Scipio Aemilianus. Chapter 2 centred on the musical politics of the late Republic, emphasising in particular the role of music in framing the contest between *optimates* and *populares*. Whereas *optimates* like Cicero sought to keep music controlled, *populares* used music to incite their supporters, as the rhetorical tactics of Gaius Gracchus and Publius Clodius demonstrate. Chapter 3 was structured around another contest – namely, the contest between the Dionysian music of Mark Antony and the Apollonian music of Octavian/Augustus. Although Antony's love of music is represented in the sources as a sign of his depraved character, his patronage of musicians can be seen as a calculated strategy designed to win political support among the local populations under his control. Finally, in Chapter 4, we looked at the new political culture which the emperor Nero attempted to create through his use of music. His musicianship might have won him the support of the lower classes and the young metropolitan elite, but it came at a heavy cost: abandoned by the military and the Senate, he was remembered by posterity as a narcissistic tyrant, whose obsession with music brought shame upon the Roman people and accelerated the descent into civil war.

Nero's downfall reminds us that Roman leaders did not always get what they wanted from the game of musical politics. Indeed, there was always the possibility that their rivals or subordinates would turn the music *against* them. The ribald verses sung by soldiers during the triumph in mockery of their general were probably no more than harmless jests, taken in good spirit by the *triumphator*. But on other occasions mass singing had a rather more serious intent. Chanted acclamations (*acclamationes*) during the games, for example, served as 'a powerful tool in the expression of popular will' and 'depended on rhythm for their momentum'.[11] During the imperial period, they provided a central mode of interaction between *plebs* and *princeps*, allowing Roman spectators to express approval of the emperor or to voice complaints against him. Similarly, satirical songs used the language of music to mock certain political figures (recall, for example, the chants of Clodius' supporters against Pompey, likened by Plutarch to a trained choir). Song was an effective medium for such attacks for two reasons. Firstly, singing was a collective and spontaneous act. This provided a cloak of anonymity, since the originators of the songs were hard to detect. Secondly, the songs were easily memorised and reperformed, allowing for the rapid dissemination of politically charged messages.

Assessing the musicality of Roman acclamations and protest songs is often more challenging than one might suspect, since the language used by our sources is notoriously imprecise (the usual terms are *carmina* or *versus*). However, our picture is enriched considerably by the evidence from Late Antiquity. The early leaders of the Church exploited the medium of song as a way of both fostering group cohesion and converting heretics and non-believers to orthodox Christianity.[12] Songs of this kind could range from single repeated phrases to elaborate melodies with multiple verses. Augustine's *Psalm Against the Donatists*, composed in the 380s CE, has even been described as 'the western world's first known pop song'.[13] When Augustine reflected on the success of the *Psalm* some three and a half decades after its composition, he pointed specifically to the song's appeal among 'the ignorant and the uneducated', noting how he was able to 'fix it in their memories' by structuring it around the letters of the Latin alphabet (each of the twenty stanzas starts with a different letter of the alphabet).[14] Like other leaders before him, Augustine realised that the connection between music and memory held the key to unlocking the hearts and minds of ordinary Romans.

There is much about the musical life of ancient Rome that remains frustratingly out of reach to the modern historian. As close as we may come to rediscovering the lost sounds of Roman music, we will never be able to

---

[11] Coleman 2011: 347. [12] See Shaw 2011: 441–89; Grig 2013. [13] Shaw 2011: 476.
[14] Aug. *Retract.* 1.20 (trans. Shaw).

capture the real thing. However, if we tune our ears to the ancient sources, we can still hear the echoes of this music in the Romans' imagination and way of life. In the process, we can gain a deeper appreciation of how Roman attitudes and social practices evolved, how Roman culture converged with and diverged from Greek culture, and how Roman politicians and political dissidents presented themselves in the civic sphere. Above all, I hope that this book has made a compelling case for integrating music into the broader scope of Roman social and political history.

Bibliography

Adolf, H. (1950), 'The Ass and the Harp', *Speculum* 25: 49–57.

Alcock, S. E. (1994), 'Nero at Play? The Emperor's Graecian Odyssey', in *Reflections of Nero: Culture, History and Representation*, eds. J. Elsner and J. Masters. London: 98–111.

Aldrete, G. S. (1999), *Gestures and Acclamations in Ancient Rome*. Baltimore, MD and London.

Alexandrescu, C.-G. (2010), *Blasmusiker und Standartenträger im römischen Heer. Untersuchungen zur Benennung, Funktion und Ikonographie*. Cluj-Napoca.

Alföldi, A. and Alföldi, E. (1990), *Die Kontorniat-Medaillons*. 2 vols. Berlin and New York, NY.

Alonso Fernández, Z. (2015), '*Docta Saltatrix*: Body Knowledge, Culture, and Corporeal Discourse in Female Roman Dance', *Phoenix* 69: 304–33.

Aneziri, S. (2003), *Die Vereine der dionysischen Techniten im Kontext der hellenistischen Gesellschaft: Untersuchungen zur Geschichte, Organisation und Wirkung der hellenistischen Technitenvereine*. Stuttgart.

(2007), 'The Organisation of Music Contests in the Hellenistic Period and Artists' Participation: An Attempt at Classification', in *The Greek Theatre and Festivals: Documentary Studies*, ed. P. Wilson. Oxford: 67–84.

(2009), 'World Travellers: The Associations of the Artists of Dionysus', in *Wandering Poets in Ancient Greek Culture: Travel, Locality, and Pan-Hellenism*, eds. R. Hunter and I. Rutherford. Cambridge: 217–36.

Antcliffe, H. (1949), 'What Music Meant to the Romans', *Music & Letters* 30: 337–44.

Armstrong, D. (1986), 'Stylistics and the Date of Calpurnius Siculus', *Philologus* 130: 113–36.

Asmis, E. (1995), 'Epicurean Poetics', in *Philodemus and His Poetry: Poetic Theory and Practice in Lucretius, Philodemus, and Horace*, ed. D. Obbink. New York, NY and Oxford: 15–34.

Astbury, R. (1985), *M. Terentii Varonis saturarum Menippearum fragmenta*. Leipzig.

Astin, A. E. (1978), *Cato the Censor*. Oxford.

Auvray-Assayas, C. and Delattre, D. (eds.) (2001), *Cicéron et Philodème: La polémique en philosophie*. Paris.

Baines, A. (1960), *Bagpipes*. Oxford.

Baldwin, B. (1995), 'Better Late than Early: Reflections on the Date of Calpurnius Siculus', *Illinois Classical Studies* 20: 157–77.

Balsdon, J. P. V. D. (1966), 'Fabula Clodiana', *Historia* 15: 65–73.

Barchiesi, A. (2002), 'The Uniqueness of the Carmen Saeculare and its Tradition', in *Traditions and Contexts in the Poetry of Horace*, eds. A. J. Woodman and D. C. Feeney. Cambridge: 107–23.

(2005), 'Learned Eyes: Poets, Viewers, Image Makers', in *The Cambridge Companion to the Age of Augustus*, ed. K. Galinksy. Cambridge: 281–305.

Barja de Quiroga, P. L. (2018), 'The Quinquatrus of June, Marsyas and Libertas in the Late Roman Republic', *Classical Quarterly* 68: 143–59.

Barker, A. (1984), *Greek Musical Writings, Vol. I: The Musician and His Art*. Cambridge.

(1989), *Greek Musical Writings, Vol. II: Harmonic and Acoustic Theory*. Cambridge.

(1994), 'Greek Musicologists in the Roman Empire', *Apeiron* 27: 53–74.

(2010), '*Phōnaskia* for Singers and Orators. The Care and Training of the Voice in the Roman Empire', in *La musica nell'Impero Romano: Testimonianze teoriche e scoperte archeologiche*. Atti del secondo convegno annuale di MOISA, Cremona, 30–31 ottobre 2008, ed. E. Rocconi. Pavia: 11–20.

(2011), 'Music, Politics and Diplomacy in Hellenistic Teos', in *Music and Cultural Politics in Greece and Chinese Societies, Vol. 1: Greek Antiquity*, ed. D. Yatromanolakis. Cambridge, MA and London: 159–79.

(2014), *Ancient Greek Writers on their Musical Past: Studies in Greek Musical Historiography*. Pisa.

(2017), 'Dionysius of Halicarnassus on Rome's Greek Musical Heritage', *Greek and Roman Musical Studies* 5: 63–81.

Bartsch, S. (1994), *Actors in the Audience: Theatricality and Doublespeak from Nero to Hadrian*. Cambridge, MA.

Bartsch, S., Freudenburg, K. and Littlewood, C. (eds.) (2017), *The Cambridge Companion to the Age of Nero*. Cambridge.

Baudot, A. (1973), *Musiciens romains de l'antiquité*. Montreal.

Beacham, R. C. (1991), *The Roman Theatre and Its Audience*. London.

(1999), *Spectacle Entertainments of Early Imperial Rome*. New Haven, CT and London.

(2016), 'The Theatre of Pompey', *Classical Review* 66: 546–8.

Beacham, R. C. and Denard, H. (2003), 'The Pompey Project: Digital Research and Virtual Reconstruction of Rome's First Theatre', *Computers and the Humanities* 37: 129–39.

Beard, M. (2003), 'The Triumph of the Absurd: Roman Street Theatre', in *Rome the Cosmopolis*, eds. C. Edwards and G. Woolf. Cambridge: 21–43.

(2007), *The Roman Triumph*. Cambridge, MA.

Beard, M., North, J. and Price, S. R. F. (1998), *Religions of Rome. Vol. 2: A Sourcebook*. Cambridge.

Becatti, G. (1935), 'Timarchides e l'Apollo qui tenet citharam', *Bolletino della Commissione Archeologica Communale in Rome* 63: 111–31.

Bélis, A. (1986), 'L'aulos phrygien', *Revue Archéologique* 48: 21–40.

   (1988a), 'Les termes grecs et latins désignant des spécialités musicales', *Revue de Philologie* 62: 227–50.

   (1988b), 'Κρούπεζαι, Scabellum', *Bulletin de Correspondance Hellénique* 112: 323–39.

   (1989), 'Néron musicien', *Comptes rendus de l'Académie des Inscriptions et Belles-Lettres* 133: 747–68.

   (1999), *Les musiciens dans l'Antiquité*. Paris.

Bell, A. J. E. (2004), *Spectacular Power in the Greek and Roman City*. Oxford.

Bellia, A. (2012), *Strumenti musicali e oggetti sonori nell'Italia meridionale e in Sicilia (VI–III sec. a.C.). Funzioni rituali e contesti*. Lucca.

Bergmann, M. (2002), 'Hatte Nero ein politisches und/oder kulturelles Programm? Zur Inschrift von Akraiphia', in *Neronia VI: Rome à l'époque néronienne*, eds. J.-M. Croisille and Y. Perrin. Brussels: 273–84.

   (2013), 'Portraits of an Emperor: Nero, the Sun, and Roman Otium', in *A Companion to the Neronian Age*, eds. E. Buckley and M. T. Dinter. Malden and Oxford: 332–62.

Beschi, L. (2009), 'L'organo idraulico (*hydraulis*): una invenzione ellenistica dal grande futuro', in *La Musa dimenticata: Aspetti dell'esperienza musicale greca in età ellenistica*, eds. M. C. Martinelli, F. Pelosi and C. Pernigotti. Pisa: 247–66.

Betts, E. (2011), 'Towards a Multisensory Experience of Movement in the City of Rome', in *Rome, Ostia, Pompeii: Movement and Space*, eds. R. Laurence and D. Newsome. Oxford: 118–32.

Birt, T. (1928), *Das Kulturleben der Griechen und Römer in seiner Entwicklung*. Leipzig.

Blank, D. (2009), '*Philosophia* and *technê*: Epicureans on the arts', in *The Cambridge Companion to Epicureanism*, ed. J. Warren. Cambridge: 216–33.

Bodel, J. (2015), 'Status Dissonance and Status Dissidents in the Equestrian Order', in *Social Status and Prestige in the Graeco-Roman World*, ed. A. B. Kuhn. Stuttgart: 29–44.

Bonaria, M. (1983), 'La musica conviviale del mondo latino antico al medioevo', in *Spettacoli conviviali dall' antichita classica alle corti italiane del '400. Atti del VII Convegno di Studio*, ed. F. Doglio. Viterbo: 119–47.

Bonavia-Hunt, N. A. (1969), *Horace the Minstrel: A Practical and Aesthetic Study of his Aeolic Verse*. Kineton.

Bonner, S. F. (2012), *Education in Ancient Rome. From the Elder Cato to the Younger Pliny*. London.

Borthwick, E. K. (1969), Review of Wille, *Musica Romana: die Bedeutung der Musik im Leben der Römer*, *Classical Review* 19: 343–6.

Bradley, K. (1978a), 'The Chronology of Nero's Visit to Greece, AD 66/67', *Latomus* 37: 61–72.

(1978b), *Suetonius' Life of Nero: An Historical Commentary*. Brussels.

Braun, J. (2002), *Music in Ancient Israel/Palestine*. Grand Rapids, MI.

Brennan, B. (1988), 'Augustine's *De Musica*', *Vigilae Christianae* 42: 267–81.

Brennan, T. C. (2000), *The Praetorship in the Roman Republic*. Vol. 1. Oxford.

Briscoe, J. (2012), *A Commentary on Livy, Books 41–45*. Oxford.

Broughton, T. R. S. (1952), *The Magistrates of the Roman Republic*. Vol. 2. New York, NY.

Brulé, P. and Vendries, C. (eds.) (2001), *Chanter les dieux: Musique et religion dans l'Antiquité grecque et romaine*. Rennes.

Buchet, E. (2010), 'La grève des *tibicines*', *Bulletin de l'Association Guillaume Budé*: 174–96.

Buckley, E. and Dinter, M. (eds.) (2013), *A Companion to the Neronian Age*. Malden and Oxford.

Burden-Stevens, C. (2018), 'Reconstructing Republican Oratory in Cassius Dio's Roman History', in *Reading Republican Oratory: Reconstructions, Contexts, Receptions*, eds. C. Gray, A. Balbo, R. M. A. Marshall and C. E. W. Steel. Oxford: 111–34.

Burghart, W. D. (2018), 'Polybius' Interpretation of Plato's Arcadian Tale: Platonic Influences on Polybius' Histories', *Polis: The Journal for Ancient Greek and Roman Political Thought* 35: 127–44.

Burnett, C. (1993), 'European Knowledge of Arabic Texts about Music', *Early Music History* 12: 1–17.

Burney, C. (1789), *A General History of Music, from the Earliest Stages to the Present Period*. London.

Butler, H. E. and Barber, E. A. (1933), *The Elegies of Propertius*. Oxford.

Butler, S. and Nooter, S. (eds.) (2018), *Sound and the Ancient Senses*. London.

Cairns, F. (1984), 'Propertius and the Battle of Actium (4.6)', in *Poetry and Politics in the Age of Augustus*, eds. T. Woodman and D. West. Cambridge: 129–68.

Caldwell, J. (1981), 'The De Arithmetica and De Musica', in *Boethius: His Life, Thought and Influence*, ed. M. Gibson. Oxford: 135–54.

Calvo-Sotelo, J. C. (2015), 'Around the Origins of Bagpipes: Relevant Hypotheses and Evidences', *Greek and Roman Musical Studies* 3: 18–52.

Cameron, A. (1976), *Circus Factions: Blues and Greens at Rome and Byzantium*. Oxford.

Carettoni, G. (1956), 'Una nuova casa repubblicana sul Palatino', *Rendiconti della pontificia accademia romana di archeologia* 29: 51–62.

(1983), *Das Haus des Augustus auf dem Palatin*. Mainz.

Carrese, M., Li Castro, E. and Martinelli, M. (eds.) (2010), *La musica in Etruria: Atti del convegno internazionale: Tarquinia 18/20 settembre 2009*. Tarquinia.

Caruso, C. (2008), 'La professione di cantante nel mondo romano. La terminologia specifica attraverso le fonti letterarie ed epigrafiche', in *Epigrafia 2006*. Atti della XIVe Rencontre sur l'épigraphie in onore di S. Panciera con altri contribute di colleghi, allievi e collaborator, eds. M. L. Caldelli, G. L. Gregori and S. Orlandi. Rome: 1407–30.

Caspar, T. W. (2011), *Recovering the Ancient View of Founding: A Commentary on Cicero's De Legibus*. Plymouth.

Casson, L. (1989), *The Periplus Maris Erythraei: Text with Introduction, Translation and Commentary*. Princeton, NJ.

Castaldo, D. (2012), *Musiche dell'Italia antica. Introduzione all'archeologia musicale*. Bologna.

(2018), 'Musical Themes and Private Art in the Augustan Age', *Greek and Roman Musical Studies* 6: 96–114.

Ceccarelli, P. (2000), 'Dance and Desserts: An Analysis of Book Fourteen', in *Athenaeus and His World: Reading Greek Culture in the Roman Empire*, eds. D. Braund and J. Wilkins. Exeter: 272–91.

Celentano, F. (1913), 'La musica presso i Romani', *Rivista Musicale Italiana* 20: 243–76, (*cont.*) 494–526.

Champion, C. (2004), *Cultural Politics in Polybius' Histories*. Oxford.

(2018), 'Polybian Barbarology, Flute-Playing in Arcadia, and Fisticuffs at Rome', in *Polybius and His Legacy*, eds. N. Miltsios and M. Tamiolaki. Berlin: 35–42.

Champlin, E. (1978), 'The Life and Times of Calpurnius Siculus', *Journal of Roman Studies* 68: 95–110.

(2003a), *Nero*. London and Cambridge, MA.

(2003b), 'Nero, Apollo, and the Poets', *Phoenix* 57: 276–83.

Chaniotis, A. (2009), 'A Few Things Hellenistic Audiences Appreciated in Musical Performances', in *La Musa dimenticata. Aspetti dell'esperienza musicale greca in età ellenistica*, eds. M. C. Martinelli, F. Pelosi, and C. Pernigotti. Pisa: 75–97.

Ciotti, U. (1950), 'Rilievo romano e plutei medioevali ritrovati a Castel S. Elia', *Bollettino d'Arte* 35: 1–8.

Claridge, A. (2010), *Rome: An Oxford Archaeological Guide*. Oxford.

Clarke, J. R. (2003), *Art in the Lives of Ordinary Romans: Visual Representation and Non-Elite Viewers in Italy, 100 B.C.-A.D. 315*. Berkeley, CA and London.

(2005), 'Representations of the *Cinaedus* in Roman Art: Evidence of 'Gay' Subculture?', *The Journal of Homosexuality* 49: 271–98.

Coarelli, F. (1970–1971), 'Classe dirigente romana e arti figurative', *Dialoghi d'Archeologia* 4/5: 241–65.

Coleman-Norton, P. R. (1948), 'Cicero Musicus', *Journal of the American Musicological Society* 1: 3–22.

(1950), 'Cicero and the Music of the Spheres', *Classical Journal* 45: 237–41.

Coleman, K. M. (1993), 'Launching into History: Aquatic Displays in the Early Empire', *Journal of Roman Studies* 83: 48–74.

(2011), 'Public Entertainments', in *The Oxford Handbook of Social Relations in the Roman World,* ed. M. Peachin. Oxford: 335–57.

(2018), 'Orchestrated Violence: The Role of Music in the Roman Amphitheatre', The Eleventh Syme Memorial Lecture. Wellington: 1–38.

Collins, J. J. (1983), 'Sibylline Oracles', in *The Old Testament Pseudepigrapha. Vol. 1, Apocalyptic Literature and Testaments,* ed. J. H. Charlesworth. New York, NY: 317–472.

Comotti, G. (1989), *Music in Greek and Roman Culture.* Baltimore, MD and London.

Conte, G. B. (1994), *Latin Literature: A History.* Baltimore, MD and London.

Corbeill, A. (1996), *Controlling Laughter. Political Humor in the Late Roman Republic.* Princeton, NJ.

(2004), *Nature Embodied: Gesture in Ancient Rome.* Princeton, NJ.

Cosgrove, C. H. (2006), 'Clement of Alexandria and Early Christian Music', *Journal of Early Christian Studies* 14.3: 255–82.

Crawford, J. (1984), *Cicero: The Lost and Unpublished Orations.* Göttingen.

Crawford, M. and Cloud, J. D. (1996), *Roman Statutes.* London.

Creese, D. (2006), 'Music', in *The Edinburgh Companion to Ancient Greece and Rome,* eds. E. Bispham, T. Harrison and B. A. Sparkes. Edinburgh: 413–22.

(2009), 'Erogenous Organs: The Metamorphosis of Polyphemus' "Syrinx" in Ovid, "Metamorphoses" 13.784', *Classical Quarterly* 59: 562–77.

Crowther, N. B. (1983), 'Greek Games in Republican Rome', *L'Antiquité Classique* 52: 268–73.

Csapo, E. (2004), 'The Politics of the New Music', in *Music and the Muses. The Culture of Mousike in the Classical Athenian City,* eds. P. Murray and P. Wilson. Oxford: 207–48.

Csapo, E. and Wilson, P. (2009), 'Timotheus the New Musician', in *The Cambridge Companion to Greek Lyric,* ed. F. Budelmann. Cambridge: 277–94.

Cugusi, P. and Sblendorio Cugusi, M. T. (2001), *M. Porcio Catone Censore.* Turin.

Currie, H. MacL. (1981), 'Ovid and the Roman Stage', *Aufstieg und Niedergang der römischen Welt* II.31.4: 2701–42.

Curtis, L. (2017), *Imagining the Chorus in Augustan Poetry.* Cambridge.

D'Angour, A. (2011), *The Greeks and the New: Novelty and Imagination in Ancient Greek Experience.* Cambridge.

D'Angour, A. and Philipps, T. (2018), *Music, Text, and Culture in Ancient Greece.* Oxford.

Daly, L. W. (ed.) (1961), *Aesop without Morals: The Famous Fables, and a Life of Aesop.* New York, NY.

David, J.-M. (1983), 'L'action oratoire de C. Gracchus: L'image d'un modele', in *Demokratia et Aristokratia: à propos de Caius Gracchus: mots grecs et réalités romaines,* ed. C. Nicolet. Paris: 103–16.

De Simone, R. (1999), 'La musica nella Pompei romana', in *Homo Faber: Natura, scienza e tecnica nell'antica Pompei,* eds. A. Ciarallo and E. De Carolis. Naples: 29–30.

Delattre, D. (1998), 'The Dialogue of Greece and Rome about Music and Ethics in Philodemus of Gadara', in *Hearing the Past: Essays in Historical Ethnomusicology and the Archaeology of Sound,* ed. A. Buckley. Liége: 213–40.

(2007), *Philodemus. Sur la musique. Livre IV.* Paris.

Deppmeyer, K. (2016) 'Die Verfehlungen des Künstlers Nero', in *Nero – Kaiser, Künstler und Tyrann. Begleitband zur Ausstellung Rheinisches Landesmuseum Trier, Museum am Dom Trier, Stadtmuseum Simeonstift Trier 14.5.–16.10.2016,* ed. J. Merten. Darmstadt: 210–16.

Dessì, P. (2008), *L'organo tardoantico: storie di sovranità e diplomazia.* Padua.

Devereux, P. (2006), 'Ears & Years: Aspects of Acoustics and Intentionality in Antiquity', in *Archaeoacoustics,* eds. C. Scarre and G. Lawson. Cambridge: 23–30.

Dillon, M. and Garland, S. (2015), *Ancient Rome: Social and Historical Documents from the Early Republic to the Death of Augustus.* 2nd ed. Oxford and New York, NY.

Drabkin, I. E. (1950), *Caelius Aurelianus, On Acute Diseases and On Chronic Diseases.* Chicago, IL.

Drachmann, A. G. (1948), *Ktesibios, Philon and Heron: a Study in Ancient Pneumatics.* Copenhagen.

Drinkwater, J. F. (2012), 'Nero Caesar and the Half Baked Principate', in *The Julio-Claudian Succession: Reality and Perception of the 'Augustan Model',* ed. A. G. G. Gibson. Leiden: 155–74.

(2019), *Nero: Emperor and Court.* Cambridge.

Dugas, C. (1944), 'Héraclès Mousicos', *Revue des études grecques* 57: 61–70.

Dunbabin, K. D. (2016), *Theater and Spectacle in the Art of the Roman Empire.* Ithaca, NY and London.

Dupont, F. (2004), 'Les petites Quinquatries et la grève des tibicines', *Europe. Revue littéraire mensuelle* 904/905: 219–30.

DuQuesnay, I. M. LeM. (1984), 'Horace and Maecenas: the Propaganda Value of Sermones 1', in *Poetry and Politics in the Age of Augustus,* eds. T. Woodman and D. West. Cambridge: 19–58.

Dutsch, D. (2014), 'The Beginnings: Philosophy in Roman Literature before 155 B.C.', in *The Philosophizing Muse: The Influence of Greek Philosophy on Roman Poetry,* eds. M. Garani and D. Konstan. Newcastle upon Tyne: 1–25.

Dyck, A. R. (2004), *A Commentary on Cicero, De Legibus.* Ann Arbor, MI.

Eberhardt, J. (2018), *Ungezähmte Musen: Musikkultur in der griechisch-römischen Spätantike.* Münster.

Edelstein, L., and Kidd, I. G. (1989), *Posidonius. Vol. I, The Fragments.* 2nd ed. Cambridge.

Edmondson, J. C. (1999), 'The Cultural Politics of Public Spectacle in Rome and the Greek East, 167–166 BCE', in *The Art of Ancient Spectacle*, eds. B. Bergmann and C. Kondoleon. New Haven, CT and London: 77–95.

Edwards, C. (1994), 'Beware of Imitations: Theatre and the Subversion of Imperial Identity', in *Reflections of Nero: Culture, History and Representation*, eds. J. Elsner and J. Masters. London: 83–97.

(1997), 'Unspeakable Professions: Public Performance and Prostitution in Ancient Rome', in *Roman Sexualities*, eds. J. P. Hallett and M. B. Skinner. Princeton, NJ: 66–95.

Elsner, J. (1994), 'Constructing Decadence', in *Reflections of Nero: Culture, History and Representation*, eds. J. Elsner and J. Masters. London: 112–27.

Emerit, S., Guichard, H., Jeammet, V., Perrot, S., Thomas, A., Vendries, C., Vincent, A. and Ziegler, N. (eds.) (2017), *Musiques! Échos de l'Antiquité*. Ghent and Lens.

Ercoles, M. (2014), 'Dressing the Citharode: A Chapter in Greek Musical and Cultic Imagery', in *Greek and Roman Textiles and Dress*, eds. M. Harlow and M.-L. Nosch. Oxford and Philadelphia: 95–110.

Eximeno, A. (1774), *Dell' origine e delle regole della musica, colla storia del suo progresso, decadenza, e rinnovazione*. Rome.

Eyben, E. (1993), *Restless Youth in Ancient Rome*. London and New York, NY.

Fagan, G. G. (2011), *The Lure of the Arena: Social Psychology and the Crowd at the Roman Games*. Cambridge.

Fantham, E. (2013), 'The Performing Prince', in *A Companion to the Neronian Age*, eds. E. Buckley and M. T. Dinter. Malden and Oxford: 17–28.

Fear, A. T. (1991), 'The Dancing Girls of Cadiz', *Greece and Rome* 38: 75–9.

Feeney, D. C. (2016), *Beyond Greek: The Beginnings of Latin Literature*. Cambridge, MA.

Feldman, L. H. (1986–1987), 'Philo's Views on Music', *Journal of Jewish Music and Liturgy* 100: 36–52.

Ferguson, E. (2003), 'The Art of Praise: Philo and Philodemus on Music', in *Early Christianity and Classical Culture: Comparative Studies in Honour of Abraham J. Malherhe*, eds. J. T. Fitzgerald, T. H. Olbricht and L. H. White. Leiden: 391–426.

Ferrary, J.-L. (1988), *Philhellénisme et impérialisme: aspects idéologiques de la conquête romaine du monde hellénistique, de la seconde guerre de Macédoine à la guerre contre Mithridate*. Rome.

(2017), *Rome et le monde grec*. Paris.

Ferri, R. (2008), 'New Evidence on the Meaning of ῥωμαιστής in IG XI. 2 133: "Actor of Latin Comedies"?', *Zeitschrift für Papyrologie und Epigraphik* 166: 155–8.

Fleischhauer, G. (1965), *Etrurien und Rom. Musikgeschichte im Bildern. Band 2: Musik des Altertums, Lieferung 5*. Leipzig.

Fless, F. (1995), *Opferdiener und Kultmusiker auf stadtrömischen historischen Reliefs: Untersuchungen zur Ikonographie, Funktion und Benennung*. Mainz.

Fless, F., and Moede, K. (2007), 'Music and Dance: Forms of Representation in Pictorial and Written Sources', in *A Companion to Roman Religion*, ed. J. Rüpke. Malden: 249–62.

Flower, H. I. (2014), 'Spectacle and Political Culture in the Roman Republic', in *The Cambridge Companion to the Roman Republic*, ed. H. I. Flower. 2nd ed. Cambridge: 377–98.

Fontaine, M. (2010), *Funny Words in Plautine Comedy*. Oxford.

Fowler, D. P. (2002), *Lucretius on Atomic Motion: A Commentary on De Rerum Natura 2.1–332*. Oxford.

Franklin, J. C. (2013), "Song-Benders of Circular Choruses': Dithyramb and the 'Demise of Music", in *Dithyramb in Context*, eds. P. Wilson and B. Kowalzig. Oxford: 213–36.

Franko, G. F. (2013), "*Anicius vortit barbare*: The Scenic Games of L. Anicius Gallus and the Aesthetics of Greek and Roman Performance", in G. W. M. Harrison and V. Liapes (eds.), *Performance in Greek and Roman Theatre*. Leiden: 343–60.

Freudenburg, K. (1993), *The Walking Muse: Horace on the Theory of Satire*. Princeton, NJ.

(2013), 'The Afterlife of Varro in Horace's *Sermones*: Generic Issues in Roman Satire', in *Generic Interfaces in Latin Literature: Encounters, Interactions and Transformations*, eds. T. D. Papanghelis, S. J. Harrison and S. Frangoulidis. Berlin and Boston: 297–336.

Freyburger, G. (1986), *Fides: étude sémantique et religieuse depuis les origines jusqu'à l'époque augustéene*. Paris.

Friedländer, L. (1936), *Roman Life and Manners under the Early Empire*. 7th ed., vol. 2. Trans. J. H. Freese and L. A. Magnus. London and New York, NY.

Fröhlich, T. (1991), *Lararien- und Fassadenbilder in den Vesuvstädten: Untersuchungen zur "volkstümlichen" pompejanischen Malarei*. Mainz.

Fuchs, M. (1982), 'Ein Musengruppe aus dem Pompeius-Theater', *Mitteilungen des deutschen archäologischen Instituts (R): Römische Abteilung* 89: 69–80.

Gabba, E. (1957), 'Note sulla polemica anticiceroniana di Asinio Pollione', *Rivista Storica Italiana* 69: 317–39.

Gagé, J. (1955), *Apollon romain: essai sur le culte d'Apollon et le développement du "ritus Graecus" à Rome des origines à Auguste*. Paris.

Gallivan, P. A. (1973), 'Nero's Liberation of Greece', *Hermes* 101: 230–34.

Garelli-François, M.-H. (2000), 'Le "ludus talarius" et les représentations dramatiques à Rome', *Revue de philologie* 74: 87–102.

Garratt, J. (2019), *Music and Politics: A Critical Introduction*. Cambridge

Geel, J. (1966), *Dav. Ruhnkenii Scholia in Suetonii Vitas Caesarum*. Amsterdam.

Geffcken, J. (1902), *Die Oracula Sibyllina*. Leipzig.

Gétreau, F. (ed.) (2021), *Musique-Images-Instruments: Revue française d'organologie et d'iconographie musicale, n° 18: Représenter la musique dans l'Antiquité*. Paris.

Geue, T. (2017), *Author Unknown: The Power of Anonymity in Ancient Rome*. Cambridge, MA, and London.

Gevaert, F. A. (1875), *Histoire et théorie de la musique de l'antiquité*. Gand.

Gigante, M. (1987), *La bibliothèque de Philodème et l'épicurisme romain*. Paris.

  (1995), *Philodemus in Italy: The Books from Herculaneum*. Trans. D. Obbink. Ann Arbor, MI.

Gilula, D. (1978), 'Where Did the Audience Go?', *Scripta Classica Israelica* 4: 45–9.

Giovagnoli, M. (2014), 'Ancora sulla *societas cantorum Graecorum* (*CIL*, I^2 2519)', *Rivista di filologia e di istruzione classica* 142: 91–102.

Gleason, M. W. (1995), *Making Men: Sophists and Self-Presentation in Ancient Rome*. Princeton, NJ.

Godbolt, J. (1984), *A History of Jazz in Britain, 1919–50*. London.

Goldberg, S. M. (1995), *Epic in Republican Rome*. Oxford.

  (1998), 'Plautus on the Palatine', *Journal of Roman Studies* 88: 1–20.

  (2013), *Terence: Hecyra*. Cambridge.

  (2018), 'Theater without Theaters: Seeing Plays the Roman Way', *Transactions of the American Philological Association* 148: 139–72.

Goodman, P. J. (2018), 'Best of Emperors or Subtle Tyrant? Augustus the Ambivalent', in *Afterlives of Augustus, AD 14–2014*, ed. P. J. Goodman. Cambridge.

Goodyear F. R. D. (1984), 'The "Aetna": Thoughts, Antecedents, and Style', *Aufstieg und Niedergang der römischen Welt* II.32.1: 344–63.

Gotter, U. (2009), 'Cato's *Origines*: The Historian and His Enemies', in *The Cambridge Companion to the Roman Historians*, ed. A. Feldherr. Cambridge: 108–22.

Gowers, E. (1993), *The Loaded Table. Representations of Food in Roman Literature*. Oxford.

  (1994), 'Persius and the Decoction of Nero', in *Reflections of Nero: Culture, History and Representation*, eds. J. Elsner and J. Masters. London: 131–50.

Graf, F. (1991), 'Gestures and Conventions: the Gestures of Roman Actors and Orators', in *A Cultural History of Gesture from Antiquity to the Present Day*, eds. J. N. Bremmer and H. Roodenburg. Ithaca, NY: 36–58.

  (2009), *Apollo*. London.

Green, S. J. (2018), 'Seneca's Augustus: (Re)calibrating the Imperial Model for a Young Prince', in *Afterlives of Augustus, AD 14–2014*, ed. P. J. Goodman. Cambridge: 44–57.

Griffin, M. T. (1984), *Nero. The End of a Dynasty*. London.

  (2001), 'Piso, Cicero and Their Audience', in *Cicéron et Philodème. La polémique en philosophie*, eds. C. Avray-Assayas and D. Delattre. Paris: 85–99.

Grig, L. (2013), 'Approaching Popular Culture: Singing in the Sermons of Caesarius of Arles', *Studia Patristica* 69: 197–204.
Gruen, E. S. (1974), *The Last Generation of the Roman Republic*. Berkeley, CA.
  (1993), *Culture and National Identity in Republican Rome*. London.
Guarducci, M. (1971), 'Iscrizioni greche e latine in una taberna a Pozzuoli', in *Acta of the Fifth International Congress of Greek and Latin Epigraphy, Cambridge, 1967*. Oxford: 219–223.
Guidobaldi, M. P. (1992), *Musica e danza*. Rome.
Gülgönen, S. (2014), 'La *mimesis* musicale dans les dialogues platoniciens', *Phoenix* 68: 25–39.
Gunderson, E. (2000), *Staging Masculinity: The Rhetoric of Performance in the Roman World*. Ann Arbor, MI.
Günther, L.-M. (2002), "Griechische Bühnenkunst bei den Römischen Siegesspielen des L. Anicius (166 v. Chr.) – Klamauk oder Parodie?", in *Wiederstand – Anpassung – Integration: Die griechische Staatenwelt und Rom. Festschrift für Jürgen Deininger*, eds. N. Ehrhardt and L.-M. Günther. Stuttgart: 121–33.
Gurval, R. A. (1995), *Actium and Augustus: The Politics and Emotions of Civil War*. Ann Arbor, MI.
Gyles, M. F. (1947), 'Nero Fiddled while Rome Burned', *Classical Journal* 42: 211–17.
  (1962), '*Qualis Artifex?*', *Classical Journal* 57: 193–200.
Habinek, T. N. (2005), *The World of Roman Song: From Ritualized Speech to Social Order*. Baltimore, MD.
Hagel, S. (2008), 'Re-evaluating the Pompeian Auloi', *Journal of Hellenic Studies* 128: 52–71.
  (2009), *Ancient Greek Music: A New Technical History*. Cambridge.
Hagel, S., and Lynch, T. (2015), 'Musical Education in Greece and Rome', in *A Companion to Ancient Education*, ed. W. M. Bloomer. Hoboken, NJ: 401–12.
Hahn, A. (1905), *De Censorini Fontibus*. Jena.
Hahn, F. H. (2011), 'Performing the Sacred: Prayers and Hymns', in *A Companion to Roman Religion*, ed. J. Rüpke. Oxford: 235–48.
Hall, E. (2002), 'The Singing Actors of Antiquity', in *Greek and Roman Actors: Aspects of an Ancient Profession*, eds. P. Easterling and E. Hall. Cambridge: 3–38.
Hardie, A. (2007), 'Juno, Hercules, and the Muses at Rome', *American Journal of Philology* 128: 551–92.
Harmon, R. (2003), 'Themistocles to Philomathes: "Amousos" and "Amousia" in Antiquity and the Early Modern Period', *International Journal of the Classical Tradition* 9: 351–90.
Hartnett, J. (2016), 'Sound as a Roman Urban Social Phenomenon', in *Stadterfahrung als Sinneserfahrung in der römischen Kaiserzeit*, eds. A. Haug and P.-A. Kreuz. Turnhout: 159–78.

(2017), *The Roman Street: Urban Life and Society in Pompeii, Herculaneum, and Rome*. New York, NY.

Hawkins, J. (1776), *A General History of the Science and Practice of Music*. 5 vols. London.

Hays, R. S. (1983), Lucius Annaeus Cornutus' *Epidrome* (Introduction to the Traditions of Greek Theology): Introduction, Translation, and Notes. Unpublished dissertation, University of Texas at Austin.

Hedrick, C. W. (2015), '*Qualis Artifex Pereo*: The Generation of Roman Memories of Nero', in *Memory in Ancient Rome and Early Christianity*, ed. K. Galinsky. Oxford: 145–66.

Heilmann, A. (2007), *Boethius' Musiktheorie und das Quadrivium*. Vandenhoeck and Ruprecht.

Hekster, O. (2010), 'Reversed Epiphanies: Roman Emperors Deserted by Gods', *Mnemosyne* 63: 601–15.

Hekster, O. and Rich, J. (2006), 'Octavian and the Thunderbolt', *Classical Quarterly* 56: 149–68.

Hemelrijk, E. A. (1999), *Matrona Docta. Educated Women in the Roman Elite from Cornelia to Julia Domna*. London and New York, NY.

Henderson, J. (1989), 'Tacitus/The World in Pieces', *Ramus* 18: 167–210.

Hendy, D. (2013), *Noise: A Human History of Sound and Listening*. London.

Hersch, K. K. (2010), *The Roman Wedding: Ritual and Meaning in Antiquity*. Cambridge.

Heslin, P. (2015), *The Museum of Augustus: The Temple of Apollo in Pompeii, the Portico of Philippus in Rome, and Latin Poetry*. Los Angeles, CA.

Hinard, F. (1992), 'C. Sosius et le temple d'Apollon', *Kentron* 8: 57–72.

Hirth, F. (1975), *China and the Roman Orient: Researches into Their Ancient and Medieval Relations as Represented in Old Chinese Records*. Reprint. Chicago, IL.

Hoff, M. C. (1992), 'Augustus, Apollo and Athens', *Museum Helveticum* 49: 223–32.

Holliday, P. J. (1990), 'Processional Imagery in Late Etruscan Funerary Art', *American Journal of Archaeology* 94: 73–93.

Hollis, A. S. (2007), *Fragments of Roman Poetry, c. 60 BC–AD 20. Edited with Introduction, Translation, and Commentary*. Oxford.

Holzer, E. (1890), *Varro über Musik*. Ulm.

Homo-Lechner, C., Pinette, M. and Vendries, C. (1993), *Le Carnyx et le lyre: archéologie musicale en Gaule celtique et romaine*. Besançon.

Horsfall, N. (1982), 'Prose and Mime', in *The Cambridge History of Classical Literature, Vol. II: Latin Literature*, ed. E. J. Kenney and W. V. Clausen. Cambridge: 286–94.

(1993), 'Cleaning up Calpurnius', *Classical Review* 43: 267–70.

(1997), 'Criteria for the Dating of Calpurnius Siculus', *Rivista di filologia e di istruzione classica* 125: 166–96.

(2003), *The Culture of the Roman Plebs*. London.

Howgego, C. J. (1995), *Ancient History from Coins.* London.
Huet, V. (2007), 'Le tibicen sur les reliefs sarificiels à Rome', *Dossiers d'archéologie nº 320. Musique à Rome*: 54–7.
Humphrey, J. H. (1986), *Roman Circuses: Arenas for Chariot Racing.* Berkeley, CA.
Hunt, Y. (2008), 'Roman Pantomime Libretti and their Greek Themes: The Role of Augustus in the Romanization of the Greek Classics', in *New Directions in Ancient Pantomime,* eds. E. Hall and R. Wyles. Oxford: 169–84.
Hyde, W. (1938), 'The Recent Discovery of an Inscribed Water-Organ at Budapest', *Transactions of the American Philological Association* 69: 392–411.
Iacopi, I. and Tedone, G. (2005–2006), 'Bibliotheca e Porticus ad Apollinis', *Mitteilungen des Deutschen Archäologischen Instituts. Römische Abteilung* 114: 351–78.
Ieranò, G. (2020), 'Dionysus and the Ambiguity of Orgiastic Music', in *A Companion to Ancient Greek and Roman Music*, eds. E. Rocconi and T. A. C. Lynch. Hoboken: 37–48.
Isager, J. (1998), 'Propertius and the *Monumenta* of Actium (IV.6 as a Topographical Source)', *Proceedings of the Danish Institute at Athens* 2: 399–411.
Jacobsson, M. (ed.) (2017), *Augustinus, De Musica: With an Introduction by Martin Jacobsson and Lukas J. Dorfbauer.* Berlin.
Jakob, F., Leuthard, M., Voute, A. C. and Hochuli-Gysel, A. (2000), *Die römische Orgel aus Avenches/Aventicum.* Avenches.
James, P. (2004), 'Marsyas's Musical Body: The Poetics of Mutilation and Reflection in Ovid's Metamorphic Martyrs', *Arethusa* 37: 88–100.
Janko, R. (2000), *Philodemus: On Poems.* Oxford.
Jocelyn, H. D. (1967), *The Tragedies of Ennius: The Fragments.* London.
  (1978), Review of Lefèvre, *Der Thyestes des Lucius Varius Rufus, Gnomon* 50: 778–80.
Johnson, W. A. (2000a), 'Musical Evenings in the Roman Empire: New Evidence from a Greek Papyrus with Musical Notation', *Journal of Hellenic Studies* 120: 57–85.
  (2000b), 'New Instrumental Music from Graeco-Roman Egypt', *Bulletin of the American Society of Papyrologists* 37: 17–36.
  (2010), *Readers and Reading Culture in the High Roman Empire.* Oxford and New York, NY.
Johnston, I. (2006), *Galen: On Diseases and Symptoms. Translated, with Introduction and Notes.* Cambridge.
Jones, C.P. (1991), 'Dinner Theatre', in *Dining in a Classical Context,* ed. W. J. Slater. Ann Arbor, MI: 185–98.
Jory, E. J. (1970), 'Associations of Actors at Rome', *Hermes* 98: 224–53.
  (1981), 'The Literary Evidence for the Beginnings of Imperial Pantomime', *Bulletin of the Institute of Classical Studies* 28: 147–61.

(1988), 'Publilius Syrus and the Element of Competition in the Theatre of the Republic', in *Vir bonus dicendi peritus. Studies in Celebration of Otto Skutch's Eightieth Birthday*, ed. N. Horsfall. London: 73–81.

(1995), 'Ars Ludicra and the Ludus Talarius', in *Stage Directions: Essays in Ancient Drama in Honour of E.W. Handley*, ed. A. Griffiths. London: 139–52.

Jucker, H. (1982), 'Apollo Palatinus und Apollo Actius auf augusteischen Münzen', *Museum Helveticum* 39: 82–100.

Kaba, M. (1976), *Die romische Orgel von Aquincum (3. Jahrhundert). Musicologia Hungarica 6.* Budapest.

Kelly, H. A. (1979), 'Tragedy and the Performance of Tragedy in Late Roman Antiquity', *Traditio* 35: 21–44.

Kennell, N. M. (1988), 'ΝΕΡΩΝ ΠΕΡΙΟΔΟΝΙΚΗΣ', *American Journal of Philology* 109: 239–51.

Keyes, C. W. (1928), *Cicero: De Re Publica, De Legibus.* Cambridge, MA and London.

King, H. (2013), 'Fear of Flute Girls, Fear of Falling', in *Mental Disorders in the Classical World*, ed. W. V. Harris. Leiden and Boston: 265–82.

Klauck, H.-J. (2001), 'Do They Never Come Back? *Nero Redivivus* and the Apocalypse of John', *Catholic Biblical Quarterly* 63: 683–98.

Kleijwegt, M. (1994), '*Iuvenes* and Roman Imperial Society', *L'Antiquité Classique* 37: 79–102.

Knoepfler, D. (2004), 'Les Rômaia de Thèbes: un nouveau concours musical (et athlétique?) en Béotie', *Comptes rendus de l'Académie des Inscriptions et Belles-Lettres* 148: 1241–79.

Krenkel, W. (2002), *Saturae Menippeae.* 4 vols. St. Katharinen.

La Rocca, E. (1977), 'L'Apollo qui citharam ... tenet di Timarchides', *Bollettino dei Musei Comunali di Roma* 23: 16–33.

(1985), *Amazzonomachia: le sculture frontale del tempio di Apollo Sosiano.* Rome.

(2006), 'Dalle Camene alle Muse: il canto come strumento di trionfo', in *Musa pensosa: l'immagine dell'intellettuale nell'antichità*, ed. A. Bottini. Rome: 99–133.

La Rocca, E., Parisi Presicce, C., Lo Monaco, A., Giroire, C. and Roger, D. (eds.) (2013), *Augusto* (exhibition catalogue). Milan.

Lada-Richards, I. (2004), 'Authorial Voice and Theatrical Self-definition in Terence and Beyond: The *Hecyra* Prologues in Ancient and Modern Contexts', *Greece and Rome* 51: 55–82.

(2007), *Silent Eloquence: Lucian and Pantomime Dancing.* London.

Landels, J. G. (1999), *Music in Ancient Greece and Rome.* London.

Lange, C. H. (2009), *Res Publica Constituta: Actium, Apollo, and the Accomplishment of the Triumviral Assignment.* Leiden.

Last, H. M. (1922), 'The Date of Philodemus' *De Signis*', *Classical Quarterly* 16: 177–80.

(1953), 'The *Tabula Hebana* and Propertius II, 31', *Journal of Roman Studies* 43: 27–29.

Latham, J. A. (2012), '"Fabulous Clap-trap": Roman Masculinity, the Cult of Magna Mater and Literary Constructions of the *galli* at Rome from the Late Republic to Late Antiquity', *Journal of Religion* 92: 84–122.

(2016), *Performance, Memory, and Processions in Ancient Rome: the Pompa Circensis from the Late Republic to Late Antiquity*. Cambridge.

Laurence, R. (2009), *Roman Passions: A History of Pleasure in Imperial Rome*. London.

(2017), 'The Sounds of the City: From Noise to Silence in Ancient Rome', in *Senses of the Empire: Multisensory Approaches to Roman Culture*, ed. E. Betts. London: 13–22.

Le Guen, B. (2001), *Les associations de Technites dionysiaques à l'époque hellénistique*. Nancy.

Leigh, M. (1996), 'Varius Rufus, Thyestes and the Appetites of Antony', *Proceedings of the Cambridge Philological Society* 42: 171–97.

(2012), 'De brevitate vitae: Seneca e il mondo romano', in *Letteratura e civitas. Transizioni dalla repubblica all'impero. In ricordo di Emanuele Narducci*, ed. M. Citroni. Pisa: 341–51.

(2017), 'Nero the Performer', in *The Cambridge Companion to the Age of Nero*, eds. S. Bartsch, K. Freudenburg and C. Littlewood. Cambridge: 21–33.

Lenfant, D. (2007), 'Les "fragments" d'Hérodote dans les Deipnosophistes', in *Athénée et les fragments d'historiens*, ed. D. Lenfant. Paris: 43–72.

Lepper, F. A. (1957), 'Some Reflections on the "Quinquennium Neronis"', *Journal of Roman Studies* 47: 95–103.

Leppin, H. (1992), *Histrionen. Untersuchungen zur sozialen Stellung von Bühnenkünstlern im Westen des Römischen Reiches zur Zeit der Republik und des Principats*. Bonn.

Leutsch, E. L. and Schneidewin, F. G. (eds.) (1839), *Paroemiographi graeci*. Göttingen.

Levarie, S. (1991), 'Philo on Music', *Journal of Musicology* 9: 124–30.

LeVen, P. (2012), 'Musical Crisis: Representing Competition and Musical Judgment in Anecdotes', in *Poesia, musica e agoni nella Grecia antica. Atti del IV Convegno internazionale di MOISA, Lecce, 28–30 ottobre 2010*, eds. D. Castaldo, F. G. Giannachi and A. Manieri. Galatina: 681–92.

(2014), *The Many-Headed Muse: Tradition and Innovation in Late Classical Greek Lyric Poetry*. Cambridge.

Levene, D. S. (2005), 'The Late Republican/Triumviral Period: 90–40 BC', in *A Companion to Latin Literature*, ed. S. J. Harrison. Malden: 31–43.

Levick, B. (1983), 'The *Senatus Consultum* from Larinum', *Journal of Roman Studies* 73: 97–115.

(2010), *Augustus: Image and Substance*. Harlow.

Lightfoot, J. L. (2002), 'Nothing to Do with the *technitai* of Dionysus?', in *Greek and Roman Actors: Aspects of an Ancient Profession*, eds. P. Easterling and E. Hall. Cambridge: 209–24.

Linderski, J. (2003), '*Sic Valeas*: A Latin Injunction, the *Symphoniaci*, and the Afterlife', *Epigraphica* 65: 185–95.

Lintott, A. W. (1972), 'Imperial Expansion and Moral Decline in the Roman Republic', *Historia* 21: 626–38.

(1999), *Violence in Republican Rome*. 2nd ed. Oxford.

(2008), *Cicero as Evidence: A Historian's Companion*. Oxford.

Loman, P. (2004), 'Travelling Female Entertainers of the Hellenistic Age', *Arctos* 38: 59–73.

Long, A. A. (1995), 'Cicero's Plato and Aristotle', in *Cicero the Philosopher: Twelve Papers*, ed. J. G. F. Powell. Oxford: 37–61.

(2003), 'Roman Philosophy', in *The Cambridge Companion to Greek and Roman Philosophy*, ed. D. Sedley. Cambridge: 184–210.

Lowrie, M. (2009), *Writing, Performance and Authority in Augustan Rome*. Oxford.

Luque Moreno, J. (1997), 'Seneca Musicus', in *Séneca dos mil años después: Actas del congreso internacional conmemorativo del bimelenario de su nacimiento (Córdoba, 24 a 27 de septiembre de 1996)*, ed. M. Rodríguez-Pantoja: 77–115.

Lyons, S. (2010), *Music in the Odes of Horace*. Oxford.

Machabey, A. (1936), 'Études de musicologie pré-médiévale. Importance et valeur de la musique Latine pour l'histoire musicale du Moyen-Age', *Revue de Musicologie*, Vol. 17, No. 57, 1–21.

MacKendrick, P. (1989), *The Philosophical Books of Cicero*. London.

Mackie, N. (1992), '*Popularis* Ideology and Popular Politics at Rome in the First Century B.C.', *Rheinisches Museum für Philologie* 135: 49–73.

MacMullen, R. (1991), 'Hellenizing the Romans (2nd century B.C.)', *Historia* 40: 419–38.

Maier, H. O. (2013), 'Nero in Jewish and Christian Tradition from the First Century to the Reformation', in *A Companion to the Neronian Age*, eds. E. Buckley and M. Dinter. Malden and Oxford: 385–404.

Malik, S. (2020), *The Nero-Antichrist: Founding and Fashioning a Paradigm*. Cambridge.

Mallan, C. (2013), 'The Style, Method, and Programme of Xiphilinus' Epitome of Cassius Dio's Roman History', *Greek, Roman and Byzantine Studies* 53: 610–44.

Manuwald, G. (2007), *Cicero, Philippics 3–9*. Berlin.

(2011), *Roman Republican Theatre*. Cambridge.

Marabini Moevs, M. T. (1981), 'Le Muse di Ambracia', *Bolletino d'Arte* 12: 1–58.

Marchetti, P. (2001), 'Le substrat dorien de l'Apollon Palatin: de Rome à la Grèce et vice versa', in *Constructions publiques et programmes éditilaires en Grèce entre le IIe siècle av. J.-C. et le 1er siècle ap. J.-C*, eds. J.-Y. Marc and J.-C. Moretti. Athens: 455–71.

Markovits, M. (2003), *Die Orgel im Altertum*. Leiden and Boston, MA.
Marsh, C. (2013), *Music and Society in Early Modern England*. Cambridge.
Martina, L. (1981), 'Aedes Herculis Musarum', *Dialoghi di archeologia* 3: 49–68.
Mathiesen, T. J. (1983), *Aristides Quintilianus: On Music, in Three Books*. New Haven, CT.
  (1999), *Apollo's Lyre: Greek Music and Music Theory in Antiquity*. Lincoln.
Mayer, R. (1980), 'Calpurnius Siculus: Technique and Date', *Journal of Roman Studies* 70: 175–6.
McKinnon, J. W. (1968), Review of Wille, *Musica Romana: die Bedeutung der Musik im Leben der Römer*, *Notes* 25: 24–6.
  (1987), *Music in Early Christian Literature*. Cambridge.
Melini, R. (2012), 'The "Soundscape" of Pompeii', in *Klänge der Vergangenheit: die Interpretation von musikarchäologischen Artefakten im Kontext: Vorträge des 7. Symposiums der Internationalen Studiengruppe Musikarchäologie im Tianjin Conservatory of Music, Tianjin, China, 20–25. September, 2010*, eds. R. Eichmann, J. Fang, and L. Koch. Rahden: 361–72.
  (2014), 'Sounds from under the Ashes: The Music of Cults and Mysteries in the Ancient Vesuvian Land', in *Music in Antiquity: The Near East and the Mediterranean*, eds. J. G. Westenholz, Y. Maurey, E. Seroussi and M. Caine. Berlin: 342–61.
Milanezi, S. (2000), 'Laughter as Dessert: On Athenaeus' Book Fourteen, 613–616', in *Athenaeus and His World: Reading Greek Culture in the Roman Empire*, eds. D. Braund and J. Wilkins. Exeter.
  (2004), 'À l'ombre des acteurs: les amuseurs à l'époque classique', in *Le statut de l'acteur dans l'Antiquité grecque et romaine*, eds. C. Hugoniot, F. Hurlet and S. Milanezi. Tours: 183–209.
Millar, F. (1964), *A Study of Cassius Dio*. Oxford.
  (1995), 'Popular Politics at Rome in the Late Republic', in I. Malkin and Z. W. Rubinsohn (eds.), *Leaders and Masses in the Roman World: Studies in Honor of Zvi Yavetz*. Leiden.
  (1998), *The Crowd in Rome in the Late Republic*. Ann Arbor, MI.
Miller, J. F. (2000), 'Triumphus in Palatio', *American Journal of Philology* 121: 409–22.
  (2009), *Apollo, Augustus and the Poets*. Cambridge.
Mitchell, A. G. (2013), 'Democracy and Popular Media: Classical Receptions in Nineteenth, Twentieth, and Twenty-First Century Political Cartoons – Statesmen, Mythological Figures, and Celebrated Artworks', in *Classics in the Modern World: A Democratic Turn?*, eds. L. Hardwick and S. Harrison. Oxford: 319–49.
Moore, T. J. (1994), 'Seats and Social Status in Plautine Theatre', *Classical Journal* 90: 113–23.
  (2008), 'When Did the *Tibicen* Play?', *Transactions of the American Philological Society* 138: 3–46.

(2012), *Music in Roman Comedy*. Cambridge.

(2016), 'Music in Roman Tragedy', in *Roman Drama and Its Contexts,* eds. S. Frangoulidis, S. J. Harrison and G. Manuwald. Berlin: 345–62.

(2021), 'Meter, Music, and Memory in Roman Comedy', in *Music and Memory in the Ancient Greek and Roman Worlds*, eds. L. Curtis and N. Weiss. Cambridge: 234–58.

Moreau, P. (1982), *Clodiana Religio. Un process politique en 61 av. J.-C.* Paris.

Morgan, H. (2017), 'Music, Sexuality and Stagecraft in the Pseudo-Vergilian *Copa*', *Greek and Roman Musical Studies* 5: 82–103.

(2019), 'A Horn for Phemius: Cicero, Atticus and the Musical Culture of the Late Republican Elite', *Mnemosyne* 72: 250–72.

(2022), 'Nero's Experiments with the Water-Organ', *Classical Quarterly* 72.1.

Morgan, T. (2007), *Popular Morality in the Early Roman Empire*. Cambridge.

Morstein-Marx, R. (2004), *Mass Oratory and Political Power in the Late Roman Republic*. Cambridge.

Moss, C. (1935), 'Jacob of Serugh's Homilies on the Spectacles of the Theatre', *Le Muséon* 48: 87–112.

Mountford, J. F. (1949), 'Music', in *The Oxford Classical Dictionary*. 1st ed. Oxford: 584–91.

(1964), 'Music and the Romans', *Bulletin of John Rylands Library* 47: 198–211.

Mourgues, J.-L. (1988), 'Les Augustiani et l'expérience théâtrale néronienne', *Revue des études latines* 66: 156–81.

(1990), 'Néron et les monarchies hellénistiques: le cas des Augustiani', in *Neronia IV: Alejandro Magno, modelo de los emperadores romanos. Actes du IVe Colloque international de la SIEN*, ed. J. M. Croisille. Brussels: 196–210.

Mouritsen, H. (2001), *Plebs and Politics in the Late Roman Republic*. Cambridge.

(2017), *Politics in the Roman Republic*. Cambridge.

Mratschek, S. (2013), 'Nero the Imperial Misfit: Philhellenism in a Rich Man's World', in *A Companion to the Neronian Age*, eds. E. Buckley and M.T. Dinter. Malden, MA and Oxford: 45–62.

Müller, C. F. W. (1878), *M. Tulli Ciceronis scripta quae manserunt omnia*. Leipzig.

Murray, O. (1965), 'The "Quinquennium Neronis" and the Stoics', *Historia* 14: 41–61.

Murray, P. and Wilson, P. (eds.) (2004), *Music and the Muses: The Culture of Mousike in the Classical Athenian City*. Oxford.

Murray, W. M. and Petsas, P. M. (1989), *Octavian's Campsite Memorial for the Actian War*. Philadelphia.

Musurillo, H. (1954), *Acts of the Pagan Martyrs*. Oxford.

Naerebout, F. G. (2007), 'Das Reich tanzt ... Dance in the Roman Empire and its Discontents', in *Ritual Dynamics and Religious Change in the Roman Empire. Proceedings of the Eighth Workshop of the International*

Network Impact of Empire, eds. O. Hekster, S. Schmidt-Hofner and C. Witschel. Leiden and Boston: 143–58.

Nettl, B. (2005), *The Study of Ethnomusicology: Thirty-One Issues and Concepts.* Urbana, IL and Chicago, IL.

Newby, Z. (2016), *Greek Myths in Roman Art and Culture: Imagery, Values and Identity in Italy, 50 BC–AD 250.* Cambridge.

Nicolet, C. (1974), 'Polybe et les institutions romaines', in *Polybe (Entretiens Hardt 20)*, ed. E. Gabba. Vandoeuvres-Geneva: 209–65.

(1980), *The World of the Citizen in Republican Rome.* London.

Nisbet, R. G. M. (1961), *Marcus Tullius Cicero: In L. Calpurnium Pisonem Oratio. Edited with Text, Introduction and Commentary.* Oxford.

(1995), 'The Survivors: Old-Style Literary Men in the Triumviral Period', in *Collected Papers on Latin Literature*, ed. S. J. Harrison. Oxford: 390–413.

Nock, A. D. (1927), 'The *Lyra* of Orpheus', *Classical Review* 41: 169–71.

(1929), 'Varro and Orpheus', *Classical Review* 43: 60–61.

O'Neill, P. (2003), 'Going Round in Circles: Popular Speech in Ancient Rome', *Classical Antiquity* 22: 135–76.

Olson, D. (2007), *Athenaeus: The Learned Banqueters, Vol. II: Books 3.106e–5.* Cambridge, MA.

Östenberg, I. (2015), 'Power Walks: Aristocratic Escorted Movements in Republican Rome', in *The Moving City: Processions, Passages and Promenades in Ancient Rome*, eds. I Östenberg, S. Malmberg and J. Bjørnebye. London and New York, NY: 13–22.

Page, C. (2010), *The Christian West and Its Singers: The First Thousand Years.* New Haven, CT.

Pailler, J.-M. (2001), 'Et les aulètes refusèrent de chanter les dieux ... (Plutarque, Questions Romaines, 55)', in *Chanter les dieux: Musique et religion dans l'antiquité grecque et romaine. Actes du colloque des 16, 17, et 18 décembre 1999*, ed. P. Brulé and C. Vendries. Rennes: 339–48.

Päll, J. (2004), 'CIL IV 2305: Ein Fragment römischer Musik?', *Zeitschrift für Papyrologie und Epigraphik* 148: 313–15.

Panayotakis, C. (1995), *Theatrum Mundi: Theatrical Elements in the Satyrica of Petronius.* Leiden.

Panella, C. (ed.) (1996), *Meta Sudans I: Un'area sacra in Palatio e la valle del Colosseo prima e dopo Nerone.* Rome.

Parker, H. (1996), 'Plautus vs. Terence: Audience and Popularity Re-examined', *American Journal of Philology* 117: 585–617.

Parmeggiani, G. (2011), *Eforo di Cuma. Studi di storiografia greca.* Bologna.

Pausch, D. (2013), 'Kaiser, Künstler, Kitharöde. Das Bild Neros bei Suet 45', in *Neros Wirklichkeiten. Zur Rezeption einer umstrittenen Gestalt*, ed. C. Walde. Rahden/Westfalen: 45–79.

Pearson, A. C. (1917), *The Fragments of Sophocles.* Cambridge.

Péché, V. (1998), *Musiciens et instruments à vent de type tibiae dans le theatre à Rome (du IIIe siècle avant J.-C. au IIe siècle après J.-C.)*. Unpublished PhD thesis, École Pratiques des Hautes Études, Paris.

(2001), 'Collegium tibicinum romanorum, une association de musiciens au service de la religion romaine', in *Chanter les dieux: Musique et religion dans l'Antiquité grecque et romaine*, eds. P. Brulé and C. Vendries. Rennes.

Péché, V., and Vendries, C. (2001), *Musique et spectacles à Rome et dans l'Occident romain sous la République et le Haut-Empire*. Paris.

Pelling, C. B. R. (1979), 'Plutarch's Method of Work in the Roman Lives', *Journal of Hellenic Studies* 99: 74–96.

(1988), *Plutarch, Life of Antony*. Cambridge.

(1997), Review of Gurval, *Actium and Augustus: The Politics and Emotions of Civil War*, *Journal of Roman Studies* 87: 289–90.

(2000), 'Fun with Fragments: Athenaeus and the Historians', in *Athenaeus and his World: Reading Greek Culture in the Roman Empire*, eds. D. Braund and J. Wilkins. Exeter: 171–89.

Pelosi, F. (2010), *Plato on Music, Soul and Body*. Cambridge.

Pelosi, F. and Petrucci, F. M. (2021), *Music and Philosophy in the Roman Empire*. Cambridge.

Peppas-Delmousou, D. (1979), 'A Statue Base for Augustus (*IG* II^2 3262 + *IG* II^2 4725)', *American Journal of Philology* 100: 125–32.

Perrin, Y. (1990), 'D'Alexandre à Néron: le motif de la tente d'apparat – La salle 29 de la Domus Aurea', in *Neronia IV: Alejandro Magno, modelo de los emperadores romanos. Actes du IVe Colloque international de la SIEN*, ed. J.-M. Croisille. Brussels: 211–29.

(2018), 'Un empereur star au XXIe siècle: Néron dans la publicité et la caricature politique', in *Antiquipop: La reference à l'Antiquité dans la culture populaire contemporaine*, eds. F. Bièvre-Perrin and É. Pampanay. Lyon. Available from http://books.openedition.org/momeditions/3341 (accessed 23 December 2021).

Perrot, J. (1971), *The Organ from its Invention in the Hellenistic Period to the end of the Thirteenth Century*. Trans. N. Deane. London.

Peyras, J. (2002), 'Le Chevalier Septimianus et le Quattuor de Spolète', *Revue belge de philologie et d'histoire* 80: 159–70.

Pighi, G. B. (1941), *De ludis saecularibus populi Romani Quiritium*. Milan.

Platner, S. B., and Ashby, T. (1929), *A Topographical Dictionary of Ancient Rome*. London.

Platts, H. (2020), *Multisensory Living in Ancient Rome: Power and Space in Roman Houses*. London and New York, NY.

Pöhlmann, E. (2010), 'Musica e musicisti greci per Roma / Greek Music and Greek Musicians for Rome', in *La musica nell'Impero Romano: Testimonianze teoriche e scoperte archeologiche. Atti del secondo convegno annuale di MOISA, Cremona, 30–31 ottobre 2008*, ed. E. Rocconi. Pavia: 31–9.

Pöhlmann, E., and West, M. L. (2001), *Documents of Ancient Greek Music: The Extant Melodies and Fragments.* Oxford.

Popkin, M. (2016), *The Architecture of the Roman Triumph: Monuments, Memory, and Identity.* Cambridge.

Porter, J. I. (2018), 'Sounds You Cannot Hear: Cicero and the Tradition of Sublime Criticism', in *Music, Text, and Culture in Ancient Greece,* eds. T. Philipps and A. D'Angour. Oxford: 203–31.

Powell, J. G. F. (2006), *De Re Publica; De Legibus; Cato Maior De Senectute; Laelius De Amicitia.* Oxford and New York, NY.

Powell, J. U. (1925), *Collectanea Alexandrina.* Oxford.

Power, T. C. (2010), *The Culture of Kitharôidia.* Washington, DC.

Powley, H. (1996), 'The Musical Legacy of the Etruscans', in *Etruscan Italy: Etruscan Influences on the Civilizations of Italy from Antiquity to the Modern Era,* ed. J. F. Hall. Provo: 287–303.

Prauscello, L. (2006), *Singing Alexandria: Music between Practice and Textual Transmission.* Leiden.

(2009), 'Wandering Poetry, "Travelling" Music: Timotheus' Muse and Some Case-Studies of Shifting Cultural Identities', in *Wandering Poets in Ancient Greek Culture: Travel, Locality, and Pan-Hellenism,* eds. R. Hunter and I. Rutherford. Cambridge: 168–94.

Prêtre, C. (2000), 'La Tabula Délienne de 168 av. J.-C.', *Bulletin de Correspondance Hellénique* 124: 261–71.

Provenza, A. (2020), 'Music and Medicine', in *A Companion to Ancient Greek and Roman Music,* eds. E. Rocconi and T. A. C. Lynch. Hoboken: 351–64

Pucci, G. (2011), 'Nerone Superstar', in *Nerone,* eds. M. A. Tomei and R. Rea. Rome: 62–75.

Purcell, N. (1987), 'The Nicopolitan Synoecism and Roman Urban Policy', in *Nicopolis I. Proceedings of the First International Symposium on Nicopolis (23–29 September 1984),* ed. E. Chrysos. Preveza: 71–90.

(2013), '"Romans, Play On!": City of the Games', in *The Cambridge Companion to Ancient Rome,* ed. P. Erdkamp. Cambridge: 441–58.

Quaesten, J. (1983), *Music and Worship in Pagan and Christian Antiquity.* Trans. B. Ramsey. Washington, D.C.

Rawson, E. (1983), 'The Senatus Consultum from Larinum', *Journal of Roman Studies* 73: 97–115.

(1985), *Intellectual Life in the Late Roman Republic.* London.

(1987), '*Discrimina Ordinum*: The Lex Iulia Theatralis', *Papers of the British School at Rome* 55: 83–114.

Rawson, P. B. (1987), *The Myth of Marsyas in the Roman Visual Arts: An Iconographic Study.* Oxford.

Rea, R. (2011), 'Nerone, le arte e i ludi', in *Nerone,* eds. M.A. Tomei and R. Rea. Rome: 202–17.

Reinach, T. (1904), 'Inscriptions des îles', *Revue des études grecques* 17: 196–214.

Ribbeck, O. (1873), *Comicorum romanorum praeter Plautum et Terentium fragmenta*. Leipzig.

Richardson, L., Jr. (1977), 'Hercules Musarum and the Porticus Philippi in Rome', *American Journal of Archaeology* 81: 355–61.

(1992), *A New Topographical Dictionary of Ancient Rome*. Baltimore, MD and London.

Richlin, A. (1993), 'Not before Homosexuality: The Materiality of the *Cinaedus* and the Roman Law against Love between Men', *Journal of the History of Sexuality* 3: 523–73.

(2017), *Slave Theater in the Roman Republic*. Cambridge.

Ritschl, F. (1877), 'De M. Terentii Varronis disciplinarum libris commentarius', in *Kleine philologische Schriften (Opuscula philologica 3)*, eds. F. Ritschl. Leipzig: 352–402.

Rives, J. B. (2002), 'Magic in the XII Tables Revisited', *Classical Quarterly* 52: 270–90.

Robert, L. (1978), 'Catalogue agonistique des *Romaia* de Xanthos', *Revue archéologique*: 277–90.

(1983), 'Bulletin épigraphique', *Revue des études grecques* 96: 79–191.

Rocconi, E. (2006), 'Theatres and Theatre Design in the Graeco-Roman World: Theoretical and Empirical Approaches', in *Archaeoacoustics*, eds. C. Scarre and G. Lawson. Cambridge: 71–6.

(2015), 'Music and Dance in Greece and Rome', in *The Blackwell Companion to Ancient Aesthetics*, eds. P. Destrée and P. Murray. Malden, MA and Oxford: 81–93.

Rocconi, E., and Lynch, T. A. C. (eds.) (2020), *A Companion to Ancient Greek and Roman Music*. Hoboken, NJ.

Roccos, L. J. (1989), 'The Augustan Apollo on the Sorrento Base', *American Journal of Archaeology* 93: 571–88.

(2002), 'The Citharode Apollo in Villa Contexts: A Roman Theme with Variations', in *The Ancient Art of Emulation: Studies in Artistic Originality and Tradition from the Present to Classical Antiquity*, ed. E. K. Gazda. Ann Arbor, MI: 273–93.

Romanelli, P., and Carettoni, G. (1955), 'Nuove pitture dal Palatino', *Bolletino d'Arte* 40: 208–14.

Roueché, C. (1984), 'Acclamations in the Later Roman Empire: New Evidence from Aphrodisias', *Journal of Roman Studies* 74: 181–99.

Rowbotham, J. F. (1888), 'The Music of Ancient Rome and Its Opponent', *The Musical Times and Singing Class Circular*, Vol. 29, No. 549 (Nov. 1, 1888): 656–8.

Rüpke, J. (2006), 'Ennius' *Fasti* in Fulvius' Temple: Greek Rationality and Roman Tradition', *Arethusa* 39: 489–512.

(2018), *Pantheon. A New History of Roman Religion*. Princeton, NJ.
Rüpke, J., and Gordon, R. L. (2007), *The Religion of the Romans*. Cambridge and Malden, MA.
Russell, A. (2016), *The Politics of Public Space in Republican Rome*. Cambridge.
Rutledge, S. (2012), *Ancient Rome as a Museum: Power, Identity and the Culture of Collecting*. Oxford.
Sachs, C. (1940), *The History of Musical Instruments*. New York, NY.
(1944), *The Rise of Music in the Ancient World: East and West*. London.
Salvo, I. (2013), 'Romulus and Remus at Chios Revisited: A Re-examination of SEG XXX 1073', in *Epigraphical Approaches to the Post-Classical Polis: Fourth Century BC to Second Century AD*, eds. P. Martzavou and N. Papazarkadas. Oxford: 125–37.
Sandbach, F. H. (1982), 'How Terence's *Hecyra* Failed', *Classical Quarterly* 32: 134–5.
Schäfer, T. (1993), 'Zur Datierung des Siegesdenkmals von Actium', *Mitteilungen des deutschen archäologischen Instituts: Athenische Abteilung* 108: 239–48.
(2013), 'Ciclo di rilievi Medinaceli', in *Augusto*, eds. E. La Rocca, C. Parisi Presicce, A. Lo Monaco, C. Giroire, and D. Roger. Milan: 320–3.
Scheid, J. (1995), '*Graeco Ritu*: A Typically Roman Way of Honoring the Gods', *Harvard Studies in Classical Philology* 97: 15–31.
(2003), *An Introduction to Roman Religion*. Bloomington, IN.
Schlapbach, K. (2018), *The Anatomy of Dance Discourse: Literary and Philosophical Approaches to Dance in the Later Graeco-Roman World*. Oxford.
(2020), 'The Dance of Priests, Matronae, and Philosophers: Aspects of Dance Culture in Rome and the Roman Empire', *Greek and Roman Musical Studies* 8: 190–99.
Schnegg-Köhler, B. (2002), *Die augusteischen Säkularspiele*. Leipzig.
Schollmeyer, P. (2019), 'Ein Unfallfahrer auf dem Kaiserthron – Anmerkungen zu Neros Versagen als Wagenlenker', in *Der Herrscher als Versager?! Vergleichende Perspektiven auf vormoderne Herrschaftsformen, Kraftprobe Herrschaft, Bd. 1: 235–253*, eds. H. Grieser, H. Frielinghaus, S. Grätz, L. Körntgen, J. Pahlitzsch, D. Prechel, N. Baumann, J. V. M. P. Dias, and A. Fuchs. Gottingen: 235–53.
Schulz, V. (2019), *Deconstructing Imperial Representation: Tacitus, Cassius Dio, and Suetonius on Nero and Domitian*. Leiden and Boston, MA.
(2020), 'The Music of the Words in Roman Rhetoric', in *A Companion to Ancient Greek and Roman Music*, eds. T. Lynch and E. Rocconi. Hoboken, NJ: 365–77.
Sciarrino, E. (2004a), 'A Temple for the Professional Muse: The *Aedes Herculis Musarum* and Cultural Shifts in Second-Century BC Rome', in *Rituals in Ink: Literary and Religious Discourses in Roman Culture*, eds. A. Barchiesi, J. Rüpke, and S. Stephens. Stuttgart: 45–56.

(2004b), 'Putting Cato the Censor's *Origines* in its Place', *Classical Antiquity* 23: 323–57.

Scoditti, F. (2009), *Solisti ed esecutori nella cultura musicale romana*. Galatina.

(2010), *Musicae Latinae glossarium*. Rome.

Scullard, H. H. (1981), *Festivals and Ceremonies of the Roman Republic*. London.

Seager, R. (1972), 'Cicero and the Word *Popularis*', *Classical Quarterly* 22: 328–38.

Sear, F. (2006), *Roman Theatres: An Architectural Study*. Oxford.

Sedley, D. (2009), 'Epicureanism in the Roman Republic', in *The Cambridge Companion to Epicureanism*, ed. J. Warren. Cambridge: 29–45.

Shanzer, D. R. (1986a), 'The Late Antique Tradition of Varro's *Onos Lyras*', *Rheinisches Museum* 129: 272–85.

(1986b), *A Philosophical and Literary Commentary on Martianus Capella's De Nuptiis Philologiae et Mercurii, Book 1*. Berkeley, CA.

(2005), 'Augustine's Disciplines: *Silent Diutius Musae Varronis?*' in *Augustine and the Disciplines: From Cassiciacum to Confessions*, eds. K. Pollman and M. Vessey. Oxford: 69–112.

Shaw, B. D. (2011), *Sacred Violence: African Christians and Sectarian Hatred in the Age of Augustine*. Cambridge.

Sherk, R. K. (1966), 'Cos and the Dionysiac Artists', *Historia* 15: 211–16.

Sick, D. (1999), 'Ummidia Quadratilla: Cagey Businesswoman or Lazy Pantomime Watcher?', *Classical Antiquity* 18: 330–48.

Sider, D. (1997), *The Epigrams of Philodemus: Introduction, Text, and Commentary*. Oxford.

Simpson, C. (2000), 'Musicians and the Arena. Dancers and the Hippodrome', *Latomus* 59: 633–9.

Skulimowska, Z. (1966), 'Les instruments de musique dans le mime scénique grec en Egypte', in *Mélanges offerts à K. Michalowski*, ed. M. L. Bernhard. Warsaw: 175–9.

Skutsch, O. (1968), *Studia Enniana*. London.

Slater, W. J. (1994), 'Pantomime Riots', *Classical Antiquity* 13: 120–44.

(2004), 'Where are the Actors?', in *Le statut de l'acteur dans l'Antiquité grecque et romaine. Actes du colloque qui s'est tenu à Tours les 3 et 4 mai 2002*, eds. C. Hugoniot, F. Hurlet and S. Milanezi. Tours: 143–60.

(2007), 'Deconstructing Festivals', in *The Greek Theatre and Festivals: Documentary Studies*, ed. P. Wilson. Oxford: 21–47.

Small, J. P. (1982), *Cacus and Marsyas in Etrusco-Roman Legend*. Princeton, NJ.

Smith, B. R. (2006), 'What Means This Noise?', in *"Noyses, Sounds, and Sweet Aires": Music in Early Modern England*, ed. J. A. Owens. Washington, DC: 20–31.

Smith, P. L. (1970), 'Vergil's Avena and the Pipes of Pastoral Poetry', *Transactions and Proceedings of the American Philological Association* 101: 497–510.

Snell, B., and Maehler, H. (eds.) (1975), *Pindari carmina cum fragmentis*. Leipzig.

Sobocinski, M. G. (2006), 'Visualizing Ceremony: The Design and Audience of the *Ludi Saeculares* Coinage of Domitian', *American Journal of Archaeology* 110: 581–602.

Sommer, M. (2013), 'Scipio Aemilianus, Polybius, and the Quest for Friendship in Second-Century Rome', in *Polybius and his World: Essays in Memory of F. W. Walbank*, eds. B. Gibson and T. Harrison. Oxford: 307–18.

Stahl, W. H. (1990), *Macrobius, Commentary on the Dream of Scipio, Translated with an Introduction*. New York, NY.

Stamires, G. A. (1957), 'Some Greek Inscriptions', *Hesperia* 26: 198–270.

Starr, R. J. (1991), 'Reading Aloud: *Lectores* and Roman Reading', *Classical Journal* 86: 337–43.

Stewart, E. (2020), 'The Profession of *Mousikē* in Classical Greece', in *Skilled Labour and Professionalism in Ancient Greece and Rome*, eds. E. Stewart, E. Harris and D. Lewis. Cambridge: 269–92.

Stroux, C. (2009), 'Appendice: caratteristische musicali dell'hydraulis di Dion', in *La Musa dimenticata: Aspetti dell'esperienza musicale greca in età ellenistica*, eds. M. C. Martinelli, F. Pelosi and C. Pernigotti. Pisa: 267–9.

Syme, R. (2016), 'The Gay Sempronia', in *Approaching the Roman Revolution. Papers on Republican History*, ed. F. Santangelo. Oxford: 173–81.

Tan, J. (2013), 'Publius Clodius and the Boundaries of the *Contio*', in *Community and Communication: Oratory and Politics in Republican Rome*, eds. C. Steel and H. van der Blom. Oxford: 117–32.

Tatum, W. J. (1999), *The Patrician Tribune: Publius Clodius Pulcher*. Chapel Hill, NC.

Taylor, R. M. (2021), *Ancient Naples: A Documentary History, Origins to c. 350 CE*. New York, NY and Bristol.

Thomas, R. F. (2011), *Horace, Odes Book IV and Carmen Saeculare*. Cambridge.

Thonemann, P. (2020), *An Ancient Dream Manual: Artemidorus' The Interpretation of Dreams*. Oxford.

Tobin, F. (2013), 'Music and Musical Instruments in Etruria', in *The Etruscan World*, ed. J. M. Turfa. Oxford and New York, NY: 841–54.

Tomei, M. A. (2017), 'Il monumento celebrativo della battaglia di Azio sul Palatino', *Mélanges de l'École française de Rome* 129: 413–24.

Tomei, M. A., and Gasparri, C. (2014), *Museo Palatino: Le Collezioni*. Milan.

Tomei, M. A., and Rea, R. (eds.) (2011), *Nerone*. Rome.

Toner, J. P. (2009), *Popular Culture in Ancient Rome*. Cambridge.

(2014), *A Cultural History of the Senses in Antiquity*. London.

(2017), 'The Intellectual Life of the Roman Non-Elite', in *Popular Culture in the Ancient World*, ed. L. Grig. Cambridge: 167–88.

Townend, G. B. (1980), 'Calpurnius Siculus and the *Munus Neronis*', *Journal of Roman Studies* 70: 166–75.

Trietler, L. (1999), 'The Historiography of Music: Issues of Past and Present', in *Rethinking Music*, eds. N. Cook and M. Everist. Oxford: 356–77.

Van Nijf, O. (2001), 'Local Heroes: Athletics, Festivals and Elite Self-Fashioning in the Roman East', in *Being Greek under Rome: Cultural Identity, the Second Sophistic and the Development of Empire*, ed. S. Goldhill. Cambridge: 306–34.

Veitch, J. (2017), 'Soundscape of the Street: Architectural Acoustics in Ostia', in *Senses of the Empire: Multisensory Approaches to Roman Culture*, ed. E. Betts. London: 54–70.

Vendries, C. (1999) *Instruments à cordes et musiciens dans l'Empire romain: étude historique et archéologique (IIe siècle av. J.-C.-Ve siècle ap. J.-C.)*. Paris

(2001), 'Le couvercle du sarcophage de M. Sempronios Nikokratès "poète et cithariste" (IGUR 1326)', in *Musique et poésie dans l'antiquité. Actes du colloque de Clermont-Ferrand, Université Blaise Pascal, 23 mai 1997*, ed. G.-J. Pinault. Clermont-Ferrand: 109–22.

(2004), 'Musique romaine', in *Thesaurus Cultus et Rituum Antiquorum*, II. 397–415.

(2013), 'Questions d'iconographie musicale: L'apport des terres cuites à la connaissance de la musique dans l'Égypte hellénistique et romaine', *Greek and Roman Musical Studies* 1: 195–227.

(ed.) (2020), *Cornua de Pompéi: Trompettes romaines de la gladiature*. Rennes.

Viereck, P. (1908), 'Aktenstücke zum grieschisch-römischen Vereinswese', *Klio* 8: 413–26.

Vincent, A. (2008), 'Auguste et les tibicines', *Mélanges de l'École française de Rome* 120: 427–46.

(2016), *Jouer pour la Cité: une histoire sociale et politique des musiciens professionnels de l'Occident romain*. Rome.

(2017a), 'The Music of Power and the Power of Music: Studying Popular Auditory Culture in Ancient Rome', in *Popular Culture in the Ancient World*, ed. L. Grig. Cambridge: 149–64.

(2017b), 'Tuning into the Past: Methodological Perspectives in the Contextualised Study of the Sounds of Roman Antiquity', in *Senses of the Empire: Multisensory Approaches to Roman Culture*, ed. E. Betts. London: 147–58.

Viscogliosi, A. (1993a), 'Apollo, Aedes in Circo', in *Lexicon topographicum urbis Romae*, I. 49–54.

(1993b), 'Circus Flaminius', in *Lexicon topographicum urbis Romae*, I. 269–72.

(1996), 'Hercules Musarum, Aedes', in *Lexicon topographicum urbis Romae*, III. 17–19.

Volk, K. (2021), *The Roman Republic of Letters: Scholarship, Philosophy, and Politics in the Age of Cicero and Caesar*. Princeton, NJ.

Walbank, F. W. (1979), *A Historical Commentary on Polybius*. Vol. 3. Oxford.

(2000), 'Athenaeus and Polybius', in *Athenaeus and his World: Reading Greek Culture in the Roman Empire*, eds. D. Braund and J. Wilkins. Exeter: 161–70.

(2002), *Polybius, Rome and the Hellenistic World*. Cambridge.
Walde, C. (ed.) (2013), *Neros Wirklichkeiten. Zur Rezeption einer umstrittenen Gestalt*. Rahden/Westfalen.
Walden, D. K. S. (2014), 'Frozen Music: Music and Architecture in Vitruvius' *De Architectura*', *Greek and Roman Musical Studies* 2: 124–45.
Wallace, R. W. (1997), 'Poet, Public, and "Theatrocracy"', in *Poet, Public, and Performance in Ancient Greece*, eds. L. Edmunds and R. W. Wallace. Baltimore: 97–111.
(2004), 'Damon of Oa: A Music Theorist Ostracized?', in *Music and the Muses: The Culture of Mousike in the Classical Athenian City*, eds. P. Murray and P. Wilson. Oxford: 249–68.
Wallace-Hadrill, A. (1983), *Suetonius: The Scholar and His Caesars*. London.
Waner, M. (2014), 'Aspects of Music Culture in the Land of Israel during the Hellenistic, Roman and Byzantine Periods: Sepphoris as a Case Study', in *Music in Antiquity: The Near East and the Mediterranean*, eds. J. G. Westenholz, Y. Maurey, E. Seroussi and M. Caine. Berlin: 273–96.
Wardle, D. (2014), *Suetonius, Life of Augustus*. Oxford.
Warmington, B. H. (1969), *Nero: Reality and Legend*. London.
Webb, R. (2008), *Demons and Dancers: Performance in Late Antiquity*. Cambridge, MA, and London.
(2013), 'Professional Musicians in Late Antiquity', in *Le Status du Musicien dans le Méditerranée ancienne: Égypte, Mésopotamie, Grèce, Rome*, ed. S. Emerit. Le Caire: 279–98.
Weiss, N. A. (2018), *The Music of Tragedy: Performance and Imagination in Euripidean Theater*. Berkeley, CA.
Welch, T. S. (2005), *The Elegiac Cityscape: Propertius and the Meaning of Roman Monuments*. Columbus, OH.
West, M. L. (1992), *Ancient Greek Music*. Oxford.
(2000), 'Music Therapy in Antiquity', in *Music as Medicine: The History of Music Therapy since Antiquity*, ed. P. Horden. Aldershot: 51–68.
(2007), 'A New Musical Papyrus: Carcinus, *Medea*', *Zeitschrift für Papyrologie und Epigraphik* 161: 1–10.
Westermann, W. L. (1924), 'The Castanet Dancers of Arsinoe', *Journal of Egyptian Archaeology* 10: 134–44.
Whitmarsh, T. (1999), 'Greek and Roman in Dialogue: The Pseudo-Lucianic Nero', *Journal of Hellenic Studies* 119: 142–60.
(2004), 'The Cretan Lyre Paradox: Mesomedes, Hadrian, and the Poetics of Patronage', in *Paideia: The World of the Second Sophistic*, ed. B. E. Borg. Berlin: 377–402.
Wiles, D. (2019), 'The Environment of Theatre: Experiencing Place in the Ancient World', in *A Cultural History of Theatre in Antiquity*, ed. M. Revermann. London and New York, NY: 63–82.
Wilkes, J. (1992), *The Illyrians*. Oxford.

Wilkins, D. (2007), 'Vers une histoire sympotique', in *Athénée et les fragments d'historiens,* ed. D. Lenfant. Paris: 29–39.

Wille, G. (1967), *Musica Romana: die Bedeutung der Musik im Leben der Römer.* Amsterdam.

Williams, C. A. (2010), *Roman Homosexuality.* 2nd ed. Oxford.

Williams, G. W. (1968), *Tradition and Originality in Roman Poetry.* Oxford.

Williams, G. D. (2003), *Seneca: De Otio, De Brevitate Vitae.* Cambridge.

Williams, P. (1980), *A New History of the Organ from the Greeks to the Present Day.* Bloomington, IN.

 (1993), *The Organ in Western Culture, 750–1250.* Cambridge.

Wilson, P. (1999), 'The Aulos in Athens', in *Performance Culture and Athenian Democracy,* eds. S. Goldhill and R. Osborne. Cambridge: 58–95.

 (2002), 'The Musicians among the Actors', in *Greek and Roman Actors: Aspects of an Ancient Profession,* eds. P. E. Easterling and E. Hall. Cambridge: 39–68.

 (2004), 'Athenian Strings', in *Music and the Muses: The Culture of Mousike in the Classical Athenian City,* eds. P. Murray and P. Wilson. Oxford: 269–306.

Winkler, M. M. (2017), 'Nero in Hollywood', in *The Cambridge Companion to the Age of Nero,* eds. S. Bartsch, K. Freudenburg, and C. Littlewood. Cambridge: 318–32.

Wiseman, T. P. (1974), 'The Circus Flaminius', *Papers of the British School at Rome* 42: 3–26.

 (1976), 'Two Questions on the Circus Flaminius', *Papers of the British School at Rome* 44: 44–7.

 (1980), 'Looking for Camerius: The Topography of Catullus 55', *Papers of the British School at Rome* 48: 6–16.

 (1985), *Catullus and his World: A Reappraisal.* Cambridge.

 (1994), *Historiography and Imagination: Eight Essays on Roman Culture.* Exeter.

 (2000), 'Liber: Myth, Drama and Ideology in Republican Rome', in *The Roman Middle Republic: Politics, Religion and Historiography, c. 400–133 B.C,* ed. C. Bruun. Rome: 265–99.

 (2002), 'Ovid and the Stage', in *Ovid's Fasti: Historical Readings at its Bimillenium,* ed. G. Herbert-Brown. Oxford: 275–99.

 (2008), *Unwritten Rome.* Exeter.

 (2009), *Remembering the Roman People: Essays on Late-Republican Politics and Literature.* Oxford.

 (2010), 'The Two-Headed State: How Romans Explained Civil War', in *Citizens of Discord: Rome and Its Civil Wars,* eds. B. W. Breed, C. Damon and A. Rossi. Oxford: 24–44.

 (2012), 'A Debate on the Temple of Apollo Palatinus: *Roma Quadrata,* Archaic Huts, the House of Augustus, and the Orientation of Palatine Apollo', *Journal of Roman Archaeology* 25: 371–87.

(2013), 'The Palatine, from Evander to Elagabalus', *Journal of Roman Studies* 103: 234–68.

(2015), *The Roman Audience: Classical Literature as Social History*. Oxford.

(2016), 'Maecenas and the Stage', *Papers of the British School at Rome* 84: 131–55.

(2017), 'Politics and the People: What Counts as Evidence?', *Bulletin of the Institute of Classical Studies* 60: 16–33.

(2019), *The House of Augustus: A Historical Detective Story*. Princeton, NJ and Oxford.

Woodman, T. (1992), 'Nero's Alien Capital: Tacitus as Paradoxographer (ANNALS 15.36-7)', in *Author and Audience in Latin Literature*, eds. T. Woodman and J. Powell. 173–88. Cambridge.

Wootton, G. E. M. (2004), 'Representations of Musicians in the Roman Mime', *Mediterranean Archaeology* 17: 243–52.

Wyke, M. (1994), 'Make like Nero! The Appeal of a Cinematic Emperor', in *Reflections of Nero: Culture, History and Representation*, eds. J. Elsner and J. Masters. London: 11–28.

Yuan, J. (2005), 'Fragment with Musical Notation', *The Oxyrhynchus Papyri* 69: 45–6.

Zachos, K. L. (2003), 'The Tropaeum of the Sea-battle of Actium at Nikopolis', *Journal of Roman Archaeology* 16: 65–92.

(2007), *Nicopolis 2. Proceedings of the Second International Nicopolis Symposium*. Preveza.

Zanker, P. (1983), 'Der Apollontempel auf dem Palatin. Ausstattung und politische Sinnbezuge auch der Schlacht von Actium', in *Città e architettura nella Roma imperiale. Atti del seminario del 27 ottobre 1981 nel 25o anniversario dell'Accademia di Danimarca*, ed. K. De Fine Licht. Odense: 21–40.

(1988), *The Power of Images in the Age of Augustus*. Trans. A. Shapiro. Ann Arbor, MI.

Zecchini, G. (2007), 'Athénée et les historiens', in *Athénée et les fragments d'historiens*, ed. D. Lenfant. Paris: 19–28.

Zell, K. (1829), 'Uber die Volkslieder der alten Römer', *Ferienschriften* 2: 99–224.

Zetzel, J. E. G. (1999), *Cicero: On the Commonwealth and On the Laws*. Cambridge.

(2003), 'Plato with Pillows: Cicero on the Uses of Greek Culture', in *Myth, History and Culture in Republican Rome*, eds. D. Braund and C. Gill. Exeter: 119–38.

Zink, S. (2008), 'Reconstructing the Palatine Temple of Apollo: A Case Study in Early Augustan Temple Design', *Journal of Roman Archeology* 21: 47–63.

(2012), 'Old and New Archaeological Evidence for the Plan of the Palatine Temple of Apollo', *Journal of Roman Archeology* 25: 389–402.

Ziolkowski, J. (1999), 'The Invention of the *Tuba* (Trumpet)', *Classical World* 92: 363–73.

Ziolkowski, J. M. (2007), *Fairy Tales from before Fairy Tales: The Medieval Latin Past of Wonderful Lies*. Ann Arbor, MI.
Zorzetti, N. (1990), 'The *Carmina Convivalia*', in *Sympotica: A Symposium on the Symposion*, ed. O. Murray. Oxford: 289–307.
  (1991), 'Poetry and Ancient City: The Case of Rome', *Classical Journal* 86: 311–29.

Index

acclamations, 121, 236-7, 247
acroamata, 64, 66, 118, 186
Actium, 40, 142, 153-60, 167, 170-1, 189-90
    Battle of, 142, 155-6
    Octavian's campsite memorial at, 154, 158
    sanctuary of Apollo at, 154
actors, 9, 36, 44, 46, 54, 61, 63, 78, 80, 94, 99-100, 102-3, 105, 118-19, 134, 186, 189, 212, 216, 225, 234
Aelius Aristides, 177
Aemilius Paullus, Lucius, 48, 51-5, 57, 61-2, 65, 77, 81
    funeral of, 61
    games at Amphipolis, 55, 65, 81
    triumph of, 51, 53, 57
Afranius, Lucius, 107
Anaxenor (citharode), 163-5, 168
Antiochus IV (Epiphanes), 64-6, 71
Antonius, Marcus (Mark Antony), 41, 142-4, 153-4, 160-73, 189, 246
Apollo, 7, 40, 51, 142-63, 171, 173-6, 178-84, 200-6, 213, 224, 227, 238, 244, *See also* Temple of Apollo
    Actius (Actian), 155-8
    Augustus worshipped as, 152-3, 162, 206
    on coins, 142-3, 155-60, 204-6
    contest with Marsyas, 161-3
    Medicus (Healer), 178
    Musagetes (Leader of the Muses), 180, 182
    Nero worshipped as, 204-6
    Tortor (Tormentor), 163
    vs. Dionysus, 160-1, 163, 171
Arcadians, 21, 67-71, 73, 81, 174
Aristides Quintilianus, 83-4, 94-5
Aristotle, 25, 135, 244
Aristoxenus, 25, 89, 96, 135
army. *See* militarism
ars ludicra, 77-9
Athenaeus, 42, 45-7, 69, 191
Atticus, Titus Pomponius, 26, 97
audiences, musicality of, 5, 7, 9, 102-4, 119, 135, 191, 214-15
Augustiani, 200-1, 235-7

Augustine, 6, 15, 84, 85, 247
Augustus/Octavian, 40-1, 142-4, 147-58, 160-4, 169-71, 173, 198-206, 226, 230, 244, 246
    as Apollo, 151-3, 206
    defeat of Sextus Pompey, 144, 154
    as 'harmoniser', 176-7
    House of, 149-51
    patronage of musicians, 186-7
    reforms of *collegia*, 187-9
    rivalry with Mark Antony, 41, 160-73, 246
    triple triumph of, 200
auletes. *See* tibicen
aulos. *See* tibia

Bacchus. *See* Dionysus
bagpipes, 17, 195, 198, 216-17, 222
Bathyllus (pantomime), 185-6
Brutus, 153
bucina, 18

Caelius, Marcus, 72-3
Caligula, 217, 225
canere, vs. *cantare*, 14-15
canticum, 9, 14, 46, 198, 210, 213, 229
cantor, 77-9, 119, 121
cantus, 12, 14, 105-6, 120, 139, 202, 228
carmen, 12, 14-15, 21, 60, 73, 120, 145-6, 211-13, 219, 227-8, 230, 237, 247
Carmen Saeculare, 181-2
Cato the Elder, 5, 40, 48, 72-3, 76, 81-2, 108, 242, 244, 246
    affinity with Polybius, 76-7
    against M. Caelius, 72-3
    on *carmina convivalia*, 73, 244
chariot-racing, 5, 18, 63, 240
    Nero's passion for, 199, 223
choraules, 36, 195
chorus, 43, 56-9, 117-18, 164-5, 177, 186, 234, 237
Cicero
    accused of copying dancers, 107
    accuses opponents of dancing, 107

279

Cicero (cont.)
  against Antony's judiciary law, 165–6
  alludes to organ, 219–21
  on appropriate occasions for singing, 2, 28, 38
  attack on music in *De Re Publica*, 94–6
  on audience behaviour, 88, 90–1, 96–7, 103, 138
  client of physician Asclepiades, 31
  on early Roman drama, 89–90
  on Gaius Gracchus, 110–14
  on Greek music, 13, 21–2
  on *ludi publici*, 86–7
  on musical *ethos*, 25, 31–2
  as *musicus*, 84–5
  on *occentatio*, 120
  opposition to *ludus talarius*, 79–80
  and Philodemus, 86, 123, 125–6, 128
  and Plato, 88–9, 91–2, 94, 96, 139, 220, 244
  praises Fulvius Nobilior's devotion to Muses, 54
  on private music-making, 28, 35, 127–8, 140
  reaction to Pompey's games, 100–4
  on responsibilities of politicians, 93–4, 140, 246
  rivalry with Clodius, 116–20, 122
  on role of music in oratory, 104–6, 110
  on Twelve Tables as *carmen*, 15
  on use of lyres at ceremonial banquets, 181
  and Varro, 134–5
cinaedi, 73–6, 240
circus, 27, 42–3, 50, 56, 62, 87, 186, 198, 207, 219–20, 223–4, 233, 239
  Flaminius, 51–2, 54, 81, 179–83
  Maximus, 50–1, 239
cithara. See lyre
citharode, 26, 36, 63, 70–1, 101, 103, 163–5, 168, 172, 176, 180, 183, 192–4, 199, 201, 211, 213, 225, 227, 235, See also Apollo
Cleopatra, 142, 160, 167, 170–1, 189
  compared to musician, 169–70, 172
  music at the court of, 167–8, 187
Clodius, Publius, 86, 98, 107, 115–22, 140, 246–7
  and the Bona Dea scandal, 115–17
  at Milo's trial, 117–18
  attacked in *Pro Sestio*, 118–19, 122
collegia, 6, 30, 54, 187–9, 241
convicium, 119–20
convivium, 26, 127–8, 141, 230–2, 240, See also symposium

cornicen, 18, 36, 56, 60, 219
cornu, 9, 18, 56, 58, 221
crotalum, 18, 80
Cybele, worship of, 29, 33–4, 239
cymbala. See cymbals
cymbals, 9, 18, 29, 31, 37, 79–80, 127–9, 161, 170, 222, 243
dance See also pantomime
  in Anicius' games, 42–4, 46, 56, 61
  aspect of *mousike*, 11, 133, 240
  association with Apollo, 143
  during Anna Perenna festival, 121
  during banquets, 64–5, 107, 124, 232
  Etruscan, 21
  at Greek festivals, 63, 68–9
  moral opposition to, 38–9, 72–6, 79–80, 170, 210, 225, 228–9, 242–3, 245
  part of citharodic performance, 70
  part of Roman aristocratic education, 226, 235, 237
  pursuit of Roman emperors, 225
  in religious rituals, 29
  in Roman theatre, 5, 9, 37, 76, 79, 91, 101, 121, 137, 233
  as topic of Roman invective, 26, 106–8, 127–8, 165
  in the triumph, 57–60

Demetrius Poliorcetes, 45, 172
didascaliae, 9
Dionysius of Halicarnassus, 21–2, 29, 59, 105–6, 115, 174
Dionysus, 107, 143, 173
  vs. Apollo, 160–3, 171
  Artists of, 68, 70, 164–5, 168–9
  drums. See *tympana*
  and Mark Antony, 160–1, 164–7
drunkenness, 30, 32, 130, 166, 208, 228, 232

education, 21–7, 67, 71, 73–5, 126, 174–5, 225–8, 242
Ennius, 133–4, 173
Epicureanism, 85–6, 123–4, 126, 128–30, 136, 220, 244
ethos, 125, 135–6, 140, 244
Etruscans, 3, 18–21, 60

festivals. See *ludi*
Festus, 119
fistula, 17, 97, 110–15
Flamininus, Titus Quinctius, 64
Fleischhauer, Günther, 4
forum, 105, 113, 132, 136, 241

Augustum, 190
   singing in, 2, 28
   statue of Marsyas in, 162
Fronto, 79–81, 243
funerals, 15, 18, 60–1, 177, 242

games. *See ludi*
gender, 6, 20
   and masculinity, 32, 80–1, 106
   and musical language, 33–4, 239–40
gladiators, 5, 18, 36, 60–1, 65, 81, 219, 233, 240
Gracchus, Gaius, 86, 110–15, 122, 140, 246
Gracchus, Tiberius, 74
Gruen, Erich S., 44–5, 48, 62

Habinek, Thomas N., 4, 14–15, 73, 92, 106
Hadrian, 8, 226
harmony
   attribute of Apollo, 143, 160, 162–3, 173, 178, 183, 205
   metaphor for political concord, 95–6, 115, 176–7
   part of *ars musica*, 11, 240
   in Pythagorean thought, 95, 134, 138, 175–6
   theory of, 13–14, 90, 124, 134, 244
harp, 17–18, 22, 74–5, 116–18, 122, 163–4, 169, 172, 191, 211
Hellenisation, 19–20, 82, 245–6
Horace, 20, 35, 146, 181, 187
Horsfall, Nicholas, 5, 15, 121, 138
hydraulis. *See* organ

Isis, worship of, 18, 29, 33

Jerome, 15
Julius Caesar, 106, 115, 122, 187, 199
Juvenal, 33, 35–7, 192, 239

kitharoidia, 144, 180, 183, 189–90, 194, 197, 202, 212, 225

Lesser Quinquatrus, 30
lituus, 18
Livius Andronicus, 88–9
Livy, 21–3, 49, 52–5, 75, 180
Lucretius, 85, 121–6
ludi, 48, 52, 61, 87–9, 92, 240
   astici, 182, 184
   circenses, 87
   Etruscan origins of, 21
   focus of popular politics, 97
   Latini, 182
   organisation of, 92

   performers at, 94
   scaenici, 50, 87, 101, 182, 188, 232
   seating at, 50
   thymelici, 182, 184
Ludi Apollinares, 51, 97, 119, 122, 180, 183
Ludi Iuvenalium ('Juvenile Games'), 194
Ludi Maximi, 225, 233
Ludi Megalenses, 61
Ludi Romani, 59–60
Ludi Saeculares, 41, 178, 181–4, 189
ludius, 118, 187
ludus talarius, 77–81, 243
lyra. *See* lyre
lyre. *See also* Apollo, *kitharoidia*
   attribute of Hercules, 54, 180
   attribute of Mercury, 138, 175
   brought to Italy by Arcadians, 21, 174
   in Cleopatra's entourage, 167
   criticism of, 69, 79, 88, 90
   in dream of Septimius Severus, 177
   in Etruscan art, 20
   etymology of, 181
   female players of, 23–4, 38, 75
   instrument of Orpheus, 102
   and *ludi*, 59, 87, 95, 121, 234
   male players of, 35–7, 84, 140, 165, 168, 180, 183, 189, 208–9, 225–8
   psychological effects of, 124
   in rhetorical theory, 104–5, 117
   in *ritus Graecus*, 181
   technical knowledge of, 24, 177
   and the triumph, 57–8
   types of, 17
   in Varro's *Onos Lyras*, 86, 129–39

Macrobius, 38–9, 72–4, 185, 187
Martial, 36–7, 102–3, 222
melodies, extant, 6, 8
melody
   and acclamations, 121
   as *ars*, 103
   bending, 14
   in Christian worship, 247
   despicable, 95
   difference between Greek and Latin, 8
   and *ethos*, 32
   Latin terms for, 13
   and oratory, 105
   ornamentation, 90
   pleasurable effect of, 124
   as political tool, 122
   and rhythm, 31, 90, 103, 140
   and sensory perception, 31

melody (cont.)
   shameful, 33
Mercury, 138, 175
Mesomedes (citharode), 8, 225
metre
   in early Roman drama, 89
   and *ethos*, 14
   part of *ars musica*, 240
   in Roman comedy, 9
militarism
   in Anicius' games, 52, 56, 59–60, 81, 246
   in Antiochus' procession, 65
   and brass music, 18, 33, 48
mime, 58, 63–6, 78, 100–1, 111–12, 137–8, 233, 235
Moore, Timothy, 5, 8–9, 88–90, 176
mousike, 8, 11, 22, 54, 71, 73, 82, 89, 95, 132–3, 135–6, 174, 240
Muses, 54, 107, 133–4, 153, 179–80
musicians
   busking, 1, 28, 208, 212
   celebrity, 37, 44, 165, 168, 186, 191, 211
   status of, 34–9, 94, 188–9

Nero, 24, 39, 41, 180, 191–228, 230, 233, 235–8
   afterlife, 207–8
   as bagpiper (*utricularius*), 195, 216–17, 222
   emulation of Augustus, 198–203, 205–6
   interest in organ, 215–17, 221–2
   modern reception, 192
   musical career, 192–5
   passion for chariot-racing, 223
   rivalry with Britannicus, 230
New Music, 14, 88
Nicopolis, 154, 160, 205
Nietzsche, Friedrich, 160–1
Norbanus, Lucius, 23
notation, 8, 185
Numa Pompilius, 177, 188
numerus, 12, 31, 103, 105, 111–12, 139

Octavia, 187
Octavian. *See* Augustus/Octavian
oratory, 22, 79, 104–6, 110, 113, 140
orchestra, 43, 102, 233
organ, 9, 17, 126, 195, 198, 215–24
Orpheus, 102, 176

panpipe. *See fistula*
pantomime, 78, 184–6, 234, 237
percussion instruments, 18, 75
philhellenism, 24, 54, 82, 128
Philo of Alexandria, 176–7, 225

Philodemus, 85–6, 91, 122, 124–6, 128, 137
Philostratus of Athens, 191, 199, 207–12
phorbeia, 171
pipe. *See tibia*
Piso Caesoninus, Lucius Calpurnius (consul 58 BCE), 85, 126–9
Piso, Gaius Calpurnius (conspirator), 227
Plato, 25, 71, 76, 83, 86–123, 125–6, 135, 137, 139, 161, 221, 244
Plautus, 8–9, 45–6, 55, 73, 75, 120
Pliny the Elder, 25, 146–7, 179
Pliny the Younger, 23
Plutarch, 31, 51, 57–8, 76, 112, 117–18, 153, 160, 163–9, 171–3, 247
poetry, 1, 6, 85, 123, 126, 155
   and *mousike*, 11, 54, 133, 240
   composed by Nero, 211
Polybius
   affinity with Scipio, 76–7
   on Anicius' games, 40, 42–8, 50, 52, 56, 60–3, 65–7, 71, 81–2, 246
   on Antiochus IV, 64–5
   on Arcadian music, 67–70, 73
   aversion to sympotic music, 63–4, 75, 80
Pompilius (tragedian), 133–4
Portico of Philippus, 179–80
Propertius, 143, 145–7, 151, 159, 171, 174
prostitute, 36, 163, 210, 239, 242, 245
psaltria. *See* harp
Ptolemy I (Soter), 172
Ptolemy II (Philadelphus), 172
Ptolemy IV (Philopator), 170–1
Ptolemy XII (Auletes), 170–1
Pylades (pantomime), 185–6
Pythagoras, 25, 32, 76
Pythagoreanism, 25, 84, 95, 123, 136, 138–9, 175, 244

Quinquatrus Minusculae. *See* Lesser Quinquatrus
Quintilian, 1–2, 24, 33, 79–80, 111–15

Rawson, Elizabeth, 84, 86, 139
religion, 1, 5–6, 15, 18, 28–9, 33–4, 38, 180–1, 188–9
rhythm
   and acclamations, 121, 247
   in early Roman drama, 89–90
   effects of, 31
   and *ethos*, 14, 32
   Latin terms for, 13
   and melody, 122, 140
   and oratory, 105, 112, 122

part of *ars musica*, 11, 103, 240
  in Roman theatre, 94, 184, 243
ritus Graecus, 180-2, 184
Romulus, 21-2, 173-4

sambuca. *See* harp
scabellum, 18, 101, 222, 241
Scipio Aemilianus, 40, 48, 73-7, 82, 95, 240, 242, 246
Scopas of Paros, 146-7, 157
Seneca the Elder, 229
Seneca the Younger, 25, 27-8, 33, 129, 203, 214, 221, 228-30
Septimius Severus, 159, 177
Severus Alexander, 225
Sibylline Books, 147
sistrum, 9, 18, 171
slavery, 9, 24, 26, 30, 35, 37, 39, 73-5, 109, 111, 114, 120, 128, 187, 189, 208, 219, 241.
  See also symphoniaci
song, *See also canticum, cantus, carmen*
  during Anna Perenna festival, 121
  and archaic Rome, 5
  during banquets, 33, 73, 237
  birdsong, 123
  Christian, 247
  and dance, 57, 133, 240
  Greek vs. Latin, 8, 88, 244
  and *kitharoidia*, 145-6, 149, 227
  Latin terms for, 14-15
  and memory, 5, 121-2, 211, 228, 247
  and oratory, 79, 106, 110
  performed by Nero, 196, 208, 212-14
  as political tool, 121-2, 140, 247
  in Roman theatre, 5
  sacred to Apollo, 202, 205
  during Saturnalia, 230, 237
  as slander, 119-20
  in taverns, 1, 209
  during travel, 1
  during the triumph, 29, 60, 241
  during work, 1, 33, 135
Stoicism, 123, 125-6, 129-30, 136-7, 139, 244
Sulla, Lucius Cornelius, 23, 45, 107, 128, 169
symphonia, 12, 24, 31, 109, 129, 140, 172, 228, 242
symphoniaci, 24, 35, 109, 128, 187-9, 241
symposium, 18, 64, 66, 109, 167, 244

taverns, 1, 27, 137, 198, 209-10
Temple of Apollo
  at Actium, 154, 158
  at the Circus Flaminius, 51, 178, 180, 183
  Palatinus, 142-5, 148-51, 155, 176, 201
temples, 1, 30, 50, 54, 83, 98, 133, 147, 180, 190, 201-2, *See also* Temple of Apollo
Terence, 8-9, 46, 61
theatre, 1, 5, 25, 27-33, 45, 63, 68, 71, 86-9, 91, 96-7, 112, 118-19, 121, 130, 134-6, 138-9, 141, 164, 166, 175, 181-2, 189, 198, 202, 207, 215, 219-20, 228, 241-2, *See also* audiences
  claques, 118, 210, 237
  of Marcellus, 179-80
  at Naples, 214
  of Pompey, 40, 86, 98-104, 126, 139
  at Spoletum, 241
theatres, private, 228, 230, 237
Tiberius, 31, 177, 184
tibia
  accompanies banquets, 28, 69, 73, 128
  accompanies dancing, 44
  accompanies singing, 79, 87, 177
  brought to Italy by Arcadians, 21, 174
  in Cleopatra's entourage, 167
  depicted on *cistae*, 20
  distinguished from organ, 218
  and ecstatic worship, 29, 33-4
  effect on audiences, 91, 135
  in Etruscan art, 20
  extant remains, 9, 184-5
  finger holes, 133, 184
  in Greek theatre, 164
  healing properties, 31
  inducement to madness, 32
  instrument of Dionysus, 161
  invention of, 123
  Nero's interest in, 195
  and oratory, 105, 111-12, 114
  Phrygian, 33
  played by Elagabalus, 225
  played by Septimius Severus, 226
  role in sacrifice, 28-9, 181
  in Roman comedy, 9
  in Roman life, 15-17, 28
  in Roman theatre, 87, 134, 185-6, 234
  in the triumph, 58
  types of, 9, 33, 69, 133
  volume, 56
tibicen, 15, 18, 103, 110-12, 135, 139, 214, 219, 232
  accompanies sacrifices, 29
  Canus, 222
  in early Roman drama, 21
  Latinus, 77-9

tibicen (cont.)
   at *Ludi Saeculares*, 182
   Princeps, 186
   in Roman comedy, 46
   on strike, 30
   Syrian, 239
   in the triumph, 58
tibicina, 17, 32, 75
Tigellinus, Ofonius (praetorian prefect), 210
Tigellius (singer), 187
Timarchides of Athens, 179
Timotheus of Miletus (musician), 70–1, 88
toga, 106, 115, 117, 181–2, 199
tragedy, 20, 61, 78, 89, 176, 199, 212, 223, 234
tragoedus, 134, 194, 198, 212, 225, 227
triumph, 18, 29, 48, 55, 62, 65, 201, 241, 247
   Aemilius Paullus, 51
   Anicius Gallus, 40, 42, 45, 49–50, 52–3, 55–60, 81
   C. Sosius, 179
   Cn. Octavius, 51
   Fulvius Nobilior, 54
   Manlius Vulso, 22, 75
   Octavian, 200
trumpet, 2, 9, 18, 20, 23, 33, 56–7, 68, 155, 221, 226, *See also tuba*, *cornu*
tuba, 18, 56, 58, 171, 221
tubicen, 18, 56, 60, 214, 219
Twelve Tables, 15, 120
tympana, 9, 18, 129, 134, 239

Valerius (actor), 38
Varro, 6, 25, 85, 123
   De Musica, 85
   Onos Lyras, 86, 91, 129–40, 243
Vergil, 154, 171, 195, 216
Vitruvius, 13, 25, 137

weddings, 38
Wille, Günther, 4
Wiseman, Peter, 96–7, 101, 133, 136–9

Zorzetti, Nevio, 4, 92, 104

For EU product safety concerns, contact us at Calle de José Abascal, 56–1°,
28003 Madrid, Spain or eugpsr@cambridge.org.

www.ingramcontent.com/pod-product-compliance
Lightning Source LLC
LaVergne TN
LVHW080305260326
834688LV00039B/1140